Reporting on Business and the Economy

Louis M. Kohlmeier, Jr./ Jon G. Udell/ Laird B. Anderson

Prepared by a prestigious group of newspaper and magazine writers and editors, **Reporting on Business and the Economy** will help meet the need for accurate and objective news coverage in this vital area.

Its logically organized content offers an introduction to business and economic reporting, treatment of the major issues and their coverage, and the special reporting needs of the various news media.

Among the Features

- Written and edited by thirteen experienced journalists representing the nation's leading newspapers and magazines.

- First comprehensive treatment of the economy and business as specialized areas of news coverage.

- Written for readers from diverse backgrounds, including journalism, business, labor, and government.

- Treats reporting of inflation, energy, environmental matters, consumerism, and other business and economic issues.

- Includes a convenient glossary of terms most often used in the reporting of business and economic activity.

The Editors

Louis M. Kohlmeier, Jr., Pulitzer Prize winning journalist, was a reporter for the *St. Louis Globe-Democrat* and *The Wall Street Journal,* a syndicated Washington columnist, an editor of *Financier* magazine, and is the author of several books.

Jon G. Udell is Irwin Maier Professor of Business at the University of Wisconsin, where he also received his doctorate. He is the author of many books, papers, and studies on a variety of economic and business topics.

Laird B. Anderson, an Associate Professor in The American University's School of Communication, is a former reporter for *The Wall Street Journal, Miami News,* and the Gainesville, Ga., *Times.*

REPORTING ON
BUSINESS AND
THE ECONOMY

REPORTING ON
BUSINESS AND
THE ECONOMY

Edited by

LOUIS M. KOHLMEIER, JR.
Director, National Center for
Business and Economic Communication
The American University

JON G. UDELL
Irwin Maier Professor of Business
University of Wisconsin

LAIRD B. ANDERSON
Associate Professor, School of Communication
The American University

PRENTICE-HALL, INC., Englewood Cliffs, N.J. 07632

Library of Congress Cataloging in Publication Data

Main entry under title:
Reporting on business and the economy.

Includes bibliographies and index.
1. Journalism, Commercial. 2. United
States—Economic policy—1971–
I. Kohlmeier, Louis M. (date) II. Udell,
Jon G. III. Anderson, Laird B.
PN4784.C7R44 1981   070.4'4933'0973   80-36841
ISBN 0-13-773879-X

Editorial/production supervision and interior
  design by Frank J. Hubert
Cover design by Zimmerman/Foyster Design
Manufacturing buyer: Harry P. Baisley

Printed in the United States of America
10 9 8 7 6 5 4 3 2 1

Prentice-Hall International, Inc., *London*
Prentice-Hall of Australia Pty. Limited, *Sydney*
Prentice-Hall of Canada, Ltd., *Toronto*
Prentice-Hall of India Private Limited, *New Delhi*
Prentice-Hall of Japan, Inc., *Tokyo*
Prentice-Hall of Southeast Asia Pte. Ltd., *Singapore*
Whitehall Books Limited, *Wellington, New Zealand*

CONTENTS

v

III. *Media Requirements . . . 271*

Covering Economics for:

PREFACE

T HIS BOOK IS WRITTEN BY EXPERIENCED JOURNALISTS for aspiring journalists, and for all interested readers, viewers, and listeners who are the consumers of journalism's product. It was compiled with three premises in mind.

The first is that economic affairs—prices, jobs, taxes, and much more—increasingly affect the lives of all Americans and yet the economy and business have been neglected in journalism education. The second is that, as local, national, and international affairs grow more complex and contentious, an understanding of the economy is necessary not only to business and economic reporting but also to good reporting in political, social, and other areas of the news. The third is that, as economic and business news becomes more important, economic and business reporting becomes more exciting and rewarding.

This book does not replace any existing basic journalism textbook. The basic requisites of good reporting are and will remain an ability to write clearly and interestingly, an acquisitiveness for facts and an inquisitiveness about issues, and a conscious objectivity in putting the facts and issues into written or spoken words.

In addition, however, contemporary journalism requires a knowledge of the subject at hand. Without such knowledge, reporting tends to be shallow and superficial and, when the facts are complicated and the issues controversial, uninformed reporting may well be lacking in objectivity.

Of course, editors expect their reporters to inform themselves by asking the right questions of the right sources at the right times, which frequently are at deadline. But to be acquisitive and inquisitive are no longer enough. There probably always will be a place in journalism for the general assignment reporter who knows a little about a lot of things, but journalism has become more seriously professional than in the day of the self-trained reporter, the police blotter, and "The Front Page."

Nor does this book replace any existing economic text. An aspiring journalist will take one or several basic economics courses, in addition to English, literature, and other courses. But experts in economics, business, and other professions rarely make good reporters. Journalism exists as a profession in its own right to convey expert knowledge and opinion to the public by means of skillful and independent reporting, writing, interpretation, and analysis. A knowledgeable and fair press is essential to an informed public and to the purposes of the First Amendment.

For journalists who specialize in economic and business reporting, *The Wall Street Journal* has been a kind of teaching university that with considerable success has combined skillful writing with knowledgeable reporting. No small number of the contributing authors and editors of this book are present or former *Wall Street Journal* editors or reporters, and we herewith acknowledge our educational debt to that estimable newspaper.

However, there are limits to its capacity as a school of journalism; a survey we conducted among formal journalism schools pointed up their growing interest in the economy and business. It indicated that journalism school deans are very much interested in the economy and business as an important area of news coverage, that they feel a need for teaching and student preparation in this field, but that there is an absence of appropriate teaching materials on business and the economy.

This book is designed to meet that need. For our purposes, *the economy* is defined as the total production and consumption of goods and services in the United States, and *business* is defined as the economic system, comprising both industry and labor, that in the United States is responsible for most goods and services.

Business and economic reporting in general has been criticized as being frequently uninformed, often superficial, and sometimes lacking in objectivity. The critics have included economists, businessmen, labor leaders, and some journalists and journalism teachers. Of course, disagreement is indigenous to a free press and it is not our purpose to respond to individual criticisms. We proceed on the assumption that business and economic reporting can and should be better informed, less superficial, and more objective.

However, improved business and economic news coverage is not the responsibility solely of reporters and editors. Informed and effective communication also is the responsibility of corporate and union executives, of economists in and out of government, and of other private and public makers of business and economic policies. A few business and labor leaders have come to recognize that responsibility, by becoming more accessible to reporters and by speaking out in public, but many more have not. It is our hope that this book also will help corporate the union leaders and others to understand better the needs and roles of the media and thus to communicate more effectively with the press and, through the press, with the public.

The contents of this book are presented in what we felt would be a logical sequence of three parts, although we are aware that others will approach the contents according to their own interests and designs. Part I is an introduction, first to the universe of business and economic news reporting, and second to this nation's economic system. The second part of the book identifies major economic and business issues and defines effective reporting of those issues. Part III describes the particular requirements of newspapers, periodicals, television, and radio and discusses how each has, or has not, covered business and economic news.

In recent decades, economic and business issues have been framed in large part by national policy makers in Washington, and therefore the issues discussed in this book necessarily are framed in large part by reporting in Washington and by the coverage of major newspapers and national news organizations. However, policies made in Washington succeed or fail in all of the states, cities, and towns across the nation to which those policies apply. Local and regional reporting can reach home as national reporting cannot. Nevertheless, effective local and regional reporting must begin with an understanding of national policies.

This book therefore is not addressed only to present and future reporters who happen to work in Washington. Indeed, the challenges and the rewards of better business and economic news coverage may well be greatest in local and regional news organizations.

The preparation of this book was made possible by the financial support of two foundations, the American Newspaper Publishers Association Foundation and the Foundation for Economic Freedom, which is sponsored by the National Association of Manufacturers. In addition, we acknowledge with thanks the financial support of Dow Jones & Company, the Minneapolis Star and Tribune Company, Lilly Endowment, Inc., the Robert R. McCormick Foundation, and the Hearst Foundation.

The financial supporters and contributors have no responsibility for the content of this book, however.

The editors, who were selected to ensure that the book have both journalistic and economic validity, take responsibility for the selection and arrangement of contents. The authors, each of whom is well experienced in reporting about the issue discussed in his or her chapter, assume full responsibility for their work.

We also record here our appreciation for the assistance and encouragement that were extended by various newspaper reporters and editors, journalism teachers, and others who contributed in large and small ways to the preparation of this book. Some offered suggestions and comments when the book was first planned, others commented upon the various drafts of the manuscript, and still others assisted in the editing and typing of the manuscript. We extend our thanks particularly to James N. Sites, Stephen E. Palmedo, Jean Smith, Donna D. Stohr, William H. Oliver, and Alice G. Bickerstaff.

Finally, it is appropriate that we note the creation of the National Center for Business and Economic Communication at The American University in Washington, D.C. Although the National Center did not exist when this book was conceived, it was subsequently created to propagate and assist the improvement of business and economic journalism throughout the country.

Louis M. Kohlmeier, Jr.

A NOTE CONCERNING EDITORS AND AUTHORS

Louis M. Kohlmeier, Jr., is a former reporter for the *St. Louis Globe-Democrat* and for *The Wall Street Journal* in Washington, a Pulitzer Prize winner, a syndicated Washington columnist, an editor of *Financier* Magazine, and author of several books.

Laird B. Anderson, a former reporter for *The Wall Street Journal* in Chicago and Washington and for the *Miami News* and Gainesville (Georgia) *Times,* is in charge of the Graduate Program in Journalism and Public Affairs at The American University, Washington, D.C.

Jon G. Udell, who received his doctorate at the University of Wisconsin and is a member of the Graduate School of Business faculty at the University of Wisconsin in Madison, has authored numerous books, papers, and studies on a variety of economic and business topics.

Alfred L. Malabre, Jr., who once reported for the *Hartford Courant,* is news editor of *The Wall Street Journal* in New York and has written several books on economics and inflation as well as having contributed to *Harper's,* the *Saturday Review,* and other magazines.

Abe H. Raskin, who retired in 1977 after 43 years with *The New York Times* as a labor reporter, columnist, and editorial board member, is an associate director of the National News Council in New York and has written for *The New Yorker* and other publications.

John W. Hazard, who retired in 1976 as executive editor of *Changing Times* Magazine and earlier was a *Wall Street Journal* and *Washington Times* reporter, is a contributing editor of *Changing Times* and has written a half dozen books on economic subjects.

Roberta Hornig, who reports on energy and environmental issues for *The Washington Star,* started at the *Star* as a copy girl in 1958 after college, was promoted to the paper's national staff in 1971, and has appeared on many network television interview shows.

Ellis Haller, who joined *The Wall Street Journal* after college and was a reporter in its New York, Chicago, and Washington bureaus, moved to *U.S. News & World Report* in 1956 and became assistant managing editor, concentrating on business and financial news.

Donald I. Rogers, formerly business and financial editor of *The New York Herald-Tribune,* occupies a similar position with the Hearst Newspapers in New York and his writings include *The Day the Market Crashed,* a book published in 1972.

Harry B. Ellis, who since 1947 has been a reporter and economic correspondent with *The Christian Science Monitor* in Washington, Paris, Beirut, and Bonn, also has done radio and television commentary and has written nine books on the Middle East and other subjects.

William E. Giles, editor and vice-president of *The Detroit News,* formerly was a reporter for the *Plainfield (N.J.) Courier-News,* Southwest edition managing editor of *The Wall Street Journal,* editor of *The National Observer,* and an executive of Dow Jones & Company, Inc.

James W. Michaels, who has been editor of *Forbes* since 1961 and a journalist for some 30 years, in 1977 was honored by the New York Financial Writers' Association for "significant, long-run contributions to the advancement of financial journalism."

Dan Cordtz, economic editor of ABC News in New York and president of the Economics News Broadcasters Association, formerly was on the reporting staff of *The Wall Street Journal* and was a member of the editorial staff of *Fortune* Magazine.

ACKNOWLEDGMENTS

We wish to thank the following for the use of material appearing in *Reporting on Business and the Economy:* Barron's National Business Financial Weekly, The Boston Globe, Business Week, Cape Codder, Chicago Tribune, The Christian Science Monitor (Reprinted by permission of The Christian Science Monitor © 1978 The Christian Science Publishing Society. All rights reserved.), Detroit News, National Journal, Newsday (The Long Island Newspaper, Copyright 1978, Newsday, Inc.), The New York Times (© 1975/76/77/78 by The New York Times Company. Reprinted by permission.), David Swit, The Wall Street Journal, The Washington Post (© The Washington Post), and U.S. News & World Report.

An Overview

I

THE BROAD HORIZONS OF ECONOMIC JOURNALISM

1

LAIRD B. ANDERSON

PROBLEMS AND OPPORTUNITIES
    Economic News and Journalistic Responsibility
    Difficulties the Journalist Faces
    Opportunities in Economic and Business Journalism

THE GROWTH OF ECONOMIC AND BUSINESS NEWS COVERAGE
    Newspapers
    Broadcasting
    Magazines
    Trade Press and Newsletters

THE NEED FOR AND CHALLENGE OF IMPROVEMENT
    Public, Private, and Self Criticism
    Meeting the Challenge

B USINESS AND ECONOMIC NEWS COVERAGE is important, and it can be exciting and rewarding.

Run down a list of national and local news stories that in recent years have been awarded Pulitzer Prizes, for instance, and you will see that a substantial number directly or indirectly concern business and economic matters. Prize-winning stories have ranged from coverage of fraudulent transactions in salad oil in New Jersey to accounts of how President Lyndon Johnson's family in Washington accumulated great wealth through the ownership of broadcasting stations in Texas.

News of business and the economy is not new, but recognition of its importance is a recent development. For example, *The Wall Street Journal,* a purveyor of business and economic news for many years, took note of the increased widespread interest in its area of specialization in a page one story that began:

> The American press, much of it flush with profits but still afflicted by the post-Watergate blahs, has been seeking a fresh blockbuster to pursue. But the story it has found isn't new. It was there all the time but largely neglected—the realm of business, finance and economics.[1]

PROBLEMS AND OPPORTUNITIES

It is not difficult to understand why the importance of business and economic news is being recognized. Economic and business issues increasingly affect every home and pocketbook and in one way or another relate to

4

our physical and psychic well-being. For example, the quadrupling of world oil prices and the appearance of double-digit inflation in the 1970's shocked an entire population that had grown accustomed to relative prosperity in most of the years since World War II.

Economic News and Journalistic Responsibility

The major economic and business stories that American journalism must report and interpret—inflation, unemployment, taxes, trade, dwindling resources, and the local, state, and federal government policies affecting them—are enduring, and one conclusion is obvious: the public wants and needs more and better coverage of economic and business news.

People want to know all they can, not only about what is happening locally and nationally to prices and jobs, but why inflation and unemployment persist and how to try to cope with them in their daily lives. With rising local, state, and federal taxes and government programs that often seem to fall short of solving the problems that motivated them, the public increasingly is concerned with the role of the government in the economy. People are interested in the apparent trade-offs and conflicts between taxes and costs and between economic and other social goals such as environmental and consumer protection. They worry when the federal government, in an asserted effort to curb inflation, takes actions that result in higher interest rates on home mortgages and automobile loans. They want to know not only what is happening, but who, why, when, where, and how. They look to the print and electronic media for answers, but they have not read or heard many answers, at least until recently.

The media, of course, have not totally ignored economic and business news. Such news, of a sort, has been a staple of newspapers for many years.

Early American merchants who depended on news of ship arrivals and departures had a lot to do with the beginning of newspapers in America. But too often economic and business news still is defined and limited to relatively narrow happenings such as the reporting of corporate dividends and the printing of stock market tables, and the bigger picture is given little or no attention. News of the economy and business often has been consigned to second or third string status, lightly and briefly covered as a duty to broad reporting but viewed by many editors as complex and dull stuff; these views frequently are reflected in the depth, quality, and prominence of such stories.

Difficulties the Journalist Faces

Coverage of economics and business is not easy for several reasons. Many editors and reporters are not trained or motivated for the task. Many business leaders are not always forthcoming. Economists themselves often present conflicting viewpoints. For instance, Wassily Leontief, a Harvard economist and Nobel Prize winner, has said that "The long standing claim of economists that they knew how to control inflation is an empty pretense."[2]

Conflicts among economists on occasion have been the basis of stories or columns by frustrated reporters who try to understand the complexities, state them simply, and give them meaning. One reporter, Robert J. Samuelson, has written:

> The recent fashion has been to picture [economists] as a flock of cackling chickens, each telling the government to do something different. You should take that with a grain of salt... today's major disagreements involve moral and political judgments, not economics. Remember that economists are flesh and bones like the rest of us. They have reputations, pet theories, political and professional connections to protect and promote. They exist in a twilight zone between dispassionate objectivity and partisan or ideological advocacy. What splits them today, more than anything else, is a fundamental but rarely acknowledged difference of opinion about the hazards of inflation.[3]

Reporters, of course, may meet and deal with differences of opinion among news sources in covering all beats, from politics to sports and religion.

Still, coverage of business and economic events is not easy. The "dismal" science of economics, while an integral part of our daily lives, is often difficult to understand and riddled with complexity. Is unemployment or inflation our greatest economic problem? Is big business good or bad? Is a tax cut in the best interests of the nation and, if so, who should receive the benefits of tax reduction? Is there an energy shortage? Should there be more or less regulation of industry and prices? Should we rely more heavily on nuclear generation of electricity? Is solar energy economically feasible? Are profits too high or too low? Are wages rising too rapidly or too slowly?

The responsibility of the reporter is not to solve such questions, of course, but to report and shed light on them. But the reporter encounters difficulty in translating the vocabulary of economics and business into understandable and meaningful language. On all news beats, including certainly the sports beat, reporters must understand and explain a peculiar lexicon, but the economics and business beat seems to present an unusually large challenge with a lexicon of such terms as fiscal policy, monetary policy, incomes policy, macro-economics, and micro-economics.

Less formal and more colorful terms also crop up in government reports, news briefings, and interviews. "Stagflation" is a term that describes an economic condition in which real output declines even when prices are rising—recession and inflation at the same time. "Jawboning" is translated as the government use of persuasion to attempt to convince business and labor to moderate price and wage increases.

Another and greater difficulty in reporting economic and business news arises from the fact that our economic life is closely intertwined with other dimensions of our existence such as the physical environment, social attitudes, politics, life styles, and basic philosophies as to what constitutes the "good life" and appropriate national goals. To report well on economic events, a reporter often needs to understand both the economics involved and their interrelationships with noneconomic phenomena.

What, for example, is the relationship between economics and increased leisure time that would result from a four-day work week? Between economics and national health insurance? Between economics and water and air pollution? Between economics and nitrites that are commonly found in nature and have been used to preserve meats but that also may cause cancer?

Opportunities in Economic and Business Journalism

If business and economic news poses challenges to reporters, it also offers new opportunities in local and national reporting.

For instance, the story of New York City's financial difficulties burst into local headlines and onto local airwaves in 1975 and was followed by big stories in other larger and older cities reporting that those city governments also were in financial distress. Because of New York City's size, its financial troubles made national news, but the cumulative distress of a number of cities underscored the emergence of a national problem and a national news story. The financial problems of the cities clearly were in the making for some years prior to 1975 and the problems might well have been uncovered earlier by investigative reporting that was supported by economic training and understanding. By and large, however, the story appeared as a major event with continuing consequences and continuing stories of major significance involving such economic and social issues as local taxes and federal loan guarantees, the erosion of municipal tax bases, the flight of people and industry from urban population centers, and the ability of older and larger cities to continue to finance police and fire protection and other essential public services.

Another and still larger economic story, again essentially local or regional but with profound national implications, exploded in 1978 when voters in California went to the polls and approved a proposal known as Proposition 13 that was intended to reduce property taxes. "Tax revolt" soon became a big story in many other states. The economic and political implications were discussed at White House press conferences and in congressional debates. Another economic news story of enormous public interest that had come into being concerned not only taxes but such fundamental public issues as education, housing, and public willingness and ability to continue to finance the costs and services of governments at all levels.

The big league arrival of economic and business news is perhaps most evident in Washington, where the federal government alone has the power to coin money and the authority to pursue the goals of full employment and price stability. A presidential press conference rarely fails to include one or more questions about economic matters. An appearance by the chairman of the Federal Reserve Board or by another key government economic planner before a congressional committee rarely will fail to fill the press tables in committee hearing rooms on Capitol Hill.

In 1974, President Gerald R. Ford, having declared inflation "domestic enemy number one," convened a two-day economic summit conference in Washington at which economists and other experts from in and out of government talked about wage and price inflation. Mr. Ford himself chaired portions of the televised conference, which received widespread coverage by dozens of print and broadcast reporters. The public—and the media—got a crash course in economics. Similarly, on the international scene, widespread coverage has been given to economic summit conferences that have been attended by heads of state including President Jimmy Carter.

THE GROWTH OF ECONOMIC AND BUSINESS NEWS COVERAGE

Economic and business reporting has expanded and the number of job opportunities have increased. Major daily newspapers have expanded their coverage and hired additional reporters and editors. Broadcasting outlets, and particularly the all-news radio stations, are giving more time to news of the economy. More magazines devoted to economic news are available and their circulations have climbed rapidly. Trade periodicals and newsletters focusing on economic and business trends in specialized areas have proliferated.

Newspapers

The Wall Street Journal leads the pack in national coverage of economic and business affairs and its growth continues to set the pace. Founded in 1889 by two young New Englanders, Charles H. Dow and Edward D. Jones, the *Journal* in 1979 had 13 news bureaus in the United States, 4 in Canada, and 5 overseas. With a circulation of 1.8 million in 1979, up from 652,000 in 1960 and only 32,000 in 1940, the paper was the nation's largest, passing the tabloid *New York Daily News*.

In 1978 the *Journal* employed 224 reporters, editors, and copy readers, an increase of 27 from six years earlier. Minimum weekly starting salaries for reporters in 1980, depending on experience, ranged from $305 to $445.

A communications system linking the publication's 12 publishing plants by satellite and microwave hookup is unmatched among daily newspapers. The *Journal* itself is the flagship of a large international publishing firm, Dow Jones & Co., Inc., which runs its own news wire services and, among other things, publishes *Barrons,* a weekly business and financial paper. Dow Jones also publishes the *Asian Wall Street Journal* in Hong Kong and, through its Ottaway Newspapers subsidiary, publishes a group of general circulation daily and weekly newspapers in the United States. The group in 1978 numbered about two dozen. Despite its journalistic and financial success in the field of business and economic news, Dow Jones in 1977 ceased publication of *The National Observer,* a 15-year old national weekly general circulation newspaper, because of continuing financial losses.

In all, there were 1,764 daily newspapers in the United States in 1977. The larger ones usually devoted several pages to business and financial news, including stock market tables. It is not unusual for a metropolitan daily to employ five or more business writers and editors. Some papers are creating financial staffs or emphasizing such coverage for the first time.

As interest in economic and business news started to grow, some of the big dailies in 1977 beefed up their reporting and their staffs. For example, *The Washington Post*'s business and financial section increased coverage by 30 columns a week and hired four more reporters (two with Master of Business Administration degrees) to bring the total financial staff to 17. In Chicago, the *Sun-Times* doubled the size of its business section after the *Daily News* folded, and it increased the staff from 9 to 13. Also in the Windy City, the *Chicago Tribune* boosted its business news staff from 8 to 16, expanded the section on two days of the week, and started a separate section called Midwest Business Report, published on Wednesday. And in New York, *The Times,* after two years of preparation, started a separate "free standing" daily business-financial section produced by a staff of 75.[4]

Pay scales for business writers appear to have improved a good deal. For instance, a 1975 survey of business and financial editors, conducted by J. T. W. Hubbard, a former *Business Week* editor, found that the average pay for a business reporter with five years' experience on a 50,000 to 100,000 circulation daily was $13,740, up from $7,600 in 1965.[5] A *Los Angeles Times* editor said recently that "experienced reporters with the biggest papers often get $30,000 to $40,000 and more." Like other major newspapers, the *Los Angeles Times* in recent years has greatly expanded its business and economic news coverage. Space devoted to such coverage has been doubled over the past decade and the business and economic news staff has been expanded from 10 to 28. Moreover, economic type stories not infrequently appear on page one of the *Times*.

Not only have improvements been made by general daily papers, but the number of local and regional business newspapers has grown. Some of the newer ones include the *Chicago Business Review,* the *Kentucky Business Ledger,* and the *Alaska Journal of Commerce.* Some that have been around for a while are experiencing new growth. The *Houston Business Journal,* for example, with a circulation of about 17,000 in 1978, had experienced a 25 percent circulation boost in a year.[6] According to *The Wall Street Journal,* "The papers often get high marks from business men for their ability to bring local angles into focus, even on major national business stories."[7] One enthusiastic publisher, Rance Crain, in the midst of planning a new weekly called *Crain's Chicago Business* and hiring ten staff members to put it out, said: "Subjects that used to be in the back pages of the paper—balance of payments, wheat deals with Russia—are now in front. Financial reporting is the wave of the future."[8]

Also at the local level, general weekly newspapers are challenging dailies as a prime source of community news, including news of the local economy. In 1977 there were about 7,500 weeklies with a total circulation of nearly 38 million. Their average circulation was over 5,000 and their estimated readership was close to 152 million. As their acceptance continues to increase, some are going to twice-a-week publication. As a group, weeklies are more professionally operated and edited than in years gone by and they offer growing opportunities to aspiring reporters. Their staffs are frequently small and sometimes required to perform multiple duties, including the sale of ads, but editors and reporters realize that the strength of community newspapers, including smaller dailies, depends on detailed local coverage that readers cannot get elsewhere. This means coverage of such economic matters as budgets of city and county governments, energy problems, financial statements of banks and savings and loan associations, labor contracts with local businesses, the ups and downs of retailers, and how these things affect local purchasing power. In some small towns and cities, editors of weeklies rely on editorial boards of community leaders familiar with the pulse of the public for advice on local thinking. Some editors suggest that one way to improve local business reporting is to use such a board composed of consumers and representatives of financial institutions, labor, industry, and government to help interpret economic issues and their impact on the community.

The growth in economic and business journalism has not advanced at a rapid pace among all newspapers, of course. For instance, *Editor and Publisher Yearbook* in 1976 listed about 420 business or financial news editors on dailies; of these, 230 were carried solely in those positions but 190 had additional editorial duties such as covering autos, real estate, amusements, aviation, or science, or writing editorials. The numbers do not differ much from those of the preceding decade. The breadth of responsibilities was related to the size of the paper.

Most dailies depend on the general wire services, the Associated Press and United Press International, for nonlocal business and economic reporting. So do most radio and TV stations. For the media that wish more detailed and extensive financial and economic reporting, there are other wire services devoted almost exclusively to such news. Among them are the Dow Jones News Service (largely served by *Wall Street Journal* reporters who write for both); the Reuters economic wire, which competes aggressively with the Dow Jones wire and is operated by London-based Reuters, owner of a number of international economic and other wire news services; and the Commodity News Service, owned by Knight-Ridder Newspapers Inc., a large chain which also publishes the *Journal of Commerce.*

Critics contend that the general wire services, which are wholesale brokers of worldwide news for millions of readers and listeners, lack commitment to business and economic news coverage outside of reporting numbers—the stock market tables, corporate earnings, government statistics, and the like. While the general wires have begun to improve their coverage of business and economic news for the general public, the day-to-day reporting "on who is doing what, why and what it means still is missing," according to critic Madeline Nelson.[9]

However, Louis Uchitelle, business news editor of the Associated Press, disagreed with Ms. Nelson's analysis. "Our report includes columns that explain economics to the general reader, features that deal in business trends, profiles of key people in the financial world and other features and takeouts that explain... who is doing what, why and what it means," Mr. Uchitelle wrote in a letter to the author.

Mr. Uchitelle said that AP in 1978 employed eight business writers and editors in New York and a dozen others in bureaus around the country, including a commodities specialist in Chicago and an oil industry specialist in Houston. He said he had no exact figures on staff growth from five years earlier but that "the staff has grown, especially outside New York. We are developing a network of business news specialists in the bureaus. Their copy moves into New York and makes an important contribution to the national business news report." The wire service encourages its business reporters to continue their studies and several have recently completed special programs for business news writers and editors at Columbia University and at the Brookings Institution in Washington.

Gregory Nokes, an AP economics writer in Washington, summed up his work this way:

> We are doing a good job—relatively. In other words, we are doing a good job considering that it is an enormously complex assignment and we often find ourselves floundering in the dark on economic issues with

little guidance we can put confidence in. Space constraint is a major
problem, too, since we often must condense very complex matters into
400 words.[10]

There is some evidence that advertiser pressure continues to plague
the business coverage of some medium-size and smaller-size newspapers.[11]
To many papers, economic and business reporting still means overly heavy
reliance on wire copy, quick rewrites of company releases, and brief notices
of executive appointments and promotions with only an occasional local
assignment of substance. But journalism changes with the times and as
public interest in the economy and business continues to grow, the interests
of editors and publishers in improving coverage also will grow.

Broadcasting

In 1968 an editor at what were then the WTOP radio and television stations
in Washington approached Bob Dalton, a long-time announcer who had
been with the stations since 1951, and asked if he would be interested in
doing a business report. Mr. Dalton, who had no background in such
reporting, thereupon ventured into relatively unexplored territory for
background journalism, using *The Wall Street Journal* as his textbook and
employing lay terms and a conversational style on the air.

Ten years later Mr. Dalton carried the title "business editor." His title
and his frequent reports and summaries—Bob Dalton on Business—on the
all-news radio station, giving stock market, local and national business developments, and news of the economy, made him unique among broadcast
newspersons in the big markets. He still reads the *Journal,* but also uses the
news wires of Reuters, the Associated Press, United Press International, and
the *Journal's* business report for radio stations that was started by Dow Jones
in 1977.

In addition to his radio reports, Mr. Dalton does the on-camera business news for WDVM television in Washington. His major concern is that
he does not have enough time to do in-depth economic and business reports. Still, his reports are popular items attracting commercials and are
aggressively marketed by ad salesmen.[12]

The three commercial networks in recent years have attempted to
improve and expand their coverage of business and economics by assigning
specialists to the task. CBS News in 1975, for example, assembled a four-
man team to report on the economy. NBC News went so far as to keep
track of how many economic stories it reported—500 from the summer of
1974 to May 1975.[13] In 1978 ABC, CBS, and NBC together employed five
correspondents specializing in economic reporting. But some participants
concede that the overall performance by the networks, despite some improvement, remained spotty at best.

The record of the 740 local commercial television stations, with a few exceptions, has been much worse. On most half-hour TV news shows (26 minutes after subtracting commercial time), the audience is lucky to get a minute or two of sketchy figures or a few seconds on the ups and downs of the stock market. Economic and business news may get shortchanged on TV because of the difficulties of visual presentation. Television's reporting of the economy typically consists of a correspondent standing by a cash register reciting a few statistics without much meaning or interpretation. Time is the enemy of the broadcast news reporter and the complexities of economic matters frequently do not lend themselves to quick explanation.

There is no published census of how many television stations have reporters specializing in business and financial news. Best estimates by those close to the industry's news operations indicate there probably are not many such reporters outside the largest stations in the major markets. The stations most likely to have specialists are those with 90-minute news shows.[14]

Many TV news staffs are fairly large and stations no doubt could expand their business reporting. A survey conducted by the Radio Television News Directors Association shows that in 1976 there were just over 10 men and women on the typical TV news staff and enough part-time help to bring the full-time equivalent to more than 11. However, not all of their efforts were devoted to news gathering. Overall, salaries of TV newspeople are relatively good. In 1976 the typical weekly pay for an individual with five years' experience was $230, up 22 percent since 1972.[15]

For most of the 8,000 commercial AM and FM radio stations, with the possible exception of those with all-news formats, news of the economy and business is usually measured in seconds, and industry observers estimate that only a handful of stations employ reporters who specialize in business and economics. But there seems to be no lack of available news to help them and others along if the spirit so moves.

For instance, Associated Press Radio, which started in 1974, now has about 600 stations taking the service, and some 200 stations use the popular national Business Barometer reported and written by Alan Schaertel. Mr. Schaertel estimates the total number of stations using his report has grown from an initial 140 or so. His 90-second reports, which run eight times a day, and his 3½-minute wrap-up at the end of the day have proven to be a "most attractive feature,"[16] said Mr. Schaertel.

Additionally, *The Wall Street Journal* Business Report for radio stations can be used eight times a day in exchange for a credit line with each newscast and air time for commercials promoting the *Journal*. *U.S. News & World Report* also provides a business news broadcast service called Money Line five days a week through NBC radio.

Radio news staffs are considerably smaller than those of TV stations, and this limitation can be an opportunity or hindrance for business journalism depending on the station's news philosophy and direction. The typical radio station news staff in 1976 numbered just over one full-time person with a bit of support from a part-timer. The radio station in a major market typically employed four newsroom persons. The newsperson with five years' experience received a median paycheck of $200 a week.[17]

Opportunities for economic and business journalism in broadcasting appear most promising in the major markets. But, as Bob Dalton of WTOP radio and WDVM-TV pointed out, many producers still have to be educated to the importance of economic and business news and, particularly, to its local application.

Magazines

Periodical directories identify more than two dozen business and finance periodicals, about half of them regional in focus. Among the others are highly competitive national magazines with such familiar names as *Business Week, Fortune, Forbes,* and *Dun's Review.* Some of the less-known periodicals include *Black Enterprise, Financier, MBA Magazine, Dollars and Sense,* and *Enterprising Women.*

Most of the magazines are written for general or specific business audiences, but some, such as *Money, Changing Times,* and *Consumer Reports,* focus on the personal interests of their readers in economic, consumer, or financial affairs.

One of the best-known and fastest growing of the national magazines is *Business Week,* a weekly published by McGraw-Hill, Inc. Circulation at the end of 1978 stood at over 800,000, a substantial increase from 204,000 in 1950. The 135-member editorial staff in 1977 was expected to grow to 150 by the end of 1978 as some bureaus expanded, a few new ones were opened, and a few bureaus that had been closed were reopened.

According to the magazine's chief of correspondents, the audience also has expanded. "People understand now the interrelationship between the balance of trade and prices they pay. The economy isn't 'business' news anymore, it's just news," said Keith G. Felcyn.[18]

In addition to *Business Week,* McGraw-Hill publishes over 20 other magazines with such diverse names as *Coal Age, Power, Chemical Engineering,* and *Electrical Construction and Maintenance.*[19]

Another well-known business periodical is *Fortune,* a publication started by Time, Inc. in 1930. In the 1958–1978 period, circulation rose from 296,000 to 628,000. For many years *Fortune* remained a monthly, until in 1978 it went to twice-a-month publication, increased its editorial staff 30 percent, and opened new bureaus in Houston, Chicago, and Los Angeles. In all, *Fortune* lists about 100 editors, reporter/researchers, and correspondents on its masthead.[20] *Money,* another Time, Inc., magazine, started in 1972 with a focus on personal finance, had a circulation of over 720,000 at the end of 1977, and employed an editorial staff of nearly 50.[21]

Forbes, a third major business magazine, is noted for its sprightly writing and analysis of the financial condition of companies. The magazine's circulation rose from 228,000 in 1958 to 668,000 in 1978; that year it went from 24 to 26 issues and opened a new bureau in Chicago. It employs an editorial staff of about 100.[22]

Unique among business magazines is *Nation's Business,* published by the Chamber of Commerce of the United States. Started in 1912, the monthly magazine, in 1980 had a circulation of more than 1.3 million, which is relatively high among magazines since it is not sold at newsstands. The magazine goes to Chamber members, but also to a large number of additional readers who subscribe for a minimum of three years. According to editor Kenneth Medley, circulation of *Nation's Business* is continuing to grow rapidly.[23]

Perhaps the most influential general circulation magazines in the United States are the major news weeklies, *Time, Newsweek,* and *U.S. News & World Report.* Their combined circulation was around 7.5 million in 1976. Each, using far-flung correspondents and considerable news-gathering resources, devotes large amounts of space to economic and business news, including a fair number of cover stories. Each has economic and business writers on its staff and one, *U.S. News,* has a six-person economic unit reporting team in addition to seven writers assigned to cover finance, business, labor, and energy. Aspiring news magazine journalists usually start on the news weeklies as reporter/researchers who gather facts, write memos, and turn their copy over to senior writers and editors who put it all together with material written by other correspondents.

Trade Press and Newsletters

There is a vast array of additional economic and business publications in the form of magazines, newspapers, and newsletters that provide their readers with more specialized news, interpretation, or analysis than is available elsewhere. These publications sometimes are known collectively as the *trade press,* an area that media surveys often have overlooked or ignored; it includes publications ranging from the weekly *AFL-CIO News,* a tabloid-size newspaper published by the American Federation of Labor–Congress of Industrial Organizations, to the monthly *American Bar Association Journal,* a slick-paper magazine published by the American Bar Association. The *AFL-CIO News* lists four editors and assistant editors on its masthead while the *ABA Journal* lists an editorial staff of eleven. Other more specialized business and economic publications range from the *Harvard Business Review* through *Aviation Daily* and *Energy Daily* to the *Kiplinger Washington Letter.*

Some are published independently, either by huge publishing conglomerates or by journalistic entrepreneurs. Others are published by professional, trade, or labor organizations for their members but frequently are available also to nonmember subscribers. Some of the periodicals of such organizations are official organs reflecting the economic or political predilections of the organizations while other publications are written with reasonable objectivity. Among both the independently published and the association-sponsored periodicals, some accept advertising while others either exist on subscription income or are subsidized by the sponsoring organizations. The *AFL-CIO News,* for instance, accepts no advertising whereas the ABA *Journal* is fat with colorful ads.

Taken as a whole, the business and economic trade press is a major source of information, not only for its specialized audiences but also for other readers who can recognize a publication's political or economic bias if it exists. The trade press also is a major source of jobs. For example, the American Trucking Association publishes *Transport Topics,* a weekly printed in newspaper format that in 1978 had a circulation of 28,629 and was produced by an eight-person editorial staff. The profit-making publication, heavy with ads, includes among its readers not only association members but also many lawyers and economists who need in-depth news and information about trucking and other forms of transportation.[24]

In numbers of publications, the trade press dwarfs mass media publications. For instance, the *1978 Writer's Market* lists more than 4,000 publications that buy articles from free-lance writers, and several hundred periodicals are listed under the book's heading of trade, technical, and professional journals. More than 40 are listed under the heading of business management, finance, industrial management, and supervision.[25]

The communications industry is not without its own trade journals. A trade publication of the newspaper business, for example, is *Editor & Publisher,* a weekly with a 1978 circulation of about 26,000 that is put out by eight editors and writers. Serving the broadcasting industry is *Broadcasting,* a weekly magazine with a circulation in 1978 of about 36,000 and an editorial staff of about 20.

Newsletters, so-called because they usually are printed on letter-size paper, may be the most specialized and most overlooked type of economic and business publication; nevertheless, they appear to be among the fastest growing types of media in terms of numbers and of job potential.

Some newsletters are published independently, by large firms or by entrepreneurs, while others are published by trade associations. Newsletters typically are relatively inexpensive to print and distribute, and carry no advertising. Most cater to subscribers by offering news, interpretation, or analysis of a single subject that the mass media explore in depth only infrequently, if at all. Do you have an interest in bond prices, accounting, medical devices, banking, insurance, food processing, fertilizers, cosmetics, genetics, plumbing, printing, or privacy? There are newsletters for each—and for just about any other business or economic interest.

Although most newsletters are relatively new, small, and specialized journalistic ventures, there are some notable exceptions. The best-known and probably the oldest letter for a more general audience is the *Kiplinger Washington Letter,* which was started in 1923 by W. M. Kiplinger, a former financial reporter for the Associated Press. Mr. Kiplinger guessed right that there was a general market for a publication out of Washington with a financial orientation. The letter that started with 8,000 subscribers had more than 358,000 at the end of 1977.

The weekly publication is produced by an editorial staff of 20 editor/writers. It is written in a conversational, personal tone complete with a letter-style salutation and close. The folksy style and letter format have been widely copied by others in the newsletter industry. Some major companies, including the publishers of *Business Week, U.S. News & World Report,* and *Newsweek,* have also gotten into the newsletter act.

Originally the Kiplinger letter cost $18, and it stayed at that price until 1958. A yearly subscription in 1978 cost $42. While many other publications may copy the Kiplinger style, none matches the $14.7 million annual income derived from subscriptions. Austin H. Kiplinger, publisher and son of the founder, said the letter—he disdains "newsletter," stressing that the publication deals in analysis and not news as such—caught on during the Great Depression and experienced circulation surges during World War II, the Korean conflict, and the 1973–1974 period of rampant inflation when business and economic trends and forecasts became crucial to many people.

The Kiplinger organization also publishes a tax letter, agriculture letter, and letters dealing with economic and business trends in Florida and California. It also publishes *Changing Times,* a magazine started in 1947 as an economic advisory service to help families cope with consumer problems. The magazine, void of advertising, employs 20 editors and researchers. It grew from an initial circulation of 30,000 to about 1.5 million in 1978.[26]

Most newsletters are directed at specialized audiences. The *1977 Newsletter Yearbook Directory* listed 154 subject areas.[27] Over 100 newsletters were listed under the heading Financial/Banking/Economics/Leasing/Insurance. In all, the yearbook verifies about 1,500 subscription newsletters that solicit news releases or buy from free-lance writers, but there are many more in publication.

Howard Penn Hudson, publisher of the yearbook and even a newsletter on newsletters, estimates there are thousands of additional newsletters in print, with between 3,000 to 5,000 sold on a subscription basis. He does not estimate total circulation, which is nearly impossible to determine.[28]

Most of those listed in the yearbook do not report their circulations. Those that do usually have over 1,000 subscribers and some are well over that, a few in the 30,000 to 70,000 range. Subscription prices range from a few dollars to several hundred dollars and some subscriptions cost more than $1,000 annually. Many newsletters are located in Washington. The Washington connection, of course, lies in the passage and issuance of hundreds of confusing new laws and government regulations that need detailed explanation and interpretation. More than 1,000 editors and writers in Washington are estimated to be employed in the preparation of newsletters.

The growth in the newsletter field is demonstrated by McGraw-Hill, Inc., publisher of *Business Week*. The big corporation publishes more than 20 newsletters, most of them in the energy and health fields. The company in 1977 started four new newsletters, one of them, an eight-page weekly at $270 a year, devoted to trends in the fertilizer industry. McGraw-Hill's Newsletter Publishing Center brings in $5 million to $10 million a year in revenues. Another large publisher is the Bureau of National Affairs, now in its fiftieth year, which is based in Washington and employs an editorial staff of 450 to produce 44 publications.[29]

One publisher of several newsletters and other business information publications, Knowledge Industry Publications, Inc., has said that business's thirst for information seems unquenchable in whatever form it takes—business periodicals, books, newsletters, data bases, and loose-leaf services. The company estimated that these vehicles of information made up a $2.6 billion market in 1975, double the size of ten years before, and is predicted to grow another 60 percent to $4.5 billion by 1981. Revenues of newsletters, loose-leaf reporting services, and market research reports alone should rise from 13 percent to 20 percent of the $4.5 billion total by 1981, the company said.[30]

According to Mr. Hudson, employment opportunities in the newsletter field are very good, and some of the best reporting today is done by newsletter writers who often are true authorities in their fields. Most newsletter staffs are small, and journalists who stick with the trade often end up as owners or part owners of publications. Salaries are "competitive," Mr. Hudson said.[31]

THE NEED FOR AND CHALLENGE OF IMPROVEMENT

As the economy floundered badly in the 1970's and public concern over prices, jobs, and other economic matters heightened, journalism by and large found itself poorly equipped to cover and interpret the daily events. Many of the newspaper and broadcast reporters who were rushed into duty to report about inflation, unemployment, energy, the environment, and similar issues came from general assignment beats and were pushed into economic and business coverage by chance. Many editors did not know how to judge the significance of the events or the depth of the stories. And many readers and listeners, in industry, in labor, and in the press itself, were quick to point out the deficiencies.

Public, Private, and Self Criticism

Of course, in the post-Vietnam, post-Watergate era, virtually all institutions—including industry, labor, government, and the press itself—fell under public suspicion and the institutions became critical of one another. For instance, although *The Washington Post* and other leading organs of the press deserved and received wide acclaim for uncovering the Watergate scandal, it was not long thereafter that the press and the courts came into heated conflict over investigative reporting techniques. Conflict erupted also between the press and the business community. Some business leaders criticized the media as being anti-business and relentlessly on the lookout for corporate villains in the wake of Watergate which, among many things, had involved disclosures of many corporate political "slush funds" and of payoffs to political figures abroad.

The atmosphere of mutual distrust undoubtedly contributed to the emergence of a heated dialogue over business and economic reporting. In a 1976 address to the American Newspaper Publishers Association, Frederic W. West, Jr., vice-chairman of Bethlehem Steel Corp., asserted that "People in business have a lot of gripes about the press."[32]

Donald S. MacNaughton, chairman of the Prudential Insurance Company of America, described the mood this way in a 1976 speech: "Our country is 200 years old. We have enjoyed the fruits of the free market system for two centuries. Yet, here we are, business and the news media, like two strange dogs circling each other warily, suspicious of each other's intentions."[33] Louis Banks, a former managing editor of *Fortune,* chided both sides for the situation and asserted that "the rest of us deserve much better from both of them."[34] *The Wall Street Journal* chimed in with a front page story headed: "Does Business Want a Sophisticated Press or a Favorable One?"[35]

Labor seemed as critical as business of the press. Al Zack, the veteran public relations director of the AFL-CIO, raised his voice to criticize reporting about "trade unions, contract negotiations and collective bargaining. I think there is a great superficiality about the coverage that goes into trade union issues. There are very few schools of journalism in this country that make economics a required course for reporters. A tremendous amount a labor reporter has to know is in the field of economics."[36]

Criticism of the press is nothing new, of course, and the media might have taken comfort in the fact that criticism of economic and business reporting was coming from both industry and labor. However, journalists and journalism educators did not deny that the criticism often was valid in its broadest sweep if not in minute detail. Moreover, the broader criticism did not relate to relatively narrow issues, such as the reporting about political slush funds, but concerned the biggest issues including inflation, unemployment, energy, and the environment.

The emergence of economic and business reporting and the growth of its criticism can be traced roughly through the pages of the *Columbia Journalism Review*. Although publication of the *Review* started in 1961, the magazine did not take its first look at economic and business writing until 1966. Gerald M. Loeb, a writer and securities dealer, then wrote with gentle bewilderment: "Ever since I entered the securities field more than 40 years ago, it has surprised me to see the far greater amount of space devoted by the press to sports, amusements and other non-hard news departments in comparison with finance."[37] It was not until 1973 that the *Review* took another look, this time with a ten-page article by Chris Welles, then general editor of *Institutional Investor* magazine.

Finally in 1975, as the economy soured, the *Review* recognized journalism's neglect of economic and business reportage in two successive issues. Nicholas Von Hoffman explored the "artificial separation of business news from political and governmental news." He used the death of the big Franklin National Bank of New York to illustrate the point that ours is a political economy and journalism should recognize the connection. "The prestige and money in journalism attaches to the one-dimensional political reportage and commentary that typically issues from the White House and Capitol Hill. At most newspapers the business section is hidden down the corridor behind the partition next to the water cooler and so long as it remains this way we shall continue to supply a chaotic and trivialized brand of news to readers who are now in need of so much more," he wrote.[38]

In its next issue, the *Review* devoted 18 pages to a long look at the press and the economy. The most critical of five articles was written by Herbert Stein, a former chairman of the Council of Economic Advisers under President Nixon and later a professor of economics at the University of Virginia.[39] Some of Mr. Stein's criticisms were these:

- While there is "much good reporting of the economy in the small" (such as commodity prices and corporate dividends), the media's performance "is seriously flawed" in reporting the bigger stories.
- Economic problems often have long and complex histories, "but complicated explanations will not do for the media."
- Reporters "communicate and exploit anxiety—meaning, in this case, worry about some impending catastrophe when there is no adequate basis for being worried."
- The selection of economic data by reporters and the press's comment on the data "combine to create a one-sided picture."

Shortly after he fired off those criticisms, Mr. Stein appeared at a convention of the American Society of Newspaper Editors to voice many of the same criticisms. He and fellow panelists, public television commentator Louis Rukeyser and economist Leon T. Kendall, agreed that the state of economic journalism was not good. Many editors appearently agreed. Subsequent to the panel discussion, Michael Gartner, president and editor of the *Des Moines Register & Tribune* and a former *Wall Street Journal* editor, wrote in the ASNE *Bulletin* that "private comments indicate the editors think their papers are indeed doing a miserable job covering the current crisis."[40]

Meeting the Challenge

The many criticisms of business and economic reporting finally are being translated into action. Newspapers' quickened interest in business and economic reporting has become the subject of news stories. Myron Kandel, financial editor of *The New York Post,* writing in the *Bulletin of the American Society of Newspaper Editors,* reflected:

> Some financial sections in newspapers around the country are getting so much better that they make me proud to be on this end of the business; others are so bad they make me cringe. The sad part is that the latter group can be improved fairly easily. And with any kind of meaningful management commitment, they can make a quantum leap.[41]

The basic qualification for aspiring economic and business reporters is and will remain a fundamental ability to report and write well. But a knowledge of economic and business affairs and of the forces behind them also is necessary for response to the public need for better economic and business news and interpretation in times of inflation and unemployment.

Journalism education has a key responsibility in bringing about that response. Perhaps the growing recognition of the problems and the opportunities of business and economic reporting will attract beginning journalists and will challenge professional journalists willing to learn. The problems are large, but the opportunities are great.

NOTES—CHAPTER 1

1. *Wall Street Journal,* December 8, 1978, p. 1.

2. *Newsweek,* September 30, 1974, p. 63.

3. Robert J. Samuelson, "These Sixteen Men Have the Answers to What's Wrong With the Economy, But What Are the Right Questions?" *Washingtonian,* November 1974, p. 102.

4. Jerome Idaszak, "Today's Money Is on the Money Beat," *Quill,* June 1978, pp. 29–32.

5. J. T. W. Hubbard, "Business News in Post-Watergate Era," *Journalism Quarterly,* Autumn 1976.

6.   *Wall Street Journal,* March 30, 1978, p. 1.

7.   *Ibid.*

8.   Idaszak, "Today's Money," pp. 29–32.

9.   Madeline Nelson, "Why the Newsservices Don't Cover Business," *MBA Magazine,* September 1974, pp. 28–30.

10.   Gregory Nokes, "Economic Beat Is More Than Numbers Game," *AP Log,* May 29, 1978.

11.   Hubbard, "Business News."

12.   Interview with Bob Dalton.

13.   *Wall Street Journal,* May 15, 1975, p. 1.

14.   Interview with Len Allen, managing director, Radio/TV News Directors Association.

15.   Vernon Stone, "TV and Radio News Staffs and Salaries Surveyed," *RTNDA Communicator,* December, 1976.

16.   Interview with Alan Schaertel.

17.   Stone, "TV and Radio News Staffs."

18.   Idaszak, "Today's Money," pp. 29–32.

19.   Mc-Graw-Hill, Inc. Annual Report 1977.

20.   Idaszak, "Today's Money," pp. 29–32.

21.   Time Incorporated Annual Report 1977.

22.   Idaszak, "Today's Money," pp. 29–32.

23.   Interview with Kenneth Medley.

24.   Interview with American Trucking Association official.

25.   Bruce Joel Hillman and Jane Joester, eds., *1978 Writer's Market* (Writer's Digest Books), pp. 143–295.

26.   Interview with Austin H. Kiplinger.

27.   *The 1977 Newsletter Yearbook Directory* (Rhinebeck, N.Y.: Newsletter Clearinghouse).

28.   Interview with Howard Penn Hudson.

29.   Susan Selinger, "Newsletters: The Fourth and a Half Estate," *Washington Journalism Review,* October 1977, and McGraw-Hill, Inc. Annual Report 1977.

30.   *The 1977 Newsletter Yearbook Directory,* p. 141.

31.   Hudson interview.

32.   See *Wall Street Journal,* July 21, 1977, p. 1.

33.   Donald S. MacNaughton, "The Businessman Versus the Journalist," *New York Times,* March 7, 1976, p. 14.

34.   Louis Banks, "The Failings of Business and Journalism," *Time,* February 9, 1976, pp. 78–79.

35.   *Wall Street Journal,* July 21, 1977, p. 1.

36.   *Washington Star,* January 6, 1977, pp. 1, A-7.

37.   Gerald M. Loeb, "Flaws in Financial Reporting," *Columbia Journalism Review,* Spring 1966.

38. Nicholas Van Hoffman, "Covering Politics: The Economic Connection," *Columbia Journalism Review*, January/February 1975.

39. "The Economy," *Columbia Journalism Review*, March/April 1975.

40. Michael Gartner, "The Press Is Doing a Lousy Job in Reporting the Economy," *Bulletin of the American Society of Newspaper Editors*, May/June 1975, pp. 6–7.

41. Myron Kandel, "Financial News: Why Our Coverage Is in a Slump," *Bulletin of the American Society of Newspaper Editors*, November/December 1978.

SOURCES OF INFORMATION

American Newspaper Publishers Association
The Newspaper Center
Box 17407
Dulles International Airport
Washington, D.C. 20041

American Society of Newspaper Editors
Box 551
1350 Sullivan Trail
Easton, Penn. 18042

Associated Press Managing Editors
50 Rockefeller Plaza
New York, N.Y. 10020

Magazine Publishers Association
575 Lexington Avenue
New York, N.Y. 10022

National Association of Broadcasters
1771 N Street, N.W.
Washington, D.C. 20036

National Newspaper Association
1627 K Street, N.W., Suite 400
Washington, D.C. 20006

National Newspaper Publishers Association
770 National Press Building
Washington, D.C. 20006

New York Financial Writers' Association
Box 4306
New York, N.Y. 10017

Radio Television News Directors Association
1735 DeSales Street, N.W.
Washington, D.C. 20006

SUGGESTED READINGS

Bannock, Graham, R. E. Baxter, and Ray Rees, *A Dictionary of Economics.* New York: Penguin Books, 1972.

Engel, Louis, in collaboration with Peter Wyckoff, *How to Buy Stocks.* New York: Bantam Books, 1977.

Galbraith, John Kenneth, *Money, Whence It Came, Where It Went.* Boston: Houghton Mifflin, 1975.

Galbraith, John Kenneth, *The Age of Uncertainty.* Boston: Houghton Mifflin, 1977.

How to Read an Annual Report, publication of Merrill Lynch, Pierce, Fenner and Smith, Inc.

Samuelson, Paul, *Economics.* New York: McGraw-Hill, 1973.

Silk, Leonard, *Economics in Plain English.* New York: Simon & Schuster, 1978.

THE AMERICAN ECONOMY

2

JON G. UDELL

GOOD COVERAGE of business and economic events is not easy. The "dismal" science of economics, while an integral part of our daily lives, is often difficult to understand and is riddled with conflicts of opinion and interest.

Unfortunately, even those reporters and editors who have had courses in economics are confronted with many real-life events that go well beyond their classroom teachings. In addition, there are usually so many variables to an economic issue or event that it is difficult to apply economic principles in an attempt to interpret it.

Nevertheless, accurate and intelligent coverage of business and economic news is vital to the successful exercise of the responsibilities of a free press. The United States economy has been confronted in recent years with threatening problems of inflation and unemployment and is undergoing vast changes. In such times of transformation the citizens of a democracy need to understand the dynamic economic environment in which they live. Without intelligent coverage of economic news, the public will be ill informed, and an uninformed public is dangerous in a democratic society.

Both the complexity and importance of economics are underscored in the economics of the press itself. A free press rests primarily on two foundations: the First Amendment guarantees the *right* to report the news, and economic independence guarantees the *means* to report the news.

A free society encourages the private ownership of many competing news voices. Government may own or support a few of those voices, such as public television, but more are privately owned and controlled. This is indeed fortunate; a free society needs a diversity of independent news voices. However, private ownership, even with the constitutional protections of the First Amendment, is not sufficient. The free press must also have substantial economic independence to withstand pressures of government, industry, labor, and other interest groups that compete for public and press influence and favor.[1]

AN ECONOMY DEFINED

An economy is nothing more or less than a system by which human activity devoted to the use of land and other natural resources, of labor, and of capital, is organized to deliver a standard of living. It is, in other words, a social mechanism which organizes production, distribution, and consumption of goods and services. Such a mechanism is necessary because attainment of a socially acceptable standard of living requires an organizational structure and because the world's supply of resources is limited. This scarcity of resources gives rise to problems of resource allocation. Economics, as a discipline, is often defined as the study of the allocation of scarce resources among alternative and competing ends.

Economic Alternatives

All societies develop some economic and political system to organize the use of resources, labor, and capital for the purpose of determining what goods and services are to be produced, how they are produced, and to whom they are allocated.

At one time, economic philosophers such as David Ricardo and Karl Marx perceived labor to be the sole source of value and wealth. Marx believed that capital, in the form of labor-saving machinery and other productive assets, was merely embodied or stored labor. He was clearly in error. For example, just a stick of wood, used as a lever or hunting instrument and involving very little embodied labor, can greatly increase productivity.

Consider also a more elaborate piece of machinery—the farm tractor. It, along with other farm implements, fertilizers, and improved varieties of crops, has expanded food production greatly. As a result, one U.S. farm can supply the food requirements of over 50 families and the nation is increasingly becoming the breadbasket of the world despite a declining farm population. The increase in farm productivity made possible by the tractor and other capital assets has been many times greater than the labor required to produce them. In other words, both labor and capital are productive in transforming natural resources into a standard of living.

Because of the productivity of capital, all advanced economic systems are essentially capitalistic. They rely on accumulations of machinery and other productive assets, in tandem with natural resources and labor, to produce the nation's standard of living. In fact, the Soviet Union devotes a higher proportion of its national income to capital accumulation than does the United States.

Alternative economic systems, then, are not differentiated by the uses of natural resources, capital, and labor—all three are essential to producing a standard of living. Standards of living, of course, vary around the world for many reasons including allocations of natural resources, differences in the levels of worker skills, differences in management efficiency, restrictive cultural and social factors, and variations in the ratio of capital to labor. Essentially, however, economic alternatives turn more on social and political choices relative to the control of resources, capital, and labor.

There are basically two alternatives by which modern societies have organized themselves for the determination of what goods and services are produced, how they are produced, and to whom they are allocated.

One is government control and/or ownership of resources, capital, and labor; such controlled economic systesms are known as *socialism* or *communism*. The alternative system is organized on the basis of private ownership and direction of resources, capital, and labor; it variously is known as a *capitalistic* or *free market* or *free enterprise* economy. Economic systems rarely, if ever, are in fact purely one or the other. Essentially, however, the former relies on government planning and direction whereas the latter relies on private ownership and initiative, profit incentives, consumer choice, and the competitive forces of a free market.

The Free Economy

Consumption is the sole end and purpose of all production. The interest of the producer ought to be attended to only so far as it may be necessary for promoting the interest of the consumer.

That prescription for economic organization was not written by Ralph Nader or another contemporary consumerist, but was penned over two centuries ago by Adam Smith, the Scottish moral philosopher who had a significant impact on the development of the United States' economy as well as on those of other Western nations. Adam Smith appropriately was rediscovered by the press and the public in the course of the celebration of the American Bicentennial in 1976.[2]

Freedom of choice in both production and consumption of goods and services is the essential hallmark of a free economy. The system assumes that the social welfare is maximized when each individual is allowed to make his or her own choices in a free market.

Under this system, individual initiative and the freedom to profit thereby are the primary incentives to engage in economic activity leading to the production of goods and services. However, the needs and desires of consumers, expressed in the free market, are the major directing forces of the economy. In order to succeed, a business must have the patronage of consumers who enjoy freedom of choice. Economic freedom no less than political freedom is made meaningful through the forces of competition. It is economic competition that provides consumers with alternatives from which to choose. Competition also disciplines prices, prompts rivals to improve their products, encourages technological innovation, and forces each competitor to strive for maximum economic efficiency. Therefore, the combination of consumer choice and producer competition is the primary regulator of a free economy.

It is not just business and consumers who benefit from a free economy. So does labor. A productive economy can afford to pay good wages. In many instances, working people have organized to make sure that they secure the highest possible wages. In the United States most labor unions have been pro-free enterprise, despite periodic intrusions of socialist philosophy.

No nation has a completely free economy. Even the United States often has departed drastically from the free market model. This nation, however, has relied heavily on the conceptual vision of the free market as the type of economy that can best provide an enviable standard of living and, given the alternative, the free market has served the United States very well.

Although the nation's population is 85 times the estimated population of 1776, real product or income per person is about 18 times the estimated product per capita in 1776. Economist Solomon Fabricant put this in slightly different terms when he said that between 1776 and 1976 the volume of goods and services per person in the United States population has doubled every 50 years on the average.[3]

Another contemporary economist noted for the independence of his views, Robert L. Heilbroner, has described the "prominent features of capitalism's development as its dizzying succession of technical advances, its enormous material productivity, its irresistible global expansion."[4] As Heilbroner and other economists also have observed, the free market, given its dynamic quality, has developed in the context of business cycles that government has attempted to even out.

Government efforts to even out the peaks and valleys of employment and prices through intervention in the free market, through such measures as support prices for agriculture, wage and price guidelines, and minimum wages, have given rise to several of the major economic and business issues in the news.

BEGINNINGS OF THE AMERICAN ECONOMY

Colonists came to America for many reasons. Some were escaping political repression, others were looking for religious freedom. But the great majority, by far, were seeking economic opportunity. And in a new land, rich in natural resources, many of them found it.

The newness of America conditioned its economic life. People were not fettered by Old World traditions and ways of doing things. In America, for instance, there were no guilds—the secret, closed organizations of medieval origin that bound European craftsmen and merchants. The American craftsman learned by doing and never regarded himself as a specialist. Even the professions, such as law or medicine, were more open in America. In Europe they were considered to be abstruse undertakings requiring extensive schooling that was available only to the wealthy. In America the aspiring lawyer or doctor simply read some books and received on-the-job training in the office of an established practitioner. The Revolutionary statesman Patrick Henry was admitted to the bar after only six months of study, though the judges who examined him did make him promise to read a little more.

Most migrants to America came to farm. Several colonies offered free land as an inducement to make the Atlantic crossing. By the hundreds they poured off the boats, accepting their allotments (usually a hundred acres per "head"), and fanned into the interior. The frontier was the newest part of this land, and it too helped condition American life and ways of doing things. The often harsh and remote frontier life produced an independent, self-reliant breed of people.

Colonial governments were small and weak. To the extent that they existed at all, social services and civic regulations were undertaken by local authorities—town meetings in New England, county courts in the southern colonies. Through these bodies, roads were maintained, taverns licensed, and widows and orphans provided for. Taxes averaged about a shilling (25 cents) a year per household.

The spirit of economic and political independence engendered by the remoteness and newness of America stood in sharp contrast to the economies of European nations at the time and helped set the stage for the American Revolution. Britain and other nations were living under an economic regime of strict government regulation known as *mercantilism*. This economic philosophy, which dominated Europe in the seventeenth and eighteenth centuries, rested on the assumption that a nation's power was determined by its wealth of gold and silver. To increase national wealth, mercantilism reasoned, government must regulate agriculture and manufacturers and establish foreign trading monopolies, all to the end of maintaining a favorable balance of trade. Therefore, European governments carefully regulated trade to achieve a surplus of exports over imports. To encourage favored industries, they granted monopolies to certain businesses and subsidized others.

Mercantilism also affected notions of empire. By obtaining its necessities from colonies, a European country could avoid dependence on its rivals. In the second half of the seventeenth century Great Britain awoke to the potential of its American empire. Parliament passed a series of mercantilist regulations designed to ensure that American trade benefited the mother country. Called Navigation Acts, these laws prevented Americans from selling their products to anyone but the British. They also restricted American manufacturers in an effort to force the colonists to buy British goods.

Initially, Americans did not resist these regulations. They simply ignored them. Yankee ship captains became some of the world's most ingenious smugglers. Colonial governors found it difficult to enforce the trade laws. When a Massachusetts governor insisted on enforcing the regulations of the British crown, the colonial assembly refused to pay his salary. Trade regulations certainly were not the only cause of the American Revolution—Americans fought for their political rights as well as for their purse strings. Still, the Revolution demonstrated dramatically the profound interface of economic and political freedom. An obvious advantage of political independence was commercial freedom and the escape from British regulations and taxes.

One of the most striking coincidences of history is that Adam Smith's *Wealth of Nations,* the classic statement of economic liberalism (liberalism originally meant freedom from government regulation), appeared in the same year (1776) in which Thomas Jefferson penned the magnificent statement of political liberalism, the Declaration of Independence. The two documents rested on similar lines of reasoning. Adam Smith argued that national wealth was best promoted if the government kept "hands off" the economy, leaving individual initiative and natural laws, such as the law of supply and demand, to function freely. Jefferson warned governments to keep "hands off" the people. Human beings, said Jefferson, have certain "unalienable rights," and it was the function of government to protect these rights, not abridge them. Jefferson penned a political document whereas Smith penned an economic treatise. In a profound sense, however, both men were rebelling against the forms of government regulation embraced by mercantilism.

HOW OUR ECONOMY WORKS

Adam Smith's prescription for economic organization, the fundamental premise of the U.S. economic system, is one that emphasizes private enterprise, individual self-interest, competition, and consumer choice in a free market.

Theoretically, a free economy is consumer oriented; its major purpose is to create and deliver a standard of living with maximum possible efficiency. "Smith's system was designed to enthrone not the businessman but the consumer."[5] He did not particularly like or trust business persons, particularly "those who were forever trying to bypass the market by conspiring to fix prices and hold down wages."[6] However, the combination of individual self-interest and the forces of competition would, in Smith's view, prompt business to serve the common good.

In a free economy each individual is to have the liberty to select his or her vocation and to spend the fruits of one's labor as desired. The media of course are part of the free market; classified advertising helps workers to find employment, and display advertising helps them spend their hard-earned money. While freedom of economic choice, as of political choice, is not unlimited, individual freedom to spend the fruits of one's labor is fundamental to the operation of the free market because a private enterprise must have the patronage of customers in order to survive. If buyers have the liberty to select from a wide variety of goods and among competing suppliers of those goods, the market's reward of profit and its punishment of bankruptcy serve to enhance the common good.

The power of the consumer is demonstrated daily as some businesses succeed while others fail due to the lack of customer patronage. Consumer purchasing power, combined with freedom of selection, provides the public with a powerful voice in the economic system, although an individual buyer may be unaware of that power. The failure of the Ford Motor Company's Edsel and the success of its Mustang can be cited as evidence of the economic power of consumers. Ford could not make the Edsel succeed despite the many millions expended on advertising, personal selling, and distribution. Consumers, in effect, vetoed the Edsel, and it was withdrawn from the marketplace. A few years later, however, consumers accepted Ford's sporty Mustang and, with their dollars, elected it to a prominent place in the automobile industry.

The auto-buying public surely was interested in the story of the Edsel and the Mustang, but the press in general did not report that story with the enthusiasm and the detail that it gives to reporting the hits and errors of baseball games. Ford was punished with huge financial losses for its Edsel and was rewarded with substantial profits for its Mustang, but that part of the story was narrowly told in dry terms of corporate statistics, if it was told at all. The press, with some exceptions including *The Wall Street Journal,* did not dig into the story to find out who was responsible for the failure and the success, why one was an error and the other a hit, and where and when and how it all happened. The real story could have been as interesting as a baseball game.

That story, of course, involved Ford and millions of consumers, but there was a still bigger story in the rivalry among Ford, General Motors, Chrysler, and American Motors Corporation for the auto-buying public's attention and its dollars. There are many more such stories, unfortunately told better in display advertising than in the news columns, about competition between Kodak and Polaroid, Safeway and A&P, Gant and Arrow, United and TWA, Sheraton and Hilton, Pabst and Schlitz and Budweiser.

The point is that, while freedom of choice is the focal point of a free economy, competition is necessary to make that freedom meaningful. It is competition among suppliers that provides the consumer with alternatives from which to choose and that same competition helps to ensure that goods and services are of acceptable quality and fairly priced.

Competition

In economic life, competition may be defined as business rivalry for the patronage of consumers. It is this rivalry that prompts business firms to improve old products, develop new ones, improve efficiency, and keep prices reasonably related to costs. Theoretically, competition for the consumer's patronage eliminates inefficient enterprises and rewards those that successfully serve buyers' needs and desires. Those who succeed are moved in turn to invest additional capital in improving products and expanding plants and equipment, all of which serve the ultimate public interest by providing products, jobs, and increased efficiency.

Smith and his followers, reasoning from the experience of mercantilism, believed that without government help monopolies could not exist. But Americans soon discovered that that reasoning was not entirely correct. As early as 1810, John Jacob Astor achieved a near-monopoly of the fur trade by buying out his competitors and organizing subsidiaries of his American Fur Company.

But, as the pace of industrialization and mechanization moved ever faster in the era between the Civil War and World War I, Americans also discovered that large business organizations were highly useful. Advances in technology made large-scale production possible, resulting in enormous savings in business costs; these collectively are known as *economies of scale.* The value to consumers of production efficiencies is graphically evident in the history of the Model T Ford. In 1913, when Henry Ford first introduced the moving assembly line, a "Tin Lizzie" sold for about $1,000. A decade later it was $250, a price within the reach of many if not all Americans.

Advancing technology also made possible other kinds of production efficiencies. For example, there was *vertical integration,* a combining of all stages of production and distribution under the control of a single company to achieve greater efficiency. Among the pioneers in this form of business combination were the Chicago meat packers Swift and Armour. By controlling all phases of meat packing, including the ownership of refrigerated railroad cars, they were able even in the 1880's to move fresh beef from Chicago stockyards into New York butcher shops almost "untouched by human hand."

There are other advantages to size. Large businesses can better afford research and development for the improvement of old products and the production of new ones. Size also is related to the ability to advertise and use other promotional means to acquaint consumers with new products. As early as the 1860's, for instance, Cyrus Hall McCormick was using traveling salesmen and giving demonstrations. These promotional devices helped put McCormick reapers on many American farms.

Since the era between the Civil War and World War I, however, Americans also have been ambivalent in their feelings toward large business organizations. On one hand, the economies of scale are acknowledged and the material affluence produced by big businesses is desired by most Americans. On the other hand, there long have been fears that big business will hurt competition and lead to monopoly. In addition, big business is not always the most productive, and the frontier spirit of individualism favors the small business enterprise.

Fears of bigness and loss of competition caused Congress in 1890 to enact the Sherman Act, the nation's first antitrust law; it banned monopolies and combinations in restraint of trade. In 1914 Congress passed two more laws, the Clayton Act and the Federal Trade Commission Act, which among other things were intended to curb corporate mergers that might substantially lessen competition and to restrain unfair methods of competition.

Adam Smith presumably would have approved of the antitrust laws, even though he was wrong in believing that all monopolies are created by governments. In any event, the basic purpose of the antitrust laws is to preserve competition as a primary regulator of economic affairs and as a protector of the consumers' interests.

One of the earliest and most famous government antitrust cases came to a climax in 1911 when the Supreme Court held that John D. Rockefeller's Standard Oil Trust had acquired monopoly power, in violation of the Sherman Act, by buying up competitive oil refining companies and through other means. The court ordered Rockefeller's Standard Oil Trust broken up into a number of competing oil companies.

There have not been many monopoly cases brought under the Sherman Act, however, presumably because at least since 1911 there have been few business monopolies in the United States. The antitrust laws have been used much more—by government agencies and by private parties including many businesses themselves—against other unfair methods of competition and against mergers of competing business firms.

Still, the antitrust laws have not stopped the growth of large business organizations through internal growth and in many instances through acquisitions of companies that are not direct competitors (diversification). Ambivalence continues between a desire for the public benefits of economies of scale that large businesses can produce and a desire for larger numbers of smaller competitors.

To further complicate the question of competition, government itself has sanctioned some types of monopoly-like power by suspending certain antitrust law provisions for the benefit of agriculture, labor, and some kinds of industries. Adam Smith was not entirely incorrect.

Electric and other utilities, for example, are considered to be natural monopolies because they have fixed costs and enormous investments in generating equipment and distribution facilities. To duplicate this investment in order to have two or more competitors in a given metropolitan area would be highly inefficient. Each utility thus has a monopoly in its own area or region, and its prices are regulated by government rather than by competition.

Elsewhere, however, federal and state governments have suspended competition for social reasons that are not related to the economic justifications of so-called natural monopolies. Collective bargaining by labor and cooperative marketing by farmers are protected by certain antitrust law suspensions, for example. In some businesses, prices also are regulated by government rather than by competition. The first major federal regulatory agency was the Interstate Commerce Commission, established by Congress in 1887 to regulate railroads. Tariff regulations were later expanded to include the airline and motor carrier industries. Recently, the regulation of air fares was eased and prices abruptly declined on many routes as competition became the primary regulator.

Despite the many exceptions, competition remains fundamental to the American economic system, and adherence to the economics of Adam Smith still is the keystone of this basically free market economy.

Profits and Private Entrepreneurship

Profit is one of the most essential yet most controversial and least understood elements of a free economy. Individual self-interest often expresses itself in the desire to acquire wealth. While some moral philosophers condemn greed, they may also judge the consequences of individual self-interest as being socially desirable. "It is not from the benevolence of the butcher, the brewer, or the baker, that we expect our dinner, but from their regard to their own interest."[7]

In pursuit of profit, businesses devote productive resources—land, labor, and capital—to those goods and services most demanded in the marketplace. For example, if more beef is desired than is available, consumers will bid up the price of beef. The resulting profitability of beef will induce farmers to expand production. Once the supply is increased, competition becomes more vigorous, and prices and profits decline. Producers then shift to a more profitable line—perhaps hogs or eggs. While it works slowly and not always perfectly, this process is a continuous one, not just in agriculture but in all industries.

The economic and political freedom to profit has motivated many Americans to develop businesses and acquire property. Some of the most famous capitalists in American history began as poor men, frequently as penniless immigrants from other nations. Through the desire for profit, Andrew Carnegie, J. C. Penney, and Henry Ford, to take but three well-known examples, acquired large fortunes. David Sarnoff of NBC and Edwin Land of Polaroid are more recent examples. For each big businessman there have been thousands of smaller entrepreneurs in communities throughout the land.

The freedom to succeed also includes the freedom to fail. Profits have been described as the pleasure of economic action, and losses as the pain—the carrot and stick of industry and commerce.[8] The profit motive, whether it succeeds or fails, is a major force directing a free economy. Ultimately, consumer demand—upon which the profit motive succeeds or fails—is the primary variable in directing the allocations and efforts of private enterprise in a free competitive economy. It is for this reason that Smith concluded that each individual, in pursuing his own advantage, is "led by an invisible hand to promote an end (the common good) which was no part of his intention."[9]

The Role of Government

Even Adam Smith acknowledged that government has a role to play in a free economy. Despite his great faith in free markets and competition and his belief that government intervention in human affairs is generally harmful, he prescribed three major roles for government:

- Defense from foreign aggression.
- Administration of justice, including domestic police protection.
- Maintenance of those socially desirable public works and institutions that would not be maintained by any individual or groups of individuals because of inadequate profit.[10]

Smith also acknowledged that government, when necessary, should take measures to ensure the vitality of free and fair competition.

The United States has, of course, substantially exceeded Smith's prescriptions for government. Many of its measures smack of the mercantilistic system of government controls to which Smith so vigorously objected: pricing regulations, as in the regulation of common carrier tariffs; business licenses, restricting freedom of entry; import tariffs, which restrict free trade; and others. The government also owns a few businesses such as the U.S. Postal Service and prohibits competition from others in delivering first class mail. While it can be argued that the United States has departed too much from the free economy model (a study by economist Murray Weidenbaum has estimated that the public cost of government regulation exceeds $100 billion annually),[11] there are good reasons for some restrictions on a free economy. For example, during a time of war the resource allocations of a free market may not be in the nation's best interest. Or, when the employment practices of an economy are hobbled by discrimination, there may be no alternative to government intervention. (A more extensive examination of government's role in the economy is presented in a later chapter.)

UNDERLYING ASSUMPTIONS

As the foregoing discussion has suggested, two major assumptions constitute the philosophical basis of a free economy. The first, an economic assumption, is that under a system of individual enterprise and free choice the highest possible level of materialistic well-being is attainable. The second, a political assumption, is that individual economic freedom is highly compatible with—perhaps even essential to—the maintenance of political democracy.

Several lesser concepts help to explain these two basic assumptions.

One, known as *laissez faire,* is "to let people do" as they choose. In minimizing interference by government in individual freedom of choice and action, people will be provided with maximum freedom to pursue their own ends. This freedom will be productive because of a second assumption known as the *economic man* doctrine.

The economic man doctrine postulates that individuals are basically rational insofar as their economic affairs are concerned and that each person can best determine the best means to his or her own ends. Therefore, it is assumed that individual freedom should be allowed in selecting among vocations, investments, and consumption alternatives so long as those selections do not infringe upon the rights and safety of others or upon the social well-being.

A third assumption, which goes under the heading of *consumer supremacy,* is that consumption is the end purpose of economic activity and that a competitive business enterprise cannot survive if it fails to serve and satisfy a consumer need. A corollary is that business rivalry in a free market will regulate industry and protect consumers' interests.

While these assumptions can be and certainly have been debated, economic and political history provides substantial justification for them. Certainly the United States has enjoyed, by historical standards, a spectacular rate of economic growth. Furthermore, no nation has achieved and maintained a high degree of personal and political freedom without also providing its populace with a substantial degree of economic freedom.

Capital and Profit

Profit is the expected compensation for risking capital. With few exceptions, an enterprise cannot be initiated without some investment in buildings, tools, and equipment, although such investments are sometimes small. Numerous enterprises have begun in the basement of someone's home.

Many modern businesses require huge amounts of capital to be efficient and competitive. Even a small newspaper requires a substantial investment. A new paper mill to supply newspapers with newsprint is likely to require a billion dollar investment. Part of the necessary financing usually can be borrowed, and banks and other lenders naturally expect to be compensated by interest payments for the use of their money. But lenders normally expect some portion of a business venture to be financed by equity capital—by the owners' own money.

Similarly, equity investors in a business, be they a small group of private owners or public shareholders who have purchased stock in the business, expect to receive a return on their money—their equity—in the form of retained earnings and dividends. The investor's anticipated profit exceeds the interest rate on borrowed funds because the investor incurs a greater risk of loss: the equity investor has the last claim on the assets of an enterprise; all lenders and other creditors come first. However, the *actual* profit may well turn out to be less than the interest rate on borrowed capital; if the business does not succeed, the investor may suffer a loss of part or all of his or her investment.

In addition to the role of profit in motivating productive efforts, allocating scarce resources, and compensating equity capital owners, profit also must be observed as a measure of the performance of an enterprise. A highly profitable business has obviously succeeded from the proprietor's point of view. Assuming that the profit was honestly earned through the creation and delivery of a quality product or service in a competitive environment, profit also serves as one measure of the firm's social performance. The profit is *prima facie* evidence that the enterprise has wisely employed the scarce resources at its command and has performed a useful service to society.

A second observation relative to profit and equity capital is that the absolute amount of profit earned has little meaning. A citizen or reporter may perceive a multimillion dollar profit as huge and therefore "too much." Any such judgment, however, obviously must be predicated on the amount of investment or equity capital. For instance, a profit of $30,000 would represent a huge return for a part-time basement enterprise in which the owner had invested $3,000. On the other hand, a $30 million profit might well foreshadow the bankruptcy of a company in which equity owners had invested billions of dollars. Just a 6 percent return on a billion dollar investment would require a profit of $60 million.

A third observation to be kept in mind is that profit is a major source of capital. Typically a business distributes to its owners or stockholders dividends that represent only a portion of the firm's after-tax income. The balance, consisting of retained earnings, is reinvested in the enterprise and, in the aggregate, retained earnings are a major source of capital, job formation, and economic growth. It bears repeating that profit is essential to all modern economic systems and is not just a free market phenomenon. All advanced economies have capital costs and require further accumulations of capital to underwrite economic growth. As Peter Drucker, professor of management and author, has written, "If archangels instead of businessmen sat in directors' chairs, they would still have to be concerned with profitability, despite their personal lack of interest in making profits."[12] Drucker points out that this is equally true of the commissioners who manage the Soviet Union's business enterprises. In that nation, profit is levied and extracted from revenues as a "cost of capital tax," and the severity of the tax generally is double the profit rates of U.S. businesses.

Capital Accumulation and Economic Growth

There simply are not enough resources to produce all the goods and services that could be consumed. Therefore, a major economic problem faced by all nations is to decide what to produce and how to allocate scarce resources among all the possible alternative uses for them. As indicated earlier, a free society relies primarily upon the independent decisions of millions of consumers and producers to direct this allocation. In a centralized and controlled economy, government directs the allocation.

In a free or market-oriented economy, either a rise in demand or a decline in the supply of a given commodity or product is likely to cause a shortage simply because demand exceeds the available supply. As a result the price rises, providing an incentive for the increased production needed to help balance supply and demand. Alternatively, an excess of supply due to either too much production or a decline in demand will cause prices to fall and, eventually, production will decline.

In other words, it is the market pricing mechanism that triggers action to balance supply and demand and allocate resources in a free economy. For example, in recent years rising energy prices increased the demand for insulation materials, causing shortages and higher prices. The higher prices and profits caused resources to be reallocated to the manufacture of more insulation materials.

When the many alternative uses for a given resource exceed the available supply, the scarce resource will be allocated among those uses for which there is the greatest value and demand. The aggregate demand of most resources exceeds aggregate supply. The major contribution of the market economy is to induce producers to act efficiently, putting resources to their most valued uses. Timber resources, for example, are allocated not only to newsprint and hundreds of other types of paper but to a host of other products ranging from homes to toilet tissue.

Again, in a free economy that allocation ultimately is made by the free choice of millions of consumers. Although we may disagree with some of these free choices just as we may disagree with the outcome of a free election, the record of government-directed allocations is not admirable. Such allocations often result in resources' being used in relatively low value applications at the expense of higher value applications. This has happened in the United States during periods of price and resource controls and frequently occurs in controlled economies. In fact, several communist nations have attempted to approximate the market mechanism for pricing and resource allocation.[13] This effort has included a greater emphasis on rewards and bonuses for the managers of state-owned enterprises as well as greater attention to the demands of communist consumers. For example, the profit motive has been introduced into Yugoslavia's economy and free markets have been utilized for a portion of the agricultural production of Communist China and the Soviet Union.

Capital also is a scarce resource and capital scarcity is highly significant because economic growth and increased productivity depend in large part on capital accumulation.

Saving is the major source of capital; by not consuming all that is produced, capital is accumulated. Many individuals and families save a portion of their incomes. On average, about 6 percent of all consumer income is saved. When these savings are invested in industry or deposited in financial institutions, they are made available to finance the purchase of machines, buildings, technology, and other capital assets. Industry in turn can and does save a portion of its profits and devotes this to the purchase of productive assets.

Growth of productive capacity and production efficiency in the United States has slowed in recent years, and there has been much debate concerning the causes and consequences of the slowdown. One of the large issues in the debate is whether the rate of saving and capital accumulation in this country is or will become inadequate. U.S. Treasury Department economists have observed that the United States ranking in real economic growth is among the lowest of the industrialized countries because a relatively low share of its output is being allocated to investment. The White House Council of Economic Advisers has noted that "estimates of the growth of capacity in manufacturing industries indicate that growth has slowed in recent years" from an average of 4 percent between 1968 and 1973 to 2.9 percent from 1973 to 1977.[14]

While the causes of the slowdown may be numerous and complex, it is clear that, without adequate savings and capital, a nation in the long term is destined to experience slow growth and unemployment or underemployment. Underemployment occurs when members of the labor force must work without adequate tools and technology or must engage in low-skill occupations because the capital necessary to finance their employment in higher skill occupations is not available. Such underemployment is widespread in underdeveloped nations and frequently occurs in all nations.

Inadequate saving and capital accumulation also may be a cause of inflation. Without the ability to purchase the most up-to-date equipment, an industry becomes inefficient relative to its foreign competitors and its products become more costly. In addition, inadequate capital may cause a shortage of goods, thus forcing prices higher because of the imbalance of supply and demand.

ECONOMIC INDEXES AND INFORMATION

There are hundreds of indexes of economic activity and thousands of sources of economic information available to reporters who cover business and economic news. We have spoken of business profits as an indicator of economic activity. For instance, the annual profits and sales and other financial data of most individual corporations are available to the press from the corporations themselves or can be examined by reporters in the Washington and regional offices of the Securities and Exchange Commission.

Additional government and private indexes of economic activity will be discussed in the chapters of this book concerning business and economic issues in the news. Each chapter also lists major sources of information pertinent to the issue.

For the economy as a whole, however, Gross National Product bears discussion at this point.

Gross National Product

The most widely reported measure of an economy's performance is the Gross National Product (GNP), which is reported quarterly and annually by the Bureau of Economic Analysis of the United States Department of Commerce. The GNP is the total value of the goods and services produced by an economy in a given period. More precisely, it is the market value of all *final* goods and services produced. Actual sale prices are used as the measure of market value. Only final sales, rather than all sales transactions, are considered part of the national product. To include all sales would result in double counting. For example, a shoe manufacturer purchases leather, electricity, cloth, and other materials to produce shoes. If such transactions are included in the computation of the GNP, they will be double counted when the manufacturer sells its product to retailers and counted still again when the retailer sells the shoes to consumers.

The GNP of 1979 is estimated as follows:

		BILLIONS OF DOLLARS
Personal Consumption Purchases		$1,509.8
Durable goods	$212.8	
Nondurable goods	597.0	
Services	700.0	
Gross Private Domestic Investment		386.2
Nonresidential structures	92.3	
Producers' durable equipment	161.6	
Change in business inventories	18.4	
Residential structures	113.9	
Government Purchases of Goods and Services		476.1
Net Exports		−3.5
TOTAL GNP		$2,368.5

Note: Figures may not add due to rounding.

In most recent years the Gross National Product of the United States has risen substantially. For example, the GNP of 1979, $2.4 trillion, was about 11 percent greater than that of 1978. However, this figure includes price increases. Obviously the 8.7 percent overall rise of prices from 1978 to 1979 did not constitute real growth in the nation's economy.

To measure real growth, the GNP is "deflated" or adjusted for the change in prices. For example, real economic growth in 1979 was 2.3 percent as opposed to the current-dollar GNP increase of 11 percent.

Real GNP is typically expressed in terms of the prices prevailing in some base year, such as 1972. This is called a *constant-dollar* GNP. Other economic measures such as personal income and per capita income are also calculated in both current and constant dollars by the Department of Commerce of the United States. In economic reporting, emphasis should be given to the constant-dollar figures, which measure real changes, as well as to the combination of both real and inflationary changes included in the current-dollar figures.

Price Indexes

A price index measures changes in prices by giving the price level of a base year an index value of 100 and expressing the price level of all other years as a percentage of that. For example, if prices rise 6 percent in the year following the base year, the index value is 106.

The price index for the total economy is measured in government-compiled statistics by what are called "implicit price deflators for gross national product." Currently, 1972 is the base year used in compiling this index; thus, 1972 GNP is equal to 100 and 1979 GNP was equivalent to 165.5 in this index. Such indexes are highly useful to the reporter because inflation is one of the most significant problems and newsworthy issues of our day. The consumer and wholesale price indexes will be discussed in subsequent chapters.

Sources of Economic Information

Among the many sources of economic data for the world, nation, states, and industries, the largest source is the federal government, and especially the U.S. Department of Commerce. Two of the most useful publications for any reporter or citizen interested in economic news are *Economic Indicators* and the *Survey of Current Business,* both monthly publications available from the United States Government Printing Office in Washington, D.C. A third source which includes information on many aspects of the nation's life is the annual *Statistical Abstract of the United States*, also available from the Government Printing Office. While this book is primarily a source of historical rather than current data, it can be highly useful in providing the information necessary to interpret current economic developments.

CONCLUSION

The purpose of an economic system is to create and deliver a standard of living. The United States has primarily relied on a free market or private enterprise economy to achieve this goal. A free economy is one that relies upon individual initiative, consumer choice, and the forces of competition to direct the creation and consumption of the nation's standard of living. Private preferences, expressed through private markets and impinging upon private profit-seeking enterprises, determine what is produced and how the product is shared. A free economy emphasizes individual liberty and free markets in the attainment of a society's economic goals, rather than government ownership and control of economic resources. The latter—a controlled or command economy—is the major alternative to a free economy, at least in the world as it is today.

Profits and the pricing mechanism of a free market direct the allocation of a free economy's resources. Prices are established by the interaction of supply and demand. When prices and profits in one industry rise, relative to those of other industries, resources are attracted to that industry. The resultant increase of supply and competition brings prices and profits down; if the economy is experiencing rapid general inflation, however, absolute prices (as opposed to relative prices) may not fall.

In this process, competition serves as the primary regulator of economic activity. Thus, business rivalry and industry's need for customer patronage are the major protectors of the consumer's interests.

Although history provides substantial support for the contention that a free economy is the most productive of all known economic systems, its greatest justification may be political rather than economic. Economics is so integral a part of all human activity that it is difficult to envision a free nation without a great diversity of independently owned news voices. Furthermore, these news voices must have economic independence and security in order to pursue and publish the truth.

The economy of the United States has many problems and imperfections, many of which will be addressed in this book. Considerable controversy exists as to whether they are due to imperfections in the free market system, or to mercantilistic tendencies such as government controls, or to forces external to economics per se, such as social discrimination. The purpose of this book is not to advocate or to take sides. Its goal is to expose the reader to facts, issues, ideas, and sources that will assist the person who covers business and economic news.

NOTES—CHAPTER 2

1.   For a more extended discussion of economics and freedom of the press, see Jon G. Udell, *The Economics of the American Newspaper* (New York: Hastings House, 1978).

2.   See, for example, *The New York Times*, March 9, 1976, pp. 31, 55, "Adam Smith Led 1776 Revolution in Economics."

3.   Solomon Fabricant, "The Growth of the American Economy, 1776–2001," *Business and the American Economy, 1776–2001* (New York: New York University Press, 1976), pp. 28, 33.

4.   Robert L. Heilbroner, "Reflections (Economic Crisis)," *The New Yorker*, August 28, 1978, pp. 52–74.

5.   "Can Capitalism Survive?" *Time*, July 14, 1975, p. 52.

6.   *Ibid.*

7.   Adam Smith, *An Inquiry into the Nature and Causes of the Wealth of Nations*, ed. W. R. Scott (Surrey, England: Upcroft Books, 1925), p. 625.

8.   Claude Robinson, *Understanding Profits* (Princeton, N.J.: Van Nostrand, 1961).

9.   Smith, *Inquiry into the Nature and Causes*, vol. II, p. 206.

10.   *Ibid.*

11. See *New York Times,* June 14, 1978, p. E-3, "Regulation by the U.S.: Its Costs vs. Its Benefits."

12. Peter Drucker, *Management, Tasks, Responsibilities, Practices* (New York: Harper & Row, 1973), p. 60.

13. See Harry Landreth, "Creeping Capitalism in the Soviet Union," *Harvard Business Review,* September/October 1967, p. 36. See also *Wall Street Journal,* October 8, 1975, p. 36, an article headed "Yugoslavia's System of Letting Employees Manage Business Works Surprisingly Well."

14. Economic Report of the President, January 1978. The capacity growth estimates are from the accompanying Annual Report of the Council of Economic Advisers, pp. 66–67.

SOURCES OF INFORMATION

American Enterprise Institute
1150 Seventeenth Street, N.W.
Washington, D.C. 20036

Department of Commerce
Assistant Secretary for Policy
Washington, D.C. 20230

Brookings Institution
1775 Massachusetts Avenue, N.W.
Washington, D.C. 20005

Department of the Treasury
Assistant Secretary for Economic Policy
Washington, D.C. 20220

Congressional Budget Office
Congress of the United States
Washington, D.C. 20515

Federal Reserve Board
Office of the Chairman
Washington, D.C. 20551

Congressional Joint Economic Committee
Dirksen Senate Office Building
Washington, D.C. 20510

House Ways and Means Committee
Longworth House Office Building
Washington, D.C. 20515

Council of Economic Advisers
Executive Office of the President
Washington, D.C. 20506

Senate Finance Committee
Dirksen Senate Office Building
Washington, D.C. 20510

SUGGESTED READINGS

Budget of the United States (Annual), Office of Management and Budget, Executive Office of the President, Washington, D.C. 20503.

Caves, Richard, *American Industry: Structure, Conduct, Performance* (3rd ed.). Englewood Cliffs, N.J.: Prentice-Hall, 1972.

Economic Indicators (Monthly), Council of Economic Advisers, Washington, D.C. 20506.

Economic Report of the President together with Annual Report of the Council of Economic Advisers (Annual), Council of Economic Advisers, Executive Office of the President, Washington, D.C. 20506.

Employment and Earnings (Monthly), U.S. Department of Labor, Bureau of Labor Statistics, Washington, D.C. 20212.

Federal Reserve Bulletin (Monthly), Board of Governors of the Federal Reserve System, Washington, D.C. 20551.

Handbook of Labor Statistics (Annual), U.S. Department of Labor, Bureau of Labor Statistics, Washington, D.C. 20212.

Heynes, Paul T., *Private Keepers of the Public Interest*. New York: McGraw-Hill, 1968.

Lipsey, Richard G., and Peter O. Steiner, *Economics*. New York: Harper & Row, 1966.

Monthly Labor Review, U.S. Department of Labor, Bureau of Labor Statistics, Washington, D.C. 20212.

Petit, Thomas A., *Freedom in the American Economy*. Homewood, Ill.: Richard D. Irwin, 1964.

Statistical Abstract of the United States (Annual), U.S. Department of Commerce, Washington, D.C. 20230.

Steiner, George A., *Business and Society* (2nd ed.), New York: Random House, 1975.

Survey of Current Business (Monthly), U.S. Department of Commerce, Bureau of Economic Analysis, Washington, D.C. 20230.

White House Conference, *A Look at Business in 1990,* U.S. Government Printing Office, Washington, D.C., November 1972.

Issues in the News

II

Reporting on ...
PRICES AND
INFLATION

3

ALFRED L. MALABRE, JR.

W ITHIN THE BROAD FIELD of reporting on business and the economy, there are several major story areas that provide continuing grist for the journalist's mill. Among these is the key area of prices and inflation. Like death and taxes, inflation unfortunately seems to be always with us. It is, to use a bit of newspaper jargon, a running story, and a big running story. The reporter who comprehends just what inflation means—its various causes and its many repercussions—will be far better able than his or her colleagues to cover this important story with the skill and understanding that it deserves.

Perhaps the happy day will arrive when the American economy will no longer be plagued by inflation. The persistent rise in prices that most of us have witnessed for much of our lives hasn't always existed. And there is no reason to assume that it will go on forever. But it is with us now, and barring a most unexpected change in the economic picture, it is likely to remain in evidence for a long time to come. So the aspiring business reporter would be well advised to become as familiar with the subject of inflation as possible.

A compelling reason for attention to inflation is the increasing evidence in recent years that spiraling prices and relatively high rates of joblessness manage to subsist together. Indeed, any business or economic reporter concerned about unemployment would be prudent to understand the problem of inflation as well.

INFLATION DEFINED

Newspaper readers and television viewers know too well from experience what inflation means and what it could mean. Inflation at the rate of about 8 percent annually could mean that a year at a leading college costing $7,000 in the late 1970's will cost $32,650 in another generation. A young couple could buy an averaged-priced home and, when their present life expectancy ends, their heirs might sell it for almost $2.5 million.[1]

Inflation has been likened to a disease, complex in origin and destructive in result. Henry C. Wallich, a member of the Federal Reserve Board, has said that

> Inflation is like cancer—many substances are carcinogenic, and many activities generate inflation. The sources of inflation can be diagnosed at several levels. The familiar debate about the sources of violence provides an analogy: Do guns kill people? Do people kill people? Does society kill people? Some assert that money, and nothing but money, causes inflation—the "guns kill people" proposition. Some assert that the entire gamut of government policies, from deficit spending to protectionism to minimum wage to farm price supports to environmental and safety regulations, causes inflation—the "people kill people" proposition. Some argue, finally, that it is social pressures, competition for the national product, a revolution of aspirations, which is at the root— the "society kills people" proposition. The first view of inflation holds central bank primarily responsible; the second, the government in general; the third, the people that elect and instruct the government.[2]

What, really, does the word "inflation" mean? Webster defines it as an abnormal increase in the volume of money and credit which results in a substantial, continuing rise in the general price level. Through constant misusage in the press and elsewhere, the meaning of the word has been altered in a subtle way in recent years. It now is generally taken to mean any substantial, continuing rise in the general price level. When newspapers talk about inflation today, they usually mean rising prices—period. Any effort to gain a fuller understanding of inflation might well begin by recalling Webster's definition, for it nails down a major cause of rising prices—an abnormal increase in the volume of money and credit.

The Consumer Price Index

Before discussing in detail the major forces that tend to perpetuate the increase in the country's price level, we should explain precisely how a business reporter can best keep tabs on the price picture. Fortunately, there is a variety of readily understandable price indexes, issued by assorted agencies of the federal government, that provide useful glimpses of the overall situation. The most widely watched and most publicized of these is the *consumer price index,* known simply as the CPI.

The CPI is issued monthly by the Bureau of Labor Statistics, a division of the Labor Department in Washington. The CPI is compiled by some 400 government researchers who personally visit about 40,000 stores each month and price a "market basket" designed to represent as accurately as possible the buying habits of the American citizenry. The list of items covered is huge. It ranges from sugar to home insurance to used cars to tobacco to school books. This monthly CPI report is expressed as an index. A particular year—for example, 1967—is designated as a base of 100. Thus, if the CPI happens to equal, say, 181.5 in a particular month, this signifies that the general price level for American consumers has risen 81.5 percent since 1967.[3] The BLS report, in the fine print, also breaks the price trend down in various ways according to product or service and according to particular sections of the country.

Inflation, as recorded in the monthly consumer price index, has become a major news story of personal and immediate interest to millions of Americans. Consider, for example, this lead from a *New York Times* story:

> Washington, April 28—The national inflation rate approached 10 percent last month, the Labor Department said today. The report had the immediate effect of raising Social Security and welfare benefits for one out of every six Americans, beginning this summer.[4]

A reporter who follows the movement of the CPI each month will soon become familiar with the trend of prices in general. It should be noted, however, that an array of additional price indexes also is available. For example, the Bureau of Labor Statistics also issues several indexes that trace price movements at various stages of processing and distribution before items reach the retail level. The *wholesale price index,* for instance, measures price changes at the wholesale level and is of importance because wholesale price movements tend to foretell coming changes in consumer prices.

The Commerce Department issues a quarterly price index, forbiddingly called the *gross national product deflator.* Despite its arcane title and relative infrequency, the GNP deflator is the most comprehensive inflation yardstick available because it is derived from the gross national product, the broadest statistical measure we have of overall economic activity. The GNP deflator accurately reflects, at least in theory, price trends through all levels of the country's economy, not just at the neighborhood store.

Both the Bureau of Labor Statistics and the Commerce Department maintain exceedingly helpful press relations personnel in Washington and other major cities around the nation. These individuals see to it that interested newspapers are amply supplied with the latest price index reports in full detail. Moreover, they stand ready to help reporters clarify statistics if any elaboration is required.

Money and Prices

To cover the continuing story of prices and inflation well, however, a reporter must do more than simply relay to readers the government's latest price reports. A first step is to appreciate the main forces underlying the general price climb. Webster mentions money and credit. Let us first consider the matter of money.

The relationship between money and prices can be sketched in basic terms. If the supply of money remains unchanged but the quantity of goods and services available for purchase rises, the price of those goods and services will tend to fall. Conversely, and more to the point here, if the supply of money increases but the quantity of goods and services remains the same, prices will tend to climb. In effect, more dollars will be competing for an unchanging amount of items to buy. Accordingly, to track the unfolding inflation picture, a reporter should try to stay abreast of money supply developments and the evolving relationship between the money supply trend and overall economic activity in the country.

Fortunately, keeping tabs on the money supply is a fairly easy matter. Each week the Federal Reserve Board issues a report that provides, along with other information, the precise level of the money supply and its rate of growth or decline. Actually, there are several measures of the money supply; the two most common are called M-1 and M-2. The former defines the money supply as currency in circulation plus checking account or demand deposits at commercial banks. The latter embraces M-1 and also includes savings account deposits at the banks. Thus, M-2 is a somewhat larger figure each week than M-1, but the two statistics tend to move in the same direction from week to week. For simplicity's sake, we will focus on M-1, the most widely followed measure of the money supply.

Business analysts have found that in the long run, for healthy, inflation-free economic growth, a moderate, steady rate of expansion in M-1 is desirable. This growth ideally should be compatible with the economy's physical capacity to expand, which in turn depends on the country's available resources of material, machinery, labor, and other such fundamentals. The growth of the money supply can be closely regulated by the Federal Reserve, and in the next section we will see how this is done. Studies have placed the capacity of the economy to expand comfortably in the neighborhood of 3 percent a year. Thus, a noninflationary rate of money supply growth would also be in that neighborhood. Sharply higher monetary growth rates would tend to aggravate inflation. Lower growth could eventually lead to the opposite of inflation—deflation. Unfortunately, deflation, or a shortage of money, may cause a recession or depression such as that of the 1930's. Between 1929 and 1933, the money supply in the United States declined by one-third.[5] Thus, for every $100 of bank deposits and currency owned by people in 1929, only $67 were available in 1933.

THE ROLE OF THE FEDERAL RESERVE

Some economists, including Milton Friedman, argue that the Federal Reserve reduced the money supply when it should have been expanded during the Great Depression. However, the tendency of the Federal Reserve in subsequent decades was to expand the money supply considerably faster than the 3 percent or so at which the economy can comfortably grow year after year without undue strain on its various fundamental resources. It was no coincidence that prices generally were on the rise throughout the time of swift monetary expansion.

Why has the Federal Reserve allowed such excessive monetary growth if the eventual effect is clearly to aggravate the price spiral?

Let us go back again to the dictionary definition of inflation. You will recall, it mentions credit as well as money. Credit means, quite simply, borrowing. There are many forms of borrowing, of course, but the form that bears most directly on the problem of inflation is governmental borrowing. The federal government now almost every year spends more than it takes in through taxes and other revenues. The difference—the deficit in the federal budget—must be made up largely through borrowing if Uncle Sam is to keep paying his bills. In recent years, annual federal budget deficits have topped the $50 billion mark, compared with surpluses ranging as high as $14 billion in the early post-World War II years.

Federal borrowing to make up the deficit is done, typically, through issuance by the Treasury Department of short-term bills, medium-term notes, and long-term bonds. These securities are periodically sold to investors ranging from giant commercial banks to individual small investors.

There are, however, practical limits to the amount of borrowing that the Treasury can do in this way. It obviously competes directly with efforts by corporations and other borrowers to raise funds. A heavy demand for borrowed funds tends to drive up interest rates sharply and thus to increase the cost of money. Sharply higher interest rates cause a variety of unpleasant repercussions, particularly in businesses such as home building; the fortunes of the building industry are especially sensitive to interest rates because construction normally is financed largely by long-term borrowing.

How Money Is Created

When Treasury borrowing needs are especially heavy, the Federal Reserve can step in to try to prevent spiraling interest rates. It can "purchase" some government securities itself; in effect, the Federal Reserve creates a credit that the Treasury uses to pay government debts. The phrase that economists apply to this procedure is "monetizing the debt." It is an appropriate description. The upshot of such action is to create new money in the economy. This helps to fund the government deficit and may ease interest-rate pressures as well, at least for a while. However, experience shows that in the longer run the creation of money is inflationary precisely because the money supply has been expanded through the debt-monetizing procedure.

Ironically, interest rates eventually rise as well, in most instances, because high interest rates and high rates of price increase tend to go hand in hand. Lenders, fearing a depreciation in the value of repayment dollars as the money supply grows swiftly, naturally will seek high interest rates from borrowers in order to offset the anticipated depreciation.

It is this willingness of the Federal Reserve to accommodate the borrowing needs of the Treasury—to monetize at least part of the federal debt year after year—that helps explain the perennially excessive growth of the money supply. To put some numbers on what has been happening, M-1 rose through much of the inflation-ridden first half of the 1970's at rates more than double the economy's natural growth potential of 3 percent or so annually.

The message here for the reporter who wants to keep on top of the inflation story is clear. Watch the money supply figures closely each week, but also keep firmly in mind the importance of federal spending patterns. Remember that a crucial relationship exists between the borrowing needs of the federal government and the shape of Federal Reserve monetary policy. For example, in 1976 the federal deficit required the government to either borrow or create new money at an average rate of $190 million a day for each day of the year. In addition, the government had to borrow still more money to repay old debts that had reached maturity. In addition, one should recognize the fundamental link between the economy's ability to expand comfortably, the trend of the money supply, and developments on the price front.

Money Supply Mechanics

At this point we should briefly outline the mechanics of how the Federal Reserve regulates the level of the money supply. There are several approaches available under the law, and each is employed from time to time, with varying success.

The Constitution gives to the federal government the sole power to coin money and Congress has delegated the money supply power to the Federal Reserve Board. The Federal Reserve has the power to raise or lower the interest rate it charges commercial banks that occasionally borrow from it. Raising this interest rate tends to constrict the money supply because the higher price reduces the demand for money in the private sector. Lowering the rate has the opposite effect. The Federal Reserve also can raise or lower the so-called reserve requirements that banks must keep on hand and thus cannot lend out to customers. Typically, the banks are required to keep on reserve a specified percentage of their customers' deposits. If the reserve requirement is raised, the money supply is restricted because the banks must build their reserves to meet the new requirement. Lowering the requirement has the opposite effect; it expands the ability of banks to lend money.

When banks lend, the money supply is expanded through what economists call a *multiplier effect*. If banks are instructed to maintain cash reserves of 15 percent against their deposits, for example, the theoretical limit of the multiplier effect for an original deposit of $1,000 works out to $6,667. This happens because diminishing fractions of the original $1,000 are lent and re-lent through the banking system. This arrangement is called a *fractional reserve* banking system.

In addition, the Federal Reserve can affect the size of the money supply through buying or selling government securities. The decisions are made by a Federal Reserve unit called the Federal Open Market Committee, which meets in Washington every two or three weeks. The buying procedure acts to pump money into the economy, as the Federal Reserve pays out money for the securities it buys. The process of selling securities has the effect of drawing money out of public hands, as private buyers pay the Federal Reserve; this serves to reduce the size of the money supply.

While an understanding of the role of money and credit is necessary background for intelligent coverage of the inflation story, "Fed watching" by reporters need not be arcane, as the lead of this *Wall Street Journal* page one story shows:

> Washington—The Federal Reserve System, a seeming monolith under the leadership of Arthur Burns, increasingly appears a house divided under the regime of G. William Miller.
>
> A growing minority of top policy makers are pressing for stronger action against inflation. Specifically, they want to do more to curb the growth of the nation's money supply even at the risk of a recession. And they appear to be making headway.
>
> Their maneuvers hardly amount to a full-fledged civil war. Rather, they are fighting a quiet battle here in the Federal Open Market Committee, the Fed's chief monetary policy unit. The chief dissenters on the committee—an organization little known to the public—are Mark H. Willes, Willis J. Winn and Ernest T. Baughman, whose names are scarcely household words.[6]

PRICES AND PRODUCTIVITY: THE WIDGET EXAMPLE

Before discussing the enormous importance of the inflation story and ways it can best be tackled, we should perhaps glance briefly at several other factors that bear on the price picture. Consider first the matter of productivity and pay. Productivity is a measure of worker efficiency. It is frequently expressed in terms of a worker's hourly production of widgets or whatever. To appreciate the relationship between productivity and pay, and ultimately the link to inflation, a glimpse at life inside a widget factory may be instructive. A widget worker, let us say, receives an hourly pay increase of 10 percent, but he also manages to increase his hourly production of widgets by 10 percent. The upshot is that the per-widget cost of his labor remains unchanged. As a result, the pay increase places no new pressure on the widget company to raise widget prices. However, suppose that the worker's hourly output rises only 5 percent instead of 10 percent. The result is that the per-widget cost of his labor increases 5 percent—the difference between a 10 percent pay boost and 5 percent productivity advance. In this situation, the widget company must increase prices to try to offset the labor-cost climb.

The widget example makes clear the important role that productivity plays in controlling inflation. In recent decades, productivity has been rising, on average, at a rate of slightly over 2 percent annually.[7] Very recently, there have been indications that this long-term growth rate may be declining below the 2 percent level.

Unfortunately, year after year the productivity gains of most American workers have trailed the size of their pay boosts. Labor costs, as a result, have risen sharply. And, not surprisingly, many companies have come under intense pressure to increase their prices to offset the cost climb. Many firms, unable to make price increases stick, have seen their profitability erode. Some have been forced to close their doors. Many, still in business, have felt compelled to skimp on other spending, such as for new production equipment.

The irony here is that skimping on new equipment has itself tended to slow productivity, inasmuch as new equipment is a primary means for advancing productivity. There may be some validity to the popular view that productivity depends on worker attitudes—lazy workers mean low productivity and eager-beaver workers mean high productivity. But a far more important factor affecting the level of worker productivity is the quality of equipment available in factories. It is distressing to note that the average age of machinery in the United States is considerably greater than the average age of machinery in such competing industrial lands as Japan and West Germany.

INTERNATIONAL AND MILITARY CONSIDERATIONS

The question of international economic competition is another consideration to be weighed in any effort to understand inflation. American-made goods compete against goods made elsewhere in the world. In the process, America takes in dollars for goods and services that it sells abroad and pays out dollars for goods and services purchased from foreign sources. If the United States continually pays out more than it takes in, one effect is to weaken the international value of the dollar. As its value declines, the cost to Americans of imported goods and services tends to increase.

For example, it will take more dollars to buy a car made in West Germany because the dollar is worth less in terms of the West German mark. To the extent that imports constitute an important part of what Americans buy—and increasingly this is the situation—inflation will worsen in the United States. Unhappily America has indeed been paying out more dollars for imports—particularly for foreign oil—than it has been taking in for exports. As would be expected, the international value of the dollar has declined over the years, and ultimately inflationary pressure has tended to intensify.

Another important consideration in any appraisal of inflationary forces within the U.S. economy is the matter of military spending. American defense outlays have been vast over the years, and such spending seems bound to continue at high levels for years to come.

Military expenditures, of course, are a major factor in the borrowing problems of the federal government. But such spending exerts a doubly inflationary impact on the economy, because such outlays do little to expand the nation's supply of goods and services. Yet, a defense worker may be paid as much as or more than one who turns out washing machines. Both receive money each week to buy whatever they want or need in their daily lives. But only one, the appliance worker, produces an item that fills a need in the civilian marketplace. As we have already indicated, a highly inflationary situation results if money available to purchase goods and services rises far more rapidly than the actual supply of goods and services in the marketplace. The defense worker's paycheck therefore constitutes a particularly inflationary form of remuneration.

It can be argued that other relatively inflationary paychecks are those going to other workers whose labors also do not contribute to the economy's offering of goods and services. Of course, so-called transfer payments to persons on welfare and other nonproducers, such as retired workers, also are apt to be particularly inflationary.

EFFECTS OF INFLATION

The inflation story affects our lives enormously, more than we may perceive. It does not take much digging by a reporter to find the human side of this story. *The Washington Post* sent one of its business reporters across the country to see how inflation affects Americans, and the trip resulted in a series of articles. But newspapers do not have to venture out of their own communities to illustrate inflation's impact locally. Here is how the final *Post* story, a summary of the reporter's observations, began with a back-home lead:

Daniel and Veronica live in a well-tended, three-bedroom townhouse near Fairfax Circle on an annual salary of $24,000, which is what Dan draws as a drug salesman.

Once, Dan and Veronica thought $24,000 was a lot of money. But that was a long time ago, before a lot of things—before hamburgers started selling at steak prices, before weekend vacations to the Shenandoah Valley started costing more than a week's pay, before Heather (their three-year-old daughter) was born.[8]

One major criticism to be made of press coverage of the inflation story in general is that the full ramifications on our pocketbooks have not been sufficiently explained. To underscore the importance of the topic, a reporter can use the so-called "rule of 70." Take the annual rate at which prices generally are rising. You can use, for example, the CPI. Then divide the particular rate of increase into the number 70. The answer is the number of years that it will take, if inflation stays at the same rate, before the dollar in your pocket will be worth 50 cents. If the CPI rises year-in and year-out at 7 percent, for instance, your dollar will lose half its buying power in ten years. That is something to think about the next time you hear an economist or political leader reassure us that the inflation rate is "only" 6 or 7 percent.

Detriment to Poor and Rich

It hardly needs to be noted that serious economic and social dislocations are bound to occur when a currency, whether it be the dollar or some other tender, loses a large fraction of its value within a relatively short span of time. People hesitate to save. Instead, there is an urge to rush out to acquire tangible assets with money that appears likely to buy less tomorrow than today. Long-term economic growth in an economy such as ours depends heavily, of course, on the propensity to save. Savings provide much of the financing needed each year by home builders, manufacturing concerns, and other businesses. The propensity of people to spend rather than save may have the immediate effect of buoying consumer goods industries, but in the long term this tends to slow down capital accumulation, productivity growth, and job formation. Moreover, the spending spree itself may come eventually to an unhappy end as debt obligations and spiraling prices become too onerous.

Inflation's detrimental impact takes many forms.[9] One particularly insidious aspect is that inflation weighs most heavily on the poor and the middle class. The very rich often possess the financial sophistication to cope with inflation. They have the wherewithal to employ high-priced tax lawyers, investment advisers, and the like. Consequently, they may be able to keep at least one step ahead of the price spiral. Less affluent citizens generally lack financial sophistication. As a result, their buying power often cannot keep pace as prices climb.

It is for such reasons, studies show, that inflation has served over the years to widen, rather than close, the gap between America's very rich and the rest of us.[10] The millionaire buys real estate and precious metals, for example, which often appreciate rapidly with inflation. The washerwoman religiously puts as much of her weekly pay as possible into a savings bank. The account pays, perhaps, 5.5 percent interest a year, fully taxable, while the CPI keeps climbing at an annual rate of, say, 6.5 percent. The value of the poor woman's savings melts away on account of inflation though she may not even realize it. In contrast, the millionaire has a real asset which may appreciate more rapidly than inflation.

Of course, the market price of real estate, precious metals, rare stamps, antiques, old masters' paintings, and other real assets can decline rapidly. Therefore, no form of savings or investment is safe in a period of rapid inflation. However, studies show that the value of all these items rose far faster than the consumer price index during a recent ten-year period of steep inflation.[11]

The Chaos of Runaway Inflation

The repercussions of inflation, when it gets utterly out of hand, can be glimpsed by recounting the situation in Germany in the early 1920's, when that nation's price level was soaring because of a drastic increase in the German money supply. The raw statistics of Germany's inflation make awesome reading. In August 1922 the country's money supply totaled 252 billion marks. In January 1923 the total reached 2 trillion. In September 1923 it stood at 28 quadrillion. And in November 1923 it amounted to 497 quintillion—the number 497 with 18 zeroes after it. The country's general price level, it should be added, climbed apace. At the same time, in the social arena steep increases were recorded in German crime and suicide rates. Moreover, some historians draw a connection between social stresses that developed during those years of runaway inflation—the currency eventually became worthless—and the subsequent rise of Hitler. It was not a pretty situation and it dramatizes clearly the harm that excessive inflation can cause.

Trying to Keep Up with COLA's

Journalists attempting to cover the inflation story also should be aware that any sharp rise in America's general price level affects a great number of labor contracts. They are tied directly to the CPI or some other broad price index. Many labor contracts now stipulate that when the CPI, for example, goes up during a given month, the workers covered receive offsetting pay increases. These are called *cost-of-living agreements,* or COLA's. More than 9

million workers in private industry get cost-of-living wage increases that
are contractually linked to increases in the CPI.

While COLA's may tend to help equalize things in the short run, their
long-range implications may not seem so apparent, as this excerpt from *The
New York Times* suggests:

> The cost-of-living adjustment, COLA in the language of labor con-
> tracts, is designed to protect workers' pay from inflation. But it is also
> making inflation more difficult to control.
>
> "We start seeing agreements like rail, with almost a 5 percent a year
> fixed wage increase on top of a pretty generous COLA," said Jack
> Meyer, assistant director of the Council on Wage and Price Stability.
> "That starts to get kind of scary."
>
> Indeed, with inflation now running at an annual rate of 11.4 percent,
> based on the latest quarterly figures, it is likely that unions will be
> demanding more generous living-cost clauses.[12]

Inflation, of course, has tended to erode the real value of private
pension fund payments to retired workers and their families. However, the
incomes of more than 50 million Americans, including more than 30 million
Social Security beneficiaries and retired federal civil service and military
personnel, also are linked to the consumer price index.

WAGE AND PRICE CONTROLS

No discussion of the inflation story would be complete without some
attention to the issue of wage and price regulations and controls.

Time and again throughout history, in the United States and elsewhere, political leaders have turned to wage and price controls to try to stop
inflation. And time and again, the controls programs have failed. They have
failed for much the same reason that you cannot keep a pot of water indefinitely from boiling over simply by placing a lid across the top. Eventually,
the lid will blow off unless you also turn down the flame. In much the same
manner, price controls will eventually crumble and inflation will resurface
unless noninflationary economic policies, including a more moderate expansion of the money supply, are pursued.

Knowledgeable and observant journalists have attempted to report the
small and large frustrations of attempts to control or regulate wages and
prices. This lead from *The Wall Street Journal* summed up the attempts made
by the Council on Wage and Price Stability in 1978 to monitor wage and
price increases:

> Washington—Barry Bosworth, the government's chief inflation
> fighter, may be the most frustrated man in town.

The 35-year-old economist is director of the White House's Council on Wage and Price Stability, and for nearly a year he has led a frequently lonely battle against inflation. Along the way, he has been sniped at by business executives and labor chiefs, who suspect he is leading them down the trail to wage and price controls, and by some administration officials who think he puts his economics ahead of his politics.[13]

Another aspect of the frustration and confusion was conveyed in this *Wall Street Journal* lead:

Washington—A tiny new government agency is stirring a ruckus here by criticizing its big brothers in the bureaucracy.

The agency is the Council on Wage and Price Stability, a 10-month-old organization that is supposed to keep track of inflationary developments. It has a staff of only 40, a budget of less than $2 million a year, and it lacks authority to prohibit, change or even delay price and wage actions. About all it can do is complain.[14]

Why do political leaders keep resorting to controls programs despite the sorry record? Price controls essentially are a political response to an economic problem. Many Americans apparently still believe that controls can work. This belief seems to reflect a lack of knowledge about the dismal record of controls. At times when inflation becomes extremely painful, publicly and thus politically, any old horse medicine with enough ballyhoo can begin to look like a bona fide cure. But the history of price control efforts, going back many centuries around the world, records a dismal failure.[15]

Controls have not worked in the United States because in the end we reside within a relatively free society whose economy is still governed to a considerable extent by supply and demand. If Americans want something badly enough, they will find a way to obtain it, controls or no controls. Jawboning and the like are merely forms of controls, albeit watered down.

The press could have done more in the past to try to make readers see the inability of controls programs to stop inflation. This aspect of the inflation story makes less spectacular headlines than, for instance, President Richard Nixon's dramatic and ill-fated decision on August 15, 1971, to freeze prices and wages.

American authorities no doubt will continue from time to time to resort to new price-control efforts. When they do, the diligent reporter will naturally be compelled to spell out for readers the precise bureaucratic details of what prices are frozen at what levels for how long, and so on. But the reporter also should strive to keep readers abreast of the fundamental forces of inflation, including monetary and fiscal developments, productivity trends, and the like. These are the factors that will ultimately determine the long-range outlook for inflation. It is also essential during a period of controls to monitor the actual execution of all the directives coming out of Washington. Are they being carried out properly? Is any cheating going on, by corporations or by unions? Are black markets arising? Are shortages materializing where goods simply cannot be produced, distributed, and sold at prices mandated by Washington? How effectively does the bureaucracy police its own price and wage regulation?

CONCLUSION

The inflation story, as we have seen, is exceedingly wide-ranging. It encompasses strictly economic matters, such as the movement of M-1 and the size of the federal budget deficit. It also embraces a variety of imponderables, from crime and suicide levels to the distribution of wealth between rich and poor. It is, in many respects, an intensely political story. It is a story that affects transactions at the labor-management bargaining table. Indeed, it is a story with boundless dimensions, one that can be told in countless ways and that touches the lives of all of us.

Historical perspective is naturally important to full understanding of the country's inflation problem. Looking back over the post-World War II era, we can readily see that the price problem has been getting worse. In much of the postwar era the yearly increases in the consumer price index rarely exceeded 2 percent, and in some years—for instance, 1949 and 1954—it actually dropped slightly. However, in some recent years it has risen at annual rates of more than 10 percent. Double-digit rates of increase became prevalent in late 1973—by no coincidence, about the time that imported oil first became extremely costly by prior standard. Since then, torrid inflation rates have become a familiar part of the economic scene.

Precisely because the subject has become so large in historical terms and so boundless in its dimensions, it affords the enterprising journalist a vast choice of approaches. An article about inflation can be done in an interesting fashion or in a dull fashion. The effort and skill of the reporter will determine the result. Even the many statistics that go into the inflation story—and what can be duller than economic statistics?—can be presented to readers in an interesting way. Consider, for example, the many articles that have appeared in *The Wall Street Journal* concerning inflation. It tries mightily to make the figures palatable; moreover, there is an effort to put the whole inflation question into some perspective and to impart some basic understanding of the subject.

There are, of course, a great number of articles and books that focus on the subject of inflation. Many would doubtless be useful to an aspiring business journalist. Not surprisingly, many are written by economists, and these tend to employ terms that may seem arcane to English or journalism majors who would just as soon skip such matters as diffusion indexes and regression series. However, more and more books and articles dealing with the matter of rising prices are being written for the layman.

Whether you are covering inflation, unemployment, or some other aspect of the nation's economic scene, there is simply no substitute for learning as much as you can about the subject. Then, in language that readers can understand and may even find interesting, you should do your level best to impart your knowledge, with all the enthusiasm you can possibly muster.

NOTES—CHAPTER 3

1. Henry C. Wallich, in an address at Fordham Graduate School of Business, New York, June 28, 1978.

2. *Ibid.*

3. In the consumer price index currently published by the Bureau of Labor Statistics, 1967 prices are equal to 100. The 1929 prices were equal to 51.3 on the index and 1977 prices stood at 181.5.

4. Clyde C. Farnsworth, "Consumer Prices Up by 0.8% for March; 3-Month Rate is 9.3%," *New York Times,* April 29, 1978, p. 1.

5. The Federal Reserve Board is the source of money supply statistics. Total deposits and currency at the end of 1929 were $54.7 billion and by the end of 1933 had declined to $42.6 billion.

6. Lindley H. Clark, Jr., "Reserve System Panel Splits as a Minority Urges Tighter Money," *Wall Street Journal,* September 27, 1978, pp. 1, 36.

7. Productivity figures are published regularly by the U.S. Department of Labor's Bureau of Labor Statistics.

8. Bradley Graham, "An Increasing Frustration Over Inflation," *Washington Post,* August 6, 1978, p. G1.

9. See Alfred L. Malabre, Jr., *America's Dilemma: Jobs Versus Prices* (New York: Dodd Mead & Co., 1978).

10. One such study of the uneven effects of inflation on various classes was prepared by Lester C. Thurow, professor of economics at Massachusetts Institute of Technology, and appeared in *The Wall Street Journal,* July 6, 1978, p. 22. A primary source of data concerning income levels is "Households Money Income in 1976," Bureau of the Census, Department of Commerce.

11. See, for example, a study dated July 3, 1978, prepared by Solomon Brothers, a New York based investment firm.

12. Jerry Flint, "Cost-of-Living Adjustments Create Difficulties in Controlling Inflation," *New York Times,* August 1, 1978, p. A10.

13. Robert S. Greenberger, "Chief of Price Council Leads a Lonely Battle to Damp Living Costs," *Wall Street Journal,* April 1, 1978, p. 1.

14. Timothy D. Schellhardt, "The Watchdog of the Watchdogs," *Wall Street Journal,* June 10, 1975, p. 18.

15. See "A Trap to Avoid," in Malabre, *America's Dilemma*, for a history of price control efforts going back many centuries.

SOURCES OF INFORMATION

American Enterprise Institute
1150 Seventeenth Street, N.W.
Washington, D.C. 20036

Brookings Institution
1775 Massachusetts Avenue
Washington, D.C. 20036

Bureau of the Census
U.S. Department of Commerce
Suitland, Md. 20233

Bureau of Labor Statistics
U.S. Department of Labor
Washington, D.C. 20212

The Conference Board
845 Third Avenue
New York, N.Y. 10022

Congressional Budget Office
U.S. Congress
Washington, D.C. 20515

Council of Economic Advisers
Executive Office of the President
Washington, D.C. 20506

Council on Wage and Price Stability
Executive Office of the President
Washington, D.C. 20506

Federal Reserve Board
Assistant to the Board for Public Affairs
Washington, D.C. 20551

Office of Management and Budget
Executive Office of the President
Washington, D.C. 20506

SUGGESTED READINGS

Clark, Lindley, *The Secret Tax*. Homewood, Ill.: Dow Jones-Irwin, 1976.

Costanzo, G. A., "The Great American Seed-Corn Banquet," a paper on inflation in the form of an assignment to graduating seniors, published as a pamphlet by Citicorp, 399 Park Avenue, New York, N.Y. 10043.

Fellner, William, ed., *Contemporary Economic Problems*. Washington, D.C.: American Enterprise Institute for Public Policy Research, 1977.

Friedman, Milton, "What Will Happen to This House Divided?" *Enterprise: Journal of the National Association of Manufacturers,* March 1978, pp. 3–5.

"Fueling Inflation: The Price Input," a statement on inflation adopted by the AFL-CIO Executive Council at its spring 1978 meeting, appearing in *AFL-CIO American Federationist,* July 1978, pp. 1–2. See also in the same issue, Anne Draper, "Measuring Inflation: An Analysis of the CPI," pp. 3–8.

"The Great Government Inflation Machine," Special Report, *Business Week,* May 22, 1978, pp. 106–50.

Kuehner, Charles D., ed., *Capital and Job Formation: Our Nation's 3rd Century Challenge*. Homewood, Ill.: Dow Jones-Irwin, 1978.

Malabre, Alfred L., Jr., *America's Dilemma: Jobs Versus Prices*. New York: Dodd Mead & Co., 1978.

————, *Understanding the Economy: For People Who Can't Stand Economics.* New York: Dodd Mead & Co., 1976.

Owen, Henry, and Charles L. Schultze, eds., *Setting National Priorities: The Next Ten Years.* Washington, D.C.: Brookings Institution, 1976.

Simon, William E., *A Time for Truth.* New York: Reader's Digest Press and McGraw-Hill Book Company, 1978.

Reporting on . . .
WAGES AND
EMPLOYMENT

4

ABE H. RASKIN

INFORMED PRESS COVERAGE of employment and wages requires that reporters have some knowledge not only of economics and politics but also of sociology, for wage and employment issues in the United States as well as in other democratic nations have been influenced greatly by the rise of organized labor.

The American labor movement was born in struggle. The very first recorded strike, by fishermen employed off the coast of Maine, occurred in 1636 and was classed as a mutiny. Until 1842, more than a half-century after the Declaration of Independence and the ratification of the Bill of Rights, unions were viewed by the courts as illegal conspiracies in restraint of trade. Workers who banded together to seek higher wages or improved working conditions found themselves obliged to combat not only their employers but also a hostile united front of judges, the police, and the press.

Much has changed since then.

HOW ORGANIZED IS LABOR?

Unionism's size and strength manifest themselves in so many ways today that the phrase "big labor" has become a journalistic cliché. Yet the reality is that the great bulk of the labor force remains outside union ranks.

Organized and Unorganized Labor

In the 1970's only one worker in every five belonged to a union and the ratio was declining.[1] A quarter-century ago one worker in every four held a union card; the belief among union leaders that this proportion was too low was among the principal spurs for the decision of the American Federation of Labor and Congress of Industrial Organizations to end 20 years of civil war and unite under one roof in 1955.

The hope that their merger would bring a new tide of unionization akin to the one that brought millions into unions in the New Deal years never materialized. But the fact that unionism has failed to grow as rapidly as the number of jobholders is misleading: in many areas organization has been moving forward at a brisk pace, and changing technology in other areas has reduced the number of union members without diminishing the economic power unions are able to bring to bear in their relations with employers or the community.

The paradoxes of great strength and growing weakness that beset the labor scene create pitfalls for the reporter. Every newspaper can expect at least a dozen letters a year from readers objecting to the use of the word "labor" as a descriptive for organized labor. The writers invariably note that the embracing term implies that unions speak for all workers when in fact they represent directly a dwindling minority.

Even in the organized sector of the economy, there are divisions that make for confusion. The AFL-CIO, which embraces more than 100 affiliated unions with a total of 13.5 million members, is accorded primary status in the White House and on Capitol Hill as legislative spokesperson for all labor. However, the two largest unions in the country—the International Brotherhood of Teamsters, with 2 million members, and the United Automobile Workers, with 1.5 million members—are both outside the federation. So are many smaller unions, including the United Mine Workers, a union rich in history.

A further element of confusion arises from the trend among many professional associations, especially organizations of teachers, nurses, and other employees of civil service or nonprofit agencies, to take on most of the characteristics of unions even to the extent of calling strikes. Perhaps the most conspicuous shift of this kind is the one that slowly transformed the National Education Association from a conservative organization in which a dominant voice was exerted by school administrators into a group that rivals the American Federation of Teachers in militant representation of classroom teachers. The association's total membership has grown to a point that puts it close to the teamsters in size.

Traditional unions still represent the great majority of workers in such basic industries as steel and autos. However, nonunion operation has cut into many union strongholds in other industries. Notable among them is construction.

Under the heading "Trade Unions Losing Grip on Construction," a page one story in *The New York Times* in 1977 reported:

Los Angeles, Dec. 11—The building trades unions, long the strongest segment of organized labor, are losing their control of the construction industry.

By the thousands, workers "put their union cards in their pockets or their shoes and go to work nonunion," because that is the way they can find jobs, says Robert A. Georgine, president of the building and construction trades department of the American Federation of Labor and Congress of Industrial Organizations.[2]

The building trades unions have lost their grip even in the big cities, where the unions once exercised total control over hiring to an extent that often bordered on collusion with contractors to exclude competition. In the late 1970's at least half of all construction was being performed under nonunion conditions, and in small-home building the portion exceeded 90 percent.[3]

The Effects of Technology

A similar decline in unionization has occurred in coal mining, a field in which employment has expanded rapidly as the country has sought to reduce its dependence on imported oil for use by electric utilities and other large fuel consumers. The United Mine Workers remains strong in its heartland, the Appalachian region, but the opening up of vast new fields in the West and the displacement of many deep mines by strip-mining operations have reduced the flow of union-mined coal to less than half of the national total. The surface mines have produced another challenge to the UMW. The techniques used to extract coal in these mines are essentially those used to excavate earth, and such construction unions as the International Union of Operating Engineers and the International Brotherhood of Electrical Workers have won bargaining rights for many strip miners.[4]

Changing technology has required both unions and industry to adapt. For example, the containerization of ship cargo has revolutionized the loading and unloading of ocean-borne freight. Merchandise, already crated in large containers when it reaches the dock, can be loaded on ships by large cranes; fewer dockworkers are needed than in the days when merchandise was shipped in smaller boxes and crates. In order to protect the dock workers whose jobs were jeopardized, the International Longshoremen's and Warehousemen's Union entered into a pioneering pact with West Coast ship operators and stevedores in 1960. After a series of costly strikes on the Atlantic and Gulf coasts, the International Longshoremen's Associations there adopted the same basic approach. The result in the Port of New York has been an arrangement under which longshoremen with seniority status are guaranteed full pay for 2,080 hours a year even if there are no ships for them to load, and they are assured an income of close to $20,000 a year.

But there is a gloomier side to this arrangement from the union's view. The use of huge cranes to swing cargo aboard ship, in standard-sized crates piled one atop another, has made it possible to handle a record volume of freight with fewer than half the workers the port employed before the 1970's. New York Shipping Association records show that in August 1978 the number of longshoremen employed in the Port of New York had declined to fewer than 11,000, as against 25,500 on September 30, 1964. Man-hours of work in loading and unloading ships dropped from 42 million in 1964 to 19 million in 1977.

The same kind of personnel shakeout is taking place in many newspapers and commercial printing plants as computers, lasers, and sophisticated electronic devices displace printing practices carried over from the early days of the Linotype. Thus, unions that trace their origins to the dawn of the Republic find themselves compelled by the obliteration of craft lines to accept a lingering death warrant. Printing trades sign contracts safeguarding the jobs and pension rights of existing employees, but with little expectation that any sizable number of new craftsmen will be required by an industry on its way toward one-step movement from a writer's original copy to delivery in the subscriber's home via the television screen or electronic printout, all without the interposition of human hand.[5]

Growth of Public Employment

Equally dramatic adjustments occur as the base of the economy shifts increasingly away from the production of goods and raw materials toward emphasis on services. Shortly after World War II an economic watershed was crossed when, for the first time, the number of Americans employed in services inched ahead of those employed in production. By 1978, just three decades later, the turnaround had gained such momentum that seven workers out of every ten in an employed work force of 94 million were engaged in providing services, from data processing to shining shoes.[6]

The biggest growth area in the postwar period has been state and municipal employment, with education and health services in the forefront. That growth has now leveled off, and in big cities like New York the pressure of tight budgets and an exodus of tax-paying residents are causing the public employee job total to edge downward. Nevertheless, civil service unions continue to grow while most other unions stand still or decline. Nearly half of the country's 9.5 million state and local government workers now belong to unions, and the ratio is even higher among the 2.5 million federal workers.[7] One result of this rapid expansion was that the American Federation of State, County and Municipal Employees, an AFL-CIO affiliate which had fewer than 300,000 members enrolled in 1967, passed the million member mark in April 1978. The last quarter-million came in a single gulp through the absorption of an independent union of New York State public employees.[8]

The circumstances of that marriage of convenience underscore the importance of background in reporting on the labor front. On the surface, the two unions had been the bitterest of rivals for a quarter century. What brought them together was no sudden excess of mutual affection but rather the political orphanage that descended on the independent union when its chief protector in Albany, Nelson A. Rockefeller, quit the governorship in 1973 to become Vice-President. In the ensuing years the unaffiliated group found itself being cannibalized through raids on its membership by such strong AFL-CIO units as the teachers, the service employees, and the laborers. The movement en masse into the organization that had originally been its fiercest detractor was designed to insulate it against more outside raids of this sort.

The merger catapulted the union of state, county, and municipal employees into first place in point of size among the affiliates of the AFL-CIO. Its expanded roster of dues payers enabled it to move slightly ahead of the United Steelworkers of America, which has jurisdiction over workers in aluminum, copper, iron ore, lead, zinc, can manufacturing, and metal fabricating as well as those employed in basic steel. The spurt of the public employees to top rank in the Federation (though they still trail the teamsters and auto workers in the overall listing) makes graphic the speed with which white-collar and professional employment is eclipsing blue-collar jobs in the labor force.

How successfully organized labor reshapes its recruiting approaches in ways that appeal to the needs and wants of these newcomers to the workplace will determine whether unions move forward or backward in their impact on the economy and on society. The degree of that success will be an important area of observation for labor reporters.[9]

WAGES: HOW MUCH IS ENOUGH?

The emergence of chronic inflation and unemployment as afflictions of the economy has added a new dimension to public interest in the contracts arrived at through collective bargaining. Every president in the post-World War II period has pleaded for restraint on the wage front, sometimes through mandatory controls, but more often through guidelines establishing a percentage standard as a flexible ceiling on pay increases or through "jawboning," a process of persuasion applied with varying degrees of coercion by the occupants of the White House. Organized labor's experience with such programs under both Democratic and Republican presidents has convinced it that, outside of war emergencies, the chief effect of controls or percentage guidelines is to hold down wages without arresting the rise in prices.

The reporter's responsibility to put the wage bargain into perspective for the reader is complicated by the absence of any universally accepted measuring rod on what constitutes a fair settlement. The nearest approach to a scientific yardstick is the one adopted in 1948 by General Motors and the United Automobile Workers and now widely used in many other industries. It embodies a "progress sharing" formula designed to guarantee full-time workers an annual improvement in purchasing power equal to the long-term general rise in the productivity of American industry. One part of the formula involves a cost-of-living escalator that neutralizes the erosive impact of inflation by allowing hourly pay rates to go up or down automatically in response to fluctuations in the Consumer Price Index as computed by the federal Bureau of Labor Statistics. The other part uses an annual "improvement factor" fixed at 3 percent; this figure is not geared to the specific productivity of General Motors or the auto industry, but rather reflects annual growth of overall national productivity in the two decades following World War II.

Two circumstances have operated to keep the GM formula from functioning with metronomic precision as a balance wheel for equity on the wage front. One is that the formula has been enriched by the rapid growth in pensions, employer-financed health benefits, time off with pay, and other fringe benefits that now represent between 30 and 40 percent—and sometimes close to 50 percent—of basic wage costs in many unionized companies. The other distortive element is that national productivity has slipped in the last decade to less than the rate incorporated in the GM pattern.

The wage scramble is further complicated by the substantial gaps in average pay between workers in two types of industries; in one type the market control tends to be concentrated in a handful of large, well-established companies; the other type of industry is characterized by much greater diffusion and volatility of ownership. A recent study by the International Ladies Garment Workers Union accents the extent to which the economy has been split into two tiers, with workers in such fields as steel, autos, oil refining, and aluminum consistently earning wages more than double those prevailing in apparel and textile manufacture, retail trade, and the bulk of the service trades. The disparities in income are widened by an even greater gulf between the fringe benefits financed by employers in the "have" and "have not" industries.[10]

Yet another complication in assessing the wage balance is the potential impact of each union settlement on the particular industry's ability to remain competitive in foreign trade, whether in export sale of its own products or in defending domestic markets against overseas invasion. Many

American industries with pay scales at or close to the federal minimum wage are already in danger of extinction because they cannot match the prices set by foreign producers with pay rates far below what can legally be paid here.

WOMEN AND THE CHANGING WORK FORCE

Pressure for changes in the split-level wage structure that locks millions into jobs close to the poverty level is bound to be a matter demanding increased journalistic attention in the years immediately ahead. That is principally because a high proportion of these jobs tend to be filled by women, many of them black or Hispanic, and the next phase of the women's revolution almost certainly will focus on attempts to upgrade the status and earnings of these women at the bottom of the skill and income ladder.

More than 40 million of the 97 million Americans in the work force in 1979 were women. In 1950 there were 18 million women in a total work force of 60 million.[11] Nearly half of all wives now work and six families out of every ten have more than one wage earner. The tidal force of that influx is slowly breaking down the invisible fences that penned women into dead-end jobs as typists, file clerks, waitresses, laundry workers, and laborers in other relatively low-paid fields. A vanguard of women have inched into executive posts in government and business. The executive council of the AFL-CIO long remained an all-male sanctuary, but the Federation's leaders quietly sought a way to elevate a woman to the charmed circle without too grossly breaching the sacrosanct rules that govern succession. Women have penetrated the skilled construction trades; they are at the wheel of huge over-the-road trucks; they are digging coal in underground mines.

The entry of women into the work force has been a human interest story as well as an economic one in local and national news. *The Wall Street Journal,* for example, in 1978 ran an eight-part, page-one series of articles on "Women at Work."[12] A box explained, "Once a small minority, American women who hold a paying job soon may outnumber those who stay at home. This is the first in a series of articles exploring the changes that trend is bringing to our economy, our institutions and the everyday conduct of our lives."

The first article in the series began:

> With their help, the country survives $6,000 cars and $60,000 three-bedroom bungalows. They are one reason why schools are closing and child-care centers are jammed. Businesses court them, yet they have forced many a manager to re-think the rules of business. And in millions of homes, they have brought wholesale changes in everything from eating habits to the institution of marriage.

They are the nation's working women, 41 million strong and growing. . . .[13]

The vast sweep into the job market of younger workers, both men and women, which caused enormous problems and adjustment for industry and society in the last decade, has begun tapering off. But the imprint of the generation that came out of the baby boom after World War II will continue to be pronounced in reshaping the workplace.[14] The ironclad work schedules traditional in industry are less popular with the new breed. This is especially true of working mothers who are seeking to balance home and job responsibilities. A key item of news development will be the kinds of accommodation employers make to workers' desire for more flexible workdays and workweeks. Part-time employment has become more common, partly in response to many women's preference for limited schedules and partly because employers find the use of "temporaries" and part-timers a way to cut the mounting burden of fringe costs. Fifteen million workers are now employed on a part-time basis, one-sixth of all jobholders.[15]

A special problem in need of watching by the press is the sharp rise in the number of families headed by women and the depressed economic state in which a disproportionate number of these families live. A 1977 survey by the Bureau of Labor Statistics showed that nearly one out of seven American families was headed by a woman and that well over half of these women were in the labor force. One out of three of the female-headed families had an income below the officially defined poverty level. Among husband-wife families, the ratio was only one out of eighteen. For youngsters the pinch of such poverty is especially harsh. Among families with children, the median income for those headed by women was only one-third the median for husband-wife families.[16]

INNOVATIONS IN THE WORKPLACE

The boundaries of collective bargaining have broadened over the years to include thousands of subjects beyond wages and working hours. The most spectacular development in pushing out the negotiating horizon has been the evolution since World War II of a far-flung program of employer-financed Social Security under the union label. Industrial pension systems, almost unknown before the war, now have reserves in excess of $280 billion and provide 30 million workers with a cushion of old-age protection beyond that provided by Uncle Sam.[17] Industrial health, hospital, and life insurance plans steadily expand in the range of benefits and in cost. Dental, optical, and psychiatric care are often included as well as basic medical service for workers and their families.

Pensions and ERISA

The great bulk of pension funds have been managed with no hint of scandal, but some, notably the huge Central States Teamsters pension fund, have been a happy hunting ground for corrupt elements.[18] To eradicate such abuses and to establish stricter standards of financial responsibility in all aspects of benefit fund administration, Congress in 1974 passed the Employee Retirement Income Security Act (ERISA), which has created a raft of new problems while it eased many of the old ones. The evolution of operating rules under this complicated law represent a fertile field for journalistic tilling. Of late, reportorial attention has also been directed to a new trend in union application of pension reserves that could profoundly influence the power balance in industrial relations: billions of dollars have been used in jointly trusteed labor-management funds for such diverse purposes as the purchase of municipal securities to keep New York City out of bankruptcy and as a financial club to force policy changes by corporations that are on union "unfair" lists.

Beyond the questions raised by this incipient shift in union tactics are even more fundamental questions the nation will have to grapple with as the assets and obligations of the private pension programs grow ever more mountainous and the volume of guarantees underwritten by the federal government rises. At some point the cumulative burden imposed on the nation's resources by the maintenance of an elaborate structure of private, civil service, and military retirement programs, all existing apart from the basic Social Security system, is bound to bring moves to integrate them all inside a single framework.[19]

Fringe Benefits and the Four-Day Week

How swiftly innovative ideas take hold in collective bargaining has recently been demonstrated anew in the rapid spread of prepaid legal services—plans under which workers are guaranteed qualified lawyers to represent them in cases ranging from disputes with their landlords to tax audits and divorce cases. These were frowned upon by the bar until the Supreme Court declared them legal in 1971 as an exercise of First Amendment rights; the number of such plans then went from one to 3,500 in six years. Some unions finance the legal service programs out of union dues, but the trend is sharply toward incorporating them in the regular union contract with the employers paying the bill in the same way that they do for employees' hospitalization and life insurance.

The most far-reaching changes sought in recent years aim at guaranteeing lifetime income security and at instituting a four-day basic workweek with no cut in weekly pay. Economists question whether either objective can be achieved without cost increases that would wipe out jobs by making

American goods noncompetitive in world markets; nevertheless, some significant breakthroughs toward both goals were made by major unions. In 1976 *Business Week* reported:

> The giant United Steelworkers union, the largest in the AFL-CIO, is about to inject an explosive new issue into collective bargaining. In his keynote speech to its convention in Las Vegas this week, retiring President I. W. Abel said that the union will seek "a lifetime security program for steelworkers."[20]

The union did not achieve its complete goal. But in its 1977 agreements with steel and aluminum makers, the United Steelworkers took its first steps toward assuring that veteran employees would get permanent income in case of plant shutdown or other forced layoff.[21] The United Auto Workers negotiated additional workless days with pay in its major 1976 pacts, raising to 40 days a year the number for which its members are paid without having to show up on the assembly line. That brought the auto union within hailing distance of getting a four-day schedule on a year-round basis and thus intensified labor pressure on Congress to lower the 40-hour standard originally fixed in 1938 by the Federal wage-hour law.

Experiments in Co-determination

Still another novel thrust in labor-management relations will be occupying journalists in the next decade. This is the trend, already well advanced in Western Europe, to give workers and their unions a more direct voice in industrial decision making. Thus far there is almost no evidence that American labor is seriously interested in the most dramatic expression of this trend—the inclusion of workers on corporate boards of directors. In West Germany, as a heritage of British and American allied military government immediately after World War II, the law requires that half of all the membership of supervisory boards be made up of workers. Other Common Market countries have adopted somewhat similar plans.

However, in the United States labor has shied away from such representation, even though the United Auto Workers did make a successful demand for at least one director in its negotiations with ailing Chrysler Corporation in 1979. The dominant view among American unions has been that formal participation in boards of directors would impair their integrity in representing their own members.

Whatever the future of that approach to co-determination, there are persistent signs that both labor and management in this country will be moving toward greater worker input regarding the work conditions at the job and plant level. General Motors and the UAW have for several years been working together on plans to involve assembly line employees and others in tests of autonomous work teams, redesign of tools, pay systems and production methods, and other projects directly related to the safety and security of their own jobs. Similar experiments have been undertaken in many other plants and communities, by management alone in nonunion enterprises and jointly by management and labor where unions speak for the workers.[22]

It would be an exaggeration to contend that these experiments have yet proven either their durability or their worth, but reporters will have an important role in communicating whatever is learned about what makes some tests work and others fail. The ways in which workers are brought into active involvement in functions traditionally sacrosanct to employers will be of wide interest, as will the dividends—or lack of dividends—in employee satisfaction and efficiency. The same will be true of the evolution of employee stock ownership plans and other forms of profit-sharing, with or without tax preferences.[23]

PUBLIC POLICY IN THE WORKPLACE

Even though the AFL-CIO and the National Association of Manufacturers are equally effusive in their declarations that government should keep hands off labor-management relations, the federal presence in the workplace has been an assertive one through all the years since the New Deal. Indeed, the start came even earlier with passage of the Railway Labor Act of 1926 establishing orderly patterns for union recognition, collective bargaining, and strike settlement in the nation's railroads. In 1932, Herbert Hoover's last year in the White House, Congress passed the Norris-La Guardia Act outlawing certain anti-union practices by industry and drastically limiting the right of judges to enjoin strikes.[24]

But the real turning point came when the 1933 National Industrial Recovery Act included provisions encouraging unionization and collective bargaining, along with a floor under wages and a ceiling on working hours, as part of Franklin D. Roosevelt's "Blue Eagle" plan for industrial revival through codes of fair competition. By the time the Supreme Court in 1935 struck down the act as unconstitutional, unions in mining, men's and women's clothing, and many other fields hard hit by the Great Depression had picked themselves up off the floor and signed tens of thousands of new members.

The gap left by invalidation of the NRA codes, promulgated by the National Recovery Administration under the 1933 act, was quickly filled by a succession of New Deal laws, most of them enacted by Congress over bitter employer resistance; these put a firm statutory foundation under collective bargaining, created a Social Security system of old age and survivor insurance and a federal-state partnership in unemployment insurance, and made minimum wages and maximum hours in interstate commerce a permanent concern of Uncle Sam.

The Minimum Wage

The original Fair Labor Standards Act of 1938 fixed the minimum pay floor at only 25 cents an hour, but postwar inflation pushed the minimum up to $2.65 by the start of 1978, to $2.90 in 1979, and to $3.10 at the beginning of 1980.

Many economists argue that the floor is now so high that each increase causes employers to squeeze out workers through the substitution of labor-saving machinery or reorganization of operations. The Department of Labor says its studies do not confirm such adverse consequences on opportunities for those at the bottom of the skill and experience ladder, but the years immediately ahead are likely to see various experiments aimed at achieving a balance between decent wage standards and the fostering of entry-level jobs in an economy dedicated to full employment.[25]

The debate over the degree to which a higher federal minimum wage helps or hurts disadvantaged workers, especially youngsters looking for their first job, became particularly fierce in 1978 after the statutory pay floor had jumped from $2.30 an hour to $2.65 in a period of high unemployment and inflation. G. William Miller, newly appointed by President Carter as chairman of the Federal Reserve System, urged that a second increase to $2.90, already scheduled for January 1, 1979, be postponed. A similar suggestion came from Treasury Secretary Michael Blumenthal. Secretary of Labor Ray Marshall and the AFL-CIO strongly demurred, however. The increases were not postponed.

Secretary Marshall pointed to federal figures showing that total employment had gone up by 1.6 million in the first half-year after the minimum wage was increased. Included were 150,000 more jobs for teenagers. However, most industry leaders and many economists outside management and labor noted that the economy was still on the upgrade from a 1974–1975 recession and insisted that the increase in employment would have been substantially greater if the minimum wage had remained at its old level. "The economy always adds some jobs during a period of growth," declared Professor Walter E. Williams of Temple University, who had been a consultant on the minimum wage to the Congressional Joint Economic Committee.

Multiple Government Interventions

The range of government intervention in industrial affairs has become encyclopedic. Among the laws that generate newspaper, radio, and television stories in profusion are Title VII of the Civil Rights Act of 1964, prohibiting discrimination in employment on the basis of race or sex, and the Occupational Safety and Health Act of 1970, authorizing federal authorities to establish and enforce standards to reduce deaths and injuries from industrial accidents and to curb the use of carcinogens and other toxic substances that damage health and often cause birth defects.

Despite virtually unanimous agreement on the virtuousness of their purposes, both laws have become increasingly controversial. Enforcement of Title VII to broaden opportunities for women, blacks, and Hispanics has led to wide charges of "reverse discrimination" by white males. In similar fashion, application of safety and health rules has brought widespread complaint by employers that the extra outlays needed for new equipment or less hazardous procedures push them toward bankruptcy, jeopardize jobs, and worsen inflation. The tug-of-war is not likely to end quickly, and the White House usually finds itself in the role of final arbiter in disputes among Cabinet officers and other administrators on how forceful the government ought to be on these issues.

Environmental rules governing industrial establishments also frequently spawn controversy of the same sort. In some situations the union and the company are on the same side in opposing government mandates they feel will stifle jobs or force plant closings. In others the union is the prime mover in urging a government crackdown in the interest of the health of its members and of the community in which they live.

Old Rights and New Controversies

The foundation stone of governmental involvement in labor-management affairs was the Wagner Labor Relations Act, passed in 1935 to broaden and legitimize the principles of collective bargaining that had had their insecure beginnings in the invalidated NRA codes of fair competition. This Magna Carta of the modern labor movement gave workers the right of free choice on whether to have a union, required employers to accord exclusive bargaining rights to majority unions, and established a National Labor Relations Board to conduct employee elections and monitor unfair labor practices by employers.

It was the Wagner Act that provided the principal impetus for unionization of the steel, auto, and other mass production industries, until then bastions of the open shop. But in the period immediately after World War II a rash of strikes in every sector of the economy, coupled with a tide of inflationary wage settlements, caused a revulsion in popular sentiment. Responding to charges that the Wagner Act had swung the pendulum too far in favor of labor, in 1947 Congress passed, over President Truman's veto, the Taft-Hartley Act, which was aimed at redressing the balance. The new law prohibited the closed shop, under which no worker could be hired unless he or she belonged to the dominant union, but it left employers and unions free to negotiate union-shop agreements, under which newly hired workers were obliged to join the union within a specified time. However, even this right was qualified by a provision that permitted individual states to outlaw all forms of compulsory unionism by enacting so-called right-to-work laws of their own. Such laws in 1978 existed in twenty states, most of them in the South and Southwest.

Taft-Hartley also established a list of unfair labor practices by unions that were subject to "cease and desist" orders by the NLRB in the same manner as those established against employers by the original Wagner Act. Secondary boycotts, under which unions called strikes against one employer to bring pressure on another, were made illegal and the Labor Board was empowered to seek court injunctions to halt strikes that grew out of interunion battles over jurisdiction. The 1947 law had an even more important provision for injunctive relief. It authorized the President of the United States to obtain an 80-day no-strike order from the federal courts whenever he felt an industrial tie-up might imperil the national health or safety.[26]

The next major revision in the basic labor law came in 1959 when revelations of gangster penetration and undemocratic practices in the International Brotherhood of Teamsters and several smaller unions impelled Congress to pass the Landrum-Griffin Labor Reform Act. Concerned primarily with the internal affairs of unions, the law contains a "bill of rights" for union members. Its purpose is to prohibit abuses of power by autocratic or corrupt officials, and that aim is reinforced by provisions for federal review of disputed union elections and a sizable catalogue of requirements for disclosure of union finances, contracts, and fiduciary arrangements.[27]

In 1977, under the double spur of a shrinkage in union membership and the favorable political climate created by the election of President Carter and a union-backed majority in Congress, organized labor decided to concentrate all its legislative muscle on enactment of a bill that would reverse the negative thrust labor viewed as responsible for both Taft-Hartley and Landrum-Griffin. Its goal was a law that would bring the rules governing unionization and bargaining back into close consonance with the initial precepts of the Wagner Act.

Relying heavily on its frustration in trying to organize the Southern textile empire of J. P. Stevens & Co., labor won President Carter's backing for a bill intended to ensure speedier employee elections and provide stiffer penalties against violators of the labor laws. The President gave his endorsement only after the AFL-CIO had agreed to drop a section nullifying the right of the states to enforce right-to-work laws, as well as another provision that would have enabled unions to obtain certification on a show of membership cards without any election.

What emerged was a measure that most impartial experts and all six living ex-Secretaries of Labor, both Republican and Democratic, viewed as a relatively modest recasting of established labor-management practices. Nevertheless, the bill's consideration on Capitol Hill in 1978 touched off the fiercest political battle between industry and labor in the three decades since passage of the Taft-Hartley Act. The unions insisted that the measure's sole purpose was to make real the rights of free choice and collective bargaining supposedly guaranteed to workers more than four decades earlier. Employers called it a union "power grab" intended to put the government into the role of rescuer for a labor movement sliding downhill in membership and prestige.

A filibuster in the Senate, strongly supported by almost all elements of business, small and large, finally forced the bill back into committee, but the intensity of the conflict left a heritage of ill will that will long affect labor-management relations and require close press scrutiny in the years ahead.[28]

Organized Labor at the Crossroads

The labor movement is very much at a crossroads, with no present certainty on whether it will rise or fall in size and power in the next decade. Equally uncertain is whether its relations with industry will move in the direction of long-term peace pacts and closer collaboration on matters of public policy or back toward bitter confrontations on the picket line and in the legislative arena on the 1930's model.

Note already has been taken of the trend in many basic fields toward cooperative arrangements. But the opposite trend has been assertive too in more recent years. Employers have been taking a more aggressive posture at many bargaining tables. Where once unions did all the demanding, management now comes in with demands of its own for a giveback by the union of concessions it got in past contracts. Changing technology and increased availability of nonunion labor have enabled many employers to keep operating in the face of union strike calls, instead of taking the posting of a picket line as a mandate to shut down.

The nation's newspapers have already emerged as a microcosm in this trend toward trial by combat. In this day of electronic printing, many publishers have concluded that craft separations on the union side put management in a strategic position to move for changes in restrictive union rules without risking suspension of publication. Covering that kind of story puts the reporter much on the spot; however, no personal embarrassment, much less compromise of professional integrity, need ensue if both the reporter and the editors treat the conflict as just another news story to be covered for its news value. See, for example, the 17-column, blow-by-blow account in *The New York Times* that told its readers why New York's newspapers were blacked out for 116 days by a printers' strike in 1962–1963.[29]

Union organization of local, state, and federal government employees also came to a crossroads of its own as taxpayers, plagued by inflation, resisted the higher costs of government generally and higher wages for unionized public employees in particular. For example, *The New York Times* in 1977 reported:

> Los Angeles, June 1—Policemen and firemen here got some good news the other day: Under a wage formula that has been in use for 52 years, their annual base pay will rise shortly to $20,358.
>
> They also got some bad news: Two city councilmen and a half-dozen taxpayers' associations, deploring what they called "runaway" wages for public employees, opened a campaign aimed at repealing the law setting the wage formula.[30]

FOCUS ON THE WORKER

In addition to being aware of all the intricacies of organized labor and formal labor-management relations, it is important to remember that the reporter's sphere of concern also covers workers outside unions. Since such workers outnumber those in unions by three to one in the nonfarm work force and by four to one if all workers are counted, their needs and problems cry out for press attention.

Workers Outside Union Ranks

Interestingly, the nonunion group is made up, in considerable measure, of workers at opposite poles of the income, education, and skill scale. Unions are weak among professional employees and among the best-educated and best-paid white-collar employees, though that differentiation has been somewhat reduced by the mass unionization of teachers and civil service professionals. Unions are also weak among many of the least secure workers in the economy, those with little or no schooling and skills. In the last few years millions of illegal aliens have been added to the crowded ranks of these seekers after low-end jobs.

Despite the sharp increases made in the minimum wage, many of these unskilled workers remain in the ranks of the working poor, obliged to supplement their meager earnings with public welfare allowances. The high turnover among these workers in the light manufacturing and service industries, the comparatively small size of their establishments, and the frequency with which their employers go out of business have caused most unions to ignore them. That has left the labor field largely to racketeers who offer the employers "sweetheart contracts," under which they get immunity from legitimate unionization at cut-rate.

Among more advantaged workers, the lack of union penetration has been less the product of slack effort than of no persuasive argument as to why such workers would be better off with unions. Part of the holdback, unquestionably, has its roots in the public's identifying unions with blue-collar workers. But the extent to which computerization and other advances in technology have introduced assembly-line techniques into white-collar and professional activities makes that an increasingly blurred dividing line.

The slim inroads unions have made among upper-rank workers are better explained by unions' failure to modernize either their approaches or their definition of the mission they pursue. That mission can still be summed up essentially in Samuel Gompers' single word, "More." In a period when inflation gobbles up pay increases before workers can get to the supermarket to spend them, that is scarcely a comprehensive enough slogan. Many in the new generation of union leaders recognize that inadequacy. Whether they can evolve new goals with greater appeal will be a central question of the 1980's.

Employment and Unemployment

The labor reporter will have to be a scorekeeper not only in this effort by labor to reshape its objectives but also in the society's efforts to bring down unemployment and the runaway rise in living costs. The nation made an amorphous commitment to full employment in the Employment Act of 1946, and from time to time since then Congress has debated whether that commitment should be made more specific, such as with the Humphrey-Hawkins Act, establishing a 4 percent target for joblessness.

The practicality of that target remains much in dispute. But even more vigorous dispute surrounds the validity of the figures currently used to determine how high unemployment actually is. In 1978, with the official unemployment rate hovering around 6 percent, the federal government was spending $17 billion on public works, public service jobs, and other stimulus programs keyed to the idleness figures. Yet there was almost universal agreement that the methods used to determine how many workers were jobless in any given locality were highly unreliable.

A Presidential commission was appointed to make recommendations for revising both the methodology and the concepts used in tallying the unemployed. Among the questions that needed to be decided was whether workers who have stopped looking for work out of discouragement should be excluded from the total, as they have been, or be counted. Another question was whether a hardship factor should be included in the statistics to recognize the differing impact of unemployment in families with only one breadwinner as against the 60 percent of families that have two or more employed members.

The Consumer Price Index, the mythical market basket of goods and services that serves as the chief barometer of the rise or fall of inflation, was also undergoing revision. A basic change took place early in 1978 to make it reflective of the spending habits of all urban and suburban consumers, roughly 80 percent of the population. Until then the index had been confined to urban wage earners and clerical workers, a sampling only half as large. However, the base data used in the survey were already badly out of date and the federal Bureau of Labor Statistics adopted a procedure for more frequent checks of what the average citizen buys.

The trustworthiness of these figures is of more than academic interest. A change of 1 percent in the index can trigger a billion-dollar transfer of income. Reference was made in an earlier chapter to the 60 percent of major union contracts that contain cost-of-living escalator clauses, or COLA's geared to the CPI. Similar indexing affects retirement benefits of millions of Social Security recipients and also of federal pensioners, both civilian and military. Also affected is a broad list of other payments, from food stamp allotments to child-support payments under divorce settlements.[31]

And those millions are but part of the potential audience for informed reporting on wages and employment.

NOTES—CHAPTER 4

1. *Statistical Abstract of the United States*, 1977, p. 418.

2. *New York Times*, December 12, 1977, p. 1.

3. *Ibid.*

4. *New York Times*, March 28, 1978, p. 53.

5. *New York Times*, July 29, 1974, p. 12.

6. The shift in job ratios is reflected in the monthly series, "Employment and Earnings," published by the Bureau of Labor Statistics.

7. In Release USDL 77-771, issued on Labor Day, 1977, the Department of Labor reported that 4,521,000 employees of state and local governments belonged to unions. Among federal employees the figure was 1,332,000. The figures had been compiled for the 1977 edition of the department's *Directory of National Unions and Employees Associations.*

8. *New York Times*, May 2, 1978, p. 20. The report of the AFL-CIO Executive Council to the Federation's 1977 convention in Los Angeles showed (on page 50) that the AFSCME had grown from 99,000 at the time of the labor movement merger in 1955 to 685,000 by 1977. A series of absorptions and election victories carried the membership past the million mark early in 1978.

9. For a basically optimistic assessment of the current status of organized labor, see Derek C. Bok and John T. Dunlop, *Labor and the American Community* (New York: Simon & Schuster, 1970).

10. "The Other Economy: America's Working Poor," Gus Taylor, assistant president of the International Ladies Garment Workers Union. The study was sponsored by the David Dubinsky Foundation and published as a special issue of *The New Leader*, May 1978.

11. See "Employment and Earnings for June 1978," *Bureau of Labor Statistics*, p. 24. See also *Statistical Abstract of the United States*, 1977, p. 391.

12. The series appeared between August 28 and September 22, 1978.

13. Alfred L. Malabre, Jr., "As Their Ranks Swell, Women Holding Jobs Reshape U.S. Society," *Wall Street Journal*, August 28, 1978, p. 1.

14. Robert W. Bednarzik and Deborah P. Klein, "Labor Force Trends: A Synthesis and Analysis," *Monthly Labor Review*, October 1977.

15. "Employment and Earnings for June 1978," *Bureau of Labor Statistics*, p. 31.

16. Beverly L. Johnson, "Women Who Head Families, 1970–1977," *Monthly Labor Review*, February 1978.

17. *New York Times*, June 25, 1978, Financial section, p. 2.

18. The Central States Teamster pension fund was investigated in 58 volumes of testimony and seven reports filed between 1957 and 1960 by the Senate Select Committee on Improper Activities in the Labor and Management Field, headed by Senator John L. McClellan of Arkansas.

19. For background on the interplay of the public and private systems of retirement protection, see Robert M. Ball, *Social Security Today and Tomorrow* (New York: Columbia University Press, 1978), Chapter XIV.

20. "The Steelworkers' Pitch for Lifetime Security," *Business Week*, September 13, 1976, pp. 82, 85.

21. *New York Times*, April 10, 1977, p. 1.

22. David Jenkins, *Job Power* (Garden City, N.Y.: Doubleday & Co., 1973). Also, Paul Dickson, *The Future of the Workplace* (New York: Weybright & Talley, 1975).

23. For an appraisal of the work environment in the 1980's as forecast by a variety of experts, see *Work in America: The Decade Ahead*, ed. Clark Kerr and Jerome M. Rosow (New York: Van Nostrand Reinhold, 1979).

24. For a history of governmental policies affecting labor from the New Deal to the mid-1970's, see "Federal Policies and Worker Status Since the Thirties," ed. Joseph P. Goldberg, Eileen Ahern, William Haber, and Rudolph A. Oswald (Madison, Wisc.: Industrial Relations Research Association, Series 1976).

25. *Wall Street Journal*, August 15, 1978, p. 48.

26. Harry A. Millis and Emily Clark Brown, *From the Wagner Act to Taft-Hartley* (Chicago: University of Chicago Press, 1950).

27. An excellent compendium of all current legislation affecting labor is provided by Benjamin J. Taylor and Fred Witney, *Labor Relations Law*, 2nd ed. (Englewood Cliffs, N.J.: Prentice-Hall, 1975).

28. A sample of the fierce resentment the battle stirred on the union side is contained in a speech delivered by Lane Kirkland, AFL-CIO secretary-treasurer, at a "Work in America" seminar at Arden House, Harriman, N.Y., May 24, 1978.

29. *New York Times*, April 1, 1963, p. 1.

30. "Opposition to Raises for Public Workers Found Growing in Many Cities," *New York Times*, June 2, 1977, p. 15.

31. For a discussion of some current problems affecting the federal price indexes, see Edward Meadows, "Our Flawed Inflation Indexes," *Fortune*, April 24, 1978.

SOURCES OF INFORMATION

Bureau of Labor Statistics
U.S. Department of Labor
Washington, D.C. 20212

Bureau of the Census
U.S. Department of Commerce
Suitland, Md. 20233

Council on Wage and Price Stability
Executive Office of the President
Washington, D.C. 20506

Employment Standards Administration
U.S. Department of Labor
Washington, D.C. 20210

Environmental Protection Agency
Public Affairs Office
Washington, D.C. 20460

Equal Employment Opportunity
Commission
Director of Public Affairs
Washington, D.C. 20506

Federal Mediation and Conciliation Service
Information Director
Washington, D.C. 20427

National Labor Relations Board
Director of Information
Washington, D.C. 20570

National Mediation Board
Executive Secretary
Washington, D.C. 20005

Occupational Safety and Health
Administration
U.S. Department of Labor
Washington, D.C. 20210

SUGGESTED READINGS

Beirne, Joseph A., "The Role of Labor in Politics," *Washington Post,* October 10, 1973, p. 17.

Bok, Derek C., and John T. Dunlop, *Labor and the American Community.* New York: Simon & Schuster, 1970.

Dickson, Paul, *The Future of the Workplace.* New York: Weybright & Talley, 1975.

Jenkins, David, *Job Power.* Garden City, N.Y.: Doubleday & Co., 1973.

Kennedy, Robert F., *The Enemy Within.* New York: Harper & Brothers, 1960.

Kerr, Clark, and Jerome M. Rosow, eds., *Work in America: The Decade Ahead.* New York: Van Nostrand Reinhold, 1979.

Kirkland, Lane, "Free Trade Unions-Force for Democracy," *AFL-CIO American Federationist,* April 1978, pp. 1–5.

Kistler, Alan, and Charles McDonald, "The Continuing Challenge of Organizing," *AFL-CIO American Federationist,* November 1976, pp. 8–13.

Millis, Harry A., and Emily Clark Brown, *From the Wagner Act to Taft-Hartley.* Chicago: University of Chicago Press, 1950.

Monthly Labor Review, U.S. Department of Labor, Washington, D.C.

Raskin, A. H., "Democracy in Unions: Grudging Acceptance," *New York Times,* February 6, 1977, p. E2.

Roberts, Chalmers M., "Despotism to Anarchy: The Decline of the UMW," *Washington Post,* March 15, 1978, p. 15.

Sheridan, Walter, *The Fall and Rise of Jimmy Hoffa.* New York: Saturday Review Press, 1972.

Worklife, U.S. Department of Labor, Washington, D.C. (published every other month).

Reporting on ...
PRODUCTS, SERVICES, AND CONSUMERISM

5

JOHN W. HAZARD

A REPORTER EMBARKING ON COVERAGE of the infinitely varied array of products and services offered by business, and on the reaction to them known as "consumerism," faces a complex interaction of claims, counterclaims, regulations, legislation, and legal actions.

Consider, for example, the claims and counterclaims that swirled in the 1970's around the proposal that Congress create a consumer protection agency.

Congress in the 1960's and early 1970's had passed significant legislation creating new federal agencies that were charged with enhancing the safety and efficiency of autos and other consumer products. Then Ralph Nader and other consumer advocates began to press for the creation of a consumer protection agency that would not itself have any direct regulatory functions but would represent the consumer interest before all other federal agencies. The supporters of the proposal argued that existing agencies, despite their mandates from Congress, had not acted consistently in the consumer or public interest. Business opponents of the proposal claimed that another new agency was unnecessary and uneconomic.

Bills that would create the consumer agency passed the Senate or House five times in seven years, but by increasingly narrow margins. Finally, in early 1978, a watered-down, compromise version that was strongly supported by Mr. Nader, President Carter, and the Democratic leadership in Congress came to a crucial House vote. The proposed consumer protection agency was defeated by a vote of 227 to 189.

The next morning the defeat of the bill was reported on the front page of *The New York Times* in a story with this lead:

> Washington, Feb. 8—The House of Representatives today shattered for the foreseeable future consumers' hopes for a Federal agency to represent their interests when it rejected creation of such an office.[1]

The same morning, the story with a significantly different lead was reported in *The Wall Street Journal:*

> Washington—In an important symbolic test, the House decided that it's more appealing to be against the bureaucracy than for the consumer.[2]

Both stories went on to quote members of Congress who explained the vote in terms of a rising public reaction against "bureaucracy" and "big government." The first lead made no reference to that reaction. The second and shorter lead conveyed the meaning of the House vote and, at the same time, avoided taking sides between the claims of proponents and opponents of the proposed consumer protection agency.

The rise and fall of the proposal to create a consumer protection agency in Washington well illustrates both the need and the difficulty reporters of consumer affairs will find in maintaining an unbiased view. How do you go about it? The most important element of good reporting in any beat is to understand the subject and its history. W. M. Kiplinger, a veteran newspaperman and founder of the *Kiplinger Letter,* said that fundamental education is more important than the techniques of journalism. The techniques that also must be learned are to touch all bases, to hear all sides, and to report the pertinent facts in an accurate and perceptive manner that best serves your publication or broadcast station and, above all, the reader, listener, or viewer who is the "consumer."

CONSUMERS AND CONSUMERISM DEFINED

The story of the proposed consumer protection agency also illustrates that consumer affairs, while often described narrowly, also can be defined very broadly. Broadly defined, consumer affairs embrace not only the necessities and amenities of everyday living, but also economics, politics, and a host of other forces that bear on the production and consumption of myriad goods and services.

The consumer is everyman and everywoman. We may not all be voters or even taxpayers, but everyone is a consumer. Ironically, because the term is amorphous, the audience for consumer news has been defined traditionally in narrow ways. Consumer news has been compartmentalized into automotive news, real estate news, food news, and so forth. In other words, it often has been viewed by both editors and readers as an extension of a daily newspaper's advertising sections, and consumer news thus defined has not won many, if any, journalism prizes.

Advertising is not to be decried. For one thing, it pays the salaries of most print and broadcast journalists. For another, it performs a valuable economic function. Some advertising may exaggerate or even mislead, but the fundamental function of advertising is to bring buyers and sellers together and that function obviously is valuable and indeed inevitable.

Americans have in the past obtained most of their consumer news about autos, food, real estate, and other goods and services from advertising. Recently, however, many newspapers, periodicals, and broadcast outlets also have begun to provide consumers with interesting news of goods and services in novel formats that are not simply extensions of advertising sections. The formats often take the form of "style," "living," or "home" sections of newspapers and magazines. Similar formats have been adopted in radio and television broadcasting.

The new formats appear to reflect heightened public interest in the quality and price of goods and services, and that interest presumably is related to inflation and to the rise of what is called consumerism. The terms "consumer" and "consumerism" should not be confused, however.

We have said that a *consumer* is every person. *Consumerism* describes a somewhat amorphous movement that is both political and economic in nature and that has emerged with identifiable leaders, organizations, and objectives. The movement has been marked in recent years by sharp and expanding probing of quality, safety, and prices, along with a skepticism concerning the methods and motives of businesses. The complex movement has involved hundreds of grass-roots groups of citizens, educators, and lawyers; influential national organizations; local and state government agencies, and federal government agencies and departments administering ever more complex consumer laws and regulations.

The business community's attempts to cope with consumerism have involved corporate "consumer affairs" or "public affairs" or "government affairs" offices and executives as well as trade associations and the Better Business Bureau. City councils and state legislatures, as well as Congress, have become involved. The courts have become deeply involved through the filing of many small claims for allegedly unsafe or defective products. Both legislatures and courts have grappled with efforts to adjudicate such claims more efficiently, for example by grouping the claims under so-called "class action" lawsuits.

The media often are in the middle of the maze and the reporter covering the consumer beat finds it a real problem to maintain perspective. Ralph

Nader and other leaders of the consumerist movement have seemed always on the offensive and their objectives often have had political goals of consumer protection legislation. Business has seemed always on the defensive and has seemed to be swimming against a tide of news about unsafe products, potentially harmful ingredients in foods and drugs, and recalls of millions of autos, tires, and other products. Business has complained that the bad news always gets the big play. Business people, whether or not guilty of offering questionable goods and services, feel that their responses to attacks receive less prominence than the initial thrusts.

Katherine Graham, chairman of The Washington Post Company, has responded to the business criticism that bad news is displayed more prominently than good news. She said in a speech before a business group that the criticism

> assumes that there is a great mass of something called "good news" that the media aren't covering. The system doesn't work that way. By definition, news is the dramatic, the disastrous, and the unusual. When millions of workers go home at night without being poisoned on the job, or when new cars do not break down, that is important—it is seldom news. . . .
>
> That is not to say there is nothing that news companies can improve. You can certainly ask—indeed, demand—coverage that is accurate, fair, and grounded in real understanding of events. You can ask for much better economic coverage, an area in which much of the press has been quite superficial until recently.[3]

As she suggested, business provides consumers with a multitude of goods and services that do not ordinarily make the news because safety, quality, and price are taken for granted. Some goods and services in the over $2 trillion American economy are of questionable safety, quality, or price. But consumer and consumerism news, as a part of business and economic coverage, should be "accurate, fair and grounded in real understanding of events."

THE CONSUMER MOVEMENT

Consumerism is not entirely new as a popular or political movement. Given the fact that private business always has supplied Americans with most of the necessities and amenities of day-to-day living, relations between producers and consumers for many decades have been matters of some public interest.

Many years ago, when businesses were smaller and more local, relations between producers and consumers were more personal. As companies and corporations have grown, those relationships have become more impersonal and distant. Nonetheless, both official and self-appointed spokesmen for the consumer interest appeared on the public scene more than a century ago and various consumer movements have emerged at various times in American history.

A History of Consumerism

Concern with the consumer interest has its roots deep in the nation's past. Thomas Jefferson labored to develop a weights and measures law. Through most of the first century of U.S. history, consumer goods were relatively simple and their quality was not difficult to determine. As production centers became more remote from customers, and products and their ingredients became more complex, the demand arose for better labeling, warranties, and controls. In 1850 a pure food and drink law was enacted in California.

The pioneer consumer advocate was Harvey W. Wiley, who served as chief chemist in the U.S. Department of Agriculture in 1883. He found instances of pepper extended with dust and coffee mixed with acorns. In 1902 Dr. Wiley conducted the first test of food additives and obtained publicity by feeding 12 young chemists, known as the Poison Squad, a diet of adulterated foods. At the same time the American Medical Association was uncovering ineffective or dangerous drugs. Soothing syrup for infants was found to contain morphine and opium.

Upton Sinclair's *The Jungle,* published in 1906, was a novel about a Lithuanian peasant who emigrated to the United States and took a job in a meat-packing house in Chicago. A socialist periodical financed Sinclair while he spent seven weeks among the stockyard workers. His fellow socialist, Jack London, saw the book as an appeal for socialism and wrote that "What *Uncle Tom's Cabin* did for the black slaves *The Jungle* has a large chance to do for the white slaves of today." But the public ignored the socialist implications. What shocked readers was the relatively incidental descriptions of how sausages were made, how the stockyards smelled, and how hogs that had died of cholera were allegedly made into lard. The book was a best seller and was partly responsible for Congress's passage in 1906[4] of the Food and Drug Act and the Federal Meat Inspection Act.

Prior to World War I, Congress enacted various other laws of interest to consumers. Improving on the work of Thomas Jefferson, Congress in 1901 set up the National Bureau of Standards to develop accurate and uniform techniques of measurement of time, temperature, light, and so forth. Other laws included the Federal Trade Commission Act of 1914, which created an agency to protect business and consumers against unfair competition.

In the depression years of the 1930's, F. J. Schlink founded Consumers

Research, a laboratory for testing the efficacy of consumer products. Products were rated and results were published with brand names in the *Consumer Bulletin*. Some years later a splinter group formed Consumers Union, which began publishing *Consumer Reports* and became by far the larger of the two organizations.

Also during the depression period, the New Deal in Washington took various actions relative to the consumer interest. The New Deal's efforts under the National Industrial Recovery Act of 1933 to raise prices may not in retrospect appear to have been in the consumer interest and the act subsequently was declared unconstitutional by the Supreme Court. When the efforts were undertaken, however, President Roosevelt set up various consumer boards to advise the National Industrial Recovery Administration. During the New Deal period, Congress passed other laws, such as the Securities Act of 1933 and the Food, Drug, and Cosmetic Act of 1938, that were more clearly intended to protect consumers.

The 1938 law was passed in part because of the work of Ruth de Forest Lamb, who during the New Deal was employed as a consumer representative in the Department of Agriculture. She put together an exhibit of posters, bottles, and labels illustrating horror stories in connection with cosmetics and other food and drug products. One of her illustrations related to a product known as B & M External Remedy, which was made of turpentine, ammonia, eggs, and water and was advertised as a cure for "tuberculosis, pneumonia, flu, peritonitis, cancer, locomotor ataxia, infantile paralysis" and assorted other dread diseases.[5]

When World War II came, President Roosevelt created the National Defense Commission, a business and labor advisory group, and included among its members a consumer member, Harriett Elliott of the University of North Carolina. After the war, Governor Averill Harriman of New York appointed Dr. Persia Campbell, an economics professor, to his staff as a consumer adviser.

The many state and federal actions that had been taken in the consumer interest apparently were not very effective, however, In 1956 *Changing Times* listed 20 of the most common consumer complaints: bait advertising, fictional prices, fraudulent food freezer plans, debt adjusters, earn money at home schemes, vending machine franchises, correspondence schools that promised the prospective student would pass civil service exams, money back guarantees, phony medical cures, phony labels, "hi-fi" sets that were not hi-fi, home improvement plans ("your home has been selected as a display house"), photo salesmen ("your child has been selected"), encyclopedia salesmen, itinerant nursery and tree "experts," cemetery lot salesmen, phone charity solicitations, coupon books, unordered merchandise, and sales of Florida and Arizona real estate by mail to out-of-state buyers.[6]

The Modern Consumer Movement

The most recent rise of consumerism might be dated from 1960, when John F. Kennedy was campaigning in New Hampshire for president. He made a remark about consumer rights and was surprised by the strongly favorable reaction. Shortly thereafter, he grasped the issue and devoted a whole speech to it in New York.[7] After his election, President Kennedy in March 1962 sent a message to Congress outlining his proposed Consumer Bill of Rights. The proposal embraced the right to safety, to be informed, to choose, and to be heard.[8]

Thereafter a 12-member Consumers' Advisory Council was created to study consumer needs and, after John Kennedy died, President Lyndon Johnson brought Esther Peterson to the White House as consumer adviser to his "Great Society" programs. In the meantime, Dr. Frances Kelsey of the Food and Drug Administration made headlines by blocking American use of thalidomide, a drug that had been used abroad and had been associated with deformities among children.

Ralph Nader flashed onto the screen in 1965 with his book *Unsafe at Any Speed.*[9] With all due credit to Nader, his thesis was not exactly new. In April 1953, James K. Knudsen, ICC Commissioner and U.S. Transportation Administrator, had warned:

> Already we are too far along the wrong road toward high powered engines and excessive speed.... Already 1953 models are at least 10 years ahead of the road system they must use.... Motor accidents are a scandal. Americans are rivalling Louis XVI in the emphasis on luxury. In 1952, auto accidents cost more lives than all yet lost in Korea. The public, encouraged by the auto makers, have gone power mad. Let's put the spotlight on safety.[10]

But in 1953 the public was not ready for change. By 1966 it was, and the National Traffic and Motor Vehicle Safety Act established safety standards for tires and autos.

The flood of consumer legislation had begun in 1961 with the Truth-in-Packaging Act. In 1962 came the Hazardous Substance Act for labeling of drugs. Other new laws covered consumer goods packaging and labeling and lending.

In 1967 a newspaper feature called *Action Line* was syndicated to assist consumers in resolving their complaints. That year also a professor at Arizona State University formed the Confederation of Consumer Organizations.

In the early 1970's, state and local governments began creating consumer protection agencies, many attached to the offices of state attorneys.

Father Robert J. McEwen of Boston University called an assembly of 200 consumer organizations which led to the formation of the Consumer Federation of America, largely financed by labor unions.[11]

By 1977, consumer organizations had proliferated to such an extent that a directory of federal, state, and local consumer offices published by the U.S. Department of Health, Education and Welfare contained the names of over 650 of them.[12] The Consumer Federation of America's research center that year convened a conference attended by over 250 activists from 38 states.[13]

The creation of additional consumer-oriented federal agencies continued into the early 1970's. Congress created the Consumer Product Safety Commission in 1972 to establish product safety standards and to ban sale of noncomplying products. Another new agency with consumer-related concerns was the Occupational Safety and Health Administration, which Congress established in 1973 to develop and enforce worker safety and health regulations. Other new federal laws related to poison prevention, product warranties, and consumer credit. Under Presidents Ford and Carter, consumer representation offices were set up in all federal departments.

As we have seen, however, the creation of additional agencies came to a stop, at least temporarily, later in the 1970's when Congress gradually lost its enthusiasm for a consumer protection agency and the proposal was defeated by the House in 1978. The public and political turn against "bureaucracy" and "big government" also was evidenced in various other ways, such as the vote in California for Proposition 13, which curtailed state authority relative to property taxes.

THE BUSINESS RESPONSE

Business never has found it easy to respond effectively to organized consumer movements, perhaps because of the nature of business. As was pointed out in other chapters, business firms are required by antitrust laws to compete, and the competitive ethic frowns on united fronts that may tend to diminish competition.

Reactions of Companies

Certainly the most effective, but the least visible, responses are those made by individual business firms to individual customers. The nostalgia of the mom and pop grocery or drug or hardware store, for instance, is associated with the ability of the dissatisfied customer to demand and get satisfaction directly from the owner. Larger companies many years ago also set up more formal arrangements to deal with customer dissatisfaction. Some offered guarantees and warranties of various kinds. Montgomery Ward & Company, for example, guaranteed that all merchandise ordered from its catalogues was sent "subject to examination." Its competitive rival, Sears, Roebuck & Company, promised "satisfaction or your money back."

To protect themselves and their customers, large retailers also set up methods of testing merchandise they purchased from manufacturers. For example, Macy's, the large New York department store, began operating its own testing laboratory in 1947 to measure the quality and durability of products offered to it by manufacturers.[14]

Consumer movement leaders have tended to paint all of business with a broad brush, but obviously the chain store cannot survive any better than the mom and pop grocery without customers. In 1956 Fred Lazarus, president of Federated Department Stores, Inc., told his employees: "Never treat complaints casually. Get rid of the source of complaints. The customer is always right. If you're a clerk, call the boss personally on complaints. One complaint wipes out the profit on four to eight sales."

Developments in technology and distribution have required manufacturers themselves to adopt sophisticated quality controls. High-technology consumer products—such as color television sets, stereos, and personal computers—that are deficient in quality will lead to consumer claims, recalls, and probably to loss of sales to competitors. Quality control also has become more important to manufacturers with the rapid spread of leasing whereby manufacturers of computers, copiers, automobiles, and some other products are exposed first-hand to the quality and service problems of their customers.

When large numbers of deficient products are sold, the manufacturer's aggregate costs can be substantial, even if each individual customer's claim is relatively small. Small claims courts, long promoted by the Chamber of Commerce of the United States as a means of settling consumer complaints, now exist in many cities and handle individual claims up to $500 without the use of a lawyer. When a defendent company loses, it must pay court costs as well as satisfying claims. The business community generally has opposed the alternative development of class action lawsuits, where lawyers sue on behalf of large numbers of small claimants.

Deficient products also can lead to voluntary or involuntary recalls. Some companies, to preserve their good names and goodwill, have developed elaborate voluntary recall programs. For example, when Corning Glass Works realized that one of its coffee percolator models was defective, it launched a comprehensive recall program. It produced in-store displays explaining how to identify the model and how to get a cost-free replacement. The wording of the announcement had been tested in Corning's laboratory. A daily telephone survey of consumers, followed by a mail survey, measured the recall campaign's effectiveness.

Individual companies also started other programs to improve products and their acceptance. Eastman Kodak Company, for example, created a program offering customers free advice in service centers along with minor camera equipment adjustments and repairs. Litton Industries, Inc. began voluntarily to label its microwave ovens with information concerning energy efficiency. American Motors Corporation used feedback programs to test customer response. Atlas Van Lines tried to open personal dialogues between management and customers. Westinghouse Electric Corporation, Scovill Manufacturing Company, and some other makers of consumer appliances set up "hot lines," supplying customers with toll-free numbers for information or complaints.

Individual business efforts to resolve individual customer complaints seem never to have been wholly satisfactory, however. Even assuming that some companies have satisfied their customers, other businesses have not. Some undoubtedly have not tried. In business, as in all walks of life, there are some loafers, a number of cheats, and a few crooks.

Industry Responses

In response to consumers and consumer movements, businesses for many years have tried to work together, notwithstanding the requirements of competition. The antitrust laws have said that businessmen cannot get together to fix prices, and the laws have sometimes frowned on product standards and other devices that are useful for consumer protection. Nonetheless, the antitrust laws generally have not prevented business collectively from trying to police itself to weed out those who engage in questionable practices. Some laws indeed have required self-policing, such as those governing the securities industry.

Better Business Bureaus represent one of the oldest and largest voluntary efforts by business to police itself. The effort originated in 1911 with the formation by a group of New York advertising men of a "Vigilance Committee" to check into fraudulent advertising. The idea was picked up by professional admen in other cities too, not so much to protect the public as to protect business from the erosion of public confidence in commercial advertising. The committees were the forerunners of Better Business Bureaus that operate in more than 100 cities and have four basic functions:

- to provide a collection point for public complaints about advertisers and sellers;
- to check the validity of public complaints;
- to act as umpire in bringing together competing businesses and in promoting voluntary rules of fair play;
- to alert the public to deceptive practices and products.[15]

Better Business Bureaus have remained local, voluntary organizations, supported financially by local businesses, however, and therefore their performance has varied. As the consumer movement grew in the 1960's, the local bureaus attempted to respond to it. They received some 9 million inquiries and complaints in 1971.[16] A national organization called the Council of Better Business Bureaus spent nearly $2 million to upgrade selected local bureaus, but *The New York Times* in 1972 reported that, "Despite an intensive and well-funded one-year effort to improve the image of the nation's Better Business Bureaus, they are still widely regarded by some consumer groups as ineffectual..."[17]

For many years, of course, various industries have had their trade associations, such as the Appliance Manufacturers Association, National Retail Merchants Association, and the Southern Furniture Manufacturers Association. Many of these associations also tried to respond to the consumer movement. The Southern Furniture Manufacturers Association set up the Furniture Industry Consumer Action Panel. Several other associations jointly formed the Major Appliance Consumer Action Panel. The panels, usually made up of nonindustry people, largely from the academic world, have met periodically to develop educational programs and to address complaints that manufacturers and retailers had not been able to resolve.

Business efforts to respond to consumers and consumerism were of sufficient magnitude that a new breed of Washington consultant was born. The consumer consultants to business, a few of whom had been consumer advisers to the White House or to federal agencies, included Virginia Knauer & Associates, Edie Fraser & Associates, and Jean Judge & Associates. The growth in the number of business advisers on consumerism inspired the organization in 1973 of the Society of Consumer Professionals in Business.

Business reaction to the consumer movement and to the political and government pressures it helped to foster was often greeted with skepticism or cynicism. Certainly the reactions produced some results, however. Voluntary recalls, such as the one by Corning Glass Works, seemed successful. Some industry-wide reactions also seemed to work. An example was the movie industry's adoption of ratings by which people could decide for themselves whether or not to see movies containing sex or violence. In part the movie industry was attempting to protect itself against the flood of pornographic movies that threatened government regulation of the entire industry. The threat of regulation was in the minds of many businessmen and surely it influenced their reaction to consumerism. For example, Thomas A. Murphy, the chairman of General Motors Corporation, in 1976 told a business audience:

We know that every shoddy product, every neglected service, every reason for complaint is worse than bad business. It invites more regulation by government. Adverse public opinion, the antecedent of government regulation, has been shaped to a great degree by the failures of business to satisfy the customers. Other factors are involved, but much of the public's antipathy toward big business is rooted in the American consumer's own bad experience in the marketplace. To the extent that it is rooted there, it can be remedied only there.[18]

THE GOVERNMENT RESPONSE

Federal and state legislatures over many decades have enacted many different kinds of consumer protection laws, as we have seen. A number of significant new laws were passed by Congress in the 1960's and early 1970's, but then a reaction set in and Congress refused in 1978 to create yet another agency.

The pendulum never swings one way forever. Some consumer experts believe that in the foreseeable future government regulation of business will continue to grow on a rising wave of consumer expectation. Other experts believe that adverse public and political reaction to the growth of bureaucracy and to the public cost of regulation will mean less government regulation of business in the future. We have no crystal ball, but the future of the confrontation among consumerism, business, and government surely will continue to be a major news story and business and economic journalists therefore should understand the issues involved.

Consumerism at a Climax

The consumer movement may have marched toward a climax as the decade of the 1970's wore on. Many new consumer protection laws had been passed in the 1960's and early 1970's when there was a large Democratic majority in Congress and Republican Presidents Richard Nixon and Gerald Ford were in the White House. Presidents Nixon and Ford had had misgivings about some, but not all, of the new consumer laws. When Jimmy Carter was elected President in 1976, Ralph Nader and other consumer movement leaders were optimistic that the consumer protection laws would be enforced more vigorously and sympathetically.

Early in 1977 *The New York Times* summed up the movement's expectations in a story headed, "Carter's Raiders: The Outsiders Are In."[19] President Carter had appointed to government positions a number of men and women who were friends and followers of Mr. Nader, some of whom had become known as "Nader's Raiders." Mr. Carter appointed consumerist Michael Pertschuk to be chairman of the Federal Trade Commission, for instance. Carol Tucker Foreman, former executive director of the

Consumer Federation of America, became an Assistant Secretary of Agriculture for consumer and nutrition services. Joan Claybrook, a former lobbyist for Mr. Nader, became administrator of the National Highway Traffic Safety Administration.

The consumerists quickly found, however, that administration of government programs and agencies was considerably more complex than anticipated. They also encountered rising public and political distrust of government bureaucracy. These difficulties led to a falling out, for a time anyway, between Mr. Nader and some of his former followers. At one point, Mr. Nader called for Joan Claybrook's resignation.[20] Mr. Nader himself ran into unaccustomed criticism.[21]

Two contradictory trends then developed. The consumerists serving within the Carter administration by and large tried to administer regulations vigorously, but often in the face of a growing sentiment against more government regulation of business. The sentiment was reflected in various statements and actions of the White House and of Congress.

Despite those sentiments, the consumerists in government scored some impressive victories. Joan Claybrook presided over what was then the largest consumer product recall in history. Firestone Tire & Rubber Company agreed to replace an estimated 7 million of its "500" steel-belted radial tires.[22] The recall of the allegedly defective tires was said to cost Firestone more than $200 million. By the time the recall agreement was signed and sealed, Mr. Nader no longer was calling for Ms. Claybrook's resignation.

A number of other consumer programs were not administered so impressively, however. The laws that had been passed in the earlier decade encountered increasingly difficult scientific as well as bureaucratic and political problems.

For example, the Department of Agriculture had been inspecting meat since 1906 and for many years nitrite had been used with government approval to preserve and color cured meat. In the late 1970's, academic studies showed that nitrite combined with certain chemicals could form nitrosamines, a family of chemicals that produced cancer in laboratory rats. Nitrite therefore was assumed capable of producing cancer in humans. The very large difficulty faced by Assistant Secretary of Agriculture Carol Tucker Foreman and other government officials, however, was that nitrite for many years also had been known to protect humans against the formation of botulinum toxin, a deadly food poison.[23]

Another rather startling example concerned a chemical commonly known as Tris. Congress in 1953 had passed the Flammable Fabrics Act to bar from interstate commerce wearing apparel made of highly flammable fabrics. In 1971 the government issued a regulation requiring manufacturers of children's sleepwear to comply with the act and by 1976 almost all such sleepwear was made of polyester treated with Tris, a flame-retardant chemical. At about that same time, a National Cancer Institute study produced evidence that Tris was a cancer-causing agent. Some manufacturers then stopped using Tris. In early 1977 the Consumer Product Safety Commission banned the sale of Tris-treated children's apparel.[24]

The Big Story, To Be Continued

The scientific difficulties were perhaps the largest, but they were not the only problems encountered by government attempting to establish regulations—and by journalists attempting to cover the increasingly complex consumer protection issues.

The Consumer Product Safety Commission, five years after its creation in 1972, had issued safety standards for only three products: matchbook covers, backyard swimming pool slides, and architectural glass used in building construction. Democratic Senator Wendell H. Ford of Kentucky, who was chairman of the Senate Consumer Subcommittee, conducted hearings and concluded that the commission had "serious leadership deficiencies, with an over-emphasis on management and an under-emphasis on safety." He recognized that some members of Congress felt that "the public interest would be best served by abolishing the commission entirely" and added that there were "compelling arguments to put the commission out of its misery."[25]

Congress did not then abolish the Commission, but Senator Ford promised continued surveillance by Congress of that agency and others. Oversight was necessary, he said, "because if laws now on the books aren't working, new laws and more laws can only compound the problems that exist and take twice as long to correct over the long haul."[26]

That type of skepticism led to more careful monitoring of many agencies and to greater efforts to weigh the public costs against the public benefits of government consumer protection programs. A number of agencies themselves, sensing the political climate, began to roll back some regulations. Congress in 1978 passed legislation under which the Civil Aeronautics Board would be abolished five years hence and airline passengers would be protected by competition rather than by government regulation.

Still, the future course of consumer protection remained unclear. The conflict between government regulation and free market competition is discussed at length elsewhere in this book. We simply emphasize here that reporters covering the consumer beat should understand the complexities and the contradictions of the conflict. It is worth noting, for example, that while less regulation of airlines and of some other industries seemed the order of the day, new government regulations and standards were being imposed regarding hospital costs specifically and wages and prices in general.

The contradiction was illustrated by Democratic Senator Edward M. Kennedy of Massachusetts, who led the fight in Congress for airline deregulation and also fought for legislation to contain hospital and medical costs and for national health insurance legislation.

Airline and hospital costs involve different economic as well as political issues, of course, and consistency of government policy may or may not be desirable. Be that as it may, all business and economic journalists could take to heart this advice offered by Senator Kennedy:

> Unless the public achieves a greater understanding of how its welfare is affected by complex economic policies, there is little possibility for responsible government.
>
> I do not mean to suggest that traditional consumer reporting is not important. At the same time, however, I do not believe that the media can content itself with merely filling in the gaps not covered by *Consumer Reports*. In this area, like other areas of reporting, the easy drift to the trivial and superficial should be replaced by a greater emphasis on the central consumer concerns that lie at the heart of our economy.
>
> Consumer reporting can make its greatest contribution by enabling the public to participate intelligently in the debates on complex economic issues. It must search out the consumer interest in the dark corners of the tax code, in energy policy, and in the intracacies of competition, regulation and antitrust policy.[27]

COVERING THE BEAT

Covering the consumer beat, no less than covering other economic and business news, requires caution and imagination as well as sources and background.

For background, journalists might well read books such as *Our Times* by Mark Sullivan, published in 1926, and *The Americans, The Democratic Experience*, written in 1973 by Daniel J. Boorstin, who later became Librarian of Congress.

To keep up with current information, you might watch *The Wall Street Journal* and trade publications such as *The Daily News Record, Women's Wear Daily, Merchandising Week, Automotive News,* and *Advertising Age.* These publications generally are written for business rather than consumer audiences, but an enterprising reporter can find in such publications tips and ideas for stories that appeal strongly to the consumer interest.

Information and story ideas can be found also in press releases, speeches, and legislative testimony as well as in such consumer publications as *Changing Times, Consumer Reports,* and *Consumer Bulletin.*

Consumers Are People

Estelle Jackson, who started writing a consumer affairs column for *The Richmond Times-Dispatch* in 1966, has said that her best story ideas come from readers. If one reader has a problem, it probably is bothering others as well. In reporting there is no substitute for first-hand experience, and in writing there is no substitute for real names.

"Government agencies provide good leads," Ms. Jackson said, such as information from the state Division of Motor Vehicles on how to avoid buying a stolen car:

> Consumer issues in government are important, but people are more interested in the nitty-gritty issues such as discounts at motels and auto rental agencies; the best buys in wines; how much liquid is in cans of string beans; which banks give you notice before slapping on an overdraft service charge; what happens to dormant accounts in banks; what auto repairers really charge per hour.[28]

After a local consumer affairs reporter is established, readers and listeners probably will call or write with complaints that can provide good story ideas, after they are checked and double-checked. There are two sides to most stories and reporting both sides is essential, not only for fairness to sources and readers but for avoiding libel problems. Peter Weaver, who began in 1969 writing a nationally syndicated consumer affairs column, has cautioned that careless reporting on the consumer beat could offer potentially serious libel problems. Mr. Weaver said that he has used a tape recorder for greater accuracy in reporting and found that their use generally is acceptable to news sources. He advised listening to the tape immediately after an interview to note any inflections or exaggerations that might not be evident on a typed manuscript of the recording.[29]

Good reporters naturally distinguish between facts and rumors or statements that purport to be facts. Every reporter should be constantly reminded of the need for caution. For example, *Newsday,* under the headline "Drug Firms Accused of Skirting Law," published an article with this lead:

> Drug manufacturers already have found a way to get around a law that was designed to save consumers money on the price of prescription drugs, according to one of the authors of the bill. A drug industry spokesman denied the charge.
>
> The new law, which will take effect April 1, is expected to save consumers an average of 300 percent in prescription costs by encouraging the purchase of drugs under their generic names rather than their more expensive brand names.[30]

Such laws were legitimate consumer news and they were controversial in New York and elsewhere. The *Newsday* reporter checked with the accused drug industry before writing his story. That was insufficient caution, however, inasmuch as the new law could hardly save consumers 300 percent. If they saved 100 percent, they would get their drugs free.

Rumors can be used as news on the consumer beat, provided they are handled with caution and due respect for the libel potential. For example, rumors that McDonald's Corporation added earthworms to its hamburgers to increase protein content became news when the company itself tried to dispel the rumors by acknowledging them as rumors but no more than that. In the Atlanta area, the company offered customers who bought one "Big Mac" an additional one free and ran full-page newspaper ads telling of the sales promotion.[31]

Skepticism Versus Cynicism

Because the consumer beat often brings reporters into contact with highly contentious people and issues, it is especially important to avoid taking sides or appearing to be biased. Some consumer movement leaders take a cynical view of business and some business leaders take a cynical view of consumerists, and the feelings of both run deep. Journalists obviously should reject cynicism and maintain a healthy skepticism toward news sources on all fronts.

Jane Wilson, of Federal-State Reports, Inc., a publishing concern in Arlington, Virginia, has offered this advice:

> Establish yourself as a nonpartisan, not only in what you write, but also in what you say. All your sources must trust you. You cannot play both ends against the middle, or be a sort of counterspy. Sources will respect you for having listened as carefully to their adversaries as you did to them. Some reporters pose their questions as though they agreed wholeheartedly with the opposition point of view. My attitude toward a source ranges from slightly sympathetic to slightly dubious, but stays pretty close to neutral.[32]

Perhaps more skepticism has been needed in reporting the arguments surrounding governmental efforts to protect consumers. Consider, for example, this story from *The Washington Post* which begins with the reporter's apparently uncritical acceptance of the argument that state government can and should regulate auto repair shops in the consumer interest:

> Richmond, Jan. 21—Getting the Virginia General Assembly to approve legislation for the regulation of car-repair garages has proved about as difficult as shipping a block of ice across the Sahara Desert by camel.

Supporters of the legislation have maintained that horror stories about
auto repairs and their costs are the most numerous of all consumer
complaints. But the atmosphere in the General Assembly has been so
unremittingly negative that in past sessions all bills aimed at regulating
garages or repairmen have died in committee.

With this dismal legislative history in mind, Del. Raymond E. Vickery
(D-Fairfax) and a group of his colleagues have drafted a bill this
year. . . .

The first note of skepticism appears sixteen inches of type later, on the
jump to page 5, when the story reaches the argument that, under the bill,
the state may be unable to regulate auto repair shops effectively enough to
protect consumers:

Yet DMV (Division of Motor Vehicles) Commissioner Hill says: "If
we're going to ride herd on 10,000 businesses, it does not make any
sense to license them unless we follow up and check on them." There is
no provision in the bill for routine policing of the garages the DMV
would license.

"As a result," Hill says, "I question whether the bill is going to do what
they (its supporters) say it will."[33]

Not only is journalistic skepticism necessary for reporting both sides
of an issue fairly, but a reporter's natural skepticism can properly take a
hand in writing as well. Consider this story, also from *The Washington Post,*
reporting on the progress of a federal proposal to regulate auto hood ornaments:

The way things are going over at the Department of Transportation,
they are going to have to hire a regulator to referee arguments between
regulators over how to regulate.

This time they are arguing over, among other things, just how important a regulation about automobile hood ornaments is.[34]

The story went on to say that, while the National Highway Traffic
Safety Administration was talking about regulating "vehicle exterior pro-
trusions," another office in the Department of Transportation was suggesting that spring-loaded hood ornaments are not unsafe and saying, "imagine
the fun reporters can have poking fun at regulators who want to outlaw the
last vestiges of this great tradition." The point is that, if government regulators themselves disagree, reporters should not accept uncritically all government promises of consumer protection.

Another example of a reporter's healthy and independent skepticism appeared in a *Wall Street Journal* story, one that only nominally was a news story, concerning a proposed government regulation of a new type of potato chip. The story was not written as a straightforward, dull, and unskeptical report of a proposed regulation. The lead was skeptical, but not cynical:

> Washington—When is a potato chip a potato chip?
>
> The Food and Drug Administration has finally decided this momentous issue—a subject of considerable concern to potato chip makers, if not munchers.[35]

Keep Your Balance

Reporters covering consumer affairs must think for themselves and not accept either the clichés or the cynicism they will encounter. Again, this means reporting both sides and writing with balance. But in addition it means thinking independently about story possibilities and looking in unexpected places.

One popular cliché is that chain supermarkets have put locally owned grocery stores out of business. Certainly the chains had enormous effects on local retailers, but the power of the chains came into question with the financial difficulties of Great Atlantic & Pacific Tea Company and of some other chain supermarkets. Those developments led *The Wall Street Journal* to a story that was headed "Independent Grocers Outsell the Big Chains By Adapting to Markets."[36] The story reported that "Chains lost 320 supermarkets from their ranks last year, while independents added 740." Some of the stores, especially in inner city neighborhoods, had been abandoned by chains and successfully reopened by independents.

Whatever the future of the three-sided struggle among consumerists, business, and government, the consumer beat surely will continue to grow more important as consumer goods and services become more sophisticated and more costly. Some of the stories will grow out of issues that loom large in consumers' lives and others will be where you find them.

An illustration of an issue that complicates the lives of consumers and producers was the discovery in 1977 by some General Motors customers that the big auto maker was installing Chevrolet engines in Oldsmobile cars. Substitution of parts is an integral aspect of economies of production, and car manufacturers for many years had used some of the same parts on their different auto makes, but Oldsmobile owners felt cheated upon finding Chevrolet engines in their cars and more than 100 sued General Motors.

A *Wall Street Journal* story reported:

> Earlier this year, Bryan Byars, a 41-year-old Corinth, Miss., accountant, laid out about $7,200 cash for a new Oldsmobile Delta 88. "I

wasn't used to paying that much, but I felt it was a well-built car with a reliable engine," he says. Now, Mr. Byars only wants to get rid of his Olds, and he vows he will never buy another General Motors Corp. car.

What went wrong with the car? Nothing. It's just that the Olds is powered by a Chevrolet engine instead of Oldsmobile's long-ballyhooed Oldsmobile Rocket V-8 engine.[37]

As corporations grow larger, partly through acquisitions of other producers, and as production costs rise, consumer issues growing out of part substitution and product differentiation may well loom larger.

Other consumer stories will be where you find them. This example was distributed by *The Christian Science Monitor:*

Washington, D.C.—In Louisiana, chatting from a public telephone booth still costs only one nickel.

However, in Michigan and 11 other states, a coin phone call already is a two-dime investment. And it is considered only a matter of time before all states move to the higher fare.[38]

Consumer interest in news of products and services that people need or want, ranging from telephone service to potato chips and all kinds of food, clothing, and shelter, has grown as standards of living have increased. Public interest in such news appears to have grown more as inflation has threatened standards of living.

However, consumer interest in product and service news has not been well served by puff stories that companies want to see. Nor has it been served by unsophisticated and unskeptical stories that tend to disparage whole classes of products or services.

Independent, fair, and sophisticated reporting on consumer products and services is a challenge that has not been well met. But meeting it can be rewarding to the media as well as the public.

NOTES—CHAPTER 5

1. "House Rejects Consumer Agency," *New York Times,* February 9, 1978, pp. 1, 20.

2. "Consumer Bill Killed by House in 227–189 Vote," *Wall Street Journal,* February 9, 1978, p. 2.

3. The remarks of Ms. Graham, made before The Conference Board, appear in *Business Credibility, The Critical Factors,* a publication of The Conference Board, ed. Phyllis S. McGrath, New York, 1976, p. 24.

4. For a fascinating account of American society and politics and of the economy between the turn of the century and 1925, see Mark Sullivan, *Our Times* (New York: Charles Scribner's Sons, 1926).

5. See Ruth de Forest Lamb, *American Chamber of Horrors* (New York: Rinehart, 1936), p. 81.

6. *Changing Times,* September 1956, pp. 8–12.

7. Remarks of Senator John F. Kennedy, Concourse Plaza Hotel, Bronx, New York, November 15, 1960, printed in *Speeches, Remarks and Press Conferences and Statements, John F. Kennedy,* Senate Report 994, 87th Congress, 1st Session, pp. 900–902.

8. *Public Papers of the President of the U.S., John F. Kennedy, 1962* (Washington, D.C.: Government Printing Office, 1963), pp. 93–95.

9. Ralph Nader, *Unsafe at Any Speed* (New York: Grossman, 1965).

10. See *Changing Times,* April 1953, p. 19.

11. "A Program for Consumer Federation of America," Rev. Robert J. McEwen, S. J. (Washington, D.C.: Consumer Federation of America, 1967).

12. *Directory of Federal, State and Local Government Consumer Offices,* Department of Health, Education and Welfare, published by the Government Printing Office, 1977. The directory was published annually beginning in 1973.

13. See "Action Faction," published by the Paul H. Douglas Research Center of the Consumer Federation of America, 1977, pp. 23–27.

14. *Changing Times,* March 1947, p. 9.

15. *Changing Times,* February 1956, pp. 43–45.

16. "Better Business Bureaus Seek to Counter Criticism," *New York Times,* May 22, 1972, pp. 1, 38.

17. *Ibid.*

18. Thomas A. Murphy, in an address before the Associated Industries of New York, Lake Placid, September 24, 1976.

19. *New York Times,* April 20, 1977, pp. C1, C9.

20. "Nader Calls on Ex-Colleague to Resign Safety Post," *New York Times,* December 1, 1977, p. 33.

21. See, for example, "'Naderism Is Running Amuck' With Its Rake," *New York Times,* December 8, 1977, p. 24.

22. The final agreement was announced November 29, 1978, in a Department of Transportation press release.

23. For a concise statement of the nitrite issues, see "Statement on Nitrites," issued jointly by the U.S. Department of Agriculture and the Food and Drug Administration, August 11, 1978.

24. For an explanation of the Tris controversy and its aftermath, see the statement made June 14, 1978, by James F. Merow, Civil Division, U.S. Department of Justice, before the Subcommittee on Administrative Law and Governmental Relations, Committee on the Judiciary, House of Representatives.

25. Senator Ford, in an address before the Product Safety Conference, Alexandria, Virginia, June 6, 1978.

26. *Ibid.*

27. Senator Kennedy, at an awards ceremony marking the fourth annual National Press Club Competition for Excellence in Consumer Reporting, Washington, D.C., September 20, 1977.

28. Interview with Estelle Jackson, 1978.

29. Interview with Peter Weaver, 1978.

30. *Newsday,* January 19, 1978, p. 13.

31. See "McDonald's Says Rumors of Worms Still Hurting," *Wall Street Journal,* December 12, 1978, p. 10.

32. Interview with Jane Wilson, 1978.

33. *Washington Post,* January 22, 1978, pp. B1, B5.

34. *Washington Post,* November 9, 1978, pp. C1, C2.

35. "FDA's Definition of a Potato Chip Is: a Potato Chip," *Wall Street Journal,* November 25, 1975, p. 8.

36. *Wall Street Journal,* November 28, 1978, pp. 1, 22.

37. "Engine Switch Brings 125 Suits Against GM, and Practice Continues," *Wall Street Journal,* July 27, 1977, pp. 1, 17.

38. The story, from *The Christian Science Monitor,* as it appeared in the Lansing, Michigan *State Journal,* March 7, 1977, p. 2.

SOURCES OF INFORMATION

Consumer Federation of America
1012 14th Street, N.W.
Washington, D.C. 20005

Consumer Information Institute
1225 19th Street, N.W.
Washington, D.C. 20036

Consumer Product Safety Commission
1111 18th Street, N.W.
Washington, D.C. 20207

Consumers Union
256 Washington Street
Mount Vernon, N.Y. 10550

Corporate Accountability Research Group
1346 Connecticut Avenue, N.W.
Washington, D.C. 20036

Council of Better Business Bureaus, Inc.
1150 17th Street, N.W.
Washington, D.C. 20036

Federal Trade Commission
Pennsylvania Avenue at Sixth Street
N.W.
Washington, D.C. 20580

Food and Drug Administration
U.S. Department of Health, Education and Welfare
5600 Fishers Lane
Rockville, Md. 20852

National Bureau of Standards
U.S. Department of Commerce
14th Street and Constitution Avenue
Washington, D.C. 20230

SUGGESTED READINGS

Boorstin, Daniel J., *The Americans, The Democratic Experience.* New York: Random House, 1973.

Consumerism, The Next Five Years, Corporate Communications Department, Springs Mills, Inc., P.O. Box 70, Fort Mill, S.C. 29715.

Directory of Federal, State and Local Government Consumer Offices, compiled annually by the Department of Health, Education and Welfare and published by the Government Printing Office, Washington, D.C.

Epstein, Samuel S., and Richard D. Grundy, *Consumer Products Hazards: The Roles of Congress, the Executive and the Courts in Public Policy*. Boston: Massachusetts Institute of Technology, 1973.

Kaufman, Herbert, *Red Tape: Its Origins, Uses and Abuses*. Washington, D.C.: The Brookings Institution, 1977.

Nader, Ralph, *Unsafe at Any Speed*. New York: Grossman, 1965.

Sullivan, Mark, *Our Times*. New York: Charles Scribner's Sons, 1926.

Reporting on . . .
RESOURCES, ENERGY, AND THE ENVIRONMENT

6

JON G. UDELL
and
ROBERTA HORNIG

T HE ENVIRONMENT AND NATURAL RESOURCES are relatively new areas of public and journalistic concern; they have emerged only in the last decade as reporting beats.

Environmental stories had been mostly the province of the outdoors editor and coverage was sporadic. There was little about the environment considered to be newsworthy except for an occasional spectacular event such as the "killer fog" that descended on Donora, Pennsylvania, in 1948 when static atmospheric conditions prevented dispersement of poisonous chemicals in the air and resulted in 19 deaths and the illness of nearly half the town's population of 14,000.

The supply of natural resources, including energy, commanded even less attention. There were a few exceptions, as when the Supreme Court ruled in 1954 that the federal government had authority to regulate the wellhead price of natural gas flowing in interstate commerce or when President Dwight D. Eisenhower in 1959 imposed import quotas on foreign oil. But the press by and large reported such stories as political or legal events rather than as developments relating to energy resources.

The environmental and natural resource issues grew from different roots, but both have major economic implications from many intertwining branches.

THE EMERGENCE OF ENVIRONMENTALISM

In the process of feeding, clothing, and sheltering themselves, humans have always altered the natural environment to some degree. The human race can be as destructive as severe weather, volcanic eruptions, and other natural forces that greatly alter the environment. Such destruction was widely evident long before the birth of modern technology and the emergence of environmentalism as a major public and political issue. The cities of medieval Europe, for instance, were symbols of human progress and enlightenment, but they also polluted the environment with filth and disease.

The age of industrialization and urbanization brought further material progress and environmental pollution, although advancing technology may be either helpful or harmful to the environment, as sanitation systems vividly illustrate.

In the nineteenth century the environmental costs of human progress concerned American naturalist John Muir. However environmentalism as a public and political issue dates back only to the 1960's, when many protest movements were underway.

In 1962 appeared Rachael Carson's influential book, *Silent Spring,* protesting among other things the widespread agricultural use of pesticides.[1] It was followed in the decade by many other books, articles, and broadcasts concerning aspects of environmentalism ranging from population growth to trash collection. One such book was Paul B. Erlich's *The Population Bomb.*[2] An article in *U.S. News & World Report* appeared under the heading, "Why the U.S. Is in Danger of Being Engulfed by Its Own Trash."[3] *The Progressive* published a piece, titled "Why the Birds Cough," which spoke of tons of pollutants being discharged into the air.[4] Still another book said that the acidic winds of New York City had done more damage to Cleopatra's Needle, the 224-ton granite obelisk in the city's Central Park, than the previous many centuries of its existence in Egypt.[5]

The environment developed into a popular and, in retrospect, almost faddish issue. Events around the country in 1969 included these:

- Mini-skirted women in New York picketed shops selling coats made of skins of leopards, a diminishing species.
- In Minnesota a Mother's Day protest was staged at the site of a planned nuclear power generating plant along the Mississippi River.
- At the Universities of Minnesota and California, students held mock funerals for internal combustion engines to protest auto air pollution.
- Students from Maryland to North Carolina convened at Richmond to protest the pollution of Virginia's rivers.

A large oil spill in California helped to catalyze the issue. The spill, resulting from an accident on a drilling platform five miles offshore from Santa Barbara, blackened 35 miles of California beaches. The spill was widely and prominently reported in newspapers across the nation. Such spectacular events no longer were covered only sporadically.

As public interest and alarm grew, Congress rushed to enact environmental legislation. The Environmental Protection Act of 1969 created the Environmental Protection Agency to consolidate, strengthen, and coordinate federal environmental protection and rehabilitation efforts. Within the following year, Congress passed three other major antipollution laws. The Clean Air Act for the first time established levels of pollutants that could be discharged from industries, power plants, and automobiles. The Water Quality Improvement Act initiated a large public works program under which grants were made to states and municipalities for construction of waste treatment plants, and a permit system was established to regulate the types and amounts of wastes discharged into waterways. The Resource Recovery Act recognized garbage and other solid wastes as pollutants and authorized federal grants to state, local, or regional agencies for construction of solid waste disposal facilities and for demonstration of resource recovery and recycling systems.

As news coverage of all those events increased, reporters learned a new vocabulary. The *environment* may be defined as the sum of all living and nonliving factors affecting organisms, including human beings. *Ecology* is the study of the relationships of organisms with their environment. An *ecosystem* is a complex of plant and animal life and the physical environment in which changes are interrelated.

THE ENVIRONMENTAL ISSUE

The Roots of the Problem

Ecological problems frequently are attributed to the convergence of three forces: population concentration, economic affluence, and modern technology. While there is truth in this attribution, the problems obviously are much more complex.

Some, such as Paul Erlich, have emphasized the detrimental effects of population growth.[6] An increasing number of people certainly tends to increase pollution. However, to concentrate on diffusing the so-called "population bomb" of the United States would be analogous to concentrating on a hand grenade while the fuse of a bomb continues to burn. If U.S. population growth were to cease, there would still be pollution and environmental problems. On the other hand, if the nation's population were to increase by four and one-half times, the United States would have a population density equal to that of France. To reach the density of England, the U.S. population would have to increase tenfold. Despite their great concentrations of population, the environmental condition of the French or English surely cannot be described as hopeless. As a matter of fact, London appears to have considerably less air pollution today than it had a century ago.

Pollution is not just a product of population growth, it is also a by-product of a rising standard of living. The real Gross National Product of the United States has grown far more in the period after 1950 than in the preceding 330 years between that year and the landing of the Pilgrims in 1620. Because of technology, the by-products of today's production and consumption frequently are more harmful than those of the Pilgrims. Our forefathers had no complex man-made pesticides, automobile exhausts, or nondegradable plastics.

The Many Sides of the Issue

The above observations have prompted some to condemn both economic growth and technological progress. There are those who maintain that any tampering with the natural state of the world is harmful and that man's acquisitive desire must be controlled or changed.[7] That position, like any other at the extremes of an issue, should be viewed with caution.

Material progress has frequently despoiled nature, but in nature itself there are instances of deterioration and indeed of deadly poisons. An active volcano, for example, is a great air polluter; a major eruption can produce more particulate and sulfur discharges than all the world's coal-burning chimneys. Our lakes, even without man-made pollution, are in a natural state of eutrophication that can be retarded by mechanical or chemical means. In other words, tampering with nature can be beneficial to the environment. Fire lanes in forests, for example, help to prevent destructive forest fires, many of which are induced by nature itself.

The elimination or control of man's acquisitive desire for wealth and material progress is quite unlikely. Material progress and an expanding economy have brought with them undesirable side effects, to be sure, but they have also brought many benefits including improved health care and increased longevity, a vast education system, and a higher standard of living that embraces not only health, education, and welfare but indoor plumbing, central heating and air conditioning, and an abundance of fresh, refrigerated foods.

Most of us would not welcome a return to the "good old days" when storekeepers put cats in the store at night to catch mice in the cracker barrel. Nor would we welcome return of outdoor toilets and of smokey coal and wood stoves for heating and cooking. With the technology of a century ago, many of our cities would be engulfed in dirt and horse manure. Our groundwater as well as our rivers and lakes surely would be contaminated. Furthermore, a withdrawal of labor-saving technology would recreate conditions under which large families once again would be an economic asset and more rapid population growth would thereby be encouraged.

It should also be noted that an expanding economy is needed to underwrite the costs of many social objectives in the areas of poverty, health, unemployment, and equitable standard of living. In fact, an expanding economy is needed to help finance the horrendous cost of cleansing the environment.

Thus, eliminating human desire for material progress and wealth seems most unlikely. Even if economic acquisitiveness were controlled and technological growth retarded, the desire to improve material welfare is so integral a part of our lives that it is difficult to envision personal and political freedom under any system of rigorous economic controls. Thomas Jefferson once observed, "Freedom is the right to choose, the right to create for oneself the alternatives of choice. Without the possibility of choice and the exercise of choice, man is but a number, an instrument, a thing." Furthermore, there is little evidence from highly controlled societies that economic control has produced many environmental advantages. Within our own nation, government appears to have had more success in prompting private industry to reduce its environmentally detrimental practices than it has in forcing government-owned and controlled facilities, such as municipal sewage systems and federal defense establishments, to abate pollution. It would appear to be politically easier to force a private individual or company to curtail its pollution than to ask taxpayers to finance pollution abatement practices by government.

There are, of course, extremists on the other side of the issue who refuse to recognize the potential hazards of pollution. More frequently, however, there are those who are ambiguous when it comes to cleaning up the environment. In a sense, we are all environmentalists who do not want our nests soiled. However, when confronted with the costs and inconveniences of cleaning up our own emissions, trash, and other pollutants, we may take the position that our own effluent is not hazardous and the benefits flowing from environmental investment do not justify the costs and inconveniences.

Companies frequently claim that they cannot afford to meet environmental standards, that enforcement would put them out of business and their employees out of work. In such instances, a persuasive industry-labor coalition may be formed and environmental regulators may find the coalition difficult or impossible to ignore. Similarly, the reporter is confronted with a potent multidimensional issue in gathering a complete story.

Economic Implications

The benefits of preserving the integrity of our physical environment, in terms of aesthetic pleasure, preservation of health and even of life, are largely immeasurable; the costs, however, are largely measurable and enormous. The costs are both direct and indirect. The *direct* costs that can be measured or estimated with some accuracy are those paid by government (taxpayers), and those paid by industry and ultimately largely borne by consumers.

A 1976 study prepared for the U.S. Council on Environmental Quality by Chase Econometric Associates, Inc., estimated that in the 1976–1985 period the total direct costs of federal pollution control programs resulting from laws enacted since 1970 would be about $290 billion.[8]

The study found that in 1976 government spending accounted for about 13 percent of pollution abatement expenditures, while private industry and consumers accounted for the remaining 87 percent. One major item was the higher price of automobiles due to mandated emission controls. Private industry's capital investment in 1977 for pollution control was estimated at $7.5 billion; the six industries accounting for most of the outlays were electric utilities, petroleum, chemicals, nonferrous metals, paper, and steel.

There are many other cost studies confirming the enormity of the direct costs of environmental control. The Bureau of the Census, for example, estimates that federal, state, and local governments in the 1976 fiscal year spent a total of $8.9 billion on environmental control. Water quality control accounted for $6.2 billion of the total, solid waste and other land quality control amounted to $2.3 billion, and air quality and other programs accounted for the remaining $400 million.[9]

The *indirect* costs of environmental quality controls may be greater, although they are more difficult to estimate. The sums spent on environmental controls divert capital that otherwise might be spent on new factories and equipment to improve the productivity of American industry. A Brookings Institution study calculated that business productivity in 1975 was 1.8 percent lower than it would have been if business had been operating under 1967 standards.[10] Pollution controls appear also to have discriminated against smaller businesses and smaller cities, which have a more difficult time meeting the costs. The Chase Econometric study commented that smaller industries, such as foundries and electroplaters, "have numerous marginal plants whose basic economic weakness makes environmentally related closings likely." The same study noted "increasing concern that small communities may have difficulty in financing local expenditures for sewage treatment and drinking water."

The dilemma between a cleaner environment and the costs of producing that environment has involved more than estimates and studies. For example, steel mills once spewed 200,000 tons of dirt and dust annually into the air over Birmingham, Alabama, but the mills also provided the city with jobs and taxes. In 1976 the last of the open hearth furnaces at United States Steel Corporation's Ensley Works was closed on order of the Environmental Protection Agency.[11] The closing of the Ensley Works, which had been operating since 1907, was vigorously protested by the company, the United Steelworkers, and local and state officials. However, pollution control was deemed by the federal agency to be of greater importance than the 300 jobs that were lost.

The Environmental Protection Agency has not been wholly insensitive to protests of its proposed regulations. In 1975, for instance, the agency suspended a proposal that it review local plans for construction of new shopping centers, office and apartment buildings, and parking garages that it felt would generate additional auto pollution.[12] The proposal was vigorously protested by many mayors, land developers, hotels, churches, and some members of Congress.

Nevertheless, the enormous costs of environmental controls continued to accumulate and became a larger issue with the growth of inflation in the 1970's. The Environmental Protection Agency was pressed by the White House and Congress to try to weigh the costs against the benefits of its regulations.

The agency and others attempted to make cost/benefit analyses. A study completed in 1978 at Carnegie-Mellon University estimated that through 1985 the cost of auto emission controls would be $11 billion whereas the benefits would be only $5 billion, and also concluded that the costs of industrial smokestack emission controls would be $9.5 billion whereas the benefits would be $16.1 billion.[13]

The administrator of the Environmental Protection Agency in 1978 conceded that the impact of environmental regulation on inflation was "minimal but growing" and contended that "the benefits, computed or not computed, exceed the costs."[14]

The economic costs of environmental regulation are offset to some extent by economic as well as aesthetic benefits. For example, a city that treats its sewage presumably reduces the costs that another city downstream on the same river incurs in processing its drinking water. Less air pollution should help reduce personal health costs and building maintenance costs. In addition, the jobs lost in various industries because of pollution are to some degree offset by the growth of new industries and technologies created to improve the environment.

Recycling

In many instances pollution is resources being wasted. The recapture of pollutants and waste materials can yield economic benefits. Recycling long has been practiced in some industries where it has been economically and technologically feasible. It has been estimated that more than 40 percent of the country's copper is derived from recycling. Almost half its lead, 25 percent of its aluminum, 14 percent of its zinc, and about 20 percent of its paper and paperboard are recycled.[15] In other instances, however, recycling has not been economical.

As the President's Council on Environmental Quality has pointed out, most resource recovery "is still done through the separation of recyclable materials from wastes by householders, office workers and others at the source of waste generation." Of the roughly 9 million tons of materials that have been recycled each year, more than 90 percent was wastepaper, according to the Council.[16] Recycling has not bulked larger as a solution to the environmental problem because it would require complex technologies with high capital costs.

One of the most notable recycling success stories is provided by the aluminum industry. Aluminum Company of America and Reynolds Metals Company, which together account for approximately 64 percent of U.S. aluminum production, have collected record numbers of used aluminum beverage containers for recycling. In 1976 Alcoa recycled 1.6 billion and Reynolds 2.4 billion cans, or one out of every four aluminum cans manufactured.[17]

In our throwaway society, however, recycling has been a fledgling industry at best. In many instances recycling simply is not economical. However, the rising cost of resources and technological advances will undoubtedly lead to more recycling in the future.

Further Complications of Environmental Reporting

As aspiring reporters will find, the environmental beat is complex and will grow more complicated and controversial with the persistence of inflation. Emission control and fuel economy standards have added hundreds of dollars to the price of an automobile. The banning of DDT has given rise to questions concerning future supplies and costs of food and forest products. Some forests have been newly invaded by insects and, if alternative ways are not found to control forest infestation, the results ultimately could include more costly homes, newspapers, and other wood and wood pulp products.

Concern with the environment always has been a health issue, but that issue has grown more complex and controversial as pollutants increasingly have been linked to cancer. As a result, environmental reporting has intruded more and more on the health and medical beats.

Chemicals have been used for many years to preserve foods, to purify drinking water, and for other beneficial purposes, but they have become a matter of public and press concern in part because of a number of well-publicized incidents in recent years. For example, the flame-retardant chemical known as Tris, which had been used to make children's sleepwear safer, was banned by the Consumer Product Safety Commission after it was found to induce cancer in laboratory test animals. The pesticide Kepone caused a scare after it was found to be toxic not only to employees of the Virginia plant where it was produced but also to nearby residents and to people eating fish from the river into which it was discharged with other municipal waste. PCB, or polychlorinated biphenyl, chemicals became the focus of concern after several incidents including one in Michigan where several hundred people showed persistent ill effects, including swollen joints, abdominal pains, and memory loss, three years after eating contaminated animal products.

In response to the chemical concern, Congress passed two laws, the Safe Drinking Water Act of 1974 and the Toxic Substances Control Act of 1976. The former required the fixing of water standards to protect humans from pollutants ranging from raw sewage to toxic chemicals. The latter gave government agencies broad authority to control the production, distribution, and use of all potentially hazardous chemicals and provided for testing of suspect chemicals before they became widely used and economically important.

According to the Council on Environmental Quality, there are some 3.5 million known chemical compounds. Of these, about 70,000 are in commercial use. As of 1977, some 6,000 had been tested and less than 10 percent of these were found to have carcinogenic potential. "Many of these complex chemicals do a great deal of good and little harm, but some are among the most persistent substances ever introduced into our environment," the Council said. It also noted that the toxicity of chemicals often has been discovered only

> after their widespread use and after they have become important to jobs, commerce or agriculture. The number of carcinogens—in particular the number to which there is widespread population exposure—may be quite small. Nevertheless, because exposures are thought by many cancer researchers to have irreversible and additive or synergistic effects, widespread exposure to even low levels of individual chemicals is of grave concern.[18]

Some pesticides found to be carcinogenic in test animals have been banned or suspended by the Environmental Protection Agency. These include pesticides commonly used in agriculture, such as DDT, dieldrin, aldrin, and heptachlor. Many other pesticides, herbicides, fungicides, antibodies, and hormones that have been vital ingredients of agricultural productivity have been questioned.

To ban all suspect chemicals would disrupt the economy, eliminating products and jobs, reducing productivity, and raising prices. In addition, the banning of chemicals that are suspected carcinogens would raise health problems of other kinds. For example, banning of nitrates and nitrites under the Toxic Substances Control Act could lead to spoilage of bacon and other processed meats and to an increase in botulism poisoning. Banning of chlorinated compounds under the Safe Drinking Water Act could also lead to serious health problems. Chlorine has been identified by the Environmental Protection Agency as a suspected carcinogen, but chlorine conventionally has been used as a water purifier.

The dilemma has been duly noted by the Council on Environmental Quality:

> The recent detection of small amounts of carcinogens in drinking water raises doubts about chlorination as a primary disinfection technique. Chlorinated organic compounds are numerous among the known and suspected carcinogens found in drinking water. The likelihood that these compounds may be formed during the chlorination process creates a dilemma. On the one hand, it is important to limit human contact with cancer-causing agents; on the other, it is essential to keep waterborne infections at their current low levels.[19]

The press is in no position to evaluate the conflicting claims of scientists, environmentalists, and industry concerning the dangers and benefits of chemicals. However, it is in a position to attempt to report all sides of these complex issues.

Complexity notwithstanding, the many sides of environmental reporting all involve people and the controversy itself can be fascinating and newsworthy. Consider the newsworthiness of sewage, for instance. Many sewage treatment plants have been built to eliminate the pollution of our waterways, but the plants have produced their own kind of foul, mud-like waste called sludge. What to do with it? Some cities, such as Los Angeles, experimented with using the black residue for fertilizer and thereby created a new issue inasmuch as sludge contains pollutants, often including toxic chemicals. Other cities fought with their suburbs in attempting to find places to bury their sludge. Still others, such as Philadelphia and Camden, simply hauled it off and dumped it into the Atlantic Ocean, thereby generating more controversy.

The Washington Star in the spring of 1970 received a telephone call from a Cape May, New Jersey, clammer who was outraged over Philadelphia and Camden's sludge dumping. He asserted that the sludge literally was burying and suffocating clams on the ocean bottom and destroying his livelihood. A *Star* reporter and photographer went to Cape May and attended a clammers' protest meeting, held in a local bar. They then took a boat ride 13 miles out into the Atlantic where the clammers showed their evidence. The *Star* published the resulting story and pictures. A week later officials of the Environmental Protection Agency took the same trip and, some years and many media stories later, the agency took steps to ban ocean dumping of sludge and other wastes.

THE RESOURCE ISSUE

Reporting on energy and other resources is similar to reporting on the environment in that both areas are relatively new to journalism and both are complex and controversial. As we have seen, the two areas also are intertwined. Recycling of disposable beer cans, for example, helps to clean up the environment and to conserve resources. On the other hand, the use of coal as a substitute for natural gas would serve energy purposes but could conflict with the objective of cleansing the air.

The environmental beat and the resources and energy beat are quite different in one important respect. Environmental reporting concerns people. People care about the air they breathe, the water they drink, and the land on which they live, walk, and ride. Except in times of perceived crisis, resources and energy have no such broad and interested constituency.

Certainly people related personally to a crisis on the evening of November 9, 1965, when a massive electric power failure plunged into darkness 30 million people in an area that stretched from the Atlantic Ocean to Lake Huron and from Canada to Pennsylvania. People cared when the Arab oil embargo of 1973–1974 caused a gasoline shortage and long lines at gas stations. People cared in the winter of 1977–1978 when extreme cold weather triggered a natural gas shortage that caused schools and factories in the Midwest to close temporarily. But in each instance, when the crisis was perceived to have passed, public concern diminished. For example, large automobiles were almost unsaleable during the Arab oil embargo but rapidly regained popularity following it. Great concern did not arise again until the gasoline shortages of 1979 and the associated escalation of petroleum prices.

There probably are several reasons for the fluctuation of public interest in resource issues. One is that resource shortages are not readily apparent much of the time. Another is that experts have divergent and sometimes conflicting positions concerning the causes and seriousness of the problems. A third reason is that government officials and energy company executives have failed to make the connection, in terms the public can comprehend, between U.S. energy consumption and the nation's economic future.

In terms of public interest, then, the press faces a large challenge in reporting about energy and perhaps a larger challenge in reporting about other resources. The fact is that energy and resource issues may in the long run be more important than environmental issues to the nation's social and economic security and stability.

The Issue in Perspective

For more than 500 years so-called experts have been predicting doom in which the world would run out of food, energy, and other resources. Such predictions necessarily have rested on known resources existing at a particular time in history and on assumptions concerning future population, consumption, technology, and productivity. As recently as the early 1970's ominous predictions concerning the future supply of many resources were made by the Club of Rome, a private, international organization of scientists, economists, and industrialists, in a study titled *The Limits to Growth.*[20] Using computer simulations based on various assumptions concerning population growth, food supplies, technological developments, and resource reserves, the study predicted "the state of the future world." Under the most optimistic set of assumptions, a collapse of the world social order by roughly the year 2050 was forecast. Fortunately for us all, errors in the simulations were discovered and the predictions were substantially revised.[21]

Serious and even deadly shortages of food and other resources have occurred at various times throughout history, but the predicted doom has not arrived; the omniscience of the so-called experts of each generation has been blessedly incomplete. The predictions have been unable to take into proper account the inventiveness of humankind, which is to say its capacity for adaptation to alternative resources, technologies, and life styles. Allocation of resources also involves social, political, and economic forces that may or may not be foreseen.

Perhaps the most fundamental error inherent in the predictions of doom has been the confusion of two basic economic concepts: scarcity and shortage.

A *scarcity* exists when the world simply does not hold as much of something as we all would like, such as gold and pretty girls. Most commodity scarcities are managed by the pricing mechanism; prices are used to allocate the scarce commodity among its many users. As a result, supply is adequate to meet demand at the prevailing price.

A *shortage* exists when the amount that people want is greater than the available supply at the prevailing price. Though willing to pay that price, people cannot find enough to buy, either because suppliers are not willing to sell more at the current price or because they simply cannot obtain more due to some temporary disruption of supply.

The doom prophets, in other words, have assumed worldwide scarcities of resources. But the problem with energy and most other world resources has been with shortages. The world has not run out of resources, but has experienced shortages of supplies at prevailing prices.

If the world market were truly free, commodity prices would rise to a level at which additional production would become profitable and supply would increase until demand was met at a market-clearing price, or until an alternative commodity became available at a lower price. For example, world oil prices would increase until production met demand or until energy production met demand at a lower price. But the market, particularly for energy, has not been truly free. It has from time to time and place to place been overtaken by monopolies, cartels, and a great variety of governments' regulations. The effects of the various governmental and private interventions have been to raise and lower energy prices and to produce seemingly endless disagreement among the so-called experts.

The U.S. government in 1911 broke up the old Standard Oil Trust that was found by the Supreme Court to be a monopoly existing to raise and maintain oil prices. In 1938 the federal government began regulating natural gas prices and in 1954 regulation was expanded by the Supreme Court to wellhead prices of natural gas. One purpose of that regulation was to keep natural gas prices relatively low, despite rising demand. On the other hand, in 1959 the White House imposed import quotas on foreign oil for the presumed purpose of preventing domestic oil prices from falling too low.

Meanwhile, world demand for energy grew at then prevailing prices. Proven domestic reserves of oil and natural gas declined relative to rising demand, and U.S. imports of oil and later of natural gas in liquified form increased. Finally, demand and supply at then prevailing prices became so imbalanced that in 1973 the cartel of Middle East and other governments known as the Organization of Petroleum Exporting Countries, or OPEC, was able to impose quadrupled oil prices on the United States and other oil-importing nations.

In a world of rising demand for many resources and of rising expectations among underdeveloped nations, other groups of nations possessing various kinds of natural resources tried to band together and emulate the oil cartel's success in raising prices. For example, 11 nations that produce bauxite, the ore from which aluminum is made, banded together to form the International Bauxite Association. It was the oil cartel, however, that was most successful in raising prices in 1973 and thereafter. The result has been substantially higher petroleum prices and significant economic and political repercussions.

Government's Response

The oil embargo imposed by Arab nations against the United States came in the wake of the 1973 Arab-Israeli war. The agreement by 11 of the 13 member nations of OPEC to cut their oil exports was primarily an attempt to force governments in the United States as well as Europe to retreat from their pro-Israeli positions.

The boycott was more impressive as an act of economic than political strength, however. It confirmed the vulnerability of America via its dependence on foreign oil. Annual per capita use of energy in the United States had increased from the equivalent of about 40 barrels of oil in 1955 to 60 barrels in 1970. Spot shortages of gasoline and home heating oil had cropped up before 1973 and in April of that year President Nixon delivered to Congress the first of many energy messages that would come from the White House. He ended the oil import quotas that had been in effect since the Eisenhower years, appointed an energy consultant to the White House staff, and directed the Interior Department to step up the leasing of offshore federal lands for oil and natural gas drilling by private industry. In October 1973 the Arab boycott began and, although the United States at the time was getting from the Middle East only about 6 percent of the 17.4 million barrels of oil it consumed daily, President Nixon in November announced a 15 percent reduction in home heating oil and gasoline deliveries to retailers; and he also established the Federal Energy Administration. In 1974 he proposed Project Independence, his plan to reduce United States' dependence on foreign oil.

The embargo lasted only six months, but between October 1973 and early 1974 OPEC raised its prices fourfold. When the embargo was lifted in March 1974, the symbolic gasoline lines disappeared and so did the American public's perception of an energy crisis. But world oil prices did not decline. They exacerbated the inflation of 1974 and 1975, an inflation that helped to cause the deepest U.S. recession and highest unemployment in four decades. Energy then became a subject of great economic concern.

Public and political wrath over higher oil and gasoline prices initially centered on multinational oil companies that for years had operated in the Middle East. They reported large profit increases in 1974 and their executives were hauled before congressional committees to explain why they seemed to prosper at public expense. They were accused of complicity in the embargo; they denied guilt. That controversy ended in an impasse, but the much larger controversy continued over what the United States would do to protect itself from world oil prices and shortages in the future.

In January 1975 President Ford told Congress that "We must embark upon effective programs to conserve energy and develop new sources if we are to reduce the proportion of our oil imported from unreliable sources."[22] At t'·. end of 1975, Congress passed the Energy Policy and Conservation Act which, while a far cry from what President Ford had asked, established fuel efficiency standards for new automobiles and trucks, beginning with 1978 models.

In the first major policy initiative of his new administration, President Carter in April 1977 proposed to Congress an elaborate national energy program. He sought to raise U.S. domestic oil prices to world levels through tax mechanisms. He proposed among other things to tax industries and utilities that failed to switch from oil and natural gas to coal or other more abundant energy sources. More than a year later Congress passed energy legislation, but it differed in many respects from what the President had asked for. Perhaps the most significant difference was that, while President Carter had asked for continued government regulation of natural gas rates, Congress decided on eventual deregulation. At President Carter's request, Congress in 1977 also created a new Department of Energy that consolidated many federal regulatory, research, and conservation programs relating to oil, natural gas, coal, nuclear, solar, and other forms of energy. The Energy Department began with a first-year budget of more than $10 billion and a staff of 19,800.

Political and Economic Problems

In June 1978 a *Wall Street Journal* headline said, "Ailing Agency: Department of Energy, After 8 Months on Job, Fights Many Problems" and a subhead asked, "Is It the Most Hated Bureau?"[23]

Some of the problems stemmed of course from the difficulty of attempting to pull together and control different agencies that, according to the *Journal,* were scattered in 20 Washington buildings. Other problems resulted from the sheer complexity of the energy program passed by Congress. But the administration of federal energy policy also faced much more fundamental problems. The creation of the Department of Energy represented probably the greatest single leap forward of federal regulation in the history of American government, even though the energy legislation looked toward eventual deregulation of natural gas. The energy program also anticipated the spending of many more billions of dollars by government, industry, and consumers. And the difficulties of regulating and spending wisely were immensely complicated by the absence of a public perception of an energy crisis and therefore the absence of constituency in support of the energy program.

Underlying the difficulties faced by the Department of Energy in administering the national energy program enacted in 1978 was a fundamental economic disagreement among the experts.

The pessimistic viewpoint, propounded by the first Energy Secretary, James R. Schlesinger, and others, was that, if a world energy crisis was not at hand, it was coming. The United States must conserve oil and natural gas and develop alternative energy sources because in the 1980's or 1990's the principal oil-exporting countries, such as Saudi Arabia, would have great difficulty in meeting the increase in demand expected throughout the world. The result in a decade or so would be competition between the United States and the U.S.S.R. for scarce worldwide oil supplies, and that would lead to dangerous conflict and possibly to war.[24]

An opposing viewpoint, generally taken by the petroleum industry and the business community, was that there are abundant supplies of oil, natural gas, and coal available in the United States, if only government policy would allow prices to rise sufficiently so that producers would have adequate financial incentives to search for and develop these reserves.

There appeared to be evidence supporting both points of view. In support of the latter view, domestic U.S. oil exploration increased dramatically as worldwide oil prices rose. The number of new wells drilled, which had declined from nearly 40,000 in 1960 to 20,000 in 1973, shot up to more than 30,000 in 1976. However, in possible support of the former view, the increase in production from newly discovered U.S. wells was not enough to offset declining output from existing wells; still, the price of "old" oil from these wells was curtailed to a small fraction of the import price. In any event, U.S. imports continued to swell. Between 1972 and 1977, oil import levels rose 92 percent and the costs increased from $5 billion in 1972 to $45 billion in 1977. U.S. dependence on foreign sources continued to grow, and by 1977 imports filled almost half of U.S. domestic petroleum demand.[25]

There were other, related conflicts in points of view and in policies. One of enormous significance to the public and the press was the conflict between government energy policies and anti-inflation policies.

A basic policy premise is that higher energy prices will encourage greater production and prompt conservation which in turn will eventually reduce U.S. dependence on foreign energy sources. But higher energy prices also contribute to greater inflation and, as a matter of immediate political and economic priority, inflation is often perceived as the nation's overriding problem.

The higher prices of oil, natural gas, and electricity have slowed the growth of energy consumption, especially by industry, but also have contributed to inflation. In addition, government energy policies contributed indirectly in various ways to inflationary pressures.

Consider, for example, the fuel efficiency requirements imposed by the 1975 Energy Policy and Conservation Act on auto and truck manufacturers, beginning with 1978 models and extending through the mid-1980's. The manufacturers began to address the law by building smaller and lighter cars that consumed somewhat less fuel, but the industry in 1977 estimated that the research, technology, and materials required to meet mid-1980's fuel efficiency standards would cost an estimated $50 billion.[26] These costs presumably would be passed on to consumers and would add to inflationary pressures.

Another private study estimated in 1977 that the cost of converting the nation's industrial and utility boilers from oil and natural gas to coal would cost between $106 billion and $135 billion by 1985.[27] Inasmuch as increased coal use would pollute the environment, the costs of converting to coal would be increased by smokestack "scrubbers" and other antipollution devices. Most or all of those costs are passed on to consumers, in still higher electric bills and in the prices of a wide variety of consumer goods and services.

In short, the energy story is complex and controversial. It involves virtually every American and yet remains a reporting challenge; the full scope of the energy crisis has been perceived but dimly, if at all, by most Americans.

Further Complications of Energy Reporting

Energy has been described as "the umbilical cord that connects the economy to society."[28] It is a major ingredient of almost all production and many consumption activities. Our transportation vehicles, appliances, television sets, heating systems, and lighting all require energy. When the supply is cut off, as in an electrical outage, production ceases, our lives are abruptly altered, and modern society teeters on the edge of chaos until power is restored.

As might be expected, there is a high correlation between economic growth and energy consumption. The ratios can vary with changing technology and the amount of energy conservation or waste. It has been estimated that a 2 percent growth of energy consumption is required for every 3 percent growth of the economy. An annual energy growth rate of about 4 percent would be required to produce the 5.5 percent to 6 percent rate of economic growth necessary to sustain reasonably full employment. Because of compounding, this would mean a doubling of the energy supply every 18 years. Even with slower economic expansion and more efficient energy utilization, a 2 percent energy growth rate would require a doubling of the supply every 35 years.

In fact, total U.S. energy consumption increased at an average annual rate of 4 percent between 1958 and 1972, then declined slightly from 1973 through 1975, and in 1976 and 1977 again increased at an average annual rate of 4.3 percent.

Oil and natural gas in recent years have accounted for about three-quarters of total U.S. energy consumption. Coal has supplied about 18 percent of our energy needs. Nuclear energy, used to generate electricity, has accounted for 3 percent of total supply, and the balance has come from solar, geothermal, hydroelectric, and miscellaneous sources.

The use of energy resources can be divided into four categories. *Residential and commercial use,* for heating, lighting, and air-conditioning homes, offices, stores, schools, and so forth, in recent years has consumed about 34 percent of all energy. *Transportation* of people and goods has accounted for about 26 percent of energy consumption, represented by gasoline, diesel fuel, aviation fuel, heavy fuel oil, and liquefied petroleum gas. *Industrial use* in mining and manufacturing has consumed about 32 percent of all energy used. And 8 percent of energy resources have been consumed in *nonenergy applications,* such as the use of oil, gas, and coal as feedstock, or raw material, in the production of asphalt, lubricants, fertilizers, and other petrochemicals.

Total U.S. energy consumption amounted to the equivalent of more than 38 million barrels of oil daily in 1977, as compared with 33 million barrels in 1970. Even assuming increased conservation and somewhat slower economic growth, a 2.3 percent annual increase in U.S. energy demand has been projected, meaning a demand equivalent of 51 million barrels daily by 1990.

Quite obviously, then, if economic growth and nearly full employment are to be maintained, and if U.S. dependence on foreign oil is to be reduced, the nation will have to conserve energy and turn increasingly to alternative energy sources.

Conservation, by such means as better home insulation, more fuel-efficient autos, and thermostats set lower in winter and higher in summer, is a partial solution to the energy supply problem. According to one projection, overall U.S. energy requirements by 1990 will be 25 percent lower than they would have been without conservation efforts. However, even with these savings amounting to the equivalent of 17 million barrels of oil per day, energy usage in 1990 still is expected to grow to 51 million barrels daily.

The news media play a major role in helping consumers to save energy. Articles and broadcasts concerning the importance of conservation, methods of conservation, and the savings to be realized are instrumental in prompting conservation efforts. However, care should be utilized in presenting the economics. The reporter should not unquestioningly accept the claimed savings of a given measure or device. For example, if you added together the reported savings claimed from storm windows and doors, electronic furnace ignition, caulking, lower thermostat settings, extra insulation, and other publicized measures, you might get the impression that the homeowner could reduce heating bills by over 100 percent. Still, careful reporting of reliable cost and savings estimates can guide the homeowner to realize substantial economies while helping our nation to conserve energy resources.

Assuming that conservation alone will not resolve the energy problem, the United States in the near future, probably during the remainder of this century, will have to turn to alternative fuels already at hand, primarily coal, nuclear energy, and hydroelectric power. Substantial use of solar and other more exotic forms of energy probably will not come until the next century unless there are major technological breakthroughs.

The United States has abundant coal supplies. Coal constitutes an estimated 93 percent of the country's fossil fuel reserves, although it has accounted in recent years for only 18 percent of energy consumption. Government and industry have called for a doubling of coal production by 1990 and have encouraged the switch from oil and natural gas. Government also has tried to encourage experimentation with technologies capable of converting coal to gas.

Before coal production goals can be met, though, a number of problems must be dealt with.

One is logistical. It concerns transportation eastward of increased production from coal fields, most of which are in the West. The adequacy of railroad transport is questionable and the potential of coal slurry pipelines is unknown.

The most profound difficulty, however, remains the conflict between coal and the environment. Coal is a polluting fuel, and the country's clean air laws often have hampered its burning. The burning process can be cleaned up, through the use of smokestack scrubbers, but these are expensive. In addition, the disposal of scrubber sludge may pose a greater environmental problem than the chimney gases.

As coal production increases, both energy and environmental reporters will be interested in how the conflict between energy and environment is resolved. The environmental costs of coal are great. They include disturbance of scenic Western lands, heavy demands on scarce Western water for production of oil and gas from coal, air pollution from sulfur compounds and toxic trace metals, and large amounts of waste heat spewed into water and air. In addition there are two federal laws that create expenses. One is a mine safety law aimed at drastically reducing the number of accidents in coal mines. The other is a strip mining law requiring industry to restore as much as possible the land laid barren through mining.

Many countries view nuclear power as their only real energy alternative. The United States was once among them, but the country has had difficulty getting its nuclear program off the ground. In 1979, nuclear power plants provided approximately 12 percent of the U.S. supply of electricity, a figure substantially below what nuclear proponents had anticipated ten years earlier.

U.S. reserves of uranium are estimated to be 32 percent of our total reserves of conventional fuel sources. More specifically, uranium reserves are estimated to be ten times greater than American oil reserves, fifteen times greater than natural gas reserves, and half as large as the nation's coal reserves.

The nuclear industry suffered immense growing pains, beginning in the late 1950's when nuclear power plants first were touted as the answer to the country's energy problem. Initially, government monopoly of nuclear power impeded the growth of the industry. Public distrust of nuclear power became the major problem in the 1970's. At first, the opponents were a minority, but their vigorous persistence was enough to compel seven states in the mid-1970's to raise on their election ballots the question of limiting future nuclear power development. Those referenda were defeated, but antinuclear forces continued their protests.

On March 28, 1979, there was an accidental loss of coolant from the core of a nuclear power plant at Three Mile Island, Pennsylvania. A combination of mechanical and operator errors produced several days of anxiety and near hysteria. Despite the fact that the reactor was eventually cooled with no loss of life, public fears of nuclear energy generation were greatly aroused, and those fears were further enhanced by the then popular movie *The China Syndrome.* The construction of new nuclear plants was abruptly brought to a halt. At that time there were 88 uncompleted nuclear plants with construction permits representing an estimated $50 billion investment in partially completed facilities.[29]

Some viewed the accident at Three Mile Island as proof that the plants should not be completed; others viewed it as proof that a nuclear reactor can successfully withstand a series of mechanical and operator errors without causing a loss of human life. One noted proponent of nuclear energy, Dr. Edward Teller, pointed out that "we know more about controlling radiation than we do about controlling the pollutive effects of burning coal" and "If you sat next to a nuclear power plant for a whole year, you would be exposed to less radiation than you would receive during a round-trip flight in a 747 from New York to Los Angeles."[30]

At the same time, other noted scientists disagreed on the safety of nuclear energy. The safety of nuclear reactors was not their only concern. Another centered on the use of nuclear power for military weapons. Still another concern was disposal of nuclear wastes.

A distressing fact concerning peaceful uses of atomic power is that they utilize materials that can be translated into military weapons. India, for example, manufactured an atom bomb out of materials from a research reactor. The American government worried for years about such military applications, and in 1977 President Carter enunciated an antiproliferation policy that was intended to discourage additional nations from joining "the plutonium club." The policy proposed that access to nuclear fuel be limited to those nations that had agreed to the terms of a nonproliferation treaty. About 90 countries had ratified the treaty by the end of 1979, but important countries that had not indicated agreement included India, Brazil, and Argentina.

Additionally, the United States has encountered great difficulty in trying to find ways of disposing of spent nuclear fuel that is no longer capable of powering electric plants but remains radioactive. Apparently, the technology exists for reprocessing spent fuel plutonium so that it can again be used to generate electricity. This recycling also would reduce the volume and danger of nuclear wastes. Proposals for the federal government to develop a nuclear waste treatment facility have been defeated several times.

The peaceful uses of atomic energy have been an issue in the news almost since the end of World War II, when it was hoped that the atom that was dropped on Hiroshima would henceforth be used to improve the lot of all mankind. Three decades later, that hope was only partially realized and many fears remain. The story will continue to unfold and, given its profound beginnings, there are perhaps few news stories that it is so important to cover on all sides if the nation is to resolve the issues that surround peaceful applications of atomic energy.

The development of hydroelectric power as a partial alternative to oil and natural gas also has become enmeshed in environmental concerns, although not so emotionally as coal and nuclear power. Much of the Pacific Northwest relies on energy supplied by large dams and hydroelectric generators. Government policy has been to increase hydro production of energy in other parts of the nation, such as New England, where 112 hydrosites were abandoned after 1941 because other sources of power became more economical. With soaring oil and natural gas prices, such sites once more became economically feasible. But construction of new dams encountered vigorous opposition because of concerns about wildlife and fish and the flooding of lands behind dams. Even if the dams were permitted, they would supply only a small portion of the power needed.

The problems associated with coal, nuclear power, and hydroelectric power have caused the nation to turn toward new energy sources as long-term answers to the energy problem. When President Carter in April 1977 announced his original energy plan, he said that "America's hope for energy to sustain economic growth beyond the year 2000 rests in large measure on the development of renewable and essentially inexhaustible sources of energy." To that end, government already has invested substantial sums in research and development of exotic energy sources such as solar, geothermal, wind, biomass, and fusion.

Solar energy has captured public and press imagination undoubtedly because the sun is there, solar energy is clean, and solar technology is not entirely new. It was used widely in Florida in the 1940's for heating water and was abandoned when cheap natural gas became available in the state. Solar energy may be practical in most parts of the country for water heating. Solar space heating and cooling have remained costly, however. The hardware for home solar heating usually requires an investment of at least $10,000 and conventional backup heating and cooling systems still are required, even for solar hot water.

One potential of solar energy is in its use to generate electricity, and solar electric technologies are in various stages of development. For example, photovoltaic systems were used in U.S. space explorations to make solar electric energy economically practical by reducing costs and reducing the amount of space that has been required by solar energy hardware. These are major obstacles. For example, a solar generating project being constructed in Arizona had an estimated $1.60 per kilowatt hour cost, 20 times that of conventional fuels at that time.

Geothermal energy comes from the natural heat in the earth's crust. Its potential is considerable, particularly in the West, but it has been significantly used in only one area. Geothermal steam from geysers in northern California has helped to meet electric generating needs of some cities in the area. Other forms of geothermal energy in the West and along the Gulf of Mexico have been considered and the U.S. government also has encouraged exploration for additional geothermal sites and development of geothermal technology. However, the environmental impact of using geothermal sources may be substantial.

Use of wind power had a long history in rural America but declined with the coming of rural electrification cooperatives. Department of Energy experts have hopes that advanced wind systems could supply energy to small electrical units, and the Department has funded wind research projects.

Biomass refers to energy derived from plant life in which the sun's rays are converted and stored. Biomass can be burned in original form, as wood is burned, but also can be converted into solid, liquid, or gaseous fuels. During World War II alcohol and hydrogen were produced by fermentation to supplement conventional fuels, and Brazil more recently has investigated use of alcohol derived from biomass as a substitute for gasoline. Potential sources of biomass energy from land and sea plant life include food processing wastes, crop remains, animal and forestry wastes, kelp, and hyacinths.

Fusion energy, from thermonuclear reactions, is a yet more exotic potential energy source, but the necessary technology appears to be some distance in the future. Fusion works the opposite of fission. Fission, the nuclear process that has powered atomic plants and bombs, results when heavy atoms are split into two parts; fusion is a process in which light atoms are fused. Both processes produce heat that is captured and moved to boilers that drive steam turbines to produce electricity. The fusion process, however, is derived from raw materials that are more commonly available than the plutonium made from uranium; furthermore, since the fusion process does not use plutonium, it could not readily be harnessed to military purposes. However, it is not known whether fusion, if successfully developed, is safer than fission.

With advancing technology, still other energy sources may be forthcoming. Perhaps elements of the sun's rays other than heat can be transformed into a viable energy source. Some scientists envision that hydrogen from water will some day be an economically feasible and nonpolluting source of energy. Still others are working on substitutes for the internal combustion engine to conserve current fuel supplies. In any event, as the prices of conventional fuels rise, the economics of previously untapped energy reserves, conversion, and more exotic energy sources will be improved. And, *if* a major technological breakthrough is achieved, energy prices may eventually stabilize or decline.

A JOURNALISTIC CONCLUSION

There are few if any issues in business and economic reporting more complex and at the same time more vital than the environment and energy resources. These issues pertain directly to our economic prosperity and quality of life and they could be related to the future of war or peace.

Solutions to environmental and energy resource problems are not obvious and conflicting opinions abound. It bears repeating, therefore, that journalists must report all sides and touch all bases if the nation is to be sufficiently informed to make the difficult choices that lie ahead.

Most environmental and energy policies are formulated in Washington, as are many other economic and business policies. However, those issues should not be regarded as being of concern only to reporters who happen to work in Washington. The policies decided in the Capitol ultimately succeed or fail not there but in the communities that comprise the nation. Therefore, all reporters who write about energy and the environment should be aware of national policies and laws; the application of those policies and laws offers opportunities and responsibilities to local and regional reporters no less than to the Washington press corps.

For example, *The Boston Globe* on a single day carried two local stories about solar heating that flowed essentially from national energy policies and laws. The two stories ran at the top of the first page of the *Globe's* business and financial section, which is titled "The Economy."[31] The story on the left side of the page flowed from a federal solar design grant program administered by the U.S. Department of Housing and Urban Development, but it was fundamentally a local story for Boston readers. It began:

> Except for small glass rooms on its south side, the newly renovated house will look like any other home on Mission Hill's Calumet Street.
>
> But the small glass enclosures will make all the difference in the 80-year-old house that is slated to be renovated by the Mission Hill Neighborhood Housing Services, Inc., a private nonprofit community organization.
>
> For the glass rooms—greenhouses or solariums—will be part of a passive solar heating system made possible under a special federal program to stimulate solar energy use in multi-unit urban dwellings.

The solar heating story on the right side of the page resulted from an interview with an official of a union that was doing its own experimentation with solar energy. Note that the reporter explained rather quickly to readers the union's particular motivation for experimenting with solar heating. The story began:

> The Sheet Metal Workers International Assn. sees gold in the sun's rays for itself as well as for the nation's homeowners.
>
> Edward J. Carlough, president of the union, claims that an experiment conducted by the union in Hartford, Conn., showed that supplemental heating by solar energy "provides early savings and fast pay-back on the investment."
>
> Carlough has been one of the early proponents of solar energy. He sees it as a means of expanding membership in the Sheet Metal Workers union while helping the United States decrease dependency on imported oil.

Energy and environmental reporting represent a difficult but surely not impossible challenge to reporters. The experts on all sides will explain to you their positions and, with skill in questioning and in writing, you can lay the issues clearly and cleanly before readers, listeners, and viewers. Require the experts to explain in understandable language not only what their positions are but how, where, when, and why their positions are of significance to the public at large. Remember that Americans have been willing to interest themselves in the environment and energy when those issues are perceived as personal pocketbook issues. Environmental and energy stories are everywhere, and they validly can be personalized and localized and thus made both interesting and important.

NOTES—CHAPTER 6

1. Rachel L. Carson, *Silent Spring* (Boston: Houghton Mifflin Company, 1962).

2. Paul B. Erlich, *The Population Bomb* (Mattituck, N.Y.: American Reprint Co., Rivercity Press, 1969).

3. "Why the U.S. Is in Danger of Being Engulfed by Its Own Trash," *U.S. News & World Report*, September 13, 1969, pp. 64–66.

4. William Stief, "Why the Birds Cough," *The Progressive*, April 1970, pp. 47–54.

5. Fred Luthens and Richard M. Hodgetts, *Social Issues in Business* (New York: The Macmillan Company, 1972), p. 189.

6. Erlich, *The Population Bomb*.

7. See Thomas D. Crocker and A. J. Rogers, *Environmental Economics* (Hinsdale, Ill.: The Dryden Press, 1971), p. 2.

8. "The Macroeconomic Impacts of Federal Pollution Control Programs: 1976 Assessment," a paper prepared by Chase Econometric Associates, Inc., for the Council on Environmental Quality and the Environmental Protection Agency, 1976.

9. *Environmental Quality Control—Governmental Finances: Fiscal Year 1974–1975*, Spe-

cial Studies No. 83, Bureau of the Census, Department of Commerce, Washington, D.C., 1977.

10. Edward F. Denison, *Effects of Selected Changes in the Institutional and Human Environment Upon Output per Unit of Input,* Reprint 335 (Washington, D.C.: The Brookings Institution, 1978).

11. *New York Times,* July 2, 1976, p. 1, and June 17, 1976, p. 13.

12. "EPA Indefinitely Suspends Parking-Related Provisions of Indirect Source Regulations," a press release of the Environmental Protection Agency dated June 30, 1975.

13. "Balancing Pollution Controls and Costs," *New York Times,* February 22, 1978, pp. 51, 57.

14. Douglas M. Costle, administrator of the Environmental Protection Agency, in a speech before The Conference Board, Washington, D.C., April 17, 1978.

15. "Recycling Responds," a publication of the National Association of Recycling Industries, Inc., 1978.

16. U.S. Council on Environmental Quality, Eighth Annual Report, issued in December 1977, p. 54.

17. *Ibid.,* p. 55.

18. *Ibid.,* p. 5.

19. *Ibid.,* p. 254.

20. D. H. Meadows and others, *The Limits to Growth: A Report for the Club of Rome's Project on the Predicament of Mankind* (New York: Universe Books, 1972).

21. *Mankind at the Turning Point: A Second Report from the Club of Rome* (New York: E. P. Dutton, 1974).

22. Economic Report of the President, delivered February 4, 1975, p. 3.

23. *Wall Street Journal,* June 13, 1978, pp. 1, 35.

24. Testimony of Energy Secretary James R. Schlesinger before the House Committee on Science and Technology, January 25, 1978.

25. Figures relative to drilling and import activity are reported in the Report of the Council of Economic Advisers, pp. 179–87, transmitted to Congress along with the Economic Report of the President, January 20, 1978.

26. See an untitled press release of the Motor Vehicle Manufacturers Association, Detroit, December 7, 1977.

27. Milt Copulos, "Coal Conversion to Increase Costs," a study for the Heritage Foundation, Washington, D.C., September 28, 1977.

28. Quoted in "Energy, the Ostrich and the Eagle," *Christian Science Monitor,* October 25, 1978, p. 3.

29. Irvin C. Bupp, "Nuclear Realities," *New York Times,* May 29, 1979.

30. *Wall Street Journal,* July 31, 1979.

31. *The Boston Globe,* August 2, 1979, p. 29.

SOURCES OF INFORMATION

American Gas Association
1515 Wilson Boulevard
Arlington, Va. 22209

Environmental Protection Agency
401 M Street, S.W.
Washington, D.C. 20460

American Petroleum Institute
1801 K Street, N.W.
Washington, D.C. 20006

American Public Power Association
600 Virginia Avenue, N.W.
Washington, D.C. 20037

Atomic Industrial Forum, Inc.
475 Park Avenue South
New York, N.Y. 10016

Edison Electric Institute
1140 Connecticut Avenue, N.W.
Washington, D.C. 20036

Energy Action
1523 L Street, N.W.
Washington, D.C. 20005

International Atomic Energy Agency
P.O. Box 590
Karntnerring 11, A-1010
Vienna, Austria

National Coal Association
1130 17th Street, N.W.
Washington, D.C. 20036

Nuclear Regulatory Commission
1717 H Street, N.W.
Washington, D.C. 20006

U.S. Department of Energy
1000 Independence Avenue, S.W.
Washington, D.C. 20461

SUGGESTED READINGS

Alexander, Tom, "The Packaging Problem Is a Can of Worms," Fortune, June 1972, p. 107.

Carson, Rachel L., Silent Spring. Boston: Houghton Mifflin Company, 1962.

Crocker, Thomas D., and A. J. Rogers, Environmental Economics. Hinsdale, Ill.: The Dryden Press, 1971.

"Energy, the Ostrich and the Eagle," Christian Science Monitor, October 25, 1978, p. 3.

Erlich, Paul B., The Population Bomb. Mattituck, N.Y.: American Reprint Co., Rivercity Press, 1969.

Government and the Nation's Resources, report of the National Commission on Supplies and Shortages, Washington, D.C., December 1976.

Luthens, Fred, and Richard M. Hodgetts, Social Issues in Business. New York: The Macmillan Company, 1972.

Meadows, D. H., and others, The Limits to Growth: A Report for the Club of Rome's Project on the Predicament of Mankind. New York: Universe Books, 1972.

Rossin, A. D., and T. A. Rieck, "Economics of Nuclear Power, Science, August 1978, p. 53.

Stief, William, "Why the Birds Cough," The Progressive, April 1970, pp. 47–54.

"Stopping Pollution Before It Stops Us," Futurist, December 1978, p. 404.

Ward, Barbara, and Rene Dubos, Only One Earth: The Care and Maintenance of a Small Planet. New York: W. W. Norton and Company, 1972.

"Why the U.S. Is in Danger of Being Engulfed by Its Own Trash," U.S. News & World Report, September 13, 1969, pp. 64–66.

Reporting on . . .
PROFITS, INVESTMENT, AND GROWTH

7

ELLIS HALLER

ONE AFTERNOON IN THE AUTUMN OF 1976, John deButts, then chairman of the nation's largest private business enterprise, issued a statement that was to make nationwide newspaper headlines and draw comments from radio and television newscasters. For the three months that ended August 31 of that year, Mr. deButts reported, American Telephone & Telegraph Company had racked up net profits of just over $1 billion. It was a landmark development. Never before had a U.S. corporation made as much as a billion dollars in a single quarter.

The record-setting pace of earnings was to be repeated by AT&T in later quarters. But far from being complacent about the trend, Mr. deButts made the startling observation that the huge profit really wasn't big enough. The telephone operating companies in AT&T's Bell System were pushing ahead with requests for increased rates for phone service, he added, because even though net earnings of more than $4 billion a year were gratifying, they still fell short of what was needed if the telephone company was to keep its service up to customers' expectations.

AT&T had more than $70 billion of capital invested in plants and equipment; it was spending a billion dollars every month to provide new telephone facilities. Yet, among the 500 largest American firms, the telephone company was 324th in terms of return to stockholders—roughly 8.9 cents on every dollar invested in the business. And the fact that AT&T had been able to net a profit of a billion dollars a quarter meant that tax collectors already had taken an almost equal amount from pretax income.

AT&T officials drew relatively little public criticism about the amount of money the company was making. In that respect they were luckier than some other corporations whose profits in recent years have had heavy play in the news. For example, as Congress grew more concerned about the nation's energy supplies in the 1970's, Senator Henry M. Jackson told officials of major oil companies that their profits were "unconscionable." President Carter characterized the earnings of oil companies as a "ripoff" of the long-suffering consumer. Spokesmen for environmental and ecological groups meanwhile were demanding that big manufacturing, mining, and processing companies divert a larger portion of their income to protecting the environment and attaining broadened social goals.

In the midst of all this controversy, the chairman of the Securities and Exchange Commission, Harold M. Williams, sounded his own warning about the size of corporate profits: Far from being shockingly high, he said, they were "dangerously low" in relation to the increasing demands society is placing on the private enterprise system. Reports of "all-time highs" in earnings were deceptive, Mr. Williams cautioned, because they failed to take into account inflation and other factors, including businesses' need for new capital to grow on.[1]

THE ROLE OF PROFITS

Whether a particular corporation's profits are "dangerously low" or are "unconscionable" can be argued, from the differing viewpoints of managers, employees, stockholders, and customers, and the arguments frequently are newsworthy. All the participants in the arguments presumably would agree, however, that corporate profits are essential to a healthy economy. The relationship of profits to other aspects of the nation's economy is not always apparent on the surface, but the interconnections are vital. In the United States, healthy business profits are a component of prosperity usually associated with high employment whereas depressed profits usually are paralleled or followed by unemployment and recession.

John Connor, chairman of Allied Chemical Corporation and former Secretary of Commerce, has put it this way:

> ... a substantial part of corporate profits goes to pay taxes, which help support the countless programs of federal and state governments. The rest of the profit dollar is what keeps our economy regenerating itself. Part of it is paid out as dividends to the millions of Americans who have invested their savings in our private enterprise system in the expectation of getting a return on that investment. And a large part of the balance is spent directly to build new plants and buy the new equipment needed to provide more jobs, and better jobs, for American working men and women.[2]

Retained profits, reinvested in a business, mean not only more and better jobs at higher pay, but innovative products for consumers at competitive prices. The result, reflected in growth in the nation's total output, contributes to a higher standard of living for everyone. Fletcher Byrom, chairman of Koppers Corporation, has noted that while the reason for a company to exist is not to make profits, "nevertheless profits are necessary if that corporation is to continue. It's like the relationship between breathing and life. No one would say that the purpose of life is to breathe, but neither is it possible to continue to live unless you are breathing."[3]

Successful businessmen and women quite naturally defend the profit system, but Mr. Byrom's simile is not necessarily overdrawn. Without profits, corporations may not be able to continue in business and workers may lose their jobs. For example, Chrysler Corporation, the nation's third largest auto manufacturer, in the late 1970's reported record corporate losses, about the time AT&T was reporting record profits, and by 1979 Chrysler was threatened with possible bankruptcy. To prevent Chrysler from going out of business, Congress in December 1979 agreed to provide the company with $1.5 billion of federal loan guarantees. In the political debate that preceded enactment of the "bail-out" legislation, the United Auto Workers strongly supported the federal aid proposal on the ground that as many as 300,000 workers might lose their jobs if Chrysler were thrown into bankruptcy.

PERCEPTIONS OF PROFITS

Differing perceptions concerning profits underscore a common pitfall for reporters who want to do an accurate and meaningful job of reporting and interpreting business and economic news. The task is at once demanding and frustrating, and it is not getting any less difficult. New methods of accounting complicate the interpretation of balance sheets and profit-and-loss statements. Demands that companies be "socially responsible" are changing the public's concept of the corporation and of the ways in which its income is used. Steady inflation in recent years has led people to believe that the increased prices contribute to fat profits for business concerns.

Confusion and Contradiction

Confusion concerning profits is central to a greater confusion over how an essentially free economy works. Dean Richard E. West of the Amos Tuck School of Business at Dartmouth College, for example, has said:

> In the kind of world in which we live, people are confronted every day with issues that relate to economics, whether they realize it or not. I'm talking about such things as the risks involved in making and marketing

products, the relationship between profits and jobs, why over-regulation can destroy incentives and discourage business growth and expansion. Yet the typical individual can't make heads or tails of what's going on in the economic sector of our society. That has been documented many times. A study done at the University of Texas showed that some 80 million people in this country are economically illiterate.[4]

Concerning profits, one long-time analyst of business news has written that "The very word conjures up images of gold, greed, and gluttony." David Sargent, president of United Business Service, added that, "Conversely, the adjective 'non-profit' when applied to an institution is a blessing of purity. It's right there in our language: The profit institution is bad, the non-profit good."[5]

Even so, few Americans argue that the profit system ought to be scrapped. Indeed, a national poll of high school student leaders in 1976 found that eight out of ten of those queried considered the U.S. system the best of all economic systems, and nine of ten believed that the profit motive is essential to the survival of the economy.[6]

Arthur Okun, senior fellow at the Brookings Institution in Washington and a former member of the White House Council of Economic Advisers has made this observation:

> In lecturing at universities, I find that many young people suspect that the bulk of profits stems from the exploitation of monopoly positions, gimmicks in advertising that either scare or mislead the public, and plain outright chicanery, rather than from serving the consumer with new, better or more efficient products. Thus, many of the cynics exonerate [such companies as] Xerox, Polaroid and Texas Instruments from their general condemnation of the profit system. We establishment types start with the presumption that a highly profitable firm must be doing something right, unless we see a case to the contrary; the anti-establishment critics start with the presumption that they must be doing something wrong, with qualifications for exceptions.[7]

Responsibilities of the Press and of Business

The press and business share responsibility for the public confusion over the role of profits, and a number of experts assert that efforts on the part of both the press and business are necessary to alleviate the confusion.

Dean Lawrence E. Fouraker of the Graduate School of Business Administration at Harvard University, for instance, has asserted that the press in some measure adds to the confusion about profits, and many corporate executives doubtless would agree.

Journalists should take responsibility for providing background or interpretation when reporting on corporate earnings . . . The crucial relationship is that profits enable an organization to renew itself, to take risks in the cause of avoiding obsolescence. To increase public understanding of these points, I'd like to see more discussion between reporters and business and financial people in a non-crisis atmosphere.[8]

On the other hand, Joseph L. Oppenheimer, vice-president of Standard & Poor's Corporation, has taken the view that business

for the most part, has done very little to reach the great mass of people with an explanation of how profits are necessary to create new jobs, expand a business, or meet consumers' needs. Business does not even do an effective job of communicating with its own middle and lower management about the free enterprise system. The press should not be expected to do this educational job for a number of reasons. For one thing, the limited number of newspapers and magazines that devote a decent amount of space to business/financial coverage are not the mass media that are read widely. Even when these publications are bought, the financial section may be skipped by many readers. The amount of space available in most publications does not allow for extensive background or interpretation; most of it must be devoted to the statistics that are news.

Increased public understanding of our economic system is going to take years. I think that it would be desirable to start education on this topic at the junior high school level and continue it through high school and college. The program can include not only straight business–economic courses, but also consumer education courses.[9]

A third view was taken by Dean Richard N. Rosett of the Graduate School of Business at the University of Chicago:

The public has an imperfect understanding of how our economic system functions, just as it has an imperfect knowledge of how airplanes fly, plants grow, automobiles run, and their own bodies function. . . . Understanding of all these things can be improved through mastery of various theoretical sciences few of us ever master. Still, the public's understanding of all these things is good enough for most practical purposes. That includes its understanding of the economic system.

Some of the press tends to reduce confusion about profits, some to increase it. I attribute those tendencies to public demand rather than to any merit or failure of the press. Sports reporting in this country is extremely good because the publisher's customers demand it. If they demanded financial and business reporting of the same quality, they would get it. Indeed there are some who demand it now and get it; witness *The Wall Street Journal.* Journalism is a business like any other. Its practitioners, in order to profit, must figure out what the customers want and produce it for them cheaply and efficiently.[10]

PROFIT DEFINED

For people in the news media, particularly those who must deal with economic and financial matters, a basic understanding of profits and their role in the business process is important. The subject doesn't have to be as complicated as many try to make it.

Just what is meant by that word "profit"? In simplest terms, it is the difference between everything a successful business takes in and everything it spends. Over a given period of time, a company earns a certain amount of money from selling its goods or services. Over that same period it has certain costs of operation: it must pay for supplies, for wages and fringe benefits, for pollution control, and for improvement of plant and equipment.

Note that there is a profit only if the business is successful; if expenses exceed revenues, there is a loss. Among the new businesses that start up each year, far more wind up with red ink than with a profit.

Without profits, some old and large businesses have gone broke too. In 1976, the same year that American Telephone & Telegraph was reporting quarterly profits of more than $1 billion, the press also reported the demise of W. T. Grant Company. The story in *The New York Times* began:

> A Federal judge yesterday signed an order providing for the liquidation within 60 days of the W. T. Grant Company, which only two years ago was the third largest variety-store chain in the United States.
>
> "I find myself compelled to sign this order," Federal Bankruptcy Judge John J. Calgay said after two days of hearings on a petition for liquidation. The 70-year-old company, after amassing debts of $1.8 billion, filed for a voluntary Chapter XI proceeding under the Bankruptcy Act last Oct. 2. It was the largest American retailing company to go into reorganization.[11]

Paul A. Samuelson, professor of economics at Massachusetts Institute of Technology, has stressed the need for looking at both sides of the equation in discussing the money business makes. In his words:

> It is misleading to talk about a profit system. Ours is a profit-and-loss system. Profits are the carrots held out as an incentive to efficiency, and losses are the risks that penalize using inefficient methods or devoting resources to uses not desired by spending consumers. . . . What does the

pursuit of profit mean? It means that the businessman, like anybody else, is trying to get as much as he can from resources at his disposal. This is not different from what a worker is doing when he changes occupations or joins a union. [12]

Because there are many theories and many aspects of profits, even learned economic thinkers differ on which ought to be given weight. Economists, accountants, statisticians, educators, and business executives offer their various views of profit.

Profits and Jobs

As we have seen in earlier chapters of this book, the American labor movement as a whole never has accepted the Marxist view of profit as simply the exploitation of labor. Indeed, various communist governments have turned to profit incentives to increase production efficiency. [13]

This country's labor leaders long have recognized the relationship between profits and jobs. It was Samuel Gompers, an early president of the American Federation of Labor, who was reported to have said, "Companies without profits mean workers without jobs. Remember, when the boss is in financial trouble the worker's job isn't safe." George Meany, president of the AFL-CIO from its formation in 1955 almost to his death in early 1980, declared in an address to a meeting of corporate executives a few years ago, "I stand for the profit system; I believe in the profit system. I believe it's a wonderful incentive. I believe in the free enterprise system completely. I believe in the return on investment. I believe in management's right to manage." [14]

When labor and management sit down at the bargaining table, both are fully aware that a union's ability to win increased wage and fringe benefits is greater when a company's profits are growing than when profits are declining. Profits that are retained in a business, rather than paid out to stockholders in dividends, also are a vital part of capital formation and thus of the job creation process. The average amount of capital per employee invested in manufacturing is about $30,000, according to estimates of economists on the staff of The Conference Board, a nonprofit business and economic research organization. However, the figure may be twice that amount after inflation is taken into account, the Board's economists also have said.

The relationship between profits and jobs is underscored by labor force demographics. Some 70,000 new jobs must be created each week—or more than 3.5 million additional jobs each year—to accommodate an expanding work force. Those are the average numbers of new jobs that will be needed in the years ahead, over and above existing jobs that open up through retirements or deaths. The additional jobs will be needed to provide for three major groups in the population: those seeking work for the first time, those thrown out of work by new machines and new technologies, and those listed as unemployed.

New jobs are needed because the nation's work force is continuing to increase, in fact more rapidly than the population. More women are coming into the labor market, either to bolster family income in the face of inflation or to seek careers that will give them a measure of self-fulfillment. During the decade ending in 1978, teen-agers also were seeking jobs in record numbers. At the same time, an unemployment rate that hovered in a range of 5 to 6 percent means that some 6 million people already in the labor force were looking for jobs.

Profits also are vital to workers who have retired from their jobs. More than 30 million beneficiaries of private pension plans have an interest in corporate profits, both as a source of corporate contributions to the pension plans and as a source of pension plan income derived from investment in corporate securities. Some 365 million life insurance policies in force in the United States also depend to a considerable extent on the dividends that profits produce.

The Economic Roles of Profits

Profits also can be viewed from different but related economic aspects. A rather practical overview has been offered by Harold S. Geneen, chairman of International Telephone and Telegraph Company until 1978:

> The only courage the businessman has got is his profits. When he has profits, he goes and builds plants, does things, creates jobs. And when he doesn't have profits, he gets scared and pulls in the roof. It's just that simple.[15]

It may not be quite that simple, but in a free market economy, goods are channeled according to ups and downs in demand and changes in consumer preference. If some product isn't being made in large enough quantity, the bidding up of prices will raise profits and spur output. If an item is in oversupply and no longer in great demand, the price falls, the profit declines, the high-cost manufacturers drop out of the market, and prices continue to come down until supply and demand are in balance. The same principle applies to services. As business consultant Harold Brayman has observed:

> If there are too many barbers, the price of haircuts may not necessarily decline, but the barbers are kept busy for a smaller proportion of their day, their earnings are lower, and they tend to drift off into other occupations or other localities. If, on the other hand, there is a great shortage of competent television repairmen, the profits which such persons make are high enough to attract new people to the field.[16]

The law of supply and demand does not always work perfectly, as other authors of this book have pointed out, and the imperfections give rise to a view of profit as a monopoly return—as money raked in by a tycoon who exploits the rest of the community. Such exploitation may be the economic result of collusion among a number of companies or may result from control of a product or service by a single company that uses its monopoly position to wring excessive profits from consumers. That monopoly positions can exist is recognized by government, which polices business under the antitrust laws and under various regulatory programs.

The Social Role of Profits

In recent years a new attitude toward profit has gained ground among economists, sociologists, and some corporate leaders. Rethinking the whole subject has become necessary in contemporary society, according to Franklin A. Lindsay, chairman of the board of Itek Corporation. "Today, new demands are being placed on business, demands that heretofore did not exist. These demands stem from growing public expectations that business must assume a much larger share of social and environmental responsibility."[17] Carl H. Madden, the late professor of business at American University, predicted that:

> By the year 2000 or so, most industries will have adapted to environmental health, safety and consumer regulation—or gone the way of the dinosaur. . . . Whether we like it or not, the world is moving away from the doctrine that business should limit its activities to classic profit making. The definition of "profit" itself is changing. The meaning of "cost" is changing. For a corporation, "costs" even now include social objectives: equality of opportunity, management of natural resources, development of human resources, attainment of a just and stable society.[18]

THE SIZE OF PROFITS

Business and economic journalists need to be aware of the diverse concepts associated with profits. But they also need to keep in mind that much of what they present to the public will be read or heard by people relatively unsophisticated in economic matters.

Facts and Fictions

Most Americans have a distorted idea of the size of profits earned by business, judging from responses to opinion polls. Few people come anywhere near the mark when asked how much profit the typical corporation makes. A typical survey by Opinion Research Corporation indicated that the public believes the average manufacturer makes 29 cents after-tax profits on each dollar of sales. The true figure, according to the Federal Trade Commission, is less than 5 cents. In the public mind, the local electric utility averages 37 cents of profit on each dollar of revenue, whereas the actual amount is about 12 cents. The average auto company, perceived as making 37 cents on the sales dollar, is lucky to get 5 cents. The typical oil company, viewed as bringing 43 cents of each dollar of sales down to net income, makes instead a bit less than 9 cents.[19]

While the popular impression is that business earns far more than is the case, people questioned in polls have said they believe that 25 cents on the dollar would be a fair profit—about five times what the average manufacturer makes. In a broad survey covering 5,900 heads of U.S. households and conducted in 1978 for *U.S. News & World Report,* respondents gave 13 cents as the amount of profit earned by the typical manufacturing company. When asked what they thought an average manufacturer's profit should be, the answer was still 13 cents. The actual amount, as noted earlier, is a bit more than 5 cents.

Another way of measuring profit is in percentage return on money invested in a business—called return upon stockholders' equity. For many businesses, this yardstick produces a higher percentage figure than return on sales. Figures from the Federal Trade Commission give these comparisons of after-tax profits for a sampling of industries:

- chemicals—7.1 percent on sales, 14.8 percent on equity;
- paper—5.4 percent on sales, 12.7 percent on equity;
- petroleum and coal—7.7 percent on sales, 13.7 percent on equity;
- motor vehicles—3.8 percent on sales, 11.3 percent on equity;
- all retail trade—2.7 percent on sales, 20.5 percent on equity.

As these percentages make clear, the rates of return on sales for some business ventures are below those that an individual can earn on money deposited in a savings account with no risk of loss. "In all probability," according to Arthur Okun, "the majority of laymen would be surprised to learn that corporate profits represent only about 8 percent of our gross national product before taxes and 5 percent after taxes." Indeed, profits after taxes expressed as a percentage of the country's total output have been declining for the past 25 years and now represent about half as large a proportion of wages and salaries as they did 25 years ago. In the first quarter of 1978, profits after taxes represented 6.4 percent of national income whereas wage and salary payments constituted 77 percent of national income. Back in 1929, corporate profits after taxes constituted nearly 10 percent of national income.

Despite all that, however, the sheer size of total profits for a particular year can look awesome. In 1977, for example, profits of all American corporations amounted to $171.6 billion. Of that amount, federal, state, and local governments took $69.1 billion in taxes, leaving $102.5 billion in net income. Stockholders received $41.2 billion in dividends and the companies were left with $61.3 billion for investment in new plants, equipment, product development, and job creation.

The Effects of Inflation

Reporters should be aware, however, that the awesome totals just quoted reflect the impact of inflation. Corporate profits in 1967 totaled $44.9 billion after taxes. If the 1977 profits after taxes ($102.5 billion) were adjusted to 1967 dollars, they would have been only $57.3 billion—not much gain over a decade in which the whole economy was growing rapidly. A dollar of profits today has so much less buying power than a few years ago that a company has to earn much more profit just to keep even.

Inflation also has distorted profits because of the way corporations account for depreciation, which accounts for wear and tear on plants and machinery, and their growing obsolescence. Depreciation is a cost that must be recovered so that companies will have the money to buy new facilities when the need arises, and so that they will not be paying taxes on what is actually a primary expense of doing business. The difficulty in all this, as the Economic Unit of *U.S. News & World Report* has expressed it, is that

> the amounts charged for depreciation are based on the cost of the machines and buildings when they were first acquired, and the businesses fall far short of the funds that will be required to buy replacements at the inflated prices that now prevail—not to mention the even higher costs that are likely to be charged years hence:
> The Big-Load Manufacturing Company, let's say, bought a metal press for $100,000 five years ago and figures on using it for five more years. As a result, it is charging depreciation at a rate of $10,000 per year. A replacement for that press five years from now will cost perhaps $200,000. Where will the extra $100,000 come from? Not out of the funds being set aside for depreciation. The money will have to be extracted from after-tax profits or from stockholders or creditors.
>
> Meanwhile ... the company is paying higher taxes by reason of the fact that its deductions for depreciation do not realistically reflect the rising values of its equipment on the current market.[20]

The Securities and Exchange Commission began recently to require certain large corporations to disclose, in footnotes to their financial statements, the effect of inflation on the value of their plant and equipment. In the case of American Telephone & Telegraph Company, for example, the value of investment in telephone plants, listed as costing $102 billion, would be $145 billion if this total investment had to be replaced at current prices.

Still further inflationary distortions of profits can result from the way a company values its inventories—the cost of the parts and materials it uses if it is a manufacturing firm, or the cost of the products on its shelves if it is a retail store. In recent years many companies have switched to an accounting method known as "Last in, first out," popularly called LIFO. Under this system, the cost of materials is based on the prices paid most recently for these items, instead of on the prices of materials that have been in inventory for the longest time. This helps a company meet some of the inventory-valuation problems that arise in a period of inflation, but it also can mean that the current higher costs of inventories are reflected in lower reported earnings.

REPORTING ON PROFITS

The important question centering on today's information explosion in the area of business news is whether reporters are doing an adequate job of getting sometimes complicated information to the reader or listener in plain English. Reporters owe it to themselves and to their readers to have at least a minimum understanding of what they are writing about. William H. Grimes, late editor of *The Wall Street Journal*, expressed it this way:

> We like to have our editors and reporters experts in just one field, which is the field of making a newspaper, of finding information and telling it. We insist that they know what they are writing about and that they tell their story in the simplest language possible. If they can't do that latter, it indicates to us that their own knowledge is incomplete and we send them back for the rest of the information.[21]

Sources of Information

The job of the business news reporter who must cope with the multifaceted aspects of profits is being made a bit easier in one respect. Government agencies such as the Securities and Exchange Commission and Federal Trade Commission are requiring corporations to give the public much more information about their operations and their finances than was the case in years past. The New York Stock Exchange, too, requires detailed reports on the earnings and the accounting methods of publicly traded firms. That is a sharp turnabout from earlier days, when many company managements gave stockholders no information at all. Many years ago the treasurer of the Delaware, Lackawanna, and Western Railroad, responding to a request from the New York Stock Exchange for data, wrote in reply: "This company makes no reports and publishes no statements."[22]

The journalist seeking information about profits of specific companies today will find no lack of sources. Publicly owned corporations, that is, those with stock traded on an exchange or in the over-the-counter market, issue detailed and often elaborate annual reports as well as shorter quarterly reports. The typical corporation will mail its reports on request to anyone who inquires, whether or not he or she is a shareholder. Most companies are happy to add the name of a business news writer to their mailing lists for financial reports and other corporate data. Two major financial services, Standard & Poor's Corporation and Moody's Investors Service, Inc., both with headquarters in New York City, publish comprehensive reports on activities of publicly traded corporations, including sales and profits comparisons. Many public libraries subscribe to these services and their reports are also available in the offices of stock brokers and securities firms. In addition, comprehensive data on corporate profits are available from the Securities and Exchange Commission and the Federal Trade Commission in Washington and at regional offices.

Much of the publicly available data on corporations reflect even more comprehensive information that all publicly held firms are required to file with the Securities and Exchange Commission. These companies must disclose financial data and other matters considered material to the companies and their stockholders. The annual corporate reports filed with the SEC, known as 10-K reports, and the less voluminous quarterly reports are available to the public and press at SEC offices. When the SEC finds out that material disclosures have not been made, its enforcement actions also make news. *The Wall Street Journal* reported in 1977, for instance:

> Washington—The Securities and Exchange Commission accused Victor Posner of arranging for six publicly held companies to pick up $1.7 million in personal expenses for himself and his two children.
>
> At the same time that the SEC filed its complaint in federal court here, Mr. Posner, his children and various Posner-controlled companies consented to an injunction related to the charges without admitting or denying guilt.
>
> The SEC complaint also charged that two Posner-controlled companies, Sharon Steel Corp. and its parent, NVF Co., misstated their corporate profit for 1974 and 1975 and filed false financial statements with the commission.[23]

How to Read Financial Statements

A reporter's ability to read a financial statement is important because a company's finances are important to the economic health and job security of its community and because business finances are important to the economic health of the nation.

To the uninitiated, a company's annual report can be a formidable document, particularly in its statistical section. The typical report starts off with a letter to shareholders, signed by the chairman or president, giving information about recent corporate developments, issues facing the management, and frequently some projections for the future. This introductory section tends to describe the firm's operations in optimistic terms and may gloss over problems that are explained in detail elsewhere in the report.

The financial section of an annual report consists of two major parts, the income statement and the balance sheet. The *income statement* covers the previous year's activities, showing whether the company made or lost money, the taxes it paid, whether there were unusual or nonrecurring expenses. Results are compared with those of the preceding year. Questions that a journalist might ask when scanning the income statement include these:

- Has there been sales growth, or have sales remained stagnant?
- Have operating costs moved higher in relation to sales?
- Have profit margins been maintained?

The annual income statement of a large corporation may be fairly lengthy, but the major elements of all company income statements are those illustrated in the following example:

	1980	1979
Net Sales	$10,000,000	$9,000,000
Operating Expenses		
Cost of Goods Sold	7,000,000	6,500,000
Depreciation	300,000	250,000
Sales and Administrative Expenses	1,000,000	950,000
Total Income	$1,700,000	$1,300,000
Interest Expenses	150,000	150,000
Income Before Federal Income Taxes	$1,550,000	$1,150,000
Federal Income Taxes	697,500	517,500
Net Income	$ 852,500	$ 632,500

Our hypothetical example would indicate a financially healthy company, with rising sales, reasonably controlled operating expenses, and a satisfactory net income or profit. A company's financial results for a particular one or two years might not be typical, however, and therefore you should look at sales and income trends over a longer period, say ten years. Usually you can find such trend figures in companies' annual reports to shareholders. Income taxes, of course, will vary with the corporate tax rate.

Normally these reports will contain, adjacent to the income statement, a statistic called "net earnings (or profits) per share." This figure is obtained simply by dividing net income, after provision for federal taxes, by the number of common shares a company has outstanding. In our example, assuming 200,000 outstanding common shares owned by public investors and management officials, earnings per share would have been $4.26 for 1980 and $3.16 for 1979. The earnings per common share figure is a handy way of expressing a company's annual financial results.

As we have suggested, corporate income statements generally are more complicated and lengthy than our example. For example, even smaller companies may have dividend or interest income that increases total income. They may have outstanding shares of preferred stock and, if so, dividend requirements on the preferred shares must be subtracted from net income in order to arrive at earnings available for common stock on which to calculate earnings per common share.

Still, the example illustrates the most important elements of all company income statements, and in general those also are the major elements reporters should look for in reading budgets of local, state, and federal governments. The major difference, of course, is that government receipts usually are derived from taxes rather than sales, and government entities pay no taxes on their receipts.

In addition to the annual income statement, the other important financial statement you will find in company annual reports is the *balance sheet*. It provides a picture of the company's financial status as of the end of its operating year, generally the calendar year. While the income statement applies to just one year, the balance sheet, in effect, mirrors the results of all prior years' income statements. *Current assets* are those that can be turned into cash. *Fixed assets* are buildings and machinery used to produce the good the company sells. On the side of the balance sheet labeled "liabilities," the *current liabilities* are bills that must be paid within a year; *long-term liabilities* are amounts owed over longer periods.

A corporate balance sheet also can be rather lengthy and complicated, but the major balance sheet items can be illustrated with our hypothetical company. In this example, the company operates on a calendar-year basis and the balance sheet represents the company's position as of December 31 of each year:

	1980	1979
ASSETS		
Current Assets		
Cash	$ 300,000	$ 200,000
Accounts Receivable	1,500,000	1,300,000
Inventories	3,000,000	2,800,000
Total Current Assets	$4,800,000	$4,300,000

Fixed Assets

Land	500,000	500,000
Buildings and Equipment	4,000,000	3,800,000
	$4,500,000	$4,300,000
Less Accumulated Depreciation	1,400,000	1,300,000
Net Fixed Assets	$3,100,000	$3,000,000
Total Assets	$7,900,000	$7,300,000
	1980	**1979**

LIABILITIES

Current Liabilities

Accounts Payable	$ 900,000	$ 800,000
Accrued Expenses Payable	550,000	500,000
Federal Income Taxes Payable	250,000	200,000
Total Current Liabilities	$1,700,000	$1,500,000

Long-Term Liabilities

Mortgage Bonds due 1995	$ 700,000	$ 800,000
Total Liabilities	$2,400,000	$2,300,000

STOCKHOLDERS' EQUITY

Common stock, $10 par, 200,000 shares outstanding	$2,000,000	$2,000,000
Capital Surplus	500,000	500,000
Accumulated Retained Earnings	3,000,000	2,500,000
Total Stockholders Equity	$5,500,000	$5,000,000
TOTAL LIABILITIES AND STOCK-HOLDERS' EQUITY	$7,900,000	$7,300,000

Again, you should be cautioned that an actual corporate balance sheet will be somewhat longer and more complicated, but our example contains most of the major elements in any balance sheet.

The reader of a balance sheet should take note of the corporation's liquidity, or its ability to meet its payrolls and pay its bills, by dividing total current assets by total current liabilities. This produces the "current ratio." If the ratio is less than 1.5, or has declined sharply within a year, this could be a danger signal. A ratio of about 2 or more indicates the firm is in good liquid position. In other words, if a company has $2 in current assets for each $1 of current liabilities, it probably is in a sound working capital position.

The "accounts receivable" line on the balance sheet also should be scanned to see if there has been a major increase in money owed the company. If so, it could indicate laxity in collecting bills, or sales to lower-quality customers in an effort to boost volume. A look at the line labeled "inventories" also is important; if they've taken a sudden jump, it could mean that the firm has a large stock of unsaleable merchandise on hand.

Finally, the footnotes to the financial statements often hold the most significant information about the company's operations and prospects. Frequently, they are worded in such technical fashion that many readers skip them. Listed may be such things as deferred costs, pension-plan liabilities, foreign-currency transactions, pending lawsuits, lease commitments, and accounting practices. All can offer clues to future developments within the company and may suggest things that should be followed up in talks with company officials.

An auditor's letter accompanying the annual report tells whether the accountants who examined the books and the financial statements have found them satisfactory. Reporters should look at the auditor's letter because, if there are potential problems, auditors are expected to mention them.

If you do not understand an income statement or balance sheet, or if you want to follow up with additional information, the place to start asking questions probably will be the office of the company's treasurer or its financial vice-president. However, the financial statements, and particularly the footnotes, may also suggest leads to possible stories dealing not with financial figures but with construction of new plants, development of new products, labor and pension matters, environmental or other government regulation issues, or with a variety of other matters. Big corporations with large public relations staffs may have specialists to answer your questions, but you may want to put your questions directly to the pertinent company officials. Or you may want to go to the top; many company chairmen and presidents are more accessible than in years past, although many remain shy of the press. Sometimes the "outside," or nonmanagement, directors of a corporation can be helpful news sources.

Digging Behind the Figures

It is important that reporters not take all figures at face value but read the footnotes and dig behind the figures when there appears reason to dig.

For a look at how a knowledgeable writer can uncover important details by digging behind the figures in an earnings report, consider the following excerpt from the weekly column "Up and Down Wall Street" by Alan Abelson in *Barron's*. Abelson was commenting on a three-month earnings statement issued by Centronics Data Computer Corporation, a manufacturer of printout devices for minicomputers.

Noting that Centronics appeared to be running into competitive pressures from rival companies, Mr. Abelson pointed to "the rather different pictures" of how well Centronics did in the second quarter of its fiscal year, depending on whether one read (1) the press release sent out to announce the company's operating results, (2) the company's more detailed report to shareholders for the same stretch, or (3) its detailed report, this one known as a 10-Q report, filed with the SEC. From Abelson's column:

> The press release, headed "Centronics Reports Record Second Quarter and Six Months," related that second quarter net after-tax income totaled $3.44 million vs. $3.14 million (in the comparable quarter a year earlier). That's a rise of nearly 10% and a 13.5% jump in per-share net, reflecting a smaller share capitalization this fiscal year than last.
>
> O.K. That's the way Centronics' earnings appeared in those long grey columns of earnings reports carried by our local gazette and in most of the brokerage house comments that we've seen as well.
>
> On to document No. 2. The report to shareholders provides the same net figures as the press release—but something else, too. That something else is pretax profits: $4.32 million in the three months ended December '77 vs. $4.33 million in the like quarter ended December '76. In other words, before taxes, Centronics' earnings were lower, seemingly just a bit, but lower nonetheless. Not, in any case, as the figures suggested, higher.
>
> Finally, the 10-Q indicates that operating earnings were not only lower but perhaps appreciably so. For included in the $4.3 million of this year's pretax earnings is a sizeable slice of the $394,000 received from settlement of a lawsuit. Even when one subtracts the $150,000 in legal costs connected with that settlement (broken out in a footnote), that still leaves nearly $250,000; the figures, in turn suggest that the second fiscal quarter this year ran a couple of hundred thousand dollars behind last year's, before taxes. Centronics was able to show higher net only because of the big drop in its tax rate, to 20% in this year's second quarter, from 28% in last year's.
>
> We might add that the company maintains that the legal settlement involved costs beyond those shown in its 10-Q, so that in reality, the apparent windfall didn't amount to very much. Of course, what's insignificant or immaterial to one eye may be significant and material to another. Precisely because of such potential ambiguity, we feel that the press release broadcasting the profits news might have found a half a line or so to inform folks that Centronics' net income was up—not because of the strength in operations, but because of a big drop in its tax rate. Even at the sacrifice of a couple of those phrases like "enthusiastic acceptance" or "substantial contracts," which did make it into the text.[24]

Questions and Answers to Keep in Mind

In dealing with profits, a journalist will find it useful to raise the following questions when preparing a story about a company's quarterly annual reports on its earnings:

- What were earnings, in total and on a per common share basis, before taxes and after taxes?
- What type of accounting was used? Does the accounting take note of the effect of inflation on the value of inventories and of corporate assets?
- Do net income figures for the current year—or comparative figures for a year earlier—contain any one-time income or outgo (such as special tax credits, income from sales of assets, special depreciation reserve, and nonrecurring charges)?
- Has the company committed itself for any large investment that may be a drain on future profits? (If a company takes on unusually heavy debt over a period of years, for example, future earnings on its stock could be affected).
- Is someone at the company—the treasurer, controller, or a similar officer—available to explain questions that need to be answered?

Though reporting on profits, as on other areas of the economy, can be a challenging task, it's by no means a discouraging one. Indeed, some respected economists believe that the extent of public misunderstanding on the subject may have been overdrawn, and that in any event there are things the communications media can do to dispel some of the myths that still prevail.

When asked for their views about what the media can do, economists in the academic and corporate communities offered various suggestions. Following are typical replies.

Walter H. Heller, professor of economics at the University of Minnesota and former chairman of the White House Council of Economic Advisers:

> On the question of profits being "at a record," that's one of the favorite phrases regarding almost all economic magnitudes. What the press might occasionally try to get across is that in any economy with a growing labor force and growing productivity per labor hour, "new records" ought to be routine. If profits and output and consumption and income aren't "the highest in history," there is something wrong![25]

Walter E. Hoadley, economist and executive vice-president, Bank of America:

> In our inflationary world, record annual dollar figures are not too surprising. But most media reports seem to reflect some delight in stressing "record high profits" as they occur; seldom do they mention "record high employment" which customarily parallels profit trends. The media should emphasize more coverage of what is actually required to

create a job, a product, or a service to show the individual and the public more linkage between their personal situation and risk-taking and investment. The media should stress the options open to our people to make money and spend or invest it, compared with the situation in other major countries.[26]

Paul W. McCracken, of the Graduate School of Business Administration at the University of Michigan and also a former chairman of the Council of Economic Advisers:

My impression is that the press is not primarily responsible for confusion about profits, investment, and jobs, except incidentally to the extent that those inveighing against profits in business get disproportionate coverage.

I would suggest, however, that the journalistic profession itself undertake a candid inquiry about the extent to which it may be faithfully reflecting the true facts—even examining the charge (which is frequently made) that the press is deliberately biased in its reporting. No writer can be criticized for having his own views and presuppositions. A charge that he is biased, however, strikes at the very heart of the profession. In that case one can plausibly say that there really is not a free pass... and under certain circumstances a government which already insists upon protecting people from things they ought not to eat, or ought not to wear, or ought not to drive, may decide that it ought to protect people from the things they ought not to read.[27]

NOTES—CHAPTER 7

1. Speech at the Gerald Loeb Awards Dinner, New York, N.Y., October 18, 1977.

2. John Connor, "Some of My Best Friends Are Republicans," *The Conference Board Record,* August 1972, pp. 24–26.

3. Fletcher Byrom, "Creating Wealth for a Better World," *The Conference Board Record,* May 1973, pp. 6–8.

4. Interview in *Association Management,* January 1978, pp. 26–28.

5. Letter to the author, February 13, 1978.

6. Poll sponsored by Educational Communications, Inc., in the summer of 1976 and circulated to members of the Business Roundtable, New York, by its Economic Education Research Group on December 15, 1976.

7. Letter to the author, February 1, 1978.

8. Letter to the author, February 6, 1978.

9. Letter to the author, February 3, 1978.

10. Letter to the author, February 7, 1978.

11. Isadore Barmash, "Judge Signs Order to Liquidate Grant Company Within 60 Days," *New York Times,* February 13, 1976, pp. 1, 49.

12. Paul A. Samuelson, *Economics,* 6th ed. (New York: McGraw-Hill Book Company, 1964), p. 608.

13. See *Washington Post,* December 22, 1975, "Castro: Profits Count," p. A-20. See also *Wall Street Journal,* March 31, 1978, "Profit Sharing to Be Part of Rumanian Industry," p. 32.

14. Address to the National Association of Manufacturers, December 9, 1955.

15. The Greer-Kandel Report, *The Insiders Chronicle,* February 2, 1978, p. 9.

16. Harold Brayman, *Corporate Management in a World of Politics* (New York: McGraw-Hill Book Company, 1967), pp. 190–91.

17. Address to XIX Annual Conference, International Association of Economic and Management Students, December 28, 1977.

18. Interview, *U.S. News & World Report,* December 27, 1976, p. 84.

19. See *Public Opinion Index,* Mid-January 1977, Opinion Research Corp., Princeton, N.J. The Federal Trade Commission publishes quarterly the "Financial Report for Manufacturing, Mining and Trade Corporations."

20. *U.S. News & World Report,* November 4, 1974, pp. 54–55.

21. "A Newspaper's Philosophy," *Wall Street Journal,* January 2, 1951, p. 8.

22. John W. Hazard, *Success with Your Investments* (Garden City, N.Y.: Doubleday & Co., 1973), p. 212.

23. "Victor Posner, Family Bow to SEC, Agree to Repay Improperly Charged Expenses," *Wall Street Journal,* September 21, 1977, p. 3.

24. "Up and Down Wall Street," *Barron's National Business and Financial Weekly,* March 6, 1978, p. 21.

25. Letter to the author, March 1, 1978.

26. Letter to the author, February 15, 1978.

27. Letter to the author, March 15, 1978.

SOURCES OF INFORMATION

The Business Roundtable
405 Lexington Avenue
New York, N.Y. 10017

Chamber of Commerce of the United States
1615 H Street, N.W.
Washington, D.C. 20062

The Conference Board
845 Third Avenue
New York, N.Y. 10022

Department of Commerce
Social and Economic Statistics
    Administration
Washington, D.C. 20233

Joint Committee on Economic Education
1212 Avenue of the Americas
New York, N.Y. 10021

Federal Trade Commission
Bureau of Economics
633 Indiana Avenue, N.W.
Washington, D.C. 20580

Moody's Investors Service, Inc.
99 Church Street
New York, N.Y. 10007

National Association of Manufacturers
1776 F Street, N.W.
Washington, D.C. 20006

Standard & Poor's Corp.
345 Hudson Street
New York, N.Y. 10007

SUGGESTED READINGS

"ABC's of the Economy," a special section in *U.S. News & World Report,* May 1, 1978.

Brayman, Harold, *Corporate Management in a World of Politics.* New York: McGraw-Hill Book Company, 1967.

Buzzell, Robert D., Bradley T. Gale, and Ralph G. M. Sultan, "Market Share—A Key to Profitability," *Harvard Business Review,* January-February 1975, pp. 97–106.

Cotter, Arundel, *Fool's Profits.* New York: Barron's Publishing Co., 1940.

Henderson, Carter F., and Albert C. Lasher, *20 Million Careless Capitalists.* Garden City, N.Y.: Doubleday & Company, 1967.

How to Read a Financial Report, a booklet published by Merrill Lynch Pierce Fenner & Smith, Inc., and available without charge from any of the firm's offices or from its headquarters office at 165 Broadway, New York, N.Y. 10006.

How We Live. New York: American Economic Foundation, 1976.

Putnam, Mabel R., *What Every Woman Should Know About Finance.* New York: Charles Scribner's Sons, 1954.

"Putting Profits in Perspective," *U.S. News & World Report,* August 9, 1978, pp. 58, 59.

Robinson, Claude, *Understanding Profits.* Princeton, N.J.: D. Van Nostrand Company, 1961.

Samuelson, Paul A., *Economics.* New York: McGraw-Hill Book Company, 1964.

Udell, Jon G., and others, *The Economics of the American Newspaper.* New York: Hastings House, 1978. See particularly Chapter 4, "Understanding Profits in the Newspaper Business."

Reporting on...
THE INSIDE
OF BUSINESS

8

DONALD I. ROGERS

T IMES HAVE CHANGED since the 1920's when William C. Durant, the entrepreneur who created the Chevrolet and became an auto magnate, hired public relations man Carl Byoir to keep his name out of the newspapers.[1]

The Chevrolet, of course, became the nation's largest selling passenger car under the aegis of General Motors Corporation, one of the world's largest manufacturing companies. General Motors hired public relations men in carloads, not necessarily to get its name into the newspapers, but because its name would be in the papers and on the evening television news anyway. Finally in 1978 Thomas A. Murphy, then chairman of General Motors, completed the turnabout from the days of William C. Durant. Mr. Murphy appeared before the National Press Club in Washington and spoke from a platform traditionally reserved for national newsmakers who are political personages or foreign dignitaries.

Mr. Murphy, we may assume, exposed himself to the press and to its sometimes barbed questions because he was interested in improving the press and public image of General Motors specifically and of big business generally. However, the more significant point, from the press's view, was that he and some other business leaders had decided to make themselves more accessible to reporters.

General Motors obviously was and is newsworthy. The company was selling more than 6 million cars and trucks annually to about as many customers worldwide. Its annual sales were more than $47 billion, from which it paid wages to some 750,000 employees and dividends to more than 1.2 million stockholders. What Mr. Murphy said and what General Motors did affected the transportation of millions of customers and the incomes of hundreds of thousands of employees and stockholders. In addition, its actions affected many other groups ranging from companies that supply General Motors with steel and other materials to pension funds that have invested in GM's bonds and stocks.

Not all corporations are as large as General Motors, by any means, but the total sales and revenues of the nation's 500 largest companies alone amounted to $1.7 trillion in 1976.[2] By way of comparison, the total federal budget in fiscal 1976 was approximately $400 billion. Of the approximately 79 million American wage and salary workers outside of agriculture in 1976, some 64 million worked in private industry while 15 million were employed by local, state, and federal governments.[3]

In the American economy, consumer goods and services are produced by business organizations that take the form of corporations, partnerships, or proprietorships, but the term "business," like "labor" and "government," is an abstraction. Those terms may be of use for purposes of rhetoric or philosophy, but they are considerably less useful to the profession of journalism.

Although there are some very large corporations that may seem to represent business and may presume to speak for business, there is no single entity or institution that embraces all of business. There are, by one measure, 14 million business entities in the American economy and the great majority of them are small businesses.

Although it has become a cliché to speak of business as a single entity or institution, the American economy is not a planned economy in the sense that a central economic planning authority exists. In some nations government performs an economic planning function by deciding how national resources will be apportioned among the production of consumer goods and services, capital needs, defense needs, and so forth. In the United States those decisions are left largely, although not entirely, to private initiative. Each business firm decides whether a market exists for the goods or services it can produce, tries to estimate or guess the size of that market, and then proceeds to compete for a share of the local, regional, or national market.

All businesses plan and in the process create goods, services, and jobs. A plumber makes certain assumptions about how many leaky faucets he can repair and a professional football club signs player contracts and waivers on the basis of certain assumptions about the seats it can sell. Those decisions of many thousands of individual businesses obviously do not have the economic impact of General Motors' planning concerning the numbers of cars it can sell. But each business is an entity unto itself. There are hundreds of trade organizations that may speak for their business members on some issues of common interest, but even the largest business organizations, such as the Chamber of Commerce of the United States and the National Association of Manufacturers, are in no sense economic planning authorities. Indeed, if business organizations attempted to coordinate production or prices, they would be in violation of antitrust laws.

To understand the inside of business, therefore, it is necessary to understand the inside of individual businesses. Each is different and the differences are the essence of the American economic system. Even General Motors and Ford Motor Company, the giants of the auto industry, are different. While General Motors for years has been run by a succession of professional managers, the Ford family has left no doubt that it has remained in control of Ford Motor Company.

In reporting on the inside of business, perhaps the most obvious and yet least recognized principle to keep in mind is that businesses are run by people. Corporations, partnerships, and proprietorships are merely shells, useful and even necessary for legal and other purposes but unrevealing of what goes on inside. Plumbers, bakers, barbers, barkeepers, and other proprietors most certainly are people, but keep in mind that the largest corporations also are run by people, even if that fact sometimes is obscured by committees and computers. As a former dean of the Harvard Business School has said: "A man's personal philosophy, his way of looking at the world and the men and women around him determine his success as a manager of things and people more than any other single factor. His basic attitudes are far more significant than the techniques he uses."[4]

In the long run, the basic attitudes of Henry Ford probably were more significant even than the techniques he used. His attitudes, as well as the impact of his company on American life, were conveyed in this *New York Times* story in 1978:

> Detroit, June 15—The Ford Motor Company, the business enterprise that has probably done more to change the American style of living than any other—not only by developing personal transportation for the masses but also through its revolutionary changes in the workplace—reaches its 75th birthday tomorrow facing challenges that rival its pace-setting achievements to date.
>
> The multibillion-dollar, worldwide automobile manufacturer, founded by the late Henry Ford and still controlled by his descendants, with his grandson Henry Ford 2d serving as chairman, introduced the first automobile priced within the reach of the masses, established the eight-hour workday and raised the minimum wage in 1914 to $5 a day.[5]

BUSINESS AND THE PRESS

Business suffers from a certain schizophrenia. It is private, but it also is public. The press, some would say, suffers from a similar disorder. But newspapers, periodicals, and broadcasting stations, being privately owned entities that exist to serve public needs, merely reflect the larger phenomenon: nearly all businesses are privately owned entities that exist to serve public needs and desires.

The confusion permeates the lexicon of business itself. The American economic system is organized around privately owned businesses, but the biggest businesses are said to be publicly held. What is meant, of course, is that the great majority of businesses are "privately held" in that they have but one or several owners whereas almost all large corporations have thousands and even millions of stockholders and thus are said to be "publicly held."

In more ways than one, business is both private and public and that fact has had profound consequences for business and economic reporting.

Businessmen traditionally have been leery of reporters, and reporters traditionally have been leery of businessmen. Their mutual suspicion has not often itself made news as it did back in 1883 when, in response to a newspaper reporter's question about railroad service, William H. Vanderbilt of the New York Central answered, "The public be damned." Business rarely has displayed publicly or even harbored privately that degree of hostility, simply because it would be bad for business.

The standoffishness of business in relation to the press undoubtedly has contributed to the traditional dullness of business news. Companies too often have given the press no more news than they were required to give by circumstances such as a strike or by laws such as the federal securities laws. Reporters too often have taken what they were given and asked no more.

In general, companies in the past took the attitude that they were private businesses and therefore their business was private. That attitude seems to have prevailed even among large corporations with thousands or millions of customers in times when businesses generally were controlled by one man or a handful of stockholders. The attitude may well have been reinforced in those days when the managers of corporations generally were entrepreneurs or financiers who were not inclined by training or custom to meet the press or the public.

In general, privately held businesses today still are more reticent than publicly held businesses. However, some large publicly held companies, run by professional managers trained as business administrators and lawyers, still wear their reticence as a sort of trademark.

For example, one publicly held corporation in the South, the largest in its state, has sales of more than $500 million annually and stock listed for public trading on the New York Stock Exchange. It is headed by a man who graduated from Harvard Law School and was a Rhodes Scholar. But, because the company sells raw materials only to other companies, it has no advertising department and, apparently as a further reflection of its particular orientation, it does not have a public relations department. When reporters ask questions, their inquiries are referred first to the legal department and then to the head of the company. The questions are infrequent and usually relate to financial matters that the company, because its stock is publicly traded, is required to disclose under federal securities laws. The succinct answers do not encourage further communication between the company and the press.

Such are the difficulties reporters face in penetrating the inside of some businesses. To be sure, most $500 million companies have public relations departments, but too often they expect press handouts to be used by reporters without further inquiry. That attitude also contributes to uninteresting business and economic news.

Some businessmen and businesswomen are coming out of their shells, however. They include not only Thomas Murphy of General Motors but John D. deButts, former chairman of American Telephone & Telegraph Company, and Irving S. Shapiro, chairman of E. I. Du Pont de Nemours & Company. Some less sizable businesses also have decided to meet the press head-on, although big businesses undoubtedly have been most prominent in breaking out of their shells.

Business people did not decide suddenly and unanimously to repudiate nearly a century later the words of William H. Vanderbilt. Nor has business decided it loved the press; a certain wariness still remains. The coming out of business cannot be described accurately as an act of altruism or contrition, either. Business decided simply, as Mr. Murphy told the National Press Club, that it had been "clobbered." It was coming out in self-defense.

Public opinion polls in the early 1970's showed clearly that business had declined in public favor. The polls also showed that public confidence in other institutions, including labor and government, also had declined. But business was losing political as well as public favor. Over business's objections, Congress in the late 1960's and early 1970's passed many new environmental, product safety, workplace safety, and other programs that impinged on business. Business came out in self-defense against what it felt was excessive government regulation.

Mr. Murphy, in his National Press Club speech, for instance, observed that "Everywhere we see too much doubt and suspicion about the business establishment. The result has been an overreaction by the overuse of the regulatory powers of government." His wariness of the press still was evident, however. "We feel," he said, "that the media tend to focus on the differences in our society—to create controversy by magnifying such differences."

Nonetheless, he agreed that:

> Business too often stands apart while others discuss and determine the great issues of our times. For too long, those responsible for the major

decisions in both the large and not-so-large corporations have isolated themselves from the realities of the political process. But . . . the day of the cloistered chief executive in business is long past.

The truth is that business has been and is being clobbered in the ideological marketplace. Past leaders of American business did not make much progress by adopting a "government-be-damned" attitude.

The point is that the objective of business, no less than that of government, must be the public's interest. People respond best to other people—not to impersonal "things" like a corporation. The union movement to them is not a button or a slogan—it's a George Meany or a Doug Fraser. And the consumer movement, of course, is Ralph Nader.

So, if they are to compete effectively in the idea market, business leaders must also be public figures.[6]

The decision of some big business leaders to get more directly involved in politics was a major news development, and the political battles between business, labor, environmentalists, and consumerists will provide material for many national and local news stories.

In the long run, however, the coming out of businesspeople may have a larger and somewhat different significance to business and economic reporting. If, as Mr. Murphy warned, "business leaders must also be public figures," then business generally will have to become more accessible to reporters who have legitimate questions about internal as well as external corporate affairs. The press then presumably will abandon its wariness of business people.

HOW BUSINESS IS ORGANIZED

Individual businesses are organized as proprietorships, partnerships, or corporations and often are categorized less precisely as either small business or big business. Many firms in the same lines of business also have organized themselves into trade associations for public relations, political, and other purposes.

It bears emphasis, however, that American business is not organized in the sense that is implied when we speak of, say, organized labor and in that sense the term "business" is an abstraction. The development and organization of business cannot be traced through a single thread of history because there has been no "business movement" comparable to the labor movement. Lacking any central direction or planning, individual businesses simply grew in an environment of economic freedom.

The fundamental point relative to understanding and reporting on business in the American economy is that individual firms are expected and indeed required to compete. There are many kinds and degrees of competition, but competition has made the American economy unique in history. By way of contrast, historian Barbara W. Tuchman, in describing fourteenth-century Europe, has written that:

> to insure that no one gained an advantage over anyone else, commercial law prohibited innovation in tools or techniques, underselling below a fixed price, working late by artificial light, employing extra apprentices . . . and advertising of wares or praising them to the detriment of others.[7]

The contrasting ideal of competition among thousands and even millions of individuals and firms is fundamental to the American economic system and to reporting on the inside of American business.

Proprietorships and Partnerships

A sole proprietorship is a business owned and managed by one person. A partnership is a business owned and managed by a relatively small group of two or more individuals. Proprietorships and partnerships were the original and basic form of business organization in America and, in terms of numbers, they remain the dominant form of business organization.

At the end of the American colonial period, over 90 percent of the population made its living from agriculture, and most of the relatively few "businessmen" were peddlers, blacksmiths, and storekeepers. The farmer and merchant had no need for stockholders, and economic activity required no business structure more advanced than the proprietorship or partnership.

The businesses of millions of store owners, architects, plumbers, lawyers, doctors, and other tradesmen and professionals, ranging from holders of fast food franchises to publishers of small newspapers, still take the form of proprietorships and partnerships. Of the 14 million business tax returns filed with the Internal Revenue Service in 1975, 10.8 million were filed by proprietorships and about one million by partnerships. Thus, of the 14 million businesses in the nation, only about 2 million are incorporated.

Not all corporations can be described as big businesses, of course. The U.S. Department of Commerce defines a small business as one employing 500 or fewer workers and, by that measure, there were roughly 10 million small businesses in the nation in 1978. These included incorporated businesses as well as proprietorships and partnerships. The 10 million firms employed 58 percent of the nonfarm work force.

A small firm may not be as newsworthy as General Motors simply because it is small. On the other hand, the people who run small businesses may be more obvious and more accessible than those who manage big businesses. People are interested in how others earn their money and even national business publications frequently run stories about small business. One business magazine's coverage in 1978 included, for instance, articles about a real feather merchant, an entrepreneur who rose from ethnic neighborhoods to successful record producer, and a firm that made good manufacturing and selling children's crayons.[8]

Although proprietorships and partnerships have continued to dominate business in terms of numbers, these forms of business organization have several basic and inherent disadvantages. They have limited life due to the death of proprietors or partners and they have limited access to large amounts of capital. The proprietorship will remain basic to a free economy that promises anyone the right to succeed in business. Partnerships probably will continue to be utilized by the medical and legal professions, advertising agencies, and other types of businesses that are based largely on personal talents and require relatively small capital investments.

Corporations

The growth of the corporation came with the urbanization and industrialization of the nation. Whereas nine out of ten persons made their living from agriculture in the colonial period, only one out of seven was living on a farm in 1953, and by 1974 only one American in 22 lived on a farm.[9] People moved to the cities and to jobs in industry, and eventually agriculture itself became more and more mechanized. In 1953 one farm worker produced enough food for 16 people; by 1974 that worker supplied 55 people.[10]

As the nation and the economy grew, new circumstances created the need for new forms of business organizations. Increasing demand on the part of consumers, steady technological progress, and the expansion of transportation facilities which made mass marketing possible all increased the need for manufactured products and their distribution. Technology and mass production economies required a form of business enterprise far different from the techniques of trade and small-scale production in use prior to the Civil War. The same forces required the development of techniques for expanding the size of business firms, for large scale financing of business firms, for mass marketing, and for supervising large numbers of workers. These forces combined to bring on the American scene the large-scale business enterprise and the corporation.

There are several reasons why business firms grow. First of all, the growth of smaller firms is an indication that the products they offer are desired in abundance by the consumer. Further growth results because large-scale production makes possible geographical division of labor. Individual plants can be built in locations where operations would be the most efficient with respect to their required raw materials, labor, and markets.

Large-scale production also makes possible the division of labor in that complex manufacturing operations can be separated into a number of simple tasks. Each individual task can be learned quickly and performed by workers or by automatic machinery. In short, large firms can utilize technological improvements such as specialization, mechanization, and standardization to reduce costs per unit and increase sales and profits.

Mass production techniques, of course, were introduced in the hope that they would result in more sales and more profits for the corporation, but most important in an economic and social sense is the fact that such innovations usually lowered prices for the consumer. Even today, we have automobiles with much improved quality over those made in 1910 at only a relatively modest increase in cost once inflation has been discounted. By contrast, the cost of housing today is considerably higher than it was in 1910 because most houses are still constructed largely by individual hand labor.[11] Mass production techniques produced important economic benefits by reducing the cost of individual units, improving their quality, and increasing variety.

The technological and financial requirements of mass production proved the corporation to be a more efficient form of business organization. It suited the needs of expanding business better than the sole proprietorship or partnership. The sale of shares of ownership permitted the accumulation of capital resources far beyond the amounts a proprietor or a partnership would be able to accumulate. Further, the corporation charter protects the individual investor against excessive risk by limiting his or her liability to the amount invested. Finally, although the individual shareholder in a corporation usually can sell his or her shares at any time without disrupting the operation of the business, the corporation theoretically has a perpetual life.

In summary, the corporation has made possible business and economic innovations including the development of mass production and of mass distribution through department and chain stores and discount houses; the integration of research with manufacturing and marketing; the employment and management of tens of thousands of workers, who frequently belong to unions and often are the beneficiaries of corporate retirement plans; and the widespread public ownership of corporations, directly through individual purchase of shares or indirectly through shareholdings by pension funds and other such institutions. On the other hand, where economies of large scale are not present, proprietorships and partnerships continue to be viable forms of business organization.

Goods and Services

Business firms also can be categorized according to what they do. The broadest categories divide industry into four groups: extractive businesses, which engage in coal mining, oil drilling, and the like; manufacturing businesses; retail and other distribution businesses; and service businesses ranging all the way from banking and insurance to auto repair.

One of the interesting and newsworthy features of the American economy concerns the growing numbers of people employed in service industries. In the early nineteenth century, 80 of every 100 working Americans were engaged in agriculture, forestry, fishing, mining, or manufacturing while the other 20 percent distributed the goods and provided services. By 1940 only 46 of every 100 working Americans were required to produce goods while 23 worked in distribution, 20 were employed in providing services, and 11 worked to keep the wheels of industry in operation.[12]

To state this another way, agriculture has become sufficiently efficient that its share of the nation's work force has declined and manufacturing productivity has improved so that its share of the labor force is also declining. Meanwhile, employment in service industries has increased rapidly. Looking ahead to the future, we can expect the product mix of industry to continue to shift from goods toward services. Essentially this trend, which has been evident since World War II, means that the demand for services has been increasing faster than the demand for goods.[13]

Those trends in employment and in consumer demand are one measure of rising living standards and of consumer affluence in the United States.

THE INSIDE OF CORPORATIONS

While proprietorships and partnerships greatly outnumber corporations, corporations do vastly more business in terms of dollar volume. Moreover, corporations' share of the total economic pie has grown steadily.

For example, in 1966 the business receipts of proprietorships amounted to $207 billion, those of partnerships $78 billion, and those of corporations $1.2 trillion. Proprietorships in 1966 thus accounted for 13.5 percent of total business receipts, partnerships for 5.1 percent, and corporations for 81.4 percent. A decade later, proprietorships' receipts were $328 billion, representing 10 percent of total business receipts; partnerships took in $137 billion, or 4 percent, and corporations' receipts were $2.8 trillion, or 86 percent of the total pie.[14]

Different Sizes and Shapes

Inasmuch as there are about 2 million of them, corporations obviously come in many different sizes and shapes. About the only thing that all have in common is in their names. Normally you will find attached to an incorporated business's name the word Corporation or Corp., Company or Co., or Incorporated or Inc. Behind the names of foreign corporations you usually will find Ltd., standing for Limited Liability, or S.A., meaning Society Anonymous.

The designations used by American corporations are no guide to their size, however. For instance, the nation's largest utility corporation prefers to be known as a company—American Telephone & Telegraph Co. Thousands of much smaller firms call themselves corporations. Sometimes the designations are combined. One of the nation's largest newspaper chains, for instance, is Gannett Company, Inc.

Many of the nation's largest corporations are publicly owned by thousands or hundreds of shareholders, but not all large corporations are publicly controlled and most of the country's 2 million corporations are privately held or controlled by families or other relatively small groups.

Consider, for example, Ford Motor Company. Ford clearly is a big business, with 1976 sales of nearly $29 billion and net profits of almost $1 billion. But the company was very firmly controlled and owned by the Ford family until Henry Ford 2nd in 1956 authorized the Ford Foundation to divest itself of some of its larger holdings of Ford Motor securities. In 1956, which was 47 years after Ford Motor Company had been incorporated, the foundation placed 10.2 million shares of Ford stock on the market as a "new issue" of shares that never before had been offered to the public. The selling prospectus stated frankly that that amount of stock would not represent control and that control was retained by members of the Ford family. Thus, while more than 10 million Ford shares became publicly owned, there was no question but that Ford Motor remained under the control and operation of the Ford family.[15]

The stocks of many large and well-known corporations in recent decades also have been sold to the public for the first time, although the descendants of their founders have held on to sufficient numbers of shares to retain effective control. An example in the newspaper business is Dow Jones & Company.

In many of the largest corporations, however, ownership is widely distributed and no single individual or group owns as much as 10 percent of the total outstanding shares. American Telephone & Telegraph's nearly 600 million shares outstanding in 1975 were owned by nearly 3 million stockholders, for example. Many other corporations not nearly so big as American Telephone & Telegraph still number their stockholders in the thousands. Anheuser-Busch, Inc., a prominent maker of beer, has reported nearly 30,000 stockholders, for instance. Pan American World Airways Inc. reported about 134,000 stockholders.

Some corporations have many more shareholders than employees. Again to take American Telephone & Telegraph as an example, its nearly 3 million shareholders in 1975 substantially outnumbered its 927,000 employees. Corporations in more labor-intensive industries may have as many as or more employees than stockholders. Colgate-Palmolive Company, maker of soaps and other consumer products has reported having 41,700 stockholders and 52,600 employees.

Such numbers are useful to business and economic reporting because they indicate the large potential audiences for business news. A corporation's customers represent another potential audience, of course. Customers and consumers usually represent the largest potential audience, especially for news of companies that make or sell consumer products.

In an age of consumerism, the public is interested in news of faulty products and services. But people also can be interested in the things they buy and use every day without complaint and in news about companies that make those things. For example, few people have heard of Binney & Smith, Inc., a relatively small corporation based in a small town, Easton, Pennsylvania, and controlled by the family of the late Edwin Binney. But *Forbes* found interesting and newsworthy story material in Easton because almost everybody is familiar with crayons and Binney & Smith makes Crayolas, the biggest selling brand of crayons.[16]

Some corporations sell only one type of product or service, while others are conglomerates making and selling a variety of goods and services. The single-product company, be it in the crayon or oil refining business, can be relatively small or large. Some companies are in only a limited phase of business while other "vertically integrated" corporations are in the extractive, processing, distributing, and retailing phases. Very large corporations in basic industries, such as oil and steel, are integrated in this way.

Corporations have grown internally and by acquiring or merging with other businesses. Most corporate growth has come through internal expansion, but corporations also have been merging for many years. Some of the largest corporations, such as General Motors and American Telephone & Telegraph, years ago respectively acquired many other auto and telephone companies, but federal antitrust law in the past several decades generally has stopped large corporations from acquiring competitors in their own industries.

For that reason and perhaps others, most mergers and acquisitions in recent years have been of the so-called conglomerate type involving corporations that are not competitors. An outstanding example was the acquisition in 1974 of Marcor Inc. by Mobil Oil Corporation. Mobil, one of the nation's largest oil companies, in a $500 million transaction, acquired Marcor, the parent company of Montgomery Ward & Company, a major retailer, and of Container Corporation of America, a large manufacturer of paper products.

A further observation to keep in mind concerning the many sizes and shapes of corporations concerns profits. In general, large corporations have large profits. Indeed, a few of the nation's largest corporations have reported annual net income exceeding $1 billion in recent years. Large profits make interesting news stories, although profits are relative to sales or revenues, corporate assets, and other measures including management efficiency. However, business and economic reporters in looking at corporate size should bear in mind that large sales or revenues do not guarantee large profits.

As explained in other chapters of this book, profits turn also on market conditions, the intensity of competition, and many other factors in addition to the volume of sales or revenue, the efficiency of management, and the productivity of workers. A rather startling and newsworthy illustration of the fact that large corporations and large profits are not necessarily synonymous has been provided by the Great Atlantic & Pacific Tea Company. A&P was the nation's largest grocery chain until 1973. In 1972 it had gross revenues of more than $6 billion, but it lost $51 million and in 1974 suffered a deficit of $157 million on revenues of nearly $7 billion.[17] Another large food retailer, Food Fair Stores, Inc., in 1978 filed under the Bankruptcy Act for protection from its creditors.

How to Find Your Way Around

Corporations remain private property, whether they are privately held by a small group or publicly held by thousands of shareholders, and that fact will continue to influence the access of the press to corporations.

Remember, however, that the corporation merely is a form of organization; it is the people inside who count. Those people in the past tended to be reticent, as we discussed earlier. Hence, most Americans probably have gained their deepest impressions of the inside of business from the works of such novelists as Upton Sinclair, Sinclair Lewis, and John Marquand, from movies such as *Network,* and from comic strips such as "Little Orphan Annie." Most of the real business leaders of the past, such as J. P. Morgan, John Rockefeller, and William Vanderbilt, were not well known to the public and, to the extent that they were known, they did not enjoy a "good press."

One commentator has written, "The epic hero of American economic history should be the entrepreneur, not the statesman, the military hero or the intellectual."[18] The Morgans, Rockefellers, and Vanderbilts seem not to be history's epic heroes, however.

On the other hand, the public impression of businessmen generally as robber barons never has been accurate. Henry Ford, for example, was not so viewed. Many another entrepreneur made good locally, built a factory, created jobs, and became a hero of sorts within his own community. Henry S. Canby, the critic, has recalled that in his boyhood days in Delaware the businessman was an admired member of the community. "Business was much more than an occupation," he wrote. "It was a philosophy, a morality and an atmosphere."[19]

The point here, for the reporter, is that businessmen, and women, are people and they are all different, no less than professors, preachers, lawyers, and people in all walks of life. Those in the highest places in business, like those in the highest positions in the university, in politics, or in any other calling, probably will be the most difficult to reach.

Reporters should attempt to establish contact with corporation presidents and chairmen, however, and, as Chairman Murphy of General Motors suggested, circumstances have made business leaders more accessible than they have been in the past. Information concerning the larger corporations has become increasingly accessible to the press in recent decades as more and more corporations have sold their securities to the public. Federal securities laws and the rules of stock exchanges have required the disclosure of a great deal of corporate information concerning not only sales, profits, dividends, and other financial information but matters relating to mergers and acquisitions, corporate operations and management, and the composition of boards of directors.

Publicly held corporations send annual reports and abbreviated quarterly reports to their shareholders, and these reports usually are freely available to reporters. Some of them contain more glossy pictures than enlightening data, but additional information is available in proxy statements, which detail matters on which shareholders will vote at their annual and special meetings, and in other documents. Proxy statements and annual and other reports, without pictures, must be filed with the Securities and Exchange Commission and with stock exchanges, and these filings are available for press inspection. Other chapters of this book will help you locate documents filed by corporations with the SEC and with other government agencies.

The various public disclosure documents filed by corporations will not tell a good reporter all he or she wants to know about the inside of business, and therefore access to corporate officials is still important. But the documents provide a definite beginning.

They disclose, for instance, the names and qualifications of the directors as well as the management officials of corporations and thus provide lists of potential sources. The documents contain such interesting information as the compensation paid to corporation management. You could learn, for example, that the fattest annual paycheck received by any corporate executive in 1976 amounted to $846,000 and was paid by International Telephone & Telegraph Corporation to its chairman, Harold S. Geneen. The comparable salary and bonus of General Motors Chairman Murphy that year was $450,000, but he received additional remuneration that brought his total 1976 compensation to $966,000. He was outranked, however, by Charles W. Lake, Jr., chief executive of R. R. Donnelley & Sons Company, a large printing firm; Lake's total remuneration in 1976 came to $990,000, including deferred compensation.[20]

Business leaders may not be paid quite as much as the stars of the entertainment and sports worlds, but large corporations are required by federal securities laws to disclose publicly more than Congress tells about its members and more than is disclosed by other types of organizations and institutions.

Even so, the required disclosures probably will not tell you all you want to know about the inside of business. They will not tell you, for instance, everything about who really runs a corporation and how and why he or she succeeds or fails.

Theoretically at least, executives who manage the day-to-day affairs of a corporation are responsible to the board of directors, which in turn is responsible to the stockholders. The stockholders meet once a year to elect directors, and sometimes more frequently to vote on mergers and other important matters.

In fact, however, the control of large corporations and even of smaller businesses is complex. While executives and managers ultimately are responsible through directors to shareholders, managements also are responsible to the company's customers and its workers. The management officials themselves often occupy several or more seats on a corporate board of directors. And boards of directors often function through audit, nomination, and compensation committees.

Contrary to what you may think, corporate managers appear not to be motivated solely or even primarily by money. Some studies have concluded that successful business managers are not individuals who need personal success in compensation or another form but who enjoy power and are capable of exercising a disciplined control and influence over other people.[21]

To look into the inside of business, reporters must look into individual companies and the men and women who run them. The results can be interesting as well as informative, as in a *Wall Street Journal* story that began:

New York—Harold Geneen was a night owl. Executives at International Telephone & Telegraph Corp. headquarters recall him arriving for work as late as noon, staying until 8 P.M. or later—and telephoning their homes at midnight or after.

They adjusted their schedules accordingly. However, last Dec. 31 Mr. Geneen, who now is 68, yielded the post of chief executive officer to Lyman C. Hamilton, aged 51.

This one is an early bird. He shows up for work at 8:15 A.M. or so, the palace hierarchy rapidly discovered. Executive work schedules were adjusted accordingly. Mr. Hamilton seems to differ from his predecessor in many intriguing ways; he is dubbed by some underlings "just a regular guy," not a term ever applied to Mr. Geneen.[22]

One useful generalization about corporate managers can be made, however. It is that, while some companies still are run by engineers, scientists, and inventors, many corporate presidents and chairmen today have come from legal, accounting, financial, or business administration backgrounds. The new breed of managers from such backgrounds probably is more aware of a need to communicate with the press and the public.

Corporations and Wall Street

Some 25 million people own shares of the stocks of publicly held corporations and millions of additional Americans have indirect interests in corporate stocks and bonds through pension funds, insurance companies, bank trust departments, and other institutions that invest in corporate securities. The wide ownership of corporate shares is the reason that many newspapers and broadcast stations carry stock market quotations, distributed by news wire services, even if they report little else in the way of business and economic news.

People who own, say, 10 or 100 shares of stock of General Motors, Colgate-Palmolive, or another corporation are interested in knowing the worth of their shares as measured by the prices at which the shares are traded daily in the stock market. In addition, stock price indexes, such as those compiled by Dow Jones, show daily and longer-term market price trends. The price trends are of public interest because they represent a composite judgment of millions of people concerning the fortunes not only of corporations but of the economy as a whole. A rising, or bullish, market is said to indicate economic optimism and a falling, or bearish, market reflects economic pessimism.

The terms "stock market" and "Wall Street" often are used synonymously, but the stock market is more of a mechanism than a place. The market is the means by which corporations sell their securities to the public and thus raise money for new plant and job creation, and it also is the means by which public investors can buy and sell—that is, trade—among themselves securities that were previously offered for public sale by the corporations, and thus are known as outstanding securities. The availability of the market enables the public to buy or sell at any time, at the current market price. Corporate securities thus are much more *liquid,* or salable, investments than, say, land or houses, and market liquidity in turn enhances the ability of corporations to raise additional money in the stock market.

The New York Stock Exchange and the American Stock Exchange both are located in the environs of Wall Street in lower Manhattan, where stocks have been traded for longer than 200 years, but the stock market also consists of the offices throughout the country that belong to securities firms that are members of the exchanges and are linked to them electronically. The stock market also consists of regional stock exchanges, such as those in Chicago, Cincinnati, and on the West Coast, and of the so-called *over-the-counter* market, which refers simply to stock trading that takes place in securities firms' offices rather than on an exchange floor.

There are, of course, other types of exchanges and markets where commodities, options, and so forth are traded.

In general, the shares of the largest and most established corporations are traded on the New York Stock Exchange. Somewhat smaller or newer corporations are traded on the American Stock Exchange. Other publicly held corporations' shares are traded in the over-the-counter market. Stocks traded on the NYSE may also be traded on regional exchanges.

As of 1978, about 26 billion shares of stock issued by 1,400 corporations were listed for trading on the NYSE. Any company whose shares are traded on a securities exchange must file with the exchange and with the Securities and Exchange Commission a listing and registration statement giving detailed information about the corporation and its operations. To be listed on the NYSE, called the "Big Board," a corporation generally must have a minimum of one million publicly held shares owned by not less than 2,000 stockholders. The publicly held shares should have a minimum aggregate market value of $16 million, and the company should have annual net income before federal income taxes of at least $2 million.

The Big Board and the American Stock Exchange, or "Amex," provide auction markets for the trading of securities where *"floor brokers,"* representing buyers and sellers, place orders to buy or sell specific shares with *specialists* who are charged with matching the buy and sell orders and with maintaining an *orderly* market, one without wild price fluctuations.

Say you wished to sell your 100 shares of XYZ Corporation stock, for example, and you told a securities firm representative in an office in St. Louis or Phoenix or elsewhere that you wanted $35 a share for the stock. This information would be transmitted to the firm's floor broker at the NYSE and he or she would then go to the specialist to find out the current *asked* price, that is, the price being sought by others wanting to sell XYZ stock, and the current *bid* price, or that offered by those wanting to buy. If the highest bid received was $34.50 a share, quoted on the exchange as 34½, your stock would remain unsold until a bid of $35 was made.

Or you might have told the representative in St. Louis or Phoenix to sell at the best price he or she could get. In that case, your XYZ stock would be sold *at the market,* or at the current bid price of $34.50.

If you want to buy XYZ stock, at a specific price or at the market price, the same procedure would be followed except that your purchase would be governed by the asked rather than the bid price on the exchange.

Of course, the stock market is considerably more complicated than that hypothetical transaction. Nevertheless, some understanding of the market is useful to all business and economic reporters. If the volume of trading in the stock of a local company is unusually high and the price is rising unusually fast, for instance, it might indicate to an informed reporter that the company is the target of a takeover by outsiders. The story might be developed through interviewing company executives and digging into filings at the Securities and Exchange Commission or at an exchange.

The stock market also offers sources of another kind to business and economic reporters. Many securities firms have on their staffs securities analysts whose job is to keep up with the affairs of corporations whose shares are publicly traded. These analysts can be valuable news sources, especially in view of the fact that some corporate executives who are reluctant to talk with the press feel that they have an obligation to keep securities analysts informed.

THE NEWSWORTHINESS OF BUSINESS NEWS

As we have seen, the inside of business has changed greatly since the time of William C. Durant. As corporations have grown and matured, their founders and heirs gradually have been replaced with a new breed of professional business managers, many of whom hold law degrees or master of business administration degrees and some of whom were Rhodes scholars. The motivations and attitudes of the new managers are not the same as those of the businessmen typically pictured in novels and movies.

The new attitudes have been reflected in the statements and positions of leaders such as Mr. Murphy of General Motors and Irving S. Shapiro, the chairman of Du Pont de Nemours & Company. "Now that relative affluence has been achieved," Mr. Shapiro has said, "people are asking that business pay more attention to quality, equity, and conservation and these new objectives require changes in many business operations."[23] Mr. Shapiro, who rose to the top of the giant manufacturer of chemicals and plastics although not a member of the Du Pont family, was by training a lawyer who earned his bachelor of science and law degrees from the University of Minnesota and who worked for the U.S. Department of Justice before joining Du Pont in 1951.

The attitudes of business executives changed as corporations went public with their shares and are changing further because of a variety of economic, social, and political factors. Business reacted to the civil rights movement and then to consumerism, environmentalism, and the women's liberation movements. The continued growth of corporations and of conglomerate mergers helped to make corporate governance as well as corporate growth into larger public and political issues. Meanwhile, inflation became the overriding issue.

Because of all of that and more, there would seem to be no doubt that business news will continue to grow yet more newsworthy.

Products and Services

Although a corporation has thousands of employees and stockholders, those constituencies are dependent ultimately upon the larger corporate constituency of customers. News of the development, sale, and prices of consumer goods and services is obviously legitimate, but such news often has been left to the advertising pages or reported in uninteresting stories written from blurbs and handouts.

Although the press generally has refrained from independent reporting concerning goods and services, some magazines such as *Consumers Reports* and some syndicated newspaper columnists such as Sylvia Porter have confirmed that an audience exists for independently reported consumer news. Especially in an era of inflation, there undoubtedly is vast audience potential in such news.

Perhaps most of the news of goods and services provided by business has emanated in recent years not from business itself nor from independent reporting but from government regulatory agencies.

Business organizations exist ultimately to serve public needs and desires for adequate quantities of fairly priced goods and services and, as we have said, in a free economic society alternatives concerning both the selling and buying of goods and services are left to private choice. The system assumes that competition will produce the widest possible choice of goods and services that are both safe and sound and are priced right. The companion doctrine of *caveat emptor,* let the buyer beware, implies that if the right product at the right price cannot be bought from one producer, it will be available from a competitive producer.

Federal and state governments over many years also have intervened in many ways to protect consumers from unsafe or undesirable goods and services, such as by licensing doctors and television repairmen, by grading meat and by guarding against price collusion by shopkeepers and corporations. Business has attempted for many years to police itself through such organizations as the Better Business Bureaus. But government regulation of business's goods and services took a new turn in the 1960's. A new consumer movement arose from various sources, including the 1965 publication of Ralph Nader's book, *Unsafe at Any Speed,* which questioned the safety of certain General Motors cars.[24]

Consumerism as a political movement promoted the creation by Congress in 1972 of the Consumer Product Safety Commission and resulted in other governmental efforts to provide the public with greater protection against unsafe autos and other consumer products. Consumerism and government regulation are discussed at considerable length in other chapters of this book. The point to be made here is that business reacted in various ways to consumerism.

Political pressures led many larger corporations to set up special staff departments to deal with the problems raised by consumerism and environmentalism. The pressures of these movements and the government regulations they produced also caused the chairmen of General Motors, Du Pont, and other corporations to express business's point of view at the National Press Club and other public places.

Government regulation of consumer goods and services will continue to evolve as an interesting story. Such regulation became controversial because its large costs were reflected in higher prices that exacerbated inflation. Another aspect of the story related more ironically to inflation. For, while federal regulation of consumer safety and health generally moved forward in the late 1970's, federal officials who were concerned with combatting inflation also concentrated on abolishing some forms of state regulation that had been enacted in the name of consumer protection. The Justice Department and Federal Trade Commission, for example, waged campaigns in the courts to abolish state-sanctioned restrictions on the medical and legal professions that had been intended to protect consumers from unsafe or unethical medical and legal practices.

Economic and Social Responsibilities

Business always has been responsible for the quantity, quality, and price of the goods and services it produces, through the doctrine of *caveat emptor,* through product liability laws, or through government regulatory and antitrust laws. In recent years, however, government has imposed a variety of additional responsibilities on corporations.

The Constitution long ago gave Congress the power to regulate commerce, and government for many years has imposed on business some responsibilities that are both economic and social in nature. Older examples include child labor laws and minimum wage laws. More recently, however, federal and state governments have imposed on business a larger variety of responsibilities that raise highly newsworthy questions about the functions of corporations.

The questions were suggested in a *Wall Street Journal* page one story, called a leader, that was headed "Changing Times" and began this way:

What is a corporation's job?

Five or 10 years ago, any business executive worth his salt would have answered without hesitation: A corporation's job is to make money for its owners. In the process, it presumably creates employment and satisfies the needs of its customers. But the central goal is profit.

Today, though, that answer is rapidly becoming an anachronism.

For an increasing number of companies, the answer—in theory, at least—is to help clean the air and water, to provide jobs for minorities, to contribute money and talent to the solution of urban problems, to be more helpful to consumers and, in general, to help enhance the quality of life for everyone. At long last, it seems, the corporation is developing a social conscience.[25]

Civil rights, environmental restrictions, and other types of social and economic laws and regulations seem to be changing the corporation from an economic organization into a socioeconomic institution. Perhaps social and economic historians of the future will conclude that the transformation was the logical next step in the development of corporations that had emerged from private to public stock ownership.

But the changing nature of corporations raises a host of questions that will engage business and economic journalism. Can the corporation that takes its social responsibilities seriously also continue to function efficiently as an economic producer of autos, refrigerators, insurance, sausages, and other consumer goods and services? Will the corporation as a socioeconomic institution come increasingly under public—which is to say government—direction and control? Also, as these and many other questions are resolved, will corporations become more involved in the political process from which the resolution will come?

Corporate Governance

The day is long past when captains of industry single-handedly ran steel mills, coal mines, and railroads. Passenger trains, of course, have come into the hands of a government-sponsored monopoly known as Amtrak, which seems to have earned a reputation even worse than that of William Vanderbilt. The federal securities laws since 1934 have influenced the way in which publicly held corporations are governed.

The securities laws do not empower the Securities and Exchange Commission to regulate directly the governance of corporations. The laws are based on a disclosure philosophy which holds that, if public shareholders and public investors know all the material facts concerning the inside of all corporations that have offered their shares for public sale, then corporations will be democratically governed and the stock markets will be kept honest. Thus, while state laws directly control corporate governance issues arising under corporation charters and by-laws, the federal securities laws have operated to inform public shareholders so they may vote intelligently on directors, mergers and acquisitions, and other matters relating to corporate governance.

Through this disclosure principle, however, the Securities and Exchange Commission has been able to exercise increasingly more influence over corporate governance. For example, the SEC has required disclosure of improper or illegal corporate payoffs to foreign figures, the intent of the embarrassing disclosure being to prevent future payoffs. As a further preventative, the SEC suggested that corporations have more directors who are independent of corporate management; it underscored its suggestion by requiring in proxy statements the disclosure of certain facts that tend to show whether directors are indeed independent.

Many questions have been raised concerning the effectiveness of corporate democracy and the answers are complicated by the fact that the public shareholders of corporations include not only individuals but pension funds, mutual funds, and other large institutional investors. The questions concerning corporate democracy, however, seem to be raised more by outsiders than small or large owners of corporate stock. Stockholders seem to have no difficulty exercising their right to throw out directors and managers of corporations that earn no profits and pay no dividends.

Questions have also been raised by outsiders who feel that corporations have not met their socioeconomic responsibilities. Ralph Nader, for example, has advocated federal chartering of corporations and direct federal regulation of the composition of corporate boards of directors.[26] He has suggested that consumerists, environmentalists, and representatives of other such interest groups have places on corporate boards.

The corporate governance issue thus appears rooted in the changing nature of corporations. However, the issue also grew in the 1970's as a direct result of disclosure by the SEC of millions of dollars of payoffs made from corporate political slush funds to foreign figures. The payments presumably were made to secure foreign sales in countries where payoffs were customary business practices, particularly when the purchasers were foreign governments. Nonetheless, the SEC disclosures embarrassed many large American corporations, particularly because the revelations came in the wake of the Watergate political scandal.

Many corporations have responded in some way to the corporate governance critics. One was Gulf Oil Corporation, which was under fire for making foreign payoffs and for other reasons. Its response was reported by *The New York Times* this way:

> The Gulf Oil Corporation, which has continually been taken to task by church groups for the social consequences of its corporate actions, has just nominated a Roman Catholic nun and Pittsburgh civic leader to its board of directors.

The move has astonished the social activists because none of them ever heard of the nominee, Sister Jane Scully, president of Carlow College, a Pittsburgh liberal arts college for women run by the Sisters of Mercy of Allegheny County.[27]

The question of who shall govern large corporations will continue to provide the material of enduring reportage and that question is in turn related to political and legal questions about the size and structure of large corporations. How big is too big? Through both internal growth and external mergers and acquisitions, corporations have continued to grow. The nation's 200 largest manufacturers increased their aggregate share of total U.S. manufacturing assets from 46 percent in 1947 to 57 percent in 1963 to more than 60 percent in the mid-1970's.[28]

Political liberals long have taken the position that bigness is bad, presumably because it injures competition and removes local control of plants and factories. Business has taken the position that bigness is not bad, essentially because it permits economies of scale that are unavailable to small business and that ultimately mean lower prices for consumers. Without taking sides, business and economic reporters can find vast quantities of news in such issues.

Consider the issue of corporate growth. Internal growth can be one measure of corporate efficiency and legitimate success. Growth through conglomerate mergers and acquisitions, which are about the only kind that antitrust law now allows large corporations, by definition does not injure competition, at least as competition traditionally has been defined by the laws. The antitrust laws thus have had great difficulty in reaching conglomerates.

On the other hand, conglomerate mergers and acquisitions would seem not to offer economies of scale such as are offered by combining two steel or auto or other competing companies in the same line of business. In fact, the purpose of conglomerate transactions is said to be diversification that makes corporate operations less subject to business cycles and thus more stable. Stability of prices and employment is of course a policy objective of government also and is stated as such in the Employment Act that Congress passed in 1946.

The issues of corporate growth, governance, and regulation all are drawing corporate executives out of their shells and into the public and political realms.

At the same time that Mr. Murphy of General Motors and other business leaders were resolving to become public figures, corporations also were forming political action committees, or PAC's, through which their executives and shareholders legally could make contributions to political candidates. Corporations such as Mobil Oil were taking positions on social and political issues in paid newspaper advertisements. And in 1978 the Supreme Court decided that corporations had a right under the First Amendment to spend their money in ads and otherwise to propagate their corporate views on political, social, and economic issues.[29]

The changing role of the corporation without question will be a continuing source of interesting and even profound news to serious business and economic reporters.

A WORD OF ADVICE

Business and economic news about corporations has not generally in the past been viewed by corporations or by the press as news about contests between adversaries. Coverage of contests between adversaries has been reserved for political and sports news.

As business leaders become public figures and as the role of corporations evolves in the political arena, the nature of business and economic news will change and coverage of the inside of business will change too. That is perhaps natural and inevitable at this time in history, but it will require an independence that has not been part of the tradition of most business and economic news reporting. And it will require knowledgeable and informed reporters, who also have not generally been part of traditional business and economic journalism.

THE BUSINESS OF AGRICULTURE

In the past, the farm sector of the American economy often was viewed as being separate from business and the economy in general. News of agriculture was of interest to farmers, of course, but not to city folks. News of grain, livestock, cotton, and other farm product prices was featured in newspapers with rural circulations, but not in large metropolitan dailies.

Some newspapers with urban circulations still have no farm editor, but the view that farm news is separate from business and economic news no longer is valid, if ever it was, and therefore the business of agriculture deserves attention in this discussion of business news coverage.

The decline in the number of U.S. farms and farm families is not a new phenomenon. As early as 1870, the number of farmers had dropped below the number of persons in other occupations and that trend has continued to a point where the portion of the population gainfully employed in agriculture is only about 5 percent. But that trend obviously does not mean that farm production has declined. It simply means that, as in any advancing economy, fewer people are required to produce the food and fiber for the rest of the population. It means there are larger farms, greater mechanization, and greater agricultural output per farmer and per acre. And it means that agriculture increasingly and in many ways has become more like other kinds of businesses.

There still are more than 1.6 million farms in the country, according to the U.S. Department of Agriculture, but frequently they no longer are small businesses. For example, Agriculture Department statistics show that nearly 10 percent of the nation's 662,000 farms that are engaged primarily in grain production have annual sales volumes of more than $100,000. Nearly 40 percent of the country's 43,000 poultry farms exceed $100,000 in annual sales of their products.[30]

At the beginning of 1980 the total real estate and other physical assets of the farm sector stood at $909 billion, as compared with $292 billion in 1970. The very large increases in farm values resulted in part from farm real estate prices, which escalated because of favorable farm income prospects as well as continuing inflation.[31]

American agriculture collectively is big business. Net cash income of the farm sector, according to the Agriculture Department, was nearly $97 billion in 1979, as compared with $38 billion in 1970.

Increased agricultural production per farmer and per acre has served to feed not only the rest of the U.S. population, but some of the rest of the world. Exports, particularly of grain, have contributed not only to favorable farm income prospects but also to U.S. international trade balances.

There are other respects in which agriculture has become big business. Some agricultural cooperatives, such as those that market dairy products and fruits, have grown into multimillion-dollar businesses that resemble corporations. Other types of food processors, corporations owned by public shareholders, also have grown very large. Yet as large as the farm economy is, farmers receive only about 40 percent of the price U.S. consumers ultimately pay for food; the other 60 percent represents processing and transportation charges.

Some newspapers have come to view the farm sector as part of their expanded coverage of business and economic news. The *Chicago Tribune,* for example, in its "Midweek Business Report" has included a page of "Commodities/Agriculture" news that incorporates an "On the Farm" column by the *Tribune*'s rural affairs editor.

Farm news naturally is influenced by geography. While the *Chicago Tribune*'s readers may be most interested in grain and hog markets, for instance, California newspaper readers may be more interested in fruit and vegetable markets and Alabama readers in cotton and broiler markets. Other geographical differences also make news. For example, while the value of farm real estate increased across the nation by an average of 14 percent in 1979, gains of more than 20 percent were reported in Arkansas, Nebraska, Colorado, and California.

As standards of living and prices have increased, agricultural news has come to attract the attention of consumers as well as producers of food and fibers, of urban dwellers as well as farm families. Agricultural news, packaged primarily for urban consumers, appears in the enlarged and improved food sections of many newspapers as well as in business and financial sections. Heightened public interest in food and food prices also has been recognized by television news. ABC-TV, for example, has aired a very well-produced and well-received TV news spot comparing supermarket chicken and beef prices and asking why consumers do not buy more relatively low-priced chicken. The answer, according to ABC's economics correspondent, is "chicken fatigue," which means that people's taste buds tire more quickly of chicken because of the composition of the meat.

Consumers' as well as producers' interest in farming has come to be recognized too by the U.S. Department of Agriculture, which, through its headquarters and regional offices and representatives throughout the country, long has been a primary source of farm news. In the United States Government Manual, the department now describes itself as serving "all Americans daily." The official description emphasizes the Department's rather newly discovered responsibility to consumers as well as its traditional responsibility to producers:

> It works to improve and maintain farm income and to develop and expand markets abroad for agricultural products. The department helps to curb and cure poverty, hunger, and malnutrition. It works to enhance the environment and to maintain our production capacity by helping landowners protect the soil, water, forests, and other natural resources. Rural development, credit, and conservation programs are key resources for carrying out national growth policies. USDA research findings directly or indirectly benefit all Americans. The department, through inspection and grading services, safeguards and assures standards of quality in the daily food supply.[32]

However, consumer interest in food and food prices also has led to interest in policies that are administered by the Department of Agriculture. Controversy over these policies has been and will continue to be newsworthy. For example, *The Wall Street Journal,* which is not a farm journal, said in a page one headline, "Federal Farm Policies Help Lift Food Prices, Many Observers Gripe." The story under that head began this way:

> Augustine Marusi, chairman of Borden Inc., aired a gripe when he addressed the company's annual meeting in April.
>
> "On April 1, the [government's] support price for milk went up 87 cents a hundred pounds, to $10.51," he said. "That's almost two cents a quart." But even though the increase raised costs for milk processors

such as Borden and thus lifted consumer prices, government inflation-watchers had just fingered the dairy companies for suspicious price increases.

Scoring the "contradiction," Mr. Marusi said, "Higher farm-support prices are politically astute, but they have only helped to put fire on an already overheating economy."

With Congress and the administration currently considering major farm-price policies, many observers are echoing Mr. Marusi's complaint. They concede that government farm policies aren't the major reason for the steep rises in food prices during the past two years, but they add that those policies are making an already-bad situation worse.[33]

For journalists, the moral of the story is that informed business and economic news reporting requires a comprehension of the inside of business, and that includes the business of agriculture.

NOTES—CHAPTER 8

1. See Donald I. Rogers, *The Day the Market Crashed* (New Rochelle, N.Y.: Arlington House, 1972), p. 12.

2. "The Forbes 500," *Forbes,* May 15, 1977, p. 156.

3. U.S. Department of Labor, Bureau of Labor Statistics.

4. Stanley F. Teele, as quoted by Phillip Grubb and Norma Loeser, *Executive Leadership* (Wayne, Penn.: MDI Publications, 1969), p. 14.

5. Reginald Stuart, "Ford Motor, at 75, Retooling at the Top," *New York Times,* June 16, 1978, pp. D1, D5.

6. Thomas A. Murphy, in remarks before the National Press Club, Washington, D.C., July 20, 1978.

7. Barbara W. Tuchman, *A Distant Mirror* (New York: Alfred A. Knopf, 1978), p. 37.

8. The articles, appearing in *Forbes,* respectively were "King of the Feather Family, February 6, 1978, p. 54; "Real Talent," December 11, 1978, p. 123; and "Color Me Golden," October 30, 1978, p. 105.

9. "The Real Facts About Food," U.S. Department of Agriculture, July 1974, p. 21.

10. *Ibid.*

11. Albert H. Sayer, Charles Cogen, and Sidney Wanes, *Economics in Our Democracy* (New York: McGraw-Hill Book Company, 1950), p. 235.

12. Herman E. Kroos, *American Economic Development* (Englewood Cliffs, N.J.: Prentice-Hall, 1956), pp. 46–47.

13. *The U.S. Economy in 1990* (New York: The Conference Board, 1972), p. 24.

14. The source of business receipt figures is the Internal Revenue Service. Compilations of such figures can be found in the annual *Statistical Abstract of the United States* or in more

abbreviated form in the *Pocket Data Book, USA,* both published by the U.S. Department of Commerce.

15. See "Dow Jones Joins the Media Conglomerates," *Business Week,* November 13, 1978, pp. 60–72.

16. "Color Me Golden," *Forbes,* October 30, 1978, p. 105.

17. For a more complete explanation of the troubles of Great Atlantic & Pacific Tea Company, see "Jonathan Scott's Surprising Failure at A&P," *Fortune,* November 6, 1978, pp. 35–44.

18. Kroos, *American Economic Development,* p. 271.

19. Quoted in Eric Goldman, *Rendezvous with Destiny* (New York: Alfred A. Knopf, 1953).

20. The compensation figures are taken from compilations appearing in *Forbes,* May 15, 1977, p. 244.

21. See David C. McClelland and David H. Burnham, "Power Is the Great Motivator," *Harvard Business Review,* March–April 1976, pp. 100–10.

22. Priscilla S. Meyer, "ITT Chief Hamilton Seeks to Shed Parts of 'Geneen Machine,'" *Wall Street Journal,* October 11, 1978, pp. 1, 34.

23. Quoted by Reginald H. Jones in "The Legitimacy of the Business Corporation," an address to the Graduate School of Business, Indiana University, Indianapolis, March 31, 1977.

24. Ralph Nader, *Unsafe at Any Speed* (New York: Grossman, 1965).

25. Charles N. Stabler, "For Many Corporations, Social Responsibility Is Now a Major Concern," *Wall Street Journal,* October 26, 1971, pp. 1, 22.

26. See Ralph Nader, Mark Green, and Joel Seligman, *Taming the Giant Corporation* (New York: W. W. Norton & Company, 1976).

27. Marylin Bender, "Nun's Nomination by Gulf Surprises Critics," *New York Times,* March 25, 1975, p. 45, 47.

28. Industry concentration ratios are from studies made by the Federal Trade Commission.

29. *First National Bank of Boston* v. *Bellotti,* 98 S.Ct. 1407 (1978).

30. "Agricultural Finance Outlook," a publication of the U.S. Department of Agriculture, AFO-20, November 1979.

31. *Ibid.*

32. *United States Government Manual,* 1979–1980, p. 105.

33. Paul Ingrassia, *Wall Street Journal,* August 14, 1979, pp. 1, 29.

SOURCES OF INFORMATION

American Enterprise Institute
1150 17th Street, N.W.
Washington, D.C. 20036

Federal Trade Commission
Pennsylvania Avenue at 6th Street, N.W.
Washington, D.C. 20580

The Brookings Institution
1775 Massachusetts Avenue, N.W.
Washington, D.C. 20036

The Business Roundtable
405 Lexington Avenue
New York, N.Y. 10017

Center for the Study of American Business
Washington University
St. Louis, Mo. 63130

Chamber of Commerce of the United States
1615 H Street, N.W.
Washington, D.C. 20062

The Conference Board
845 Third Avenue
New York, N.Y. 10022

National Association of Manufacturers
1776 F Street, N.W.
Washington, D.C. 20006

Securities and Exchange Commission
500 North Capitol Street
Washington, D.C. 20549

Small Business Administration
1441 L Street, N.W.
Washington, D.C. 20416

U.S. Department of Commerce
14th Street and Constitution Avenue,
N.W.
Washington, D.C. 20230

SUGGESTED READINGS

Golden, L. L. L., "A Dangerous Rush to Political Action," *Business Week,* September 25, 1978, p. 14.

Goldman, Eric, *Rendezvous with Destiny.* New York: Alfred A. Knopf, 1953.

Johnson, Paul, "Has Capitalism a Future?" *Wall Street Journal,* September 29, 1978, p. 10.

Kristol, Irving, "The Corporation: A Last Word," *Wall Street Journal,* January 11, 1978, p. 14.

———, "The Credibility of Corporations," *Wall Street Journal,* January 17, 1974, p. 12.

Kroos, Herman E., *American Economic Development.* Englewood Cliffs, N.J.: Prentice-Hall, 1956.

Learson, T. Vincent, "Business, in the Short Run, and Long Run," *New York Times,* June 9, 1978, p. 36.

Nader, Ralph, Mark Green, and Joel Seligman, *Taming the Giant Corporation.* New York: W. W. Norton & Company, 1976.

Sayer, Albert H., Charles Cogen, and Sidney Wanes, *Economics in Our Democracy.* New York: McGraw-Hill Book Company, 1950.

Walton, Scott D., *American Business and Its Environment.* New York: The Macmillan Company, 1966.

Wilson, James Q., "Democracy and the Corporation," *Wall Street Journal,* January 11, 1978, p. 14.

Reporting on. . .
THE INSIDE
OF LABOR

9

ABE H. RASKIN

CONTENTION AND COMPROMISE have shaped the economic no less than the political development of modern America. Unfortunately, however, the press has paid more attention to the contentiousness of labor and industry in strikes and lockouts than to the compromises reached at the bargaining table, even though it is the settlements of local and national labor-management disputes that are of far greater economic significance to the community and to the nation.

Press coverage of labor-management negotiations is a challenge to reporters, partly because of suspicions of the press, which are rooted in the history of the labor movement, and partly because of the very contentiousness that, sooner or later, gives way to negotiation and compromise. The challenge should and can be met, however. Neither the suspicions nor the contentiousness should be allowed to deter thorough and objective reporting of labor-management relations, which in these times of inflation and unemployment are of growing public importance.

ORGANIZED LABOR AND THE PRESS

Although "Big Labor" today is perceived as the counterpart of "Big Business," organized labor's contemporary attitudes have their roots in an earlier day when unions were the underdogs.[1] The view, shared by employers, judges, the police, and the press, that unions were illegal conspiracies in restraint of trade prevailed until 1842.

Unionism's outlaw status ended in that year, when Chief Justice Lemuel Shaw of the Massachusetts Supreme Judicial Court ruled in the landmark case of *Commonwealth* v. *Hunt* that there was nothing inherently unlawful in forming organizations to bring together all workers engaged in the same occupation. But that turning point opened up no broad new highway for unionism; all it did was to make it legal for any particular association of workers to use certain means for accomplishing its purposes.

That amorphous standard was only a tenuous support for organized labor in the years of meteoric industrialization from the close of the Civil War to the dawn of the twentieth century. Transcontinental rail lines opened up the frontier, providing new markets and new resources for exploitation by imaginative, aggressive entrepreneurs. Giant trusts developed in steel, oil, railroads, meatpacking, and many other fields.

The Rise of Organized Labor

National unionism got its start in that period, but many of the infant unions were baptized in blood. The Knights of Labor, organized on all-inclusive industrial lines around the slogan, "an injury to one is an injury to all," enrolled more than 700,000 members in the 1880's. They scored a spectacular victory through direct personal negotiations with Jay Gould, the swashbuckling speculator, in an 1885 strike that disrupted train movements on Gould's Wabash Railroad and other units of his Southwest System.[2]

It proved a Pyrrhic victory. A rash of strikes in the wake of the Knight's success on the Wabash led to intensified management resistance marked by the large-scale recruitment of strikebreakers, appeals to state governors for military assistance, and mobilization of community pressure against the strikers through the courts, the banks, the clergy, and the newspapers. The Knights of Labor collapsed under the assault, but even before its demise the American Federation of Labor came into being in 1886 as embodiment of the pragmatic, bread-and-butter philosophy that remains the core of American trade unionism in this high-technology era when men walk on the moon.

The seeming continuity of this evolution can be delusive, however, for those seeking to comprehend and interpret the current state of both unionism and labor-management relations. That is because one aspect of the transition remains most vivid in the mind set of most union leaders, even those who have come to power in the last half-decade. What stands out for them is the long record of conflict in the years when employers recruited private armies of thugs and industrial spies to smash unions, when workers were obliged to sign "yellow-dog contracts" under which they automatically forfeited their jobs if they joined a union, and when all the agencies of government and polite society were at the service of the boss.

Organized Labor's Self-Image

No matter how secure a union may appear, its officers usually tend to think of themselves as lineal descendants of the "martyrs" who were jailed, wounded, and slain in the formative years. Labor still vaunts its counterparts of Bunker Hill and Valley Forge—the Haymarket riot of 1886 in connection with a strike at the McCormick-Harvester plant in Chicago, the Homestead steel strike of 1892, and the Pullman railroad strike of 1894. The last left the bitterest memories of all, the use by President Cleveland of federal troops to break the strike under the guise of moving the mails.[3]

Even after the Norris-La Guardia Anti-Injunction Act of 1932 outlawed the yellow-dog contract and the Wagner Industrial Relations Act of 1935 put a bedrock of federal law under collective bargaining through unions of the workers' own choosing, unionism did not lose its atavistic sense of always having to contend with an antagonistic climate of community opinion. That climate, which fortified the employer in his opposition to its demands, was kept alive by such excesses of "law enforcement" as the shooting down of steel strikers and their families by the Chicago police in the Memorial Day Massacre of 1937.[4]

Organized labor's self-image as an orphan of the storm, misrepresented and misunderstood by the public of which its 18 million members make up so large a part, still remains paramount in its own thinking. The self-image survives even in this period when unions exercise stop-or-go power over many of the biggest businesses and the most crucial public services, when they administer billions of dollars in treasury, strike, and trust funds, and when they operate political and lobbying mechanisms of great sophistication and effectiveness.

There is little question in the minds of most top unionists about where to fix the blame for labor's depressed state in public esteem. Whatever cleavages may exist among them on economic, social, or political issues, union leaders have little difficulty in agreeing that through all of American history the press has given the country a warped view of the role of organized labor in society. As unionists see it, the whole thing is an elementary matter of economic determinism. All the instruments of mass communication—newspapers, magazines, television, and radio—are business enterprises, whose owners automatically identify with other employers whenever the interests of labor and management collide. That identification finds expression in use of the press as a vehicle for systematically defaming labor and vilifying its leaders. So goes the union jeremiad, and it has gained intensity in recent years as local monopolies have become more widespread in both print and electronic journalism.[5]

The Opposing View of Industry

Ironically, a precisely opposite view prevails among many ranking industrialists, although it would be an exaggeration to suggest that the sentiment is comparable to that among unionists in either universality or force. Nevertheless, among businesspeople active in the labor-management field the belief is widespread that, far from tipping the balance in industry's favor, the media tend to give sympathetic treatment to union positions while stinting on, omitting, or distorting those of management. In part, this feeling stems from the sense that four decades of post-New Deal acculturation have magnified the press "anti-business" attitude in all its appraisals of the enterprise system. But an even bigger factor is the conviction of many in industry that large numbers of reporters and commentators have forsworn neutrality and automatically become pro-labor through union membership in the Newspaper Guild or the American Federation of Radio and Television Artists.

Obviously, I could not conscientiously have devoted four decades to reporting and analyzing the course of labor-management relations and the proliferating range of labor's activities in almost every branch of human affairs if I felt there was basic validity to this indictment from either side. My own close observation—not merely in the relatively sheltered workshop of *The New York Times* but in exploring developments in the remotest reaches of mass communications—convinces me that publisher interference in the reportorial phases of labor coverage is negligible and in most cases nonexistent. Similarly, the unions that represent workers in journalism, both print and electronic, have endeavored to adhere faithfully to the prohibitions in their own rules and constitutions against attempts to influence what their members write in newspapers or say on the air.

The Need for Press Detachment

My sole purpose in dwelling at such length on the antagonistic attitudes held toward the media by so many in unions and industry is to impress upon those preparing for careers as reporters and commentators the need for expertise and detachment on their part to provide maximum reassurance to readers that none of these atavistic reproaches has substance. No field of economic reporting is more strewn with booby traps for the underinformed or the careless than this one. None deals with a subject matter of more consequence to the community.

The pages that follow will seek to provide some perspective on the labor reporter's function as it has burgeoned since Franklin D. Roosevelt's New Deal forced editors to a recognition that labor was news. Prior to 1932 the coverage of labor developments was primarily an extension of the police beat in most newspapers. This was principally because unionists tended to receive press attention only when they were arrested for picket-line clashes with strikebreakers or the police or were accused of extortion or underworld ties. That approach on the part of the press was itself a major contributor to the ingrained sense of bias that troubled labor.

The credit for lifting labor reporting out of the journalistic underworld belongs chiefly to one man. He was Louis Stark, a quiet former school teacher, who was assigned by *The New York Times* to its Washington bureau shortly after F.D.R. came to office in 1933. Stark had left the New York local staff of The Associated Press to join the *Times* some two decades earlier. Coverage of the Sacco-Vanzetti trial had been part of a broad experience that helped give him a deep insight into economic and political affairs. His unique understanding of labor-management relations earned him wide respect and a reputation for intelligence and fairness.[6]

When Stark got to the capital, that investment in responsible reporting proved of inestimable benefit to the *Times* and its readers. The period was one of innovative government, with new ideas of significance to millions of Americans bubbling out of secret conferences attended by unionists and industrialists unknown by the established White House press corps. Every morning editors all over the country would turn to *The New York Times* for exclusive stories on what new remedy the President was planning for dealing with some aspect of mass unemployment and a prostrate economy. Rarely would a day pass without some Stark story that had eluded everyone else in a capital crawling with enterprising journalists. His sustained record for news beats coincided with a flood of direct news that stemmed from the split between the industrial unionists and the craft unionists and with the unionization of steel, auto, and other mass production industries. These developments awakened newspapers in most major cities, and in many smaller ones as well, to the desirability of recognizing labor reporting as a demanding and productive specialty.

COLLECTIVE BARGAINING AND STRIKES

Pivotal to all relationships between unions and employers is *collective bargaining,* the endeavor through joint conference to reach agreement on wages, working conditions, and other rules that will prevail in the enterprise for the life of the contract. Scholars tend to applaud the American system of collective bargaining as the most highly developed in the world. Every bargaining pact fixes new boundary lines of authority and responsibility as between workers and management; some cover so encyclopedic a range of subjects that they are thicker than telephone directories. Operating at its best, the bargaining process translates into the industrial realm the most admirable aspects of the democratic tradition; at its worst it can inflict damage on the community as well as on those immediately involved.

Faulty Perceptions of What Is News

The criticism is frequently made—and, regrettably, with some validity—that the strengths of collective bargaining are too little understood by the public because press coverage tends to concentrate obsessively on the situations in which bargaining breaks down and strikes occur. The result is that little or no attention is paid to the 97 percent of negotiations in which the parties arrive at a meeting of minds with no interruption of work or even a serious threat of interruption. This near-vacuum of notice of tens of thousands of cases each year in which the process does exactly what it is supposed to do is bad for a reason that goes beyond the distorted impression it produces.

From the standpoint of the community, the important thing that eventuates from bargaining—whether or not there is a strike—is the character of the resulting contract: What effect will its terms have on the public in advancing or retarding price stability, productivity, and the quality of service in the activity the agreement is to govern? Unfortunately, that is a question to which, by and large, the press pays scant attention.

Even where. the size of a strike or the critical nature of the service cutoff makes the strike's day-to-day progress a focus of intense coverage, press interest often vanishes as soon as the workers go back to their jobs. In most instances there will be a sizable story when the negotiators announce that a handshake agreement has been reached, subject to ratification at a later date by the union rank and file. Part of the mystique of such announcements almost invariably is that the detailed provisions must first be communicated to the members and therefore cannot be officially revealed at the time of the settlement.

By the time ratification is complete, the news interest has drained out of the situation and the papers are prone to carry a paragraph or two giving the broad outlines of what the contract calls for. If a price boost rides along with the package, the story may be a bit longer but rarely will it contain the kind of detail needed for full understanding of anything that may be tucked away in the contract's fine print. Too often forgotten by the press is the fact that the minutiae of the agreement may have a more profound impact on the local or national economy than even the most draconian of strikes.

New York City's protracted fiscal crisis has much of its origins in improvident side agreements the city has made with its muscular civil service unions, most of which went totally unreported when made. One, sneaked across in the late 1960's in the mayoral administration of John V. Lindsey, wound up costing the municipal taxpayers a quarter of a billion dollars in one fell swoop, yet no one outside the inner circle of bargainers for the city and the unions knew anything about it until the agreement was completed.

This particular aberration grew out of a dispute over equalizing pay relationships in the Police and Fire Departments. Some of the country's most prestigious arbitrators had managed to sew the city into a system of parity arrangements that kept triggering "me too" pay increases for one group after another in the uniformed forces. Then, in line with its genius for making a bad situation infinitely worse, the city secretly committed itself to a parity formula that not even Albert Einstein could have balanced out. The whole thing was done in a footnote-letter attached to the basic police contract and, since no strike had been involved, no one in the press even noticed until the patrolmen went to court to force the city to come through with a huge chunk of back pay the citizens never knew they owed. By the time every other unionized group had been mollified, New York City had taken another long step down the trail that compelled it to become a financial ward of Uncle Sam.[7]

The Unwillingness of Both Sides to Talk

It is not just the reporter's or editor's lack of adequate exploratory will that keeps readers from better understanding what happens in collective bargaining; the obstacles are a good deal more formidable. Outside the realm of diplomatic relations between the great powers, no field compares with collective bargaining in the reluctance of the parties to let the public know what is really going on. The settled conviction of labor and management, in both public and private employment, is that the only time the rest of the world is entitled to any useful information is when an agreement has been reached and it is too late for anybody outside the charmed circle to do anything about it, no matter how damaging its economic consequences.

The steel industry is a perfect case in point. Much has changed in that industry since President Harry S. Truman first intervened in its labor relations just after World War II, proclaiming that "as steel goes, so goes inflation."[8] Yet one thing has remained immutable through all the succeeding years: The public's right to know does not exist until both sides have made their deal. That has been the one and only thing the industry and the union could always agree on.

How frustrating this mind set can become was well reflected in the industry's most gruelling conflict, the 116-day steel strike of 1959. The talks had begun with a message from President Dwight D. Eisenhower, calling on the parties to be aware of their responsibility to the national interest. The country, he said, could afford neither a shutdown of the mills nor an inflationary settlement. The chief spokesmen for the steel union and the industry solemnly affirmed their recognition that the public occupied a third seat at the negotiating table. The nation's welfare would take precedence over any selfish consideration, both declared.

The public part of the proceedings ended with release by the union of a torrent of statistics aimed at proving that every factor of profit, productivity, and living costs dictated a substantial pay increase, plus bigger pensions, more generous health protection, and myriad other benefits. The industry came forth with an answering barrage of figures demonstrating just as conclusively that the union's members were already far ahead of other American workers in the pay parade and that further gains would mean higher steel prices, reduced markets, mass unemployment, and a surrender of America's industrial supremacy to overseas rivals.

But the moment the parties got past this initial resort to gas warfare and settled down to serious bargaining, an iron curtain clanked down. Neither side would say a word to the press except that they had met and planned to meet again. At this point the reporters assigned to cover the talks felt obliged to set in motion their own ritualistic phase of what over the past decade had become a highly stylized Kabuki dance. They drafted a sonorous statement reminding the negotiators of the President's admonition to accord primacy to the public interest, a duty that could not be met if a news blackout prevailed.

The answer from the union and the industry was identical, and unyielding: the one important mission for the negotiators was to arrive at a contract, and the less anyone outside knew about the details, the less danger there was of disruptive interference by busybodies with special axes to grind. This was a category that could embrace anyone from pensioners and dissidents on the union side to the Big Three auto manufacturers or other steel-dependent businesses on the industry side.

Thus it was left up to the reporters to ferret out whatever they could on their own, a task they performed well enough to be able to inform their readers that the central issue in the original maneuvering had been quietly replaced by a vastly more explosive one. It was this shift that turned the 1959 negotiations into a kind of industrial holy war that ran for nearly four months before a Presidential injunction halted it.

In the preliminary sparring the companies had dug in on the battle cry of "no wage increase, no price increase"—a hold-the-line maxim with much appeal not only to an inflation-conscious public but also to many in the union's own rank and file who were weary of illusory pay raises that were swiftly swallowed up by increased living costs. But the industry laid the ground for an excruciating trial by combat when it abruptly dropped that strategy in favor of one that solidified the union membership in icy resistance. The new tack involved a management demand for abolition of a contract clause that froze all existing local work rules except what was individually modified through collective bargaining. These rules covered thousands of plant practices, from lunch breaks to shower arrangements. Many dated back more than a half-century, and the unionists were prepared to let the blast furnaces rust before they surrendered to the companies the unilateral right to modify or abolish any of them.

In the final agreement, negotiated with the aid of then Vice-President Richard M. Nixon and Secretary of Labor James P. Mitchell just before the 80-day no-strike injunction ran out, the companies retreated from their insistence on changing the old clause. By this time it was no secret to the country that this had become the pivotal issue, not the supposed fight to preserve the purchasing power of the dollar against further erosion by the wage-price spiral. A pay increase was part of the final settlement.[9]

Dozens of other situations might be cited in which a conspiracy of silence by parties involved in negotiations of great moment to the public had to be penetrated by the vigilance of newspaper, radio, or television correspondents unwilling to accept the bargainers' dictum that the community must be kept in the dark until after the string is knotted on the whole contract package. Regrettably, the notion of private agreements privately arrived at remains dominant in virtually all areas, even where the negotiators are dealing with the distribution of taxpayers' funds and writing into their contracts basic matters of public policy such as the size of elementary school classes or the quality of hospital care.

The Reporter's Responsibility to Report

The role of the reporter is not to acquiesce meekly in the conceit that collective bargaining is a closed shop, a private process to be conducted under protection of a "Do Not Disturb" sign. That does not mean one should make a voluntary accord impossible by barging through every delicate maneuver the parties engage in to knit together the intricate bits and pieces of an agreement. Rather, it means developing responsible sources within labor and management and also among the third parties intimately involved in industrial relations. The Federal Mediation and Conciliation Service has scores of expert mediators on its staff who can be of inestimable help in supplying trustworthy information, provided their identity as source is safeguarded. Many industries have impartial chairmen or other permanent arbitrators who pass on day-to-day disputes that are not resolved through the regular grievance machinery. They are often knowledgeable about the course of negotiations for new contracts, even though they have no direct voice in establishing the terms. Lawyers and other technicians attached to the union or industry team can also supply useful information.

Judgment on the reporter's part is required both to earn the trust of those in possession of the facts and to utilize the information gained in ways that contribute to balanced public understanding of the issues. The correspondent must be on guard, however, against getting encumbered with off-the-record confidences that deprive him or her of final decision on what or when to publish. Nor can the reporter, in the interest of maintaining cordial relations, acquiesce to bargainers' pleas that release of information before an accord has been initialed will not contribute to successful completion of the agreement. If the projected contract is one that will cheapen the value of everybody's dollar or curtail access to a vital service through a cartel-like accommodation between a union and its employers, the public is clearly better off learning of the prospect before it becomes a *fait accompli* beyond any outsider's ability to modify through marshalling of popular protest.

Four decades of intensive coverage of collective bargaining have left me unpersuaded that it is impractical to negotiate in a goldfish bowl, especially in this period of increasing insistence on openness in every area of government, education, and public life. Again and again I have encountered negotiators entrusted with power of decision who are so bereft of discernment that one would not trust them to find their way safely across the street without a Seeing Eye Dog. Why should the community have to wait until such people have done possibly irreparable damage before registering its concern?

The widespread adoption of a "sunshine law" at all levels of government has prompted a few states to open up the bargaining process in state and municipal contracts.[10] The experience is still too limited to permit conclusive appraisal, but thus far the need to be accountable from start to finish of the process has proved no obstruction to fruitful give and take in negotiations. The same approach could readily be applied to private industry, with no need for new legislation, but the resistance so widespread among unions and industries makes that an extremely remote prospect. Journalistic enterprise will have to remain the one promising instrument for piercing the veil.

CHANGES IN LABOR-MANAGEMENT RELATIONS

The vast institutional changes taking place in American society are changing more than the character of the work force. The new values, new aspirations, and new skepticism that are part of these changes are reflecting themselves in the emergence of new union leaders after a long period in which union presidents had a degree of job security beyond that of bankers, industrialists, or the heads of Ivy League colleges. For instance, when George Meany in 1979 retired as president of the AFL-CIO, he was 85 years old and still as firmly in command of the labor federation as when he presided over the merger of the American Federation of Labor with the Congress of Industrial Organizations in 1955. But he was the only member of the original executive council still active in 1979. In the preceding five years practically all the big international unions had installed new leaders, sometimes amid much turmoil. In late 1979, George Meany retired in favor of his longtime aide, Lane Kirkland, who became the second AFL-CIO president. Mr. Meany died in January 1980.

A bruising leadership fight within the United Steelworkers, for example, was reported in a 1977 *New York Times* story with this lead:

> Some people call Ed Sadlowski the Jimmy Carter of the steel mills, with his warmth and smile propelling his populist campaign for the presidency of the United Steelworkers of America.

More important, Mr. Sadlowski is a product of the steel mills, a burly street-fighter from working-class Chicago with an engaging manner and a chance at one of the biggest prizes in American labor.

His opponent, Lloyd McBride, a loyal career unionist more than 20 years older than Mr. Sadlowski, refers to Mr. Sadlowski as an upstart and a creation of public relations, and warns that if elected he will destroy the union.[11]

Mr. McBride defeated Mr. Sadlowski and personality stories in profusion have been written about the newcomers who won office in labor's upper echelon, but the more important stories are not yet written because the new leaders have yet to clarify their own thinking on one matter of overriding public importance: the ways in which they will attempt to redefine union goals and approaches to end the downhill slide in overall membership. That task of redefinition has been made doubly urgent because in many industries management is applying sophisticated new techniques for keeping unions weak.

Employers' New Attitudes Toward Unions

In a broad range of fields, including the newspapers themselves, employers who have lived under collective bargaining agreements for most of the years since the Wagner Act are questioning the virtues of these established relationships. Seminars on such topics as "Making Unions Unnecessary" and "How to Maintain Non-Union Status" are a popular feature of industry conventions. The National Association of Manufacturers, after many years of taking a back seat in labor-management relations, organized a Council on Union-Free Environment in 1977 to counsel employers who felt their businesses and their employees would be better off without unions.[12]

Counteracting such steps back toward conflict, in recent years a broad range of joint labor-management committees have developed to stimulate productivity and generally foster more cordial relations. Committees of this kind have existed in fields ranging from supermarkets to basic steel. The desire of import-threatened industries to preserve domestic jobs has been a particularly potent spur to the formation of such committees, with the double purpose of holding down domestic costs and persuading the government to limit imports.

The most substantial step in the direction of cooperative exploration of broad social issues, with a view to harmonizing the often clashing viewpoints of industry and unions, was taken early in the 1970's by a summit committee made up of George Meany and the heads of seven of the country's largest unions and the chief executive officers of eight giant multinational corporations. Among the companies were General Motors, General Electric, Du Pont, Citicorp, and United States Steel. Formed as a top-level advisory panel to President Gerald R. Ford, the group remained together outside the orbit of government under the catalytic direction of Professor John T. Dunlop of Harvard, a former Secretary of Labor, until the committee became a casualty of the heated conflict over labor law reform in 1978.

Along with such movements away from adversarial relationships have come the beginnings of a joint effort to do away with strikes by substituting reason for economic muscle in the resolution of disputes. The most notable venture toward an enduring peace arrangement of this type has been the Experimental Negotiating Agreement in basic steel, first signed in 1973 and later renewed until 1980. It was approved by the United Steelworkers of America and the major steel producers to end the "boom and bust" cycle of inventory accumulation that grew out of strike fears whenever a contract expired, a cycle that had helped turn many United States steel-dependent industries to overseas suppliers.[13]

Cooperation or Confrontation

Although the United Steelworkers and the steel producers renewed their experimental agreement, bargaining in 1977 was not as easy as had been anticipated. Under the headline, "Celebrated Steel-Labor Romance Wanes as Ailing Industry Adopts a Harder Line," *The Wall Street Journal* reported:

> Four years ago, in more prosperous times, the steel industry and the United Steelworkers union took a stroll down lovers' lane, linking arms in the celebrated, no-strike Experimental Negotiating Agreement.
>
> Now, with steel slumping and the industry under fire from the government for allowing its labor costs to rise faster than its productivity, steelmakers are taking a tougher bargaining line. As a result, the labor-relations romance appears to be over.[14]

Whether the cooperative mode or the return to confrontation tactics will be the dominant theme of industrial relations in the 1980's is decidedly conjectural. The polarization created by the 1978 battle in Congress over President Carter's proposals for labor law reform, with organized labor solidly in favor and industry equally solid against, put extremely severe strain on even the most cordial of relationships. A key task for labor reporters will be to keep alert for signals that indicate how smooth or rocky the future course will be.

LABOR AND THE COMMUNITY

The labor movement is often accused of being too parochial in its interests, but the labor reporter is likely to find him or herself engaged in recording activities that touch almost every aspect of the human condition and of the local, national, and global community.

Labor and Politics

The most obvious aspect, of course, is labor's deep immersion in politics. Unlike the labor movements of Western Europe, most of which are oriented toward socialism and closely linked to Socialist, Social Democratic, or Labor parties, United States labor—ever since the days of Samuel Gompers, the British-born cigar maker who headed the old American Federation of Labor from its founding in 1886 until his death in 1924—has maintained a role of relative independence rooted in the two-party system within a framework of capitalism.

Even in 1978 at the height of labor's irritation over the united front of industry in hostility to labor law reform, Lane Kirkland, then secretary-treasurer of the AFL-CIO, went out of his way to stress labor's distaste for nationalization or other forms of statism. "Management is singularly fortunate in this country," he declared. "Its role and status is not under serious attack by any ideology espoused by labor. The American worker is uniquely free of class consciousness or envy."[15]

In practice, for all the vehemence with which it stresses its nonpartisanship, labor is generally to be found in the Democratic camp in both national and local elections. Year-round political action was a characteristic of the old Congress of Industrial Organizations almost from its inception as a child of the New Deal, but the American Federation of Labor did not formally follow suit until the 1947 passage of the Taft-Hartley Act convinced its leaders that a full-time political apparatus was desirable to carry on what is still labor's basic political creed: "Reward your friends and punish your enemies."

The AFL-CIO Committee on Political Education (COPE) in many parts of the country has been recognized as the most effective of all instrumentalities for "getting out the vote." The decline of the big-city political machines has given the unions particular prominence in programs for getting workers and their families to register and vote. At the federation headquarters in Washington, COPE maintains an elaborate computerized bank of data on who is or is not registered to vote, arranged by unions and election districts on a nationwide basis.

No one in labor pretends that there is any necessary correspondence between the way union members vote and the way their leaders would like them to vote. Evidence in election after election is that union endorsements tend to swell the labor vote for the union's favored candidate when he is popular with the rank and file; they arrest slightly the vote against the candidate when leaders and membership basically disagree. The place where union political involvement clearly does make a difference, however, is in increasing the total voting population and in providing labor-backed candidates with a quick source of needed campaign cash. Industry, aided by recent favorable Supreme Court decisions, has been stepping up its own political action drives to counter those of labor. The legal and tactical manifestations of these rival efforts will be a continuing news focus.

Corruption Within Organized Labor

Another area of news attention which regrettably extends into every corner of the economy and of public life today is corruption within the labor movement. Since the beginning of the century petty grifters operating as labor czars have found rich pickings in various forms of extortion and plundering, especially in industries where ownership was fragmented and intense competition made employers pushovers for shakedowns by peddlers of strike insurance. The building trades, trucking, the waterfront, the apparel trades, and retail trade were usually high on the hit list.[16]

The end of Prohibition in the Roosevelt era loosed gangs of big-time crooks, headed by Al Capone of Chicago, to prey on labor as a source of illegal gain comparable to that previously produced by bootlegging. The CIO, operating in the mass industries, was relatively immune to their penetration, but many AFL unions were turned into principalities of the underworld. The grip of the racketeers was made tighter by the hands-off policy maintained by the central federation, which clung until the 1950's to the doctrine that it was powerless to intervene in the internal affairs of its autonomous international unions. A junking of that policy by George Meany helped provide impetus for the 1955 fusion of the AFL and CIO; the merger compact included provision for a permanent Ethical Practices Committee to stamp out corruption in labor.

The high point in enforcement of that commitment came in 1957 when the combined movement expelled its biggest and strongest affiliate, the International Brotherhood of Teamsters, on charges of racket domination. However, when President Eisenhower signed the Landrum-Griffin Act two years later to strengthen the federal hand in prohibiting malpractices within labor, the federation all but dismantled its own self-policing machinery. The Ethical Practices Committee became a dead-letter and the federation took the view that it is up to the law-enforcement agencies to keep unions free of crooks when their own offices and members fail in that duty.

One never-stated reason for the reversion to passivity by the parent federation is the ineffectiveness of the expulsion weapon as a corrective. The teamsters, far from withering in exile, have grown steadily bigger and stronger in the last two decades, despite a notable absence of any zeal for ridding themselves of corrupt elements. The federation's own unions, originally instructed to shun any relations with the outcast teamsters, have found themselves frequently obliged to call on them for extra muscle in strikes and organizing campaigns. In a period marked by Watergate and by recurrent reports of illegal payoffs by many of the country's corporations, the teamster experience has provided scant inspiration for more housecleaning within labor. The resulting vacuum of corrective action leaves this an area as much in need of investigative reporting as any in government or business.

The fertile field might be demonstrated with an article, titled "Can Anybody Clean Up the Teamsters?" which appeared under my byline in 1976 in *The New York Times Magazine*. It began:

> The International Brotherhood of Teamsters, the country's biggest, strongest and most investigated union, stands as a monument to the sweet uses of adversity, a testimonial to the proposition that nothing succeeds like bad publicity. For two decades it has been excoriated by Congressional investigators and Federal prosecutors as a roost for hoodlums, a looting ground where hundreds of millions of dollars in union trust funds flow into high-risk ventures under mob control.
>
> It has been exiled in disgrace from the mainstream of organized labor. Dozens of Teamster officials, including two international presidents, have been sent to prison. In a scene straight out of "The Godfather," Jimmy Hoffa, at once the most engaging and the most baleful of all the union's leaders, disappeared 15 months ago just after starting a drive to reclaim the presidency from those he had put in charge when he was hauled off to the penitentiary in 1967. With the vanished Hoffa went the secrets he had threatened to spill to the authorities about underworld influence in the union that exercises stop-or-go power over a million trucks.[17]

In all such investigations reporters can be sure they will hear the familiar caution, often coming from the most respectable sources, that getting rid of bad leaders and turning over power to a rambunctious rank and file may be injurious to the community. It is certainly true that a dictatorial union chief often is able to ram through a moderate contract, with or without bothering to get rank-and-file concurrence. And there is justice to the complaint that a double standard does characterize much public thinking about labor. Laws like Landrum-Griffin require unions to guarantee full freedom of dissent to their members, yet their leaders are berated for irresponsibility or ineffectuality when rank-and-file rebellion upsets a settlement negotiated in good faith or when fear of just such rebellion prompts the leaders themselves to hold out for unreasonable terms. The dismal experience of the United Mine Workers, a union that went from autocracy to anarchy in one jump, indicated how high the cost of democracy-run-wild could be in terms of damage to the public. A 110-day coal strike in 1978 was the acid fruit of that miscarriage of union reform. Both the union and the economy wound up on the casualty list.

But recognition of such dangers should in no way deter the reporter from the job of ferreting out abuses in unions, whether they stem from corruption, incompetence, or suppression of membership rights. The strength of a democracy lies in its capacity, often at the price of great pain, to find responsible correctives once diseased practices are exposed.

The International Labor Community

Correspondents covering national labor affairs will find that their terrain does not stop at the water's edge. A recognition of the increasing interdependence of the world economy has intensified the interest of American unions in improving their links with labor organizations overseas. One strong spur is an awareness that differences in wages and other labor standards are a factor in trade penetration. West Germany and the Scandinavian countries now have labor standards that match and in some cases exceed those of U.S. workers. But that is less true of most other industrialized countries, and the gap is enormous when wages in the developing countries are compared with those here.

The worldwide spread of multinational corporations has been a second spur toward closer ties with overseas unions. The United Auto Workers and the United Steelworkers have been in the forefront of moves to coordinate bargaining strategies with European and Japanese unions, but only the most tentative steps have yet been taken toward seeking to bargain across national boundaries or to provide meaningful assistance in strikes called by foreign labor against subsidiaries of U.S. multinationals.

One deterrent to such action is that the AFL-CIO has isolated American labor from the two most important instruments for collaboration in international labor affairs. One is the International Labor Organization, a specialized agency of the United Nations, in which representatives of governments, workers, and employers join to seek improved protection for workers and to help raise their economic standards. The United States formally withdrew from the ILO in 1977, chiefly because Meany and the federation persuaded President Carter that the agency had become a political vehicle for the Soviet and Arab blocs and that it would never reform unless this country quit.

Industry strongly supported the federation in urging a pullout, and their combined view prevailed over contrary counsel from the President's foreign policy advisers and all of this country's principal allies. The withdrawal failed to produce the hoped-for changes in ILO rules, but neither did it cause a general weakening in U.S. relations with the UN or its allies, as the State Department had feared. Developments on this front will be of special importance because many Labor Department officials view the world labor organization as a possible key to establishment of "human needs budgets" that would put a floor under wages in the developing nations and thus make the imbalance in labor costs less overwhelming.

The other major group in which the United States is an outsider is the International Confederation of Free Trade Unions. This is a coordinating body that embraces every continent, and Meany himself was primarily responsible for its formation in 1949 as a rival to the Moscow-dominated World Federation of Trade Unions. However, he led an AFL-CIO secession in 1969 in protest against exchange of fraternal delegates between the West European unions and unions from the Soviet bloc. Meany refused any relations with the Eastern European labor organizations on the ground that they are instruments of the state rather than bona fide unions.

However, the break with the international confederation is not total. Many of the largest American unions, notably in metalworking and chemicals, are active in trade secretariats that represent a bridge to the ICFTU affiliates. These secretariats may eventually become vehicles for coordinated bargaining, though industry is resisting all moves in that direction.

The AFL-CIO has an active international affairs department of its own. In past years much of its activity was focused on pressing for a global policy of militant resistance to Soviet expansionism. The federation was among the strongest supporters of the Vietnamese war, even though some of its unions aligned themselves with the doves early in that conflict. The AFL-CIO sponsors institutes in Latin America, Africa, and Asia to combat communist infiltration and to organize democratic trade unions. A more limited institute was operated in Spain and Portugal in 1978 and 1979 to counter Eurocommunism. Also, in 1976, after a decade-long absence, the federation reaffiliated with the trade union advisory council of the Organization for Economic Cooperation and Development. This alliance of unions from 23 industrialized nations could become pivotal in formulating international labor programs for combating chronic inflation and unemployment.

L'ENVOI: ON COVERING LABOR

This tabulation of the things a labor reporter ought to be familiar with may seem discouragingly formidable, yet it could be vastly extended without exhausting the subject. But don't let it dim your enthusiasm for venturing into the field. Covering the vagaries of labor and management can be a source of ceaseless fascination, and the next decade is likely to be one of the most critically important in the development of their relations—important not only for them but also for the nation.

Two basic admonitions may be helpful. One is to recognize that both sides have decided that their most significant future battles are going to be determined in large measure by public opinion. Image building has now become the preoccupation of both sides. Industry always relied heavily on advertising to get across its point of view in industrial disputes, much as it did in selling automobiles or soap. Unions up to now have not become major purchasers of institutional advertising. However, Albert Shanker, president of the American Federation of Teachers, calls the "column" he writes every Sunday, as a paid ad in the "Week in Review" section of *The New York Times,* the best investment his union ever made. George Meany took a display ad in *The Wall Street Journal* to try to build up at least a modicum of business support for labor law reform.

Reporters will have to be increasingly wary to keep from being seduced by the professional image-makers on both sides. As has already been noted, neither labor nor management has ever earned high marks for the candor of their public statements in collective bargaining or strikes. They are self-serving, not revelatory. It is the reporter's job to pierce the veil and give the reader the facts required to understand what the issues really are and what valid support there is for the position of either side. The still larger duty is to explain where the public fits into the picture, including the extent to which government may be operating to tip the balance in the community's favor or against it.

A second point worth remembering is that organized labor is not a monolithic institution, despite the unanimity that usually marks all major policy actions at the biennial conventions of the AFL-CIO. Labor's groping for new directions will undoubtedly bring a sharpening of the philosophic differences that have always existed within it. These surfaced in the 1960's when the conservative, antitax movement spearheaded by Governor George C. Wallace of Alabama enlisted strong support among unionized blue-collar workers and civil servants. It was even more apparent when coldness on the part of Meany and most other top federation officials to "new wave" influences in the Democratic Party led the central organization to adopt a policy of official neutrality in the 1972 Presidential campaign. Most of the building trades and the maritime unions lined up behind Richard M. Nixon in his successful drive for reelection, but the so-called progressive coalition that embraced the auto workers, the machinists, the communications workers, many organizations of public employees, and others rallied behind the Democratic nominee, Senator George McGovern of South Dakota. The political scars left by that division have not fully healed, though labor was nearly solid in support of Jimmy Carter after he won the Democratic nomination in 1976. The next decade is likely to see abrasive expression of such differences. It may also see a crosspull between unions representing public and private employees, as resistance to government spending increases, and also between unions in the high-wage industries and those whose members earn much less—the "haves" and "have-nots" of the work force. These tensions will all require careful reporting.

My final injunction is to steer clear of the too-easy disposition to rate union leaders in much the same fashion that we do top sluggers in major league baseball. Unionists complain that they disappear as public personalities if they do not constantly outrage all right-thinking persons by the bellicosity of their remarks at the bargaining table or by shutting down a vital industry. Usually the only union chiefs who get their pictures on the cover of *Time* or *Newsweek* or on the nightly news of the television networks are those who are leading big strikes or making some dire threat of political or economic mayhem.

Since union leaders stop being leaders if they do not get reelected, it becomes a matter of some moment for the president of a million-member union to make sure that the members don't forget he is around. And what better medium than national TV, that instant popularizer, to raise his standing with the rank and file, no matter how unflattering the commentary that accompanies his picture on the home screen?

There is plenty of solid news on the labor beat. The newspapers, television, and radio need more of it.

NOTES—CHAPTER 9

1. For an adequate understanding of the attitudinal factors discussed in this introductory section, some familiarity with labor history is helpful. The most definitive study of unionism's early struggles is contained in John R. Commons, *A Documentary History of American Industrial Society* (Cleveland: Arthur H. Clark Co., 1910). Also excellent is Philip Taft, *Organized Labor in American History* (New York: Harper & Row, 1964). Perhaps the most readable and satisfying short history is Foster Rhea Dulles, *Labor in America* (New York: Thomas Y. Crowell, 1949).

2. Taft, *Organized Labor,* pp. 84–155. See also Dulles, *Labor in America,* pp. 114–49.

3. Dulles, *Labor in America,* pp. 166–83.

4. For more illumination on labor's changing legal status as defined by the Supreme Court, an admirable reference is Elias Lieberman, *Unions Before the Bar* (New York: Harper & Bros., 1950).

5. A representative statement of the labor view is given by Lane Kirkland, secretary-treasurer of the AFL-CIO, in "The Renewed Assault on Labor," *AFL-CIO American Federationist,* July 1977.

6. For Louis Stark's life story, see *Dictionary of American Biography,* Supplement 5 (New York: Charles Scribner's Sons, 1977).

7. Details of this tragicomedy at the bargaining table can be found in "Politics Up-Ends the Bargaining Table" by A. H. Raskin, *American Assembly: Public Workers and Public Unions* (Englewood Cliffs, N.J.: Prentice-Hall, 1972), pp. 122–46.

8. For an account of the miscarriage of President Truman's first intervention in steel labor relations after V-J Day, see Robert J. Donovan, *Conflict and Crisis* (New York: W. W. Norton & Co., 1977), pp. 166–67.

9. Terms and analysis of the strike settlement may be found in *The New York Times* from January 5, through January 8, 1960.

10.   Florida was the only state that in 1978 specifically required that all public employee bargaining be held in the "sunshine." This requirement has been in effect since 1974 by act of the legislature. Wisconsin passed a 1978 municipal employment relations act with a similar "sunshine" requirement covering all bargaining, but this section of the bill was vetoed by Acting Governor Martin Schreiber. However, the final act did compel public officials and civil service unions to hold open meetings at various specified stages of collective bargaining and of the mediation/arbitration procedure prescribed if an impasse develops. In North Dakota the State Supreme Court ruled on March 31, 1977, that the collective bargaining process in state and municipal employee relations must be open at all stages because no explicit exemption was contained in the general "sunshine" law covering all of North Dakota's governmental activities. See *Midwest Monitor* (Bloomington, Ind.: The Midwest Center for Public Sector Labor Relations, November–December 1977).

11.   Lee Dembart, "Steel Union Leadership Fight Could Have Wide Effect," *New York Times*, January 17, 1977, p. 36.

12.   Typical of many such seminars held in 1978 were two directed by industrial psychologist Dr. Charles L. Hughes, under the auspices of Executive Enterprises, Inc., in Houston on January 23–24 and in Dallas on March 7–8. For a labor view, see "Opposition from the Right, a Growing Shadow" in *The Machinist*, October 1977. See also Phyllis Payne, "The Consultants Who Coach the Violators," in *AFL-CIO American Federationist*, September 1977.

13.   *New York Times*, March 30, 1973, p. 1.

14.   David Ignatius, "Celebrated Steel-Labor Romance Wanes As Ailing Industry Adopts a Harder Line," *Wall Street Journal*, October 21, 1977, p. 4.

15.   See a speech delivered by Lane Kirkland at a "Work in America" seminar at Arden House, Harriman, N.Y., May 24, 1978.

16.   For a sophisticated discussion of trade union corruption and its social context, see John Hutchinson, *The Imperfect Union* (New York: E. P. Dutton & Co., 1970). For a historical view, see Harold Seidman, *Labor Czars* (New York: Liveright Publishing Corp., 1938).

17.   A. H. Raskin, "Can Anybody Clean Up the Teamsters?" *New York Times Magazine*, November 7, 1976, pp. 31–101.

SOURCES OF INFORMATION

American Federation of Labor–Congress of
Industrial Organizations
Department of Public Relations
815 Sixteenth Street, N.W.
Washington, D.C. 20006

George Meany Center for Labor Studies
10000 New Hampshire Avenue
Silver Spring, Md. 20904

International Brotherhood of Teamsters,
Chauffeurs, Warehousemen &
Helpers Union
25 Louisiana Avenue, N.W.
Washington, D.C. 20001

National Right to Work Committee
1990 M Street, N.W.
Washington, D.C. 20036

United Auto Workers
Solidarity House
8000 East Jefferson Avenue
Detroit, Michigan 48214

United Mine Workers of America
900 Fifteenth Street, N.W.
Washington, D.C. 20005

U.S. Department of Labor
Bureau of International Labor Affairs
Washington, D.C. 20210

Labor Policy Association
1717 Pennsylvania Avenue, N.W.
Washington, D.C. 20006

National Labor Management Foundation
2000 L Street, N.W.
Washington, D.C. 20036

U.S. Department of Labor
Labor-Management Services
Administration
Washington, D.C. 20210

SUGGESTED READINGS

Bernstein, Irving, *The Turbulent Years*. Boston: Houghton Mifflin Co., 1970.

Bok, Derek C., and John T. Dunlop, *Labor and the American Community*. New York: Simon & Schuster, 1970.

Commons, John R., *A Documentary History of American Industrial Society*. Cleveland: Arthur H. Clark Co., 1910.

————, *History of Labour in the United States*. New York: The Macmillan Company, 1918.

Dulles, Foster Rhea, *Labor in America*. New York: Thomas Y. Crowell, 1949.

Hutchinson, John, *The Imperfect Union*. New York: E. P. Dutton & Co., 1970.

Lieberman, Elias, *Unions Before the Bar*. New York: Harper & Bros., 1950.

Seidman, Harold, *Labor Czars*. New York: Liveright Publishing Corp., 1938.

Taft, Philip, *Organized Labor in American History*. New York: Harper & Row, 1964.

Reporting on...
GOVERNMENT ECONOMIC POLICIES

10

LOUIS M. KOHLMEIER, JR.

W ASHINGTON BECAME THE MECCA of journalists in the days of the New Deal, when the federal government commenced growing rapidly and government programs such as Social Security began to affect the lives of virtually all Americans. The SEC, NLRB, FCC, FDIC, FMC, CAB, and other alphabet agencies were created to administer the emerging programs, and the Washington press corps grew to cover the expanding agencies, bureaus, and departments of government. Washington became still larger as a news capital during World War II and the cold and hot wars that followed, but domestic economic and social programs also continued to expand and new alphabet agencies such as EPA, CPSC, CFTC, and OSHA were created. The Washington press corps grew apace, despite the slow decline in the number of metropolitan daily newspapers across the country. For example, the number of newspaper journalists holding accreditation cards to the Senate and House press galleries increased from 917 in 1964 to about 1,300 in 1979. In addition, more than 1,000 radio and television journalists and about 920 magazine and other periodical staff members were accredited to the galleries in 1979.[1]

State and local governments have expanded even more rapidly than the federal government in recent years, and statehouses and city halls have become more important news centers. State and local government employment, for instance, stood at about 3 million in 1945 and increased steadily to 12 million in 1976. Federal civilian employment stood at 2 million after World War II, moved up to nearly 3 million in 1967 and then remained generally steady.[2]

The growth of government at all levels is illustrated even more dramatically by the increase in government spending. Total expenditures of federal, state, and local governments, including federal grants to states and municipalities, soared from about $60 billion in 1950 to $688 billion in 1977. In 1977, federal spending amounted to $423 billion while state and local government expenditures were $265 billion.[3] Federal spending alone in the past several years has accounted for almost 23 percent of gross national product, whereas federal outlays amounted to between 18 and 21 percent of GNP in the previous two decades.[4]

We have emphasized throughout this book that an understanding of government economic policies is necessary to journalists who cover politics, labor, environment, and other beats that at first glance may not seem to have much relationship to economics. This point is illustrated in a story that has been retold many times in *Wall Street Journal* newsrooms. At a White House press conference early in the New Deal, President Roosevelt fielded a policy question by telling the confused reporter to read what had been written that day by Bernard Kilgore, who then was manager of the *Journal*'s Washington bureau.

While government policies today have a bearing on most issues that in decades past were private or local matters, including crime, education, and health, the growth of government at all levels also has given rise to new kinds of issues.

In the decades since the New Deal, government at all levels has grown not only much larger but much more complex. The press, attempting to keep pace, has developed new approaches to news interpretations and new techniques of investigative reporting. Yet, even their larger and more specialized staffs cannot cover thoroughly all the government agencies. Not only have the agencies proliferated, but many of their policies and programs have become overlapping and conflicting and the complexities have given rise to new issues concerning the efficiency and effectiveness of government.

For example, more than a dozen agencies, bureaus, offices, and departments have been created over the years to administer federal transportation policies and programs. Each policy and program was adopted by Congress to improve some aspect of land, air, or water transportation. Not long after John Kennedy became President, however, he told Congress that federal transportation policies amounted to "a chaotic patchwork of inconsistent and often obsolete regulation evolved from a history of specific actions addressed to specific problems at specific times."[5]

The proliferation of costly programs such as these has led to widespread questioning of the efficiency and effectiveness of government itself. Jimmy Carter, for instance, campaigned in 1976 against what he called the "bloated mess" in Washington.[6] As President, he devoted much of his attention to government reorganization.

Press coverage of Washington tends to be concentrated on the White House and Congress, where policies are made and programs are set forth in broad outline in terms of goals and objectives. However, more consistent and thorough coverage is needed of the agencies, bureaus, offices, and departments that are charged with carrying out the policies and programs. Without a knowledge of the labyrinth of economic policies and programs and of the bureaucracy that administers them, the press is ill prepared to report the many reorganization and reform plans that have been put forward to restore public confidence in government.

THE LABYRINTH OF ECONOMIC POLICIES

A journalist who aspires to an understanding of the federal government might well start with the *United States Government Organization Manual,* a book that is revised annually by the National Archives and published by the Government Printing Office. This "official handbook" of the federal government contains the United States Constitution, describes the three branches of the federal government, and lists all the departments, bureaus, and agencies of government. It contains brief descriptions of the purposes, policies, and programs of each department, bureau, and agency along with an organizational chart for each.

The official manual is of limited use to any student of government, however. It describes the policy purposes for which departments, bureaus, and agencies were created, but contains no hint of the overlapping policies and conflicting programs that President Kennedy characterized as a "chaotic patchwork." The doubts that President Kennedy raised concerning the fulfillment of policy purposes have been repeated many times over. President Carter's Council of Economic Advisers, for instance, commented in 1977 that "Government regulates a substantial part of the economy in an effort to improve economic performance and promote individual welfare. Such regulation has created costs as well as benefits, and some anticipated benefits of regulation have never been realized."[7]

The official manual for 1979–1980 listed 12 departments and 58 agencies, commissions, and boards outside of the Executive Branch departments, but confusion persists even within government concerning the numbers. The confusion stems from the fact that there are bureaus within agencies and agencies within departments. A White House task force established by President Ford identified 86 federal regulatory agencies with economic and social goals.[8] President Carter, without reference to a total number of agencies, once asserted that their number "should be reduced to no more than 200."[9]

Standard political science and economics textbooks also are of limited usefulness insofar as they describe government policy goals without analyzing actual results. Journalists who are concerned with inflation and other economic and business issues, however, should understand the results as well as the goals of government policies.

Basic Economic Policy

The most fundamental economic policy of government in the United States is the policy that embraces economic freedom and competition. The role of the free market, described earlier in this book, dates back to the nation's beginning, and in the two centuries since then government has not often been a provider of goods and services. Although the federal government has operated the Postal Service and the Tennessee Valley Authority, and some state and municipal governments own electric, gas, and water utilities, most goods and services have been provided by private business and labor.

Government policy did not explicitly embrace competitive private enterprise as a national goal until economic freedom seemed to be threatened by private monopolies that grew out of the industrial revolution of nearly a century ago.

Congress in 1890 passed the first federal antitrust law, the Sherman Act, and in the years since, Congress has enacted several additional antitrust laws and many states have passed similar laws. The Sherman Act, which resembles constitutional law in its sweep, bars "every contract, combination in the form of trust or otherwise, or conspiracy, in restraint of trade" and prescribes criminal penalties for "every person who shall monopolize or attempt to monopolize, or combine or conspire with any other person or persons, to monopolize." The late Justice Hugo Black wrote a Supreme Court opinion containing this classic definition of antitrust policy:

> The Sherman Act was designed to be a comprehensive charter of economic liberty aimed at preserving free and unfettered competition as the rule of trade. It rests on the premise that the unrestrained interaction of competitive forces will yield the best allocation of our economic resources, the lowest prices, the highest quality, and the greatest material progress, while at the same time providing an environment conducive to the preservation of our democratic political and social institutions.[10]

Congress in 1914 passed two more antitrust laws, the Clayton Act, which among other things bars corporate mergers that "may substantially lessen competition or tend to create a monopoly," and the Federal Trade Commission Act, which bars "unfair methods of competition." Since 1914 Congress has amended the federal antitrust laws and the states have enacted many similar laws, but the Sherman Act has remained unchanged as a statement of basic and fundamental national economic policy.

The Sherman Act is enforced by the Antitrust Division of the Department of Justice through civil or criminal actions filed initially in federal district courts. The Justice Department and Federal Trade Commission have authority to bring Clayton Act cases. The FTC administers the Clayton Act and FTC Act by bringing and then deciding complaints. All FTC decisions can be appealed directly to United States Courts of Appeal and then to the Supreme Court. Antitrust cases brought by the department and commission are announced in press releases, and antitrust trials, those both in the courts or before the FTC, are open to the press.

Large antitrust cases are major news stories, but the case-by-case development of antitrust policy has not received the press attention it deserves. One reason the press has not paid more attention probably is that antitrust cases are complex; also, big antitrust trials go on for months and even years.

A larger reason, however, may well be that antitrust law is an imperfect statement of national economic policy mirroring the imperfections of the free enterprise system itself. While Congress has not altered the basic goals of the Sherman Act since 1890, Congress has passed many other laws creating exemptions from the antitrust laws and the courts have fashioned additional loopholes. The exemptions, which apply to many activities of agriculture, labor, and some kinds of businesses such as transportation and communications, have been created piecemeal by Congress and the courts in the belief that economic freedom and competition are not the best way to achieve specific economic or social goals such as stability in farm prices or in labor-management relations.

While there has been general agreement in theory on the goals of antitrust policy as set forth by Justice Black, there has been sharp disagreement whether the enforcement of antitrust laws in fact has furthered many of those goals even among businesses and industries that do not have antitrust exemptions.

Antitrust policies and theories have come a long way since the Sherman Act was passed in 1890. Antitrust enforcement originally was focused on price-fixing achieved either when a single company gained monopoly control of an industry or when groups of companies conspired in smoke-filled rooms to fix prices. Those kinds of practices were held to be violations of the Sherman Act, and most businessmen, economists, and lawyers agree that price-fixing is unfair not only to consumers but to other business people.

In one of the most famous antitrust cases brought by the Justice Department, the Supreme Court in 1911 ordered the breakup of the old Standard Oil monopoly. Other monopolies, then called trusts, also were broken up. As a result, there are no overt monopolies in the United States, except for utilities that are regulated by government. Price-fixing conspiracies have not disappeared and have continued to be prosecuted. For example, the

FTC in the late 1960's uncovered a conspiracy to fix prices of the drug tetracycline and thereafter the price of the antibiotic drug fell from $30.60 to $4.25 per 100 capsules.

As antitrust enforcers in recent years have developed new policies and theories, however, sharp disagreement concerning their economic consequences has risen among economists, lawyers, and businessmen. The *shared monopoly* theory, for example, holds that, even though no company has a monopoly in any major national industry, groups of companies without conspiring can share monopoly-like power. Some cases of corporate mergers also have become highly controversial. Mergers have been defended on the ground that large corporations can achieve the economies of scale that result in lower prices and other benefits to consumers. However, they have been attacked on the ground that a reduction in the number of competitors means less competition and thus possibly higher prices.

Antitrust doctrines and theories have been questioned in recent years in both conservative and liberal quarters. Old questions have been put forward with new force by conservative businessmen and economists, and some liberals have raised new questions.

The conservative view has been reported by *Business Week* in an article titled "Is John Sherman's Antitrust Obsolete?" It began:

> The head of the major U.S. corporation spoke feelingly: "I would be very glad if we knew exactly where we stand, if we could be free from danger, trouble and criticism." His plea could have been made yesterday, by executives of IBM, Xerox, GTE, General Motors, AT&T, Exxon, Standard Brands, Chrysler, or dozens of other large companies that have recently stood in the dock, accused of violating the nation's antitrust laws.
>
> It was, in fact, said back in 1912 by Elbert H. Gary, chairman of U.S. Steel Corp. He was giving a congressional committee his views on the need for updating the country's first antitrust law, the Sherman Act, to which Ohio Senator John Sherman gave his name in 1890. Echoing the sentiments of many executives, Gary complained bitterly of the restraints imposed by the antitrust law on his company's ability to compete in world markets. Business had grown too big and complex, Gary maintained, to be shoehorned into laws drawn from Adam Smith's economic model of many small companies competing in local markets.[11]

Whereas conservatives have taken the position that business should be free of government intervention, some liberals who have come to the conclusion that antitrust is obsolete see antitrust and competition as obstacles to government economic planning and to federal regulation of business.

For instance, liberal economist John Kenneth Galbraith has written that antitrust law is a "charade" and an "anachronism in the larger world of industrial planning."[12] Economist Galbraith also has stated his belief that the free enterprise system as well as the antitrust laws are outmoded in the "new industrial state."[13]

It is not the job of the press to resolve complex and controversial issues such as those that have surrounded basic economic policy and the antitrust laws. The role of the press under the First Amendment is to report and interpret the debate as intelligently and fully as possible. That debate over basic economic policy may well be critical to the future of economic freedom and, in Justice Black's words, "to the preservation of our democratic political and social institutions."

Fiscal and Monetary Policies

Beginning with the Sherman Act, all government economic policies impinge in one way or another on the functioning of the free market. Antitrust, however, impinges differently than all the others. Antitrust law, at least as traditionally enforced, impinged for the purpose of preserving and strengthening the free market system. Whether that purpose has been served may be debatable, but antitrust law, like criminal statutes against drunken driving and murder, impinges on the freedom of a violator for the purpose of preserving the safety and freedom of society as a whole.

Other government economic policies impinge on the free market because Congress or the courts have concluded that competition does not serve desired economic and social goals. Other chapters have discussed fiscal and monetary policies as they relate to the issues of inflation and employment. But aspiring journalists also should have an understanding of fiscal and monetary policies in the context of other major government economic policies.

Although Adam Smith presumably would have approved of the Sherman Act, at least in principle, economist John Maynard Keynes was the father of the economic theory holding that government policies, used to stimulate private economic activity, were necessary to supplement the free enterprise system as the regulator of national economic life. The Keynes philosophy came into its own during the New Deal era, when economic depression and unemployment plagued the nation. The fiscal and monetary policies he advocated were formally written into law when Congress passed the Employment Act of 1946. With that act, government in theory assumed responsibility for "maximum employment, production, and purchasing power." The policy declaration in the act states:

> The Congress hereby declares that it is the continuing policy and responsibility of the Federal Government to use all practicable means consistent with its needs and obligations and other essential considera-

tions of national policy, with the assistance of industry, agriculture, labor, and state and local governments, to coordinate and utilize all its plans, functions, and resources for the purpose of creating and maintaining, in a manner calculated to foster and promote free competitive enterprise and the general welfare, conditions under which there will be afforded useful employment opportunities for those able, willing and seeking to work, and to promote maximum employment, production and purchasing power.

The Employment Act, hedged with many conditions, was perhaps more a statement of philosophy and hope than of policy and reality. The efforts of the government to manipulate federal taxes and expenditures, budget deficits or surpluses, and money supply and interest rates have not achieved the goal of economic stability set forth in the 1946 Employment Act. As we have seen, unemployment has remained a problem and inflation has emerged as a vast new problem.

The Employment Act nonetheless has remained on the books. It created government institutions that have become important to economic policy and to economic and business journalists.

The act created two institutions to assist the President and Congress in their deliberations on the government responsibilities set forth in the act. The Council of Economic Advisers, consisting of three members, was created as a part of the White House staff to collect and analyze economic data and make policy recommendations to the President. The Joint Economic Committee, made up of seven Senate and seven House members, was set up to make continuing studies and analyses of economic trends and legislative issues. The act required the President to report to Congress annually on the state of the nation's economy, and the submission of his report, along with the annual report of the Council of Economic Advisers to the President, is a major Washington news event each January. The reports also have continuing value to journalists as sources of national economic data and for their analyses of inflation, employment, and other economic trends. The Joint Economic Committee's studies and hearings also are sources of news and of interpretive stories.

Regulation of Business

The 1946 Employment Act was a legislative landmark in the relationship of government to the private enterprise system. However, federal and state governments before and after passage of the Employment Act often impinged on the free market to try to achieve specific economic or social goals that legislators felt were not met by free market competition.

Government regulation and promotion of private business, labor, and agriculture have been pursued generally under Section 8 of the United States

Constitution, which empowered Congress to regulate interstate and foreign commerce, and under similar provisions of state constitutions relative to intrastate commerce. Regulation began early in American history when the states regulated the prices that gristmills and cotton gins charged farmers and the rates that ferry boats and bridge companies charged townfolk.[14] The federal government began to promote private commerce as early as 1806, when Congress authorized construction of the Cumberland Road, the first interstate highway. Between about 1850 and 1870 the federal government promoted private railway construction with land grants of some 130 million acres of public lands and in 1887 Congress created the Interstate Commerce Commission to regulate railroad passenger fares and freight rates.[15]

From those beginnings, federal and state regulatory policies and agencies proliferated and grew into large bureaucracies with profound economic consequences. In many respects, such governmental regulation of private business, labor, and agriculture has affected the lives and pocketbooks of Americans more directly than many laws. Yet, the press in general has covered regulatory policies and agencies with less thoroughness and less enthusiasm than it has covered other aspects of government.

Most states regulate the intrastate rates and services of telephone companies, electric and natural gas distributors, and other privately owned public utilities. States regulate banks, insurance companies, and stock brokers. Many states and cities also regulate the professions and trades through licensing procedures and price regulations, not only of doctors and lawyers but in some states of real estate brokers, barbers, and even bartenders, television repairmen, midwives, pest controllers, and well diggers. Connecticut has licensed hypertrichologists, who remove excess hair, and Hawaii has licensed tattoo artists. Some cities regulate consumer services ranging from taxicabs to massage parlors.

While state and local regulation of professions and trades often begins with the purpose of protecting consumers from unsafe, unprofessional, and unethical practices, virtually all such regulation has economic consequences resulting from governmental control of prices or rates and from restrictions on entry into a profession or trade.[16]

Essentially those same kinds of economic consequences flow, but in a much larger stream, from federal regulation of interstate commerce. Since the beginnings of railroads and of industrialization in the last century, Congress from time to time has addressed economic and social issues by creating new agencies empowered to regulate private commerce. In delegating its power, Congress typically has given the agencies sweeping mandates containing statements of broad social and economic goals and, instead of itself legislating the precise methodology for reaching those goals, Congress has delegated to the agencies the authority to write rules that have the force of law.

In general, Congress has made its broadest delegations of authority to regulatory agencies headed by multimember commissions and boards, usually of five or seven members; these are independent of the Executive Branch in that their rules and decisions are not subject to review or veto by the President. Somewhat less broad delegations often have been made to regulatory agencies that are headed by a single commissioner or administrator and are housed within an Executive Branch department but that still operate independently of the White House. All such commissioners and administrators are by statute nominated by the President and confirmed by the Senate to serve for statutory terms, usually of four to seven years, although Federal Reserve Board terms have been fixed at 14 years.

Some federal regulatory agencies control entry into transportation, communications, and certain other private industries through licensing procedures and control the rates or prices as well. Some agencies also may control mergers of companies within their industries. Other agencies regulate safety in the delivery of public services or products and still others regulate workplace and environmental safety and health. Some regulatory agencies also make grants of federal monies or award subsidies to regulated businesses and have other promotional responsibilities.

As agencies thus proliferated, many regulatory policies came into conflict with basic economic policy embodied in the antitrust laws and thus gave rise to many of the antitrust exemptions granted by Congress and to the loopholes created by the courts. Congress did not attempt to rationalize regulatory law as a whole with antitrust law nor did it try to coordinate regulatory policies with the economic goals of full employment, production, and purchasing power set forth in the 1946 Employment Act.

The confusion and apparent disagreement between Presidents Ford and Carter over the total number of federal agencies underscored the difficulty of attempting to enumerate them. However, an inquisitive reporter will be able to find the major agencies that have their headquarters in Washington. Many also have regional offices in other large cities.

Major independent federal agencies with significant economic policy functions include the following:

- The Interstate Commerce Commission, the oldest independent agency, has regulated railroad, trucking, and other domestic surface transportation industries.
- The Federal Reserve Board, created in 1913, regulates banks that are members of the Federal Reserve System. The board in addition has primary responsibility for administration of monetary policy.

- The Federal Trade Commission, established in 1914, regulates advertising and other trade practices in addition to its responsibility for enforcing antitrust laws other than the Sherman Act.
- The Federal Communications Commission, set up in 1934, regulates television and radio broadcasting and interstate telephone service.
- The Securities and Exchange Commission, created in 1934 regulates corporate securities issues and public trading in securities.
- The Federal Maritime Commission, set up in 1936, regulates rates and practices of shipping companies in U.S. foreign commerce.
- The Nuclear Regulatory Commission, successor of the Atomic Energy Commission established in 1946, regulates nuclear electric power generation and other civilian applications of nuclear energy.
- The Equal Employment Opportunity Commission, created in 1964, regulates employment practices relating to race and sex discrimination.
- The Environmental Protection Agency, set up in 1970, regulates industrial and other discharges of pollutants into the environment.
- The Consumer Product Safety Commission, established in 1972, regulates the safety of and sets standards for consumer products.
- The Commodity Futures Trading Commission, created in 1972, regulates futures contracts and the brokers, dealers, and exchanges trading them.

Major regulatory agencies and offices within the departments of the Executive Branch include:

- The Office of Comptroller of the Currency (Treasury Department), established in 1863, regulates and licenses national banks.
- National Bureau of Standards (Commerce Department), dating from 1901, establishes standards for building and other materials.
- The Food and Drug Administration (Health, Education and Welfare Department), created in 1931, regulates food and drug purity and safety.
- The Federal Maritime Administration (Commerce Department), created in 1936, administers shipbuilding and ocean shipping subsidy programs.
- The Occupational Safety and Health Administration (Labor Department), established in 1970, regulates practices, in places of business, that affect workers' safety and health.
- The Federal Energy Regulatory Commission (Energy Department), successor to the Federal Power Commission created in 1930 and renamed in 1977, regulates interstate sales of electricity and natural gas.

A more complete list of federal regulatory functions, exercised independently of presidential authority or within Executive Branch departments, would include a number of additional agencies, boards, and offices.[17] Additional independent agencies include the Federal Deposit Insurance Corporation, Federal Home Loan Bank Board, and Farm Credit Administration. Agencies within departments include the Patent Office in the Commerce Department, the Coast Guard in the Transportation Department, and the Mining Enforcement and Safety Administration in the Interior Department, for example. There are offices within both the Labor and Treasury Departments that regulate private pension plans under the Employees Retirement Income Security Act, a significant regulatory law enacted in 1974.

Regulation of Agriculture

Federal regulatory and promotional policies relative to labor and agriculture in many ways are even more pervasive and comprehensive than those regulating private business.

The enormous consequences of federal labor policies and laws have been discussed in detail in other chapters of this book. As we have seen, federal labor law evolved in part out of the legal and indeed physical conflict between organized labor and the antitrust laws. When the courts many years ago held union activities to be conspiracies in violation of the Sherman Act, Congress granted labor very large and almost complete exemption from the antitrust laws. Within the federal government, the Department of Labor in many respects is a consummate regulatory and promotional agency. The other major federal agency with labor policy responsibility is the National Labor Relations Board, an independent agency created in 1935 to conduct union representation elections among industry workers and to regulate unfair labor practices of employers and unions.

The Department of Agriculture also is a consummate regulatory and promotional agency that administers federal farm policies with enormous effects on the quantity and quality of the nation's food supply and prices. Federal farm policy also has encountered many conflicts with antitrust policy, and Congress and the courts generally have resolved those conflicts by granting antitrust exemptions to farmers and farm groups.

The Agriculture Department was established by act of Congress in 1862 to help farmers improve their economic lot and to protect farm income from the vicissitudes of weather and of pure competition. The Department's mission thus has grown more or less steadily for longer than a century and in fiscal 1979 its spending amounted to more than $20 billion.

The government's initial efforts to raise the incomes of American farmers consisted in part of higher tariffs on corn, wheat, wool, sugar, meat, and other imported agricultural products. In 1916 Congress passed the

Federal Farm Loan Act, which marked the beginning of a program of farm credit aid that became increasingly elaborate as time passed. In 1933 Congress passed the Agricultural Adjustment Act under which government controlled the amount of acreage planted in specific farm crops and subsidized farmers for acreage taken out of production. The Supreme Court threw out the 1933 act as an unconstitutional exercise by Congress of its spending and regulatory authority, but Congress then passed the Agricultural Marketing Agreement Act of 1937 and the Supreme Court sustained that effort by Congress to fix minimum prices for agricultural products.

Farm income rose in the decades after the New Deal, and Congress amended federal farm policy in various ways, but farm income stabilization has remained a primary mission of the Department of Agriculture. Federal programs to support prices received by producers of major crops are administered by the Commodity Credit Corporation, a unit of the Agriculture Department. The department's Agricultural Marketing Service, established in 1937, sets farm product grades and standards, inspects egg production, and determines minimum milk prices in certain areas. Among other things, the department provides farmers with insurance against crop losses, oversees the operation of huge farm product marketing cooperatives, engages in various research and education programs, and guards against plant and animal pests and diseases that could result in severe losses in farm yields.

Federal farm policies for many years have been of interest to newspapers and broadcast stations in farming areas, but in recent years they have drawn the interest of many more economists and journalists as farm incomes have improved and consumer food prices have risen. The relationships between federal agricultural policies and retail food prices have been disputed and debated, but public and press interest in the relationships undoubtedly will continue to grow as inflation persists.

FINDING WAYS THROUGH THE LABYRINTH

Throughout the maze of federal agencies and departments that administer economic policies and in their counterparts at the state and local levels of government, reporters will find small armies of public information and public relations officers. The best of them can help aspiring journalists in making their way through the labyrinth; the worst can block press access to policy-making commissioners and administrators.

While the agencies and departments are responsible for administration of their particular policies and programs, additional sources of news and information are available to reporters who want to dig for stories about particular policies and programs or about overall government regulation and spending.

Federal, State, and Local Government Budgets

Governmental budgets are good places for journalists to begin to acquire an understanding of the operation of economic and social policies and programs. That advice applies to reporting at the local, state, and national levels, as demonstrated by this lead from a *Wall Street Journal* article:

> Red Ink is splattered up and down and across the government's budget —right?
>
> Maybe right.
>
> It depends on which of our many governments you're talking about.
>
> Yes—if you mean the federal government. Its budget is perennially mired in ocean-deep deficit: $50 billion, give or take a bit, has been the recent rule.
>
> But no way—if you mean the 80,000-odd other governments that dot the nation: state governments, city and town governments, county governments, school-district governments, and on and on.[18]

Federal, state, and local budgets are statements of receipts from taxes and other sources and of expenditures of those receipts. Governmental budgets thus resemble corporate statements of income and expenditures, but there are some noteworthy differences beyond the fact that governments do not earn profits and frequently report deficits rather than surpluses.

One significant difference is that large corporations annually report to their stockholders and to the public the actual results of their operations in terms of profits or losses, while governmental budgets typically are annual forecasts of expected revenues, expenditures, and resulting surpluses or deficits. The federal budget that the President submits to Congress each January, at about the time he submits the economic report required by the 1946 Employment Act, is a projection of anticipated revenue and a proposal concerning the allocation of revenues and other resources to be spent by the individual departments, agencies, and other units of the federal government. While the Washington press corps traditionally has given intensive press coverage to the annual Presidential budget message, it has seldom paid much attention to the actual results of fiscal year operations of the federal government.

A second difference between corporate and government budgets is that, while corporate financial statements are designed to disclose all items of income and expense, governmental budgets do not reflect costs that are required by government regulations but are paid by business and consumers. Federal budgets reflect direct operating costs paid by taxpayers or government borrowing. They do not reflect expenditures that are required by government environmental and other economic and social regulations but that are paid for by private business in the form of lower profits or higher prices passed on to consumers.

Governmental budgets nonetheless are useful documents as starting points in understanding government spending priorities and trends among individual policies and programs. In addition, the federal budget is useful to reporters who want to know more about overall government fiscal policy and its effects on employment and inflation. Moreover, Congress and the White House in recent years have become more concerned with the actual results of fiscal operations and with costs that government regulation imposes on private business consumers.

The President's annual budget message is prepared and distributed to the press by the White House Office of Management and Budget. The annual Budget of the United States Government is a book, about 500 pages long in recent years, in which the President discusses his spending priority proposals and his estimate of the effects of total federal spending on the nation's economy. A telephone book-size appendix to the annual budget, detailing spending proposals for individual departments and agencies, also is available to the press.

The Congressional Budget Office is a useful source of news and information. The office, created by the Congressional Budget Act of 1974, was part of an attempt by Congress to relate actual federal spending to inflation, employment, taxes, and private economic activity. Journalists will find the office useful also as a source of policy studies on a wide range of economic and social issues including national health insurance, the federal role in education, government energy research, federal promotion of home ownership, and defense manpower costs.[19]

Bureaucracy and Its Paraphernalia

There are textbooks aplenty to familiarize students with the constitutional process by which Congress makes laws. Journalists who want to cover government economic policy and its administration will discover, however, that the making of law by appointed rather than elected officials is quite different.

Agencies that are independent or are housed within departments are mixtures of executive, legislative, and judicial functions blending some of the paraphernalia of all three constitutional branches. The presidentially appointed commissioners or administrators fix policy objectives and the agencies exercise other executive-like powers such as the award of subsidies. Under delegation from Congress, the agencies make law either through a legislative-like process known as rule-making or a court-like process of deciding issues on a case-by-case basis.

In making rules, the commissioners or administrators, usually on the advice of their staffs, first issue proposed rules. Such proposals must be published for public comment in the *Federal Register,* a compendium that is published daily and has grown larger than the Congressional Record of Congress's own proceedings. The agencies also may hold public hearings on proposed rules. After the comments are in, the agencies publish final rules that are applicable to entire business, labor, or agriculture groups. Rules generally are enforced through the courts.

In deciding issues case by case, the commissioners or administrators may act on their own initiative or on the basis of an application or complaint filed by an outside party. The case initially is heard by a staff official known as an administrative law judge and finally is decided by the commissioners or administrators themselves. The final decision, which applies directly only to the company or individual named in the application or complaint, can be appealed to a United States Court of Appeals and then to the Supreme Court.

CRITICISMS OF GOVERNMENT REGULATION

Government regulation of private business, labor, and agriculture has attracted political and legal controversy almost since the beginning of large-scale federal regulation nearly a century ago, and in more recent years regulation also has stirred intense controversy among economists.

The late Justice Robert H. Jackson, a New Dealer who served in high Justice Department positions before President Roosevelt appointed him to the Supreme Court, wrote in a court opinion in 1952 that the rise of regulatory agencies was "probably the most significant legal trend of the last century" and he added that attempts to rationalize the agencies with the constitutional separation of executive, legislative, and judicial powers was "a smooth cover which we draw over our confusion as we might use a counterpane to conceal a disordered bed."[20]

Delays, Scandals, and Costs

Congress often created regulatory agencies in the hope that regulators would become experts who could achieve policy goals more quickly, efficiently, or effectively than the same results could be achieved by the free market and competition. However, that belief came into serious question as regulatory agencies multiplied and their procedures became more complex.

There are many examples of the tortoise pace of regulation. The Interstate Commerce Commission, for example, consumed ten years in approving the merger of the Rock Island Railroad into the Union Pacific Railroad and, by the time the case was concluded in 1974, the ICC itself commented that "Unfortunately, Rock Island's financial condition can only be described as critical." The Federal Trade Commission once upon a time devoted 16 years to a case against Carter's Little Liver Pills.

Regulatory delays and inefficiencies often have been blamed on unqualified regulators. A 1976 Senate study concluded that "For generations, neither the White House nor the Senate sought or insisted upon the appointment of regulators from among the first ranks of our nation's leaders."[21] Many regulators are appointed who are unqualified, except in terms of political influence sufficient to command well-paying government jobs; furthermore, regulatory agency employees often leave government to take higher paying jobs with regulated industries or unions or with Washington law firms representing regulated entities. During the 1976 Presidential campaign, when Jimmy Carter inveighed against the "bloated mess" in Washington, he criticized the "sweetheart arrangement" between government agencies and the industries they regulate.[22]

The Washington press corps routinely has recorded the criticisms of regulation that from time to time have been sounded by the White House, Congress, and the Supreme Court. With some notable exceptions, however, investigative reporters have not dug deeply into the faults and foibles of government regulation, except occasionally when regulators have become involved in political scandal. Given the huge amounts of money that hang on many agency decisions, it is hardly surprising that almost every major Washington scandal in recent decades has involved improper pressures of regulatory agencies.[23] Regulatory agencies were involved to one degree or another in scandals ranging from the Sherman Adams affair that embarrassed the Eisenhower Administration to the Watergate affair that toppled the Nixon Administration.

Such scandals have been covered massively by the media, but knowledgeable and probing reporters independently have dug up newsworthy stories about regulators. For example, a *Wall Street Journal* article, headed "Agencies and Industries Show Persistent Signs of Cozy Relationships," reported:

> Washington—Early this summer, Helen Delich Bentley, chairman of the Federal Maritime Commission, thought seriously about running for the U.S. Senate in Maryland. For political help, her campaign aides freely turned to what seemed like a natural source: the shipping industry that her commission regulates.
>
> Mrs. Bentley's campaign staff dispatched letters seeking support and campaign assistance from industry lawyers who practice before her agency. Although she didn't ask directly for money, that aim was implicit—and criticism arose. In the end, Mrs. Bentley decided against running.[24]

Government regulation in more recent years has come under intense criticism also for its costs and their contribution to inflation. The criticism began in about 1970, when economists at the Brookings Institution in

Washington and at a number of universities across the country attempted to identify the costs of airline and trucking regulation that have never shown up in the federal budget but that have been imposed on business and ultimately on consumers.

As the inflation rate rose, the costs of airline, trucking, environmental, and other forms of regulation were examined also by economists inside government. The White House Council of Economic Advisers, for instance, commented in 1977 that "regulation has created costs as well as benefits, and some anticipated benefits of regulation have never been realized." Economists at the White House Council on Wage and Price Stability and in the Antitrust Division of the Justice Department also began to identify and criticize the costs of proposed new environmental, safety, and health regulations.

The off-budget costs of regulation were not easily identified and controversy grew also because regulatory agencies found it difficult to defend themselves by quantifying the benefits of regulation. Despite disagreement over the precise costs that government regulation has imposed on private business and consumers, however, the total appeared to be enormous. President Ford once estimated "the combined cost to consumers of government regulation and restrictive practices in the private sector . . . at something in the order of $2,000 per family" per year.[25] Several private studies have estimated the total cost of government regulation in 1977 at more than $100 billion.[26]

Policy Conflicts

The faults, foibles, and costs of government regulation cannot be blamed wholly on the ineptitude and inefficiency of government regulators. Many have been political hacks, but some have been intelligent men and women. An additional consideration are policy conflicts over which the regulators themselves have had little or no control. Admittedly, the uncovering of policy conflicts takes deep digging because the conflicts are buried in many laws passed years ago. Moreover, with the exception of President Kennedy, presidents and Congresses have not been eager to admit the existence of deep conflicts in government economic policies.

President Kennedy referred to one of the more striking policy conflicts when he talked about the chaotic patchwork of transportation policies. Congress years ago set forth a national transportation policy when it directed the Interstate Commerce Commission to

> provide for fair and impartial regulation of all modes of transportation, so administered as to recognize and preserve the inherent advantages of each; to promote safe, adequate, economical, and efficient service and foster sound economic conditions in transportation; to encourage the

establishment and maintenance of reasonable charges for transportation services; and to encourage fair wages and equitable working conditions—all to the end of developing, coordinating, and preserving a national transportation system by water, highway, and rail, as well as other means.

The failure of the ICC to "foster sound economic conditions in transportation" and the subsequent heavy cost to taxpayers would seem evidenced by the bankruptcies in the early 1970's of the Penn Central and more than a half dozen other railroads. Congress responded to the bankruptcies in 1976 by creating Consolidated Rail Corporation (Conrail) and providing it initially with $2 billion of federal loans and guarantees. The earlier decline of railroad passenger service had prompted Congress to create in 1971 the National Railroad Passenger Corporation (Amtrak), and federal subsidies paid to Amtrak through 1977 amounted to more than $3 billion. Conrail and Amtrak, to the extent that they have been unable to pay their own way, represent a tax-supported semi-nationalization of railroad service as an unplanned and undesired alternative to government regulation of privately owned railroads.

The railroad bankruptcies of the early 1970's arguably can be blamed to some degree on the ICC, inasmuch as the commission earlier had approved the merger of the old Pennsylvania and New York Central Railroads to form Penn Central. However, the ICC surely was not wholly to blame for the decline of rail passenger service or the railroad bankruptcies.

In the years after Congress in 1887 created the ICC to regulate the railroads' transportation monopoly, new transportation technologies produced new competition from airplanes, trucks, buses, and private autos. Without recognizing that the railroad transportation monopoly no longer existed, Congress developed new policies for the new technologies. These policies consisted largely of promotional programs under which tens of billions of dollars of federal tax monies were spent to construct interstate highways, to subsidize airlines, and to improve commercially navigable waterways. Federally subsidized competition thus contributed greatly to the decline of rail passenger service, to railroad bankruptcies, and finally to the semi-nationalization of large segments of the once private railroad industry.

Another and large policy conflict exists between laws that regulate business, labor, and agriculture, on one hand, and the antitrust laws on the other. Regulation limits or tends to inhibit competition whereas antitrust seeks to enforce competition. As we have seen, Congress and the courts have attempted to resolve some of these conflicts by creating antitrust exemptions and loopholes. But the conflicts have been resolved piecemeal and in an intense political atmosphere. Congress frequently enacted antitrust exemptions only after a conflict became real in the sense of a successful Justice Department prosecution of a regulated industry practice.

For instance, the Justice Department in the 1940's successfully prosecuted as a Sherman Act violation the railroad industry practice of fixing rates in conferences of railroad executives. The long-standing practice apparently had the tacit approval of the ICC. The railroad and trucking industries then went to Congress demanding an antitrust exemption. Congress passed the exemption, known as the Reed-Bulwinkle Act, in 1948. President Truman angrily vetoed the act and Congress overrode his veto.

Other major antitrust exemptions, all enacted in the midst of intense political pressure and controversy, include the Capper-Volstead Act of 1922, which exempted from antitrust prosecution farmer cooperatives that market agricultural products. The Norris-LaGuardia Act of 1932 conferred almost complete antitrust immunity on organized labor. The McCarran-Ferguson Act of 1945 granted antitrust exemption to insurance rate-fixing activities that were subject to state regulation.

Efforts to Reform Regulation

Criticisms of government regulation for many years have been accompanied by plans to reform individual agencies and the whole regulatory process. One of the earliest reform efforts came not long after the Interstate Commerce Commission was created. President Theodore Roosevelt in 1905 appointed a study group to "improve methods . . . to avoid conflict and duplication" in regulation.[27]

The reform attempts continued through subsequent presidential administrations and eventually resulted in enactment of the Administrative Procedures Act in 1946. That law, dealing only with the procedures of regulation and not with its policy substance, was intended to make regulatory agency procedures more uniform and fair, but it also had the effect of making the agencies slower and more bureaucratic. The reform efforts thus continued through the first and second Hoover Commissions, appointed respectively by Presidents Truman and Eisenhower, and continued still through President Carter's attempt in 1978 to address what he called "duplicative or overlapping regulations."[28]

The reform attempts were not without some effect. For example, Congress in 1976 passed the Government in the Sunshine Act, which, with certain exceptions, required multimember regulatory commissions and boards to open their meetings to the press and public and to maintain transcripts of their meetings for public review.

However, the failure of repeated attempts to reform the regulatory process also combined with inflation to give rise to a new deregulation movement. The political as well as economic necessity of curbing inflation led both Presidents Ford and Carter to appoint to some regulatory agencies men and women who as economists were known to feel strongly that government regulation was both inefficient and inflationary. The White House also proposed to Congress that government regulation of some industries, such as airlines and trucking, be rolled back. Alert reporters found that those proposals of Presidents Ford and Carter met with some unexpected reactions. As *The New York Times* in 1976 reported:

> Washington—President Ford has been winning a multitude of cheers from business audiences across the United States during the last few months by criticizing Federal bureaucrats and what he has characterized as their sometimes silly and wasteful ways.
>
> Some of the cheers have turned to boos, however, as the President has moved from the generalities of campaign rhetoric to specific recommendations on how the Administration would like to attack the allegedly wasteful shortcomings of Federal regulation.
>
> The airline and trucking industries, for example, have both expressed vehement opposition to the Administration's proposals aimed at lowering the regulatory fences that many experts argue have protected the airlines and truckers from the rigors of price competition.[29]

Despite the opposition, Congress at President Carter's urging in 1978 passed the Airline Deregulation Act providing for a rollback in airline regulation and for abolition of the Civil Aeronautics Board in 1985. As competition increased, consumers enjoyed lower air fares and, because the discount fares attracted many more passengers, the airlines enjoyed higher profits.

The Airline Deregulation Act was a milestone after many decades of federal regulatory agency growth. No one can predict how far the deregulation movement will go in years ahead, but the deregulation story may be one of the most significant economic and political developments to be reported by the Washington press corps. Similar deregulation movements have begun in many state capitols.

The deregulation movement, which leans in the direction of substituting free market competition for government regulation, could resolve the most fundamental conflict in government economic policies.

WAGE AND PRICE REGULATION

Government economic policies, as we have seen, never have been consistent with one another nor with the basic economic policy embodied in the antitrust laws. Yet, a new and larger inconsistency in economic policy developed in the 1970's with the emergence of inflation as an overriding national economic problem.

In part, inflation inspired the attacks that were made by the Ford and Carter Administrations on many of the existing forms of economic and social regulation, and inflation was largely responsible for the 1978 enactment by Congress of airline deregulation legislation. Yet, inflation at the same time inspired a new kind of government regulation of private wages and prices.

Summary federal efforts to control wages and prices as well as rents during World War II and the Korean conflict had met with uneven success, but those controls were removed after wartime government demand no longer inflated the nation's economy.

Peacetime inflation was a new phenomenon that began to appear in the 1950's and that concerned President Eisenhower. As the inflation rate continued to rise slowly, Presidents Kennedy and Johnson took informal actions in an attempt to curb price and wage increases. They set up "guideposts" that large companies and unions were supposed to observe by keeping price and wage increases within certain percentages. They invented "jawboning," the White House technique of calling in particular companies and unions to persuade them to obey the guideposts.

Informal White House intervention in wages and prices did not halt inflation, however. From 1950 to 1970 the Consumer Price Index consistently registered year-to-year increases (with the sole exception of 1954, when prices declined from 1953 levels). In 1959, when President Eisenhower spoke of making "price stability an explicit goal of federal economic policy," prices were rising at an annual rate of under 3 percent.[30] By 1970 the annual inflation rate was nearly 6 percent and in 1971 the government imposed controls on private wages and prices for the first time in the nation's peacetime history.

Wage and price regulation was imposed under the 1970 Economic Stabilization Act, which had delegated broad regulatory authority to the President. On August 15, 1971, President Nixon invoked the act and delegated his authority in turn to the Cost of Living Council. The council quickly issued hundreds of pages of wage and price regulations.

The inflation rate declined in 1971 and 1972 and the Nixon Administration began to move toward ending wage and price controls. The controls were terminated on April 30, 1974, and consumer prices that year increased 11 percent. The economic uncertainty and confusion wrought by double-digit inflation helped account for the recession and unemployment that followed. The first words in President Ford's 1975 Economic Report to Congress were, "The economy is in a severe recession." The unemployment rate in 1975 rose to 8.5 percent, which was higher than it had been since the Depression of the 1930's, and as the 1970's moved on both inflation and unemployment persisted at high levels that contradicted the economic policy goals of "maximum employment, production and purchasing power" stated in the 1946 Employment Act.

The quest for a coherent national economic policy continued. Congress in 1974 not only passed the Congressional Budget Act but also, at President Ford's request, passed the Council on Wage and Price Stability

Act. The creation of the council within the Executive Office of the President was an attempt to restrain inflation through federal monitoring of private wage and price increases.

The Council on Wage and Price Stability Act institutionalized the informal White House wage and price intervention that had gone before, but the council also did not curb inflation. The inflation rate was brought down by recession and unemployment to 9 percent in 1975 and about 5 percent in 1976, but the rate was back up to nearly 7 percent in 1977 and rose higher in 1978 and 1979 to double-digit levels.

President Carter responded first by reviving a mild form of jawboning in which companies and unions were asked voluntarily to hold down price and wage increases and then, on October 24, 1978, by tripling the size of the Council on Wage and Price Stability and proposing tax and other incentives to curb inflation.

The evolution of wage and price policy has been a major news story of continuing interest to employees, employers, and consumers throughout the nation. By and large, the press has not told the story in terms of conflicting federal economic policies, but wage and price regulation may ultimately represent the overwhelming conflict with basic and historic economic policy that in 1890 was intended to support and maintain free market competition as the regulator of the nation's economic life.

REPORTERS, POLITICIANS, AND BUREAUCRATS

To say that conflicting government economic and social policies represent a challenge to the press and its First Amendment role is to state the obvious. The press by and large has taken government at face value and shared with Congress the assumption that the theories and hopes set forth in new policies and programs will be matched by reality. To attempt to report on government economic and social policies and programs from Capitol Hill without digging into the agencies and departments, however, is akin to trying to cover a foreign war without leaving home.

Most members of Congress are not intellectually or otherwise dishonest, but economic and social policies and programs are made through the political process. Each new policy and program has its political constituency which becomes the constituency of an administrative agency or department, and these constituencies include powerful business, labor, agriculture, environmentalist, and consumerist interests. The resulting proliferation of policies, programs, agencies, and departments serves the conflicting interests of various political constituencies, but inflation does not serve the public interest.

In summary, government's assumed responsibility for economic stability, without undue inflation or unemployment, is the largest domestic news story of our times. In fact, however, it is a tremendously complex economic and political story involving political choices among economic policy alternatives. The basic choice is between free market competition and government intervention, and the policy alternatives include antitrust laws, wage and price controls, and much more.

It is not easy for reporters to place daily news events into the context of inflation and unemployment goals, but surely it can be done. Consider, for example, this story that appeared on the front page of *The Washington Post* back in 1973:

> The chairman of the Federal Reserve Board, warning that the nation must take the inflation fight more seriously, urged yesterday a vigorous effort to improve corporate competition, including new antitrust laws that "require heavier fines and penalties."
>
> Chairman Arthur F. Burns said the nation will never solve its balance-of-payments deficit, which he termed a "cancerous growth which must be cut out," unless it solves its inflation problem. He testified at a hearing of the Congressional Joint Economic Committee.[31]

Aspiring journalists can find their way through the labyrinth and there are few issues in the news more worthy of informed, independent investigative reporting than government economic policies.

NOTES—CHAPTER 10

1. Figures on gallery membership are taken from the Congressional Directory for 1964 and 1979.

2. For federal, state, and local employment statistics, see "Public Employment in 1976," a document designed GE-76, Bureau of the Census.

3. Economic Report of the President, January 1978. See the accompanying report of the Council of Economic Advisers, p. 342.

4. *Ibid.,* p. 85.

5. The President's Message on Transportation, transmitted to Congress April 4, 1962.

6. *New York Times,* September 28, 1976, pp. 1, 31.

7. Economic Report of the President, January 1977. See the accompanying report of the Council of Economic Advisers, p. 146.

8. "The Challenge of Regulatory Reform," a report submitted to President Ford by the Domestic Council Review Group on Regulatory Reform, January 1977.

9. The assertion was made in Jimmy Carter's submission to the Democratic Platform Committee, June 1976.

10. *Northern Pacific Railway* v. *U.S.,* 356 U.S. 1, 4 (1958).

11. "Is John Sherman's Antitrust Obsolete?" *Business Week,* March 23, 1974, pp. 47–56.

12. See John Kenneth Galbraith, *American Capitalism: The Concept of Countervailing Power* (Boston: Houghton Mifflin Co., 1952), and *The New Industrial State* (Boston: Houghton Mifflin Co., 1967).

13. See Galbraith, *The New Industrial State.*

14. Louis M. Kohlmeier, *The Regulators: Watchdog Agencies and the Public Interest* (New York: Harper & Row, 1969), p. 10.

15. *Ibid.*, p. 145.

16. See "State Regulation and the Federal Antitrust Laws," an address by Joe Sims, Special Assistant to the Assistant Attorney General, Hot Springs, Arkansas, December 12, 1974.

17. An inventory of 90 agencies is listed in "The Challenge of Regulatory Reform." For another inventory, see Kohlmeier, *The Regulators*, pp. 307–12.

18. Byron Klapper, "While Red Ink Floods Washington, Other Units of Government Show Big, but Fragile, Surplus," *Wall Street Journal*, August 11, 1978, p. 30.

19. The studies referred to, all issued in January 1977, are titled Catastrophic Health Insurance; Elementary, Secondary, and Vocational Education: An Examination of Alternative Federal Roles; Energy Research, Development, Demonstration, and Commercialization; Homeownership: The Changing Relationship of Costs and Incomes; and Possible Federal Roles and the Costs of Defense Manpower.

20. *Federal Trade Commission* v. *Ruberiod Co.*, 343 U.S. 470, 488 (1952).

21. "Appointments to the Regulatory Agencies (1949–1974)," a study prepared for the Senate Commerce Committee, April 1976.

22. *Washington Post*, August 12, 1976, pp. A1, A5. See also *New York Times*, September 28, 1976, pp. 1, 31.

23. See Kohlmeier, *The Regulators*, pp. 39–46.

24. Les Gapay, "Agencies and Industries Show Persistent Signs of Cozy Relationships," *Wall Street Journal*, November 1, 1974, pp. 1, 25.

25. Remarks of the President at a White House Conference on Domestic Economic Affairs, April 18, 1975.

26. See Willard C. Butcher, "$100 Billion Price Tag on Government Regulation," *Financier, the Journal of Financial Affairs*, October 1978, pp. 32–35. The article is based on estimates of economists at Chase Manhattan Bank.

27. See Harold T. Pinkett, "The Keep Commission, 1905–1909: A Rooseveltian Effort for Administrative Reform," *Journal of American History*, September 1965, p. 297.

28. President Carter's criticisms were summarized in a White House white paper, "The President's Anti-Inflation Program," October 24, 1978.

29. David Burnham, "Ford Administration Proposals for Deregulation Bringing Increasing Opposition from Industry," *New York Times*, January 2, 1976, pp. 35, 37.

30. Economic Report of the President, January 1959, p. vi.

31. James L. Rowe, Jr., "Tough Trust Laws Proposed by Burns," *Washington Post*, February 21, 1973, pp. A1, A9.

SOURCES OF INFORMATION

Administrative Conference of the United States
2120 L Street, N.W.
Washington, D.C. 20037

Civil Aeronautics Board
1825 Connecticut Avenue
Washington, D.C. 20428

Congressional Budget Office
House Annex 2
Washington, D.C. 20515

Environmental Protection Agency
401 M Street, N.W.
Washington, D.C. 20460

Federal Communications Commission
1919 M Street, N.W.
Washington, D.C. 20554

Federal Trade Commission
Pennsylvania Avenue at Sixth Street
Washington, D.C. 20580

Council of Economic Advisers Executive Office of the President Washington, D.C. 20506	*Interstate Commerce Commission* Twelfth Street and Constitution Avenue Washington, D.C. 20423
Council on Wage and Price Stability Executive Office of the President Washington, D.C. 20506	*National Conference of State Legislatures* 1405 Curtis Street Denver, Col. 80202
Department of Justice, Antitrust Division Constitution Avenue at Tenth Street Washington, D.C. 20530	

SUGGESTED READINGS

Bernstein, Marver H., *Regulating Business by Independent Commission.* Princeton, N.J.: Princeton University Press, 1955.

Cary, William L., *Politics and the Regulatory Agencies.* New York: McGraw-Hill Book Company, 1967.

Cole, Barry, and Mal Oettinger, *Reluctant Regulators: The FCC and The Broadcast Audience.* Reading, Mass.: Addison-Wesley Publishing Co., 1978.

Cushman, Herbert E., *The Independent Regulatory Commissions.* New York: Oxford University Press, 1941.

Fellmeth, Robert, *The Interstate Commerce Omission.* New York: Grossman Publishers, 1970.

Friendly, Henry J., *The Federal Administrative Agencies.* Cambridge, Mass.: Harvard University Press, 1962.

Harris, Joseph P., *The Advice and Consent of the Senate.* Berkeley: University of California Press, 1953.

Kaysen, Carl, and Donald F. Turner, *Antitrust Policy.* Cambridge, Mass.: Harvard University Press, 1959.

Kohlmeier, Louis M., Jr., *The Regulators: Watchdog Agencies and the Public Interest.* New York: Harper & Row, 1969.

Landis, James M., "Report on Regulatory Agencies to the President-Elect," printed as a document of the Senate Committee on the Judiciary, 86th Congress, 2nd Session, 1960.

"National Transportation Policy, a report to the Senate Commerce Committee by a Special Study Group on Transportation headed by John P. Doyle, Committee Print, 87th Congress, 1st Session, 1961.

Peck, Merton J., *Competitive Policy for Transportation?* Washington, D.C.: The Brookings Institution, 1965.

Schwartz, Bernard, *The Professor and the Commissions.* New York: Alfred A. Knopf, 1959.

Stigler, George J., *The Citizen and the State: Essays on Regulation.* Chicago: University of Chicago Press, 1975.

Reporting on...
INTERNATIONAL
ECONOMIC AFFAIRS

11

HARRY B. ELLIS

LATE IN 1977, American manufacturers of nuts, bolts, and screws—collectively known as the fastener industry—applied to the federal government for relief from foreign import competition. The company officials argued in Washington that fasteners from overseas, principally Japan, were cutting into domestic sales and forcing layoffs of workers. The U.S. International Trade Commission, supporting the industry's claim, recommended a 30 percent tariff increase on foreign fasteners. But President Carter early in 1978 rejected the ITC's finding, ruling that higher tariffs would be inflationary because they would raise costs for American consumers.

Thus the President, by denying relief to the manufacturers, had come down on the side of free trade. Late in 1978, however, Mr. Carter reversed himself and raised import duties on industrial fasteners. The White House said that the increase would amount to less than 30 percent and thus have "a substantially smaller inflationary impact." The increase was justified, the White House asserted, because more than 4,000 U.S. fastener industry workers had been laid off and more layoffs were threatened if import duties were not raised.

Here, in microcosm, was a problem with which every President in recent U.S. history has wrestled: how to promote free trade that benefits American consumers while protecting Americans from job losses due to imports.

The story of free trade versus protectionism is by no means new, but in recent years it has become a major issue flashing across newspaper headlines and television screens as various American industries and unions have pleaded for protection from foreign TV sets, shoes, steel, and other products.

Squeezed by these conflicting pressures, successive presidents have clung to the principle of free trade, but on a case-by-case basis have tried to help those Americans most threatened by foreign competition.

The Carter Administration, for example, in 1977 persuaded Japan to limit exports of TV sets to the United States and won agreement from Taiwan and South Korea to reduce shipments of inexpensive shoes to the American market. More broadly, the U.S. Treasury authored a complex "trigger pricing" plan to prevent Japanese and European steel companies from selling their wares below production costs in the United States.

Taiwan and South Korea were not accused of *dumping*—that is, of selling their shoes below cost; they were simply able, because of low production costs, to market their footwear at prices American manufacturers could not match. The International Trade Commission recommended substantially higher tariffs on shoes from the two Asian lands. Earlier, the U.S. Treasury had ruled that Japanese manufacturers, with the exception of the Sony Corporation, were dumping TV sets on the American market. This finding would subject Japanese sets to countervailing, or additional, customs duties.

Reluctant to impose higher tariffs at a time when many nations, including the United States, had been meeting in Geneva and trying to dismantle trade barriers, the Carter Administration negotiated "orderly marketing agreements" with Japan, Taiwan, and South Korea. These arrangements, while restrictive in the sense of reducing imports, were voluntary quota agreements reached between governments.

The steel case was different, said Anthony M. Solomon, then Undersecretary of the Treasury, because slack demand around the world had resulted in "a huge overhang of excess capacity" everywhere, impelling Japanese and European steelmakers to sell below cost in the United States to preserve jobs in their domestic steel industries. The solution for steel, as U.S. officials saw it, was to eliminate this dumping threat by setting the "trigger price" mechanism, below which foreign steelmakers could not sell in the United States without incurring "dumping duty" penalties.[1]

In each case—TV sets, shoes, steel—the Carter Administration sought a formula that would give some relief to the particular American industry, without inviting retribution against American exports and without violating the overall White House commitment to free trade. "The task," said a White House official, "is to chart a course between the principle of free trade and the needs of American workers whose jobs manifestly are being taken away by imports."[2]

In charting this course, President Carter overruled recommendations by the ITC that special protection be given to American producers of high-carbon ferrochromium, a chrome alloy used in making stainless steel. High tariffs on these products, Mr. Carter decided, would add to consumer costs in the United States and invite foreign retaliation. In these cases, White House judgment favored free trade rather than protection of domestic workers.

The United States is not alone in its dilemma on trade. Inflation, high unemployment, and slow growth characterized the economies of most industrial powers after the worldwide recession of 1974–1975 that in turn followed the fourfold increase in the world price of oil. Olivier Long, Director-General of the General Agreement on Tariffs and Trade in Geneva, warned: "The stresses involved have now become such that they seriously threaten the whole fabric of postwar cooperation in international trade policy."[3]

THE PRESS, THE PUBLIC, AND THE WORLD

The phrase "international economic affairs" probably brings to the minds of most aspiring journalists an arcane and remote world in which the gnomes of Zurich manipulate marks, francs, yen, and dollars in secret Swiss bank accounts. Even if international economic affairs are not that arcane, most journalists will not be covering the World Bank in Washington or the Organization for Economic Cooperation and Development in Paris or the other more or less remote institutions of world trade and finance. On the other hand, any aspiring journalist who expects to report on international affairs is well advised to acquire an understanding of international economic affairs. Furthermore, as world trade and its institutions have grown, they have become much more significant to economic and business news in general, locally as well as nationally.

Figuratively and literally, world trade has become the nuts and bolts of domestic jobs and prices. World oil prices have affected the lifestyles of virtually all Americans. World trade in TV sets, shoes, and other consumer products has affected prices and jobs in many American cities, large and small. International economic affairs thus have become intertwined with local and national affairs and the reporting thereof.

International trade that permits each nation to sell those products it can produce most efficiently helps to improve world living standards and to improve chances of world peace. As nations compete in the sale of their goods, world trade also reduces as well as increases job opportunities within nations. On balance, however, the number of American workers who owe their jobs to exports is far greater than the number of those who suffer from imports.

According to U.S. Treasury figures, one out of every eight manufacturing jobs in the United States produces goods for export. Each $1 billion worth of U.S. products sold overseas creates 40,000 to 70,000 jobs for American workers. One-third of all U.S. farmland grows crops for export.

More than half of American-grown wheat, soybeans, and rice is sold overseas. Exports contribute almost 10 percent to the nation's total output of goods and services.

Foreign trade not only is an essential part of the U.S. economy, but, by the number of jobs it creates, it dictates government adherence to free trade. Commerce is a two-way street. To the extent that the United States erects barriers against foreign goods, other nations may do the same against American products.

Still, some U.S. industries press for protection against imports. Thousands of American families see foreign trade from the perspective of people whose jobs have vanished beneath waves of foreign goods. Trade union leaders point to workers whose jobs in effect were exported, either because foreign manufacturers could undersell their U.S. competitors or because American firms set up operating bases overseas.

Workers certified by the U.S. Labor Department to have suffered injury from imports are eligible, under the Trade Act of 1974, for adjustment assistance, including cash allowances, training in new skills, job placement, and money to move their families. But such assistance is *ex post facto,* after the damage is done. Many workers and their employers want their jobs protected in the first place, by having the U.S. government restrict the inflow of foreign goods.

Yet, Robert S. Strauss, then President Carter's Special Trade Representative, declared in 1977 that

> the United States has been the principal beneficiary in the more than tenfold increase in world trade that has taken place over the past quarter century. World trade is about a trillion dollars annually and about one-eighth of that is ours. . . . Increased world trade can only mean a stronger United States.[4]

The importance of foreign trade illustrates why the focus of much international reporting has become economic. After World War II the work of American correspondents overseas centered on political problems—the struggle to stabilize Europe, split by the Iron Curtain; French withdrawal from Algeria; the Korean War, and the like. Economic stories began to emerge with the Marshall Plan and its economic impact on Western Europe. Those stories were followed by the effort of six and later nine European powers to weld closer links through the European Economic Community or Common Market.

As world trade quickened, and as governments groped toward an international monetary system flexible enough to cope with enormous flows of money across frontiers, awareness grew that reporters required some degree of economic expertise. Culmination of this trend came with quadrupling of oil prices by the Organization of Petroleum Exporting

Countries in 1973 and the Arab oil embargo. Much of international reporting since then has dwelt on the need of oil-importing nations—rich and poor—to adjust to a fundamentally different era based on expensive energy. The fabric of postwar international economic cooperation, and at times dissension, has brought into existence a number of international organizations that are important to economic and business journalists, even if they seem remote. They include the General Agreement on Tariffs and Trade (GATT), the Geneva-based forum within which nations thrash out the terms of international commerce; the International Monetary Fund (IMF), the Washington-based agency for overseeing the world's monetary system; and the Washington-based International Bank for Reconstruction and Development, or World Bank, and its affiliates—prime channels of foreign aid to nations in economic need. Other major multinational groupings include the nine-nation European Economic Community, headquartered in Brussels, and the Paris-based Organization for Economic Cooperation and Development (OECD), grouping 24 industrial powers. Also significant, quite obviously, is the 13-member Organization of Petroleum Exporting Countries (OPEC).

Most of these groups hold periodic conferences, usually open to press coverage, and all of them issue streams of reports on developments within their spheres. Getting on mailing lists of such organizations is vital to economic journalists.

Almost all governments maintain their own agencies to formulate national policies on trade, energy, foreign aid, monetary affairs, and other areas of international economics. For the United States, such agencies include the Departments of State, Commerce, Agriculture, Energy, and the U.S. Treasury, plus specialized units like the Export-Import Bank.

WHY NATIONS TRADE

Industrial powers must export, partly to earn money with which to pay for imports of food, commodities, and manufactures, and partly to dispose of goods their domestic markets cannot absorb. West Germany, the Netherlands, Japan, and other industrial nations of small land mass relative to population have earned a quarter or more of their national incomes from exports in recent years.

The United States, with its continental resources and huge domestic market, is less dependent on foreign trade. Even so, the share of trade in the American gross national product has almost doubled since the mid-1960's. The United States not only has become the largest exporter of food in the world, but supplies about 20 percent of all manufactures—machinery, transport equipment, chemicals, and the like—moving in international trade.[5] This percentage is down in a relative sense (the U.S. share was 27.7

percent in 1958), because Japan, West Germany, and a few other powers have moved into high export gear. But world trade itself has greatly increased, so that Americans take a slightly smaller slice of a very much bigger pie.

As American exports have grown, so has U.S. dependence on resources overseas. Americans are painfully aware that roughly half the petroleum they burn comes from foreign wells, at a cost of more than $40 billion a year. Less well-known is the reliance of the United States on foreign supplies of many of the key raw materials on which a modern economy runs. The United States buys 100 percent of its sheet mica, strontium, and columbium from overseas, as well as 99 percent of the manganese needed for metal alloys, 98 percent of cobalt, 86 percent of asbestos, 75 percent of tin, and so on down a long line of essential materials.[6] Dedication to free trade is for the United States, as for all industrial powers, a matter of necessity, not magnanimity.

"Two-thirds of our imports," the Secretary of State has said, "are essential raw materials, or goods we cannot readily produce. From automobiles to newspapers, from jet aircraft to household appliances, many of our industries depend upon imported materials."[7]

While international trade offers fundamental advantages to nations, allowing each to specialize in production of goods and services it can produce most efficiently, world trade also entails risks. Nations must pay in one way or another for the goods they import. The point was made in these paragraphs from the top of a page one *Wall Street Journal* article:

> At a drill-bit factory in Shanghai recently, a Chinese official paused before a heap of newly finished bits and confided to his American visitors, "Yours are better than ours. We want drill bits from you."
>
> It isn't just drill bits the Chinese want these days but steel mills, nuclear reactors, railroad cars, airplanes, computers, Coca-Cola and about everything else the West produces. For China is on a crash program to modernize by the year 2000 with help from its capitalist friends.
>
> Peking's buying binge—it has signed commitments this year to purchase $27 billion of technology from Japan, West Europe and the U.S.—has created great expectations among Western businessmen of a huge new market. Those expectations have been accelerated by the news that the U.S. will establish diplomatic relations with the People's Republic of China on Monday.
>
> "Any nation of over 950 million people growing at the rate of 18 million individuals a year is a tremendous market," says Donald Regan, chairman of Merrill Lynch & Co. and a recent visitor to Peking.
>
> But there are real constraints. For one thing, China can't afford everything it wants, and large revenues from its bounteous oil reserves are years away. Meanwhile, crop failures could continue to force high ag-

ricultural imports, reducing Peking's ability to pay for industrial goods.
Diplomatic relations with the U.S. should ease China's financial problems by opening the way for tariff cuts and for U.S. government and
commercial loans, but the diplomatic ties won't eliminate those problems.[8]

All nations must pay for their imports with exports or by other
means. The United States, for example, blessed with vast farmlands and
highly efficient farmers, depends on farm exports to pay for some of the
raw materials and manufactures which Americans import. Japanese,
crowded tightly into their islands, sell quality manufactures overseas to pay
for the food, oil, and raw materials they import. Thus Japan is a major
market for American grains and soybeans while the United States buys a
huge volume of Japanese cars, cameras, TV sets, and other electronic products.

The system generally works well when nations trust each other not to
raise barriers against other countries' goods in order to preserve domestic
jobs. The system breaks down—that is, the principle of specialization, or
international division of labor, is abandoned—when inefficient or noncompetitive industries demand and get protection against imports. The same is
true when subsidies or other government aids are extended to make one
nation's exports artificially low priced in another's market.

U.S. TARIFF HISTORY

The march toward a policy of free trade was gradual in the United
States. Congress passed the first national tariff in 1789, and nearly two
centuries of U.S. tariff laws mirror a seesaw struggle between those law-
makers who wanted to protect fledgling or ailing industries and those who
favored expanded commerce. The 1789 tariff was inspired by the need to
raise revenue to pay wages and other obligations of the federal government,
which, until 1787, had lacked authority to levy taxes of any kind.[9]

Provision of revenue, in other words, was the chief function of early
tariffs, which were taxes levied on imported goods—5 percent of value on
most products in the 1789 tariff. Until 1913, customs duties supplied between 50 and 90 percent of all federal revenues. With inauguration of income taxes on individuals and corporations, authorized by the ratification in
1913 of the Sixteenth Amendment to the Constitution, the revenue function
of tariffs began to decline. They now provide no more than 2 percent of the
federal government's total income.[10]

The Rise of Protectionism

As time went on protectionism loomed larger as an element in tariff policy.
The triple aims of protection were to encourage a higher degree of U.S.
self-sufficiency, to give infant industries a chance to establish themselves,

and to shield American firms from the dumping of foreign products below cost. Britain, for example, after the War of 1812 worked off a huge surplus of goods by dumping them on the U.S. market at prices that drove a number of American companies out of business and threw the whole domestic price structure out of kilter. The British action prompted Congress to pass the Tariff Act of 1816, which raised tariff rates an average of 42 percent higher than they had been before the war.

Act followed act as the century wore on, with tariff rates fluctuating according to economic conditions in general and the ability of specific American industries to lobby for protection in Congress. Generally speaking, protectionism during the nineteenth and early twentieth centuries found its natural home among Republicans, while free trade sentiment centered in the Democratic Party.

The Smoot-Hawley Act of 1930, which marked the high point of protectionism in the United States, taught the lesson that the United States could not legislate trade policy in a vacuum. Spurred originally by the desire to raise tariffs on imported farm products, the act wound up setting the highest general level of tariffs on both farm and industrial goods in the nation's experience. Swiftly America's trading partners responded by raising barriers against American exports. World trade plummeted and, in retrospect, Smoot-Hawley emerged as a contributing factor to the world depression of the 1930's. Awareness was growing, meanwhile, that protective tariff barriers, behind which American manufacturers sought shelter from overseas competition, tended to raise prices generally in the United States, to the detriment of American consumers.

Protectionist pressures that arose in the 1970's were different from those that led to Smoot-Hawley. American farmers in recent years have not generally clamored for protection against imports, though some of them— such as sugar growers and meat producers—do benefit from import restrictions. Nor is industrial demand for import relief as widespread as in Smoot-Hawley days. Recent protectionist demand has sprung primarily from specific industries and unions, such as those in steel and shoe manufacturing, which for a variety of reasons are unable to meet lower-cost foreign competition.

Local and national media reported the phenomenon of unions and companies joining together in the 1970's to raise protectionist pressures. For example, *The New York Times* in 1976 reported:

> Washington, Sept. 22—Five manufacturers and 11 unions filed a petition with the United States International Trade Commission today seeking to curb rapidly growing imports of color television sets, mainly from Japan.
>
> Imports, according to the petition, reached 29 percent of the market in

the first seven months of this year, up from 16 percent in all of 1975. The petition seeks relief in the form of import quotas.[11]

Protectionist pressures emphasize actual or perceived losses of U.S. sales and jobs, but the media have not looked as hard at the other side of the coin: the higher prices that normally are paid by U.S. consumers when tariffs and quotas reduce imports of less expensive foreign products.

The Modern Multilateral Approach to Trade

In 1918 President Woodrow Wilson, in the third of his Fourteen Points to restore world peace, had called for the "removal, so far as possible, of all economic barriers and the establishment of an equality of trade conditions among all nations." Though this vision appeared to be lost during the Harding-Coolidge-Hoover era, which spawned the Smoot-Hawley bill, Franklin D. Roosevelt later expanded the Wilsonian appeal. During the 1932 Presidential campaign he called for a reduction in tariff rates and, most significantly, called for "reciprocal tariff agreements with other nations."

The Roosevelt years launched the United States firmly on the path toward free trade, of which a first step was the Reciprocal Trade Agreements Act of 1934. In essence the act was a promise to reduce U.S. tariffs if other nations would do the same. Congress also gave the White House authority to negotiate flexible tariff rates, thus ending the need to rewrite basic tariff law each time a change was made.

By the early 1940's the United States had concluded 30 bilateral trade agreements with 25 nations, lowering tariff rates. In 1941 President Roosevelt and British Prime Minister Winston Churchill called, in the Atlantic Charter, for a multilateral effort to liberalize trade when World War II was over. Bilateralism, in other words, was giving way to a multilateral approach, realized by the General Agreement on Tariffs and Trade on January 1, 1948.[12]

Early rounds of trade talks within GATT concentrated on cutting tariffs, the most visible hindrance to a free flow of commerce. Culmination of this effort was the so-called Kennedy Round of trade negotiations held during 1964–1967, resulting in across-the-board tariff cuts averaging more than 35 percent on a wide variety of industrial goods and, to a lesser extent, on commodities and farm products.

As tariff levels fell, attention gradually shifted to nontariff barriers to trade. For example, a nation might levy low tariffs on foreign goods but hold them up at dockside with complex licensing paperwork until, in the words of a U.S. trade official, "it rusts if it's metal or rots if it's food."

Nearly 100 nations buckled down at Geneva in 1978 to the seventh round of GATT talks, popularly called the Tokyo Round, after preliminary discussions in the Japanese capital. Tariff cuts of at least 35 percent were sought, but more meaningful were the long lists of nontariff barriers tabled by members for discussion. The Carter Administration's negotiating team pressed 700 requests for trade concessions on U.S. trading partners around the world. Other countries submitted their own list of 100 ways the United States might alter American trading practices.

Quotas are a major nontariff barrier to trade. Governments, to protect native industries, may limit the types or quantities of competing foreign goods allowed in. The United States has restricted the importation of specialty steels, among other things. Japan has placed quotas on its imports of film, citrus fruits, and beef.

Sometimes the quota is coupled to other obstacles to trade. "Japanese quotas on foreign beef and citrus fruits," a White House official has said, "are an absolute barrier. But even if we could get rid of those quotas, we would run into their distribution system. They do not have supermarkets as such," the official continued, "and the Japanese distribution system makes it hard for our beef and fruit to penetrate their market."[13]

Export subsidies are a second nontariff barrier to trade. Many governments, one way or another, make it possible for their businessmen and farmers to sell goods abroad more cheaply than at home. One of the so-called export subsidies involves removal of domestic taxes from products sold overseas.

Government procurement policies are a third nontariff barrier. Governments are major buyers of goods and services and often favor native suppliers over foreign competitors. "The U.S. Government," conceded a White House trade official, "also has a Buy American policy, but at least we do it openly. Japan and some European countries do it quietly."[14]

Customs valuation procedures constitute a fourth nontariff barrier to world trade. Governments apply varying standards in assessing the value of imports, on which the final tariffs are based. For example, two nations might levy a 10 percent tariff on a particular product but determine its value in different ways. Especially galling to some nations is the so-called American Selling Price system, whereby the United States levies customs duties based not on the intrinsic value of the foreign article being imported, but on its relation to the domestic selling price of the equivalent American item. This system applies to several categories of goods including synthetic organic chemicals, rubber footwear, canned clams, and certain wool knit gloves. The Carter Administration, at the beginning of the new round of talks in 1978 in Geneva, said it was willing to work for a universal customs valuation procedure for the world.

GATT members also have sought elimination of the U.S. "countervailing duty" system, whereby the U.S. Treasury is required, under the Countervailing Duty Act of 1897, to assess an additional duty on foreign goods judged to have received export subsidies from their governments Given the difficulty of pinpointing such subsidies, and because of frictions aroused with trading partners, Treasury officials invoked the law as little as possible. In the Trade Act of 1974, however, Congress instituted a judicial review process; if the Treasury does not find injury done to an American company, the plaintiff can go to court.

Though generally the United States is a low-tariff country, it retains high tariffs on some chemicals and textiles. The American meat-import program essentially is a series of restrictive bilateral quotas worked out with meat-exporting countries.

U.S. officials can and do compile equally impressive lists of American complaints against foreign trading partners. GATT talks are a constant process of give and take, with each participant striving to exact concessions from others while preserving trade advantages for itself. Consequently, the GATT negotiations are covered closely by major American and foreign press organizations and the negotiators often have made news in U.S. cities when they have struck agreements that might affect local factories and jobs.

MULTINATIONAL CORPORATIONS

Since World War II a new feature has spread widely across the international trading landscape. The era has seen the rise of multinational corporations, with manufacturing or processing plants in two or more countries. America has taken the lead in this movement, but increasingly business people in other lands—Japan, West Germany, the Netherlands, Sweden, and Brazil among them—have built factories and bought mines around the world.

The Fall and Rise of Multinationals

The concept of multinationals is not new. Seventeenth-century British entities such as Hudson's Bay Company and the East India Company played powerful economic and developmental roles and exercised a degree of political sovereignty unmatched by today's international corporations. Two world wars nearly wiped out the multinational movement, and the rapid spread of corporations across national lines, as we know the system today, essentially dates from the recovery period after World War II.

Varied motives induce business people to expand operations beyond their own frontiers. American firms, by setting up plants inside the Common Market, became "insiders" themselves and escaped the common external tariff thrown up around the European Economic Community by its member states. U.S. products made within the EEC competed equally with European goods, unburdened by tariffs levied on foreign imports. A fruit-canning company in the United States, for example, would have to buck the common external tariff to sell its fruits within the nine EEC countries. If that company built a processing plant in France or Italy, it would be inside the Common Market. From the standpoint of the host country the new factory meant jobs, a buyer of local fruits, and a source of tax income.

Literally hundreds of American firms planted themselves inside the EEC. Some bought up shares of European firms, often buying a controlling interest. Many U.S. ventures in Europe predated the Common Market, as did General Motors' ownership of Opel in West Germany and Ford's establishment of its own affiliate in Germany. A European buying an Opel (General Motors) or Capri (Ford) was acquiring a car that had a European name but was produced by an American-owned firm. Other U.S. companies granted licenses to European firms to manufacture American products according to U.S. specifications.

The Cons and Pros of Multinationals

In some cases industrial corporations set up shop in developing lands of Asia, Africa, or Latin America to be near sources of raw materials and cheap labor. This disturbs U.S. trade union leaders, who contend that Americans lose jobs when a firm builds a plant outside the country. This is true when the U.S. company shuts down domestic operations altogether, as some TV set makers did when they switched parts and components manufacturing to Mexico, Taiwan, and other places where labor costs are low.

Some foreign manufacturers, on the other hand, have opened plants in the United States to bring their products closer to the lucrative American market. Volkswagen turns out cars at a plant in Pennsylvania; the French tire firm Michelin makes its steel-belted radials at three factories in South Carolina, with expansion plans beyond that; and at least four Japanese comanies, including Sony, manufacture color television sets in the United States.

Many American businesses claim that their building of factories overseas also creates jobs for Americans at home. J. Stanford Smith, at the time senior vice-president of General Electric Company, asserted: "Our company makes locomotives in Brazil. About half the manufacturing is done down there." But, continued Mr. Smith, the "higher technology," involving perhaps half the value of the finished locomotives, is manufactured in Erie, Pennsylvania. Without that overseas plant, he argued, Erie production would shrink and so would the number of jobs in Erie.[15]

Supporters of multinational corporations argue that investment overseas creates domestic jobs in two ways. About 25 percent of total U.S. exports, according to the National Association of Manufacturers, go to U.S. foreign subsidiaries, in the form of parts, components, and other supplies. Also, according to the NAM, a large part of many multinationals' profits are repatriated to the United States and reinvested in domestic plant and equipment.

U.S. GOVERNMENT POLICIES

The U.S. government, with the goal of expanding American exports, offers tax and other concessions to American firms trading overseas. The aim is to allow U.S. companies to compete with foreign multinationals, whose governments afford similar or more generous benefits.

Tax Policies

One major tax advantage accruing to U.S. multinational corporations is the foreign tax credit, which permits companies to subtract taxes paid to foreign governments dollar-for-dollar from their U.S. tax liabilities. The foreign tax credit benefits chiefly large American oil firms, whose tax credits reduce and in some cases eliminate U.S. income taxes. The U.S. Treasury estimates that foreign income tax credits claimed by American oil companies cost the Treasury nearly $5 billion in revenue from 1974 through 1976.[16] To cut this revenue loss, the Internal Revenue Service in January 1978 tightened the definition of foreign taxes that might be credited against U.S. tax liabilities.

A second tax policy, known as the *deferral provision*, allows companies to escape U.S. taxes on foreign profits until they are actually returned to the United States. President Carter, describing this provision as a "subsidy to exporting firms," argued that deferral "amounts to subsidizing corporations to export jobs overseas."[17]

Officials of multinational corporations reject this argument, contending that elimination of deferral would place American firms at a competitive disadvantage in world markets. "No other country in the world," said Reginald H. Jones, chairman and chief executive officer of the General Electric Company, "taxes such [overseas] income until it is repatriated, and some countries, such as France and the Netherlands, do not tax foreign-source corporate income at all."[18]

A third tax policy, known as the *Domestic International Sales Corporation provision*, enables firms to postpone indefinitely U.S. taxes on part of their export earnings. Created in 1971, the so-called DISC provision was intended to encourage American businesses, many of which were oriented toward the domestic market, to produce for export. Corporations were allowed to form DISC subsidiaries to consolidate all income earned from exports. Initially 50 percent of that income was excused from taxation. DISC, in the view of its sponsors, had two basic aims: to encourage exports generally and to neutralize provisions in foreign taxation laws that might impel U.S. firms to establish branches overseas. American exports boomed in the years immediately following 1971 and the U.S. Treasury attributed part of the export growth to DISC. However, critics soon charged that a disproportionate amount of benefit from DISC was falling to giant multinational corporations that already enjoyed other tax advantages, and Congress began to whittle down DISC benefits.

Lending and Insurance Policies

Another benefit to U.S. multinational corporations is a government agency called the Overseas Private Investment Corporation, created by Congress in 1969 as an amendment to the Foreign Assistance Act of 1961. The purpose of OPIC is to stimulate American investment in developing countries and to protect U.S. firms from the risks of such investment. To this end OPIC has two major programs, political risk insurance and investment financing.

Political risk insurance covers firms against loss from expropriation, currency inconvertibility, war, revolution, or insurrection. *Investment financing* provides loan guarantees and direct loans to U.S. investors, as well as cost-sharing by the U.S. Treasury in surveys before investment is made.

The concept of government insurance for overseas investment began in 1948 as part of the Marshall Plan effort to rebuild Europe. In 1959 the focus of government insurance was narrowed to developing countries and the insurance program was administered by the Agency for International Development, a branch of the State Department. Still needed, however, was broader coverage of risks assumed by American corporations willing to invest in poorer developing countries, whose political and economic situations often were unstable. OPIC was conceived as the answer.

OPIC in time also encountered criticism, however. It was found, for example, that a large share of OPIC insurance covered investments in nations with authoritarian regimes whose political stability and lack of labor unrest made foreign investment attractive. Hand in hand with authoritarian control often went denial of human rights to citizens of such countries. Both Congress and the White House sought ways to orient more OPIC coverage toward nations respectful of human rights and toward the poorest developing nations most in need of foreign investment.

A second U.S. government agency that promotes foreign trade is the Export-Import Bank, founded in 1945 to finance the export of American goods and services in situations where commercial financing was unobtainable. A firm competing with foreign companies for a contract in Brazil or Yugoslavia, for example, could turn to the Eximbank for credit help in the form of a loan or loan guarantee which private banks were unprepared to offer.

Such loans are designed to cost the American taxpayer nothing. The Bank borrows from the U.S. Treasury at one-eighth percent over the interest cost to Treasury of placing five- to eight-year notes on the private market. Eximbank then extends its credit in a way to cover its administrative and operating costs, to place some earnings into reserves, and to pay a dividend to the Treasury.

Eximbank loans are designed to fill specific financing gaps, where private loans are lacking, usually because the loans involve longer term risks than commercial banks normally undertake, or because the loan amounts are extremely large, or because the underdeveloped countries in which the loans are to be invested have unusually low credit ratings.

Do these lending activities increase U.S. business overseas? A U.S. Treasury study indicates that Eximbank added almost $4 billion to total American exports in fiscal year 1976. According to the Treasury, such lending is necessary to assure that the official export credit of the United States remains competitive with equivalent export credit programs of other industrial powers:

> Of our major trading partners, only Canada has a smaller official export finance program than ours. Overall Eximbank support, as a percentage of total merchandise exports from the United States, was 7 percent in 1976. Canada's ratio was 5 percent. By comparison, Germany supported 10 percent of its merchandise exports with official financing; the United Kingdom, 23 percent; France, 39 percent; and Japan, 48 percent.[19]

In these circumstances, concludes the Treasury, Eximbank support to U.S. exports is needed to offset government intervention by other powers.

BALANCE OF PAYMENTS

Ultimately nations, like individuals, must settle up. In international affairs, the settling up involves weighing the value of a nation's total exports against its total imports and paying off the difference. In recent years the large deficits in the U.S. balance of payments have made headlines around the world and chiefs of state have held economic summit conferences addressed to the problems of the dollar and of trade imbalances. Economic and business reporters need some knowledge of these complex problems because a workable international monetary system is necessary to world commerce, and world commerce in turn is necessary to the improvement of world living standards in terms of both prices and jobs.

Trade is a major, but not the only, element in a nation's balance of payments, which is the total flow of capital, goods, and services in and out of a country. Some 64 "accounts," each focusing on a particular aspect of the movement of goods, money, and services across frontiers, contribute to the U.S. balance of payments.

Two accounts, for example, cover tourism—travel receipts (the amount of money foreigners spend in the United States) and travel expenditures (money spent by American tourists overseas). This measurement long has been in deficit, for American travelers spend more money abroad than foreign tourists do in the United States.

The most widely used balance of payments measurement, comprising a number of the 64 accounts, is called the "current account balance." It includes trade (the export and import of goods), services (insurance, shipping, tourism, and the like), government grants to other nations, and interest earned on direct American investment abroad. Also included in the current account balance are some U.S. government money transfers, principally pension and Social Security payments to U.S. citizens overseas.

In 1977 the U.S. balance of trade deficit, measured on a balance of payments basis, was a record $31 billion. But the broader current account measurement was only about $20 billion in arrears, chiefly because income on direct U.S. investment abroad showed a substantial surplus. Money invested by American firms overseas, in other words, returned a flow of capital to the United States.

Balance of trade figures require a word of caution to business and economic writers. The Bureau of the Census, a section of the Commerce Department, reported the 1977 trade shortfall as $26.5 billion, compared with the $31 billion figure compiled by the balance of payments division of the same department. The reason is that sales of U.S. military equipment to other nations, amounting to billions of dollars, are included in the Census Bureau report, but dropped from the balance of payments figures. This shrinks the dollar value of American exports and produces a larger trade deficit. Also, the balance of payments compilation includes imports (principally oil) into the U.S. Virgin Islands, which the Census Bureau does not count.

The International Monetary System

Recent monetary history has been marked by a weak U.S. dollar, whose value has dropped precipitately against the West Germany mark, Swiss franc, and Japanese yen and dropped less sharply against a number of other currencies. A few years ago a dollar bought four Deutschemarks; more recently it was worth less than two. As a result, a German automobile that cost $5,000 in 1972 carried a price tag of more than $10,000 in 1978, measured in the relative value of the dollar and Deutschemark.

This explains why the operation of the international monetary systems, or the interplay among national currencies, is important to Americans in general and to reporters covering the international economic scene. A weak dollar results in higher retail prices of foreign consumer goods in the United States, including watches, tape recorders, perfumes, cameras, cars, and the like. This adds to the U.S. inflation rate. Conversely, when the dollar strengthens against other currencies, foreign goods cost Americans relatively less.

When the United States in November 1978 intervened in foreign exchange markets and took other steps to bolster the dollar, then in a dangerous slide, the *National Journal* demonstrated how the story's importance could be conveyed:

> You could have easily missed the significance of President Carter's recent decision to defend the dollar. Most people do not understand special drawing rights, "swap lines" or even the discount rate. At the mention of these mysteries, the average American flips to the sports page, the comics or Ann Landers.
>
> But do not be deceived by the jargon: Carter's decision represents a momentous turning point for the U.S. economy.
>
> Carter and his advisers have mortgaged the future to the stability of the dollar. In the process, they may have inaugurated a period of slow growth—possibly punctuated by periodic recessions—as the only realistic antidote to the dollar's chronic weakness.[20]

The basic reason for the U.S. currency's decline has been a persistent outflow of dollars from the United States, putting more dollars into the hands of foreigners than they wished to hold. Like any other commodity in surplus, the dollar cheapened in value as foreign bankers, Arab sheikhs, and corporate money managers, including American officials of U.S. multinational firms, sold dollars to buy currencies they considered stronger.

The dollar outflow was spurred by America's growing purchase of foreign oil—$45 billion worth in 1977, or $2,045 for every man, woman, and child. Before World War II the United States was a net exporter of petroleum. Beginning in 1947 imported oil began to fuel a steadily larger share of American industrial expansion. By 1957 foreign oil supplied 18 percent of domestic petroleum demand; in 1973, when the Arabs temporarily cut off oil shipments to the United States, that percentage had risen to 36.1. By 1978 almost half of all oil Americans used came from overseas.

The oil deficit was the primary, though not the only, cause of the 1977 U.S. trade shortfall of $26.5 billion. Every year until 1971 the United States had run a trade surplus by selling more goods abroad than it bought. Over the next seven years the nation's trade balance was in the red five times, culminating in the record shortfall of 1977.[21]

The dollar's troubles reflected the relative turmoil that had gripped world monetary markets since the collapse of the postwar Bretton Woods system, built around the dollar and gold. That system, conceived at the 1944 Bretton Woods conference, obliged each member nation of the International Monetary Fund, or IMF, to assign a fixed value to its currency in terms of gold. This was the *par value* of a currency. Each country then defined the *parity,* or relationship, between its currency and the dollar, centerpiece of the Bretton Woods system. The dollar in turn was valued at $35 per fine ounce of gold.

Under the fixed exchange rate system devised at Bretton Woods, each nation pegged its currency to the dollar and agreed to maintain that value within a narrow band of fluctuation. Under extraordinary circumstances a country might devalue or revalue its money—lessen or increase its value in relation to the dollar, to bring the currency back into line with market conditions. The United States, for its part, agreed to convert dollars into gold on demand, at $35 an ounce. Thus, during the postwar period, the dollar was "as good as gold."

This system progressively broke down when the United States began to spend more than it earned. Billions of surplus dollars piled up in foreign central banks, in private banks overseas, and in the holdings of multinational corporations. The United States, converting dollars into gold as promised, saw its official gold hoard shrink from $25 billion to less than half that amount. Something had to be done, for the Bretton Woods system was based on a convertible dollar, pegged at $35 an ounce of gold.

In December 1971 President Nixon ended convertibility of the dollar, or "closed the gold window," to halt the run on the nation's gold. Bretton Woods in effect was dead. Member nations of the IMF began to negotiate toward a new world monetary system. Speculators and money managers, meanwhile, continued to unload billions of dollars for stronger currencies, with governments unable to stem the rush. As disorder spread in the money markets, governments released their currencies from their IMF pledge to support the dollar at its pegged price and instead allowed their currencies to *float,* or to move up or down freely in response to supply and demand.

Twice the United States devalued the dollar, by 8.57 percent in December 1971 and by 10 percent in February 1973. By these moves President Nixon hoped to end foreign speculation against the dollar and reduce the American balance of payments deficit. A cheaper dollar, it was hoped, would boost exports of U.S. products. Also at the end of 1971 some strong currencies, including the West German mark and Japanese yen, were revalued. Devaluation of a currency lowers its value in relation to other currencies; revaluation does the opposite. Technically, the U.S. dollar's devaluations were achieved by increasing the price of gold to $38 and then to $42.22 per ounce.

Even before President Nixon closed the gold window and twice devalued the dollar, it was apparent that the Bretton Woods agreement was dying. Realizing that the dollar and gold had become too narrow a base for the world's growing circulation of money, the IMF in 1969 created *special drawing rights,* known as SDR's or "paper gold," to increase world monetary liquidity. This new reserve asset could not be crinkled in the hand like a dollar bill or clinked together like silver German marks or Saudi riyals, because it did not exist as tangible money. SDR's were simply bookkeeping entries on the accounts of member nations of the IMF, allowing each member government to borrow specified amounts of various national currencies. Each IMF member was allocated a certain volume of SDR's in proportion to that nation's contribution of money to the operating fund of the IMF.

When the IMF created SDR's in 1969, the dollar still had a par value of $35 an ounce of gold and was still the centerpiece of the world's monetary system. So an SDR was defined as equal to one dollar or 1/35 of an ounce of gold. This became progressively meaningless after the United States ended the convertibility of dollars into gold and twice devalued the dollar. Beginning July 1, 1974, the IMF began to define the SDR in terms of the composite value, computed daily, of a "basket" of 16 currencies. A single currency, like the dollar or British pound, could fluctuate erratically. So, if a nation pegged the value of its money to the dollar, as under the Bretton Woods system, it could never know from one day to the next what its money might be worth on international exchanges. But the composite value of 16 currencies, including the dollar and such stalwarts as the West German mark and Swiss franc, provided a more reliable peg for the valuation of other currencies.

The Role of Gold

As the Bretton Woods system crumbled, the maintenance of its cornerstone—a dollar "as good as gold"—also crumbled. The trouble started when speculators began converting paper money into gold at $35 an ounce in the belief that the precious metal was a safe hedge against the weakening value of paper currencies. This forced commercial users of gold—dentists, jewelers, and the defense and aerospace industries, who need between two and three tons of gold daily—to compete with speculators for limited supplies of the metal. To help meet the private demand for gold, the United States and nine other rich nations formed a gold pool, from which they supplied commercial needs on a pro rata basis.

In 1967 the British devalued their pound and there was a massive run on the gold pool. Unwilling to see their gold supplies drained further, the United States and six other nations in 1968 signed a "two-tier" agreement. The signatories agreed they would continue to settle official transactions among themselves at $35 an ounce but no longer would sell gold to the private market, which would be allowed to float up or down according to supply and demand. Thus freed, the open market price of gold shot up.

When Mr. Nixon closed the gold window and devalued the dollar, by increasing the price of gold to $38 in 1971 and to $42.22 in 1973, pressure grew to abolish the two-tier agreement. Common Market governments held that the official price of gold, $42.22 an ounce, was unrealistic and pressed for the right to settle accounts among themselves at a higher price. Commercial users of gold, plagued by soaring prices for the stuff of their trade, demanded access to official hoards.

In late 1973 the United States and other nations agreed to abolish the two-tier system. Their aim had become to "demonetize" gold, that is, to reduce its ancient and special role within the world's monetary system and allow gold to be bought and sold like any other commodity.

To summarize the complex and troublesome international monetary story: The nations of the free world that emerged from World War II agreed at Bretton Woods on a monetary system that was built on the stability of the American dollar, but the dollar in time lost its stability and was no longer "as good as gold." The instability of the dollar led to the erosion and then the abandonment of the Bretton Woods system and of the traditional role of gold in international monetary affairs. Those events led in turn to the search for a different international monetary system in which gold has no official role and yet in which the role of gold as a safe hedge against weak paper currencies cannot be ignored.

The Rise of OPEC

World agreement on a new international monetary system to replace the Bretton Woods system became much more difficult after Middle Eastern and other oil-producing nations quadrupled the world price of oil within a period of months in 1973 and 1974.

The very large increase in the price of oil imported by the United States was a major reason for the growth of U.S. trade deficits, as we have seen, and the trade deficits weakened the dollar and further eroded the international monetary system. Beyond that, however, the rise of the oil-producing nations' cartel added profound complications to plans for a new international monetary system. In general, international money matters had been primarily the concern of mature "developed" industrial nations, but the quadrupling of world oil prices demonstrated most dramatically the demands of "underdeveloped" nations for a major piece of world monetary action and income. More specifically, the system of special drawing rights, or SDR's, that was begun between 1969 and 1974 to replace the Bretton Woods system was severely shaken by the quadrupling of oil prices. The dramatically higher oil prices launched a massive transfer of wealth from the more highly developed oil-consuming nations into the coffers of the under-developed oil-producers. To confine world currencies to new fixed exchange rates, which was the plan behind SDR's, would have been pointless, for the vast amounts of money now rolling about the world defied rigid controls.

The Organization of Petroleum Exporting Countries, familiarly known now as OPEC, initially was formed in 1960 by five oil-producing states to counter or control the ability of giant international oil companies to regulate petroleum pricing. Charter members of the OPEC cartel were Iran, Iraq, Kuwait, Saudi Arabia, and Venezuela. Eight other underdeveloped oil-producing nations joined later.

For the first decade of its existence OPEC attracted little attention. In 1968 the cartel published a document outlining its chief objectives—to determine future petroleum prices and to nationalize oil operations within the borders of member states. By October 1973 pricing control was effectively in OPEC hands and the cartel started a rapid upward spiral of the cost of oil. Until the fall of 1973 the posted price of Arabian light crude (the "marker" crude, against which other grades of OPEC oil are priced) was $3.01 a barrel. In October of that year OPEC jumped the price 67 percent to $5.11 and on January 1, 1974, three months later, boosted the posted price to $11.65 a barrel. At the beginning of 1978 the posted price of Arabian light stood at $12.70.

The era of cheap energy, which had fueled the industrial world's rapid postwar expansion, appeared over. Each year billions of dollars, which otherwise might have been spent by the United States and other oil-consuming nations to provide jobs, goods, and services at home, flowed to OPEC nations.

Some of the more populous cartel members, such as Iran, Nigeria, and Indonesia, ended up with little surplus cash and, in some cases, continued to borrow capital abroad. The situation of four of the more sparsely populated Persian Gulf States—Saudi Arabia, Kuwait, Qatar, and the United Arab Emirates—was dramatically different. By 1978 these OPEC members owned roughly $100 billion in foreign assets, over and above what they needed for domestic investment.

Japan and West Germany, both heavily dependent on OPEC for their oil supplies, substantially offset the cost of their oil through the export of goods and services to oil-producing states. The United States, as we have seen, ran an enormous oil deficit, in the range of $40 billion yearly. This contrast arose partly from differing adjustment policies to the higher price of oil. Europeans and the Japanese adjusted quickly to the full shock of high oil prices by passing the costs on to consumers, while the United States adopted the "slow burn" approach, shielding consumers from the brunt of those costs. The "American shock is still to come," Bruce MacLaury, president of the Brookings Institution in Washington, said in 1978, because government action has suppressed U.S. energy prices below world levels.[22]

Underdeveloped Versus Developed Nations

The quadrupling of oil prices by the OPEC nations was not only a dramatic demand by underdeveloped nations for a larger role in international economic affairs, but also was an example that other less developed nations tried to follow.

Less developed nations were not wholly ignored by the growth of world trade over the past quarter century or so. Multinational corporations built factories and opened mines in those nations, as we noted earlier, and the results were both favorable and unfavorable. On the unfavorable side, the multinationals' activities sometimes led to charges that the companies were intervening in the internal affairs of the host country. However, C. Fred Bergsten, an assistant secretary of the U.S. Treasury for international affairs, said that in practice the attitude of most developing countries toward multinational corporations "has been much more moderate. The intense need for capital, technology, and managerial skills has encouraged a pragmatic approach to foreign investment in most countries."[23]

The investments of multinational corporations in poor lands has not satisfied those nations' economic aspirations, however. Many underdeveloped countries have attempted to gain a larger share of control over their own economic destinies by emulating OPEC.

For years governments have sought to stabilize world prices of other basic commodities, notably coffee, cocoa, wheat, tin, sugar, textiles, and olive oil. Discussions have been held in recent years to add rubber and copper to the list. But these international agreements, unlike OPEC, embrace both producers and consumers. Their general aim is to set limits within which prices for a particular commodity should be allowed to fluctuate.

In the past decade or so, and particularly since the success of OPEC, developing countries have made more aggressive efforts to tilt the world's economic system more to their advantage, and much is heard of the North-South dialogue. Poor lands of the southern hemisphere, dependent primarily on commodity exports, long have seen their economies whipsawed by changes in the market price of their raw material exports, over which they had little or no control. Nor could they influence the price of manufactured goods, which they bought from rich lands of the north.

As early as 1962 Raul Prebish, first Secretary-General of the United Nations Conference on Trade and Development (UNCTAD), called for correction of what he termed structural imbalances in North-South trade. A number of industrial nations, including the United States, responded partially to this appeal, both through foreign aid programs and what is called the Generalized System of Preferences. Under this system, industrial powers agree to import duty-free a wide range of products from developing lands. In the United States this duty-free treatment has been expanded from an original 2,000 items worth $2.5 billion to 3,000 items worth $3 billion annually.

This limited approach failed to satisfy the growing aspirations of the less developed countries, however, and, in December 1975, representatives of 27 rich and poor lands convened at Paris in the Conference on International Economic Cooperation. Eighteen months later the conference adjourned with only limited success. But during the Paris meetings there emerged a clear demand from the developing countries for a restructuring of the world economy, summed up in their call for a New International Economic Order. Reforms were demanded in four areas: a new system to stabilize commodity pricing; a wider sharing of industrial technology; relief from growing debt repayment burdens; and increases in interest-free foreign aid.

In the commodity pricing area, demands were spurred by the example of OPEC and by the success of Morocco and Jamaica in raising prices of phosphate rock and bauxite respectively. The less developed countries proposed the establishment of a common fund, to buy up stocks of 18 basic commodities. Among these would be 10 "core commodities"—coffee, cocoa, tea, sugar, cotton, rubber, jute, hard fibers, copper, and tin. Stocks would be bought up and held off the market if prices dropped below specified floors. Conversely, commodities would be released on the market if prices soared above certain ceilings.

The United States responded to the industrial technology demand by proposing centers for technological training, research, and exchange of information. Transfers of technology from developed to developing lands might flow through such centers. In asking relief from debt repayment, the developing nations, which cumulatively owed more than $200 billion, asked that their official debts—what they owe to other governments—be forgiven. Britain, Sweden, Canada, Switzerland, and the Netherlands have done just that. But the United States, whose officials insist on tackling the debt burden of non-oil-producing countries on an individual basis, rejected blanket liquidation. More than two-thirds of less developed nations' debts are owed to private banks, the rest to other governments. Poor lands must depend primarily on private lenders, even if some of their public debt is canceled. Some debtor governments, in the U.S. view, need to be prodded into living within their economic means, and debt forgiveness might relieve this pressure.

In demanding more interest-free foreign aid, the developing nations had a point, relative to the United States at least. As a percentage of gross national product, U.S. foreign aid has slipped substantially below the average of other donor nations, grouped in the Development Assistance Committee of OECD. In current dollars American foreign aid rises slightly year by year, but has declined as a percentage of GNP to about 0.25 percent, far below the 0.75 percent achieved in the early 1960's. On average, donor nations gave 0.33 percent of their GNP in 1976, with the United States ranking 13th among the 18 OECD committee members. Sweden, the

Netherlands, and Norway give more than the 0.7 percent of GNP which is the United Nations' official target.

CONCLUSIONS FOR THE PRESS

If international economic affairs ever were arcane and remote, they are no longer so. World trade, the struggles among nations to maintain and increase their shares of world trade, and the efforts of nations to devise an international monetary system that will accommodate world trade—all are intricately interwoven parts of a continuing story that commands public and press attention. A knowledge of international economic affairs is necessary to aspiring journalists in local and in global reporting.

As international trade has grown, foreign-made cars, television sets, and other consumer goods, including even ham, cheese, and butter cookies, have become commonplace in the United States, and reporters who keep that fact in mind can write more meaningfully about foreign trade issues that otherwise seem complex and remote to readers.

Consider, for example, a story that appeared in *The Christian Science Monitor* in 1978 under the heading, "Ham and Cookies Impasse May Lead to a Trade War." The story said:

> Europe and the United States are staring down the barrels of a trade war, unless sensible men on both sides of the Atlantic find an early compromise.
>
> Though the immediate problem involves ham, cheese, and butter cookies, its ramifications could ripple out to millions of dollars worth of other products and threaten the world's faltering progress toward freer trade.[24]

Another illustration, again from the *Monitor,* shows how reporters can try to make complex issues understandable and readable:

> Can something called a "countervailing duty waiver" really be one of the most important things going on in Washington now?
>
> Yes, says Robert S. Strauss, who calls the issue a time bomb that could "blow up" multilateral trade talks in Geneva and damage U.S. trade relations with Europe and elsewhere.[25]

The emergence of underdeveloped nations as both an economic and political force in international affairs raises many issues that will remain in the news for years to come. It has been stated in other chapters of this book that an understanding of economic and business issues is necessary to informed reporting in political and other areas of the news, and surely that premise applies to an understanding of international economic affairs.

The economic aspirations of less developed nations and their demands on the world's developed industrial nations already have produced traumatic political as well as economic consequences. The Arab members of OPEC launched the oil embargo of 1973–1974 to exercise leverage against supporters of Israel—principally the United States and the Netherlands—after the Arab-Israeli war of 1973, and the political ramifications of Middle East oil economics remain an issue of international concern. In other parts of the world, too, issues of war and peace may hinge on international economic affairs.

Locally as well as globally, the economic aspirations of developing nations will continue to make news. The actions of OPEC and of other nations will continue to affect the prices Americans pay for oil and other commodities and will affect American jobs.

Between 1965 and 1975, according to World Bank figures, manufactured exports by developing countries increased in value from $10 billion to $33 billion yearly, at an estimated cost of one million jobs in the industrial world. Robert S. McNamara, president of the World Bank, has called for a tripling of exports by underdeveloped "Third World" nations by 1985. Using the World Bank's basis of calculation, that increase might displace 3 million workers in industrialized nations, including the United States.

Already the United States, to preserve domestic jobs, has cut back on imports of cheap shoes from Taiwan and South Korea, two developing lands whose rapid economic progress was made possible partly by American foreign aid. OECD members, including the United States, limit textile exports from the Third World. "The pressures for protection," Alan W. Wolff, deputy U.S. trade negotiator, has said, "have been concentrated in precisely those industries in which many developing countries have built an export capacity—textiles, footwear, consumer electronics. As the industrial base of the developing countries expands, problems of this sort are likely to increase."[26]

International economic affairs and their implications for world peace and prosperity, or for conditions less sanguine, will provide many opportunities for foreign correspondents. Note this dispatch from a veteran *Wall Street Journal* reporter in the Middle East:

> Kuwait—When people talk about multinational corporations, few would think of any based in the desert sheikdom of Kuwait, with its population of a little more than a million people.
>
> One who does is Kutayba Alghanim, the 36-year-old head of the Alghanim Group, who might have been heading an American company if

he had remained in the U.S. after graduating in 1969 from the University of California at Berkeley. Instead, he returned to Kuwait, took over a family trading company with a $20 million annual turnover and transformed it into a $450 million sales company in 10 years.

His businesses range from selling automobiles to making steel buildings, from distributing frozen food to consumer finance. "Now we are multinational. In another four years we will be a billion-dollars-in-annual-sales multinational," he says.[27]

Local business and economic reporters, as well as foreign correspondents, can develop the implications of international economic developments, however. Here is how *The Washington Post* wrote such a story for its local readers:

Mortgage interest rates in the Washington area rose again yesterday, pushed to near-record highs by the Carter Administration's latest efforts to bolster the sagging dollar.[28]

At home and abroad, international economic news will provide large challenges and large opportunities to business and economic journalists.

NOTES—CHAPTER 11

1. Anthony M. Solomon, briefing reporters in the White House, December 6, 1977.

2. Alan W. Wolff, Deputy Special Representative for Trade Negotiations, April 1978, to the writer.

3. Olivier Long, in an address to the Zurich Economic Society, November 9, 1977.

4. Robert S. Strauss, in a speech before the Southern Governors Conference, San Antonio, Texas, August 31, 1977.

5. U.S. Treasury, Office of Balance of Payments, October 3, 1977.

6. U.S. Bureau of Mines, 1976 figures.

7. Secretary of State Cyrus R. Vance before the National Governors Association, Washington, D.C., February 27, 1978.

8. Karen Elliott House, "Peking's Money Woes Could Limit Any Spurt in Trade with West," *Wall Street Journal*, December 28, 1978, pp. 1, 19.

9. For a history of U.S. tariff policy see John M. Dobson, *Two Centuries of Tariffs* (Washington, D.C.: United States International Trade Commission, December 1976).

10. *Ibid.*, p. 1.

11. "Petition Asks Curb on Color TV Imports," *New York Times*, September 23, 1976, p. 8.

12. At the beginning of 1978, GATT had 83 full members, plus three provisional members and 19 "de facto" member nations that abide by GATT rules. Of GATT's members in 1978, five were Communist: Cuba, Czechoslovakia, Poland, Romania, and Yugoslavia.

13. A White House trade official commenting to the author in December 1977, when the United States and Japan were engaged in trade talks.

14. *Ibid.*

15. J. Stanford Smith, speaking to reporters in Washington, December 5, 1972.

16. U.S. Treasury figures, presented to the House Commerce, Consumer, and Monetary Affairs Subcommittee, October 1977.

17. President Carter in a speech at Cranston, R.I., February 17, 1978.

18. Reginald H. Jones, in a statement before the House Ways and Means Committee, March 6, 1978.

19. C. Fred Bergsten, assistant secretary of the Treasury for international affairs, to the International Trade, Investment and Monetary Policy Subcommittee of the House Banking Committee, March 13, 1978.

20. Robert J. Samuelson, *National Journal,* reprinted by *Washington Post,* November 14, 1978, p. D1.

21. U.S. trade figures from 1971, when the nation's trade balance first went into deficit, through 1977, as compiled by the Bureau of the Census, U.S. Commerce Department: 1971, $2 billion deficit; 1972, $6.4 billion deficit; 1973, $1.3 billion surplus; 1974, $2.3 billion deficit; 1975, $11 billion surplus; 1976, $5.9 billion deficit; 1977, $26.5 billion deficit. Figures are rounded.

22. Bruce MacLaury, to the author, February 1978.

23. C. Fred Bergsten, to the Subcommittee on Foreign Assistance, Senate Committee on Foreign Affairs, July 27, 1977.

24. Harry B. Ellis, *The Christian Science Monitor,* October 20, 1978, pp. 1, 18.

25. Harry B. Ellis, *The Christian Science Monitor,* September 22, 1978, pp. 1, 11.

26. Alan W. Wolff, speaking in Kuala Lumpur, Malaysia, February 2, 1978.

27. Ray Vicker, "Kuwaiti Multinational Firm Illustrates Expansion of U.S. Arab Business Links," *Wall Street Journal,* December 28, 1978, p. 6.

28. Jerry Knight, "Near Record Mortgage Rates Throughout Area," *Washington Post,* November 7, 1978, p. D9.

SOURCES OF INFORMATION

Agency for International Development
Public Information Office
Washington, D.C. 20523

Export-Import Bank of the United States
Public Affairs Office
811 Vermont Avenue, N.W.
Washington, D.C. 20571

Office of the Special Representative for
 Trade Negotiations
Executive Office of the President
Washington, D.C. 20506

U.S. Department of Commerce
Bureau of International Commerce
Washington, D.C. 20520

U.S. International Trade Commission
Public Information Office
Washington, D.C. 20436

U.S. Treasury Department
Assistant Secretary for International
 Affairs
Washington, D.C. 20220

World Bank *(International Bank for*   1818 H Street, N.W.
Reconstruction and Development)   Washington, D.C. 20006
Press Office

SUGGESTED READINGS

Acheson, Dean, *Present at the Creation*. New York: W. W. Norton & Co., 1969.

Balance of Payments Manual, 4th ed. Washington, D.C.: International Monetary Fund, 1977.

Barnet, Richard J., and Ronald E. Muller, *Global Reach: The Power of the Multinational Corporations*. New York: Simon and Schuster, 1974.

"Creeping Cartelization," *Business Week*, May 9, 1977, pp. 64–83.

Dobson, John M., *Two Centuries of Tariffs*. Washington, D.C.: U.S. International Trade Commission, 1976.

"Gold Up, Dollar Down: ABC's of What It Means," *U.S. News & World Report*, August 14, 1978, pp. 71–73.

Hirsch, Fred, *Social Limits to Growth*, A Twentieth Century Fund Study. Cambridge, Mass.: Harvard University Press, 1976.

Hirsch, Fred, and John Goldthorpe, eds., *The Political Economy of Inflation*. London: Martin Robertson, 1978.

Kamarck, Andrew, *The Tropics and Economic Development*. Baltimore: Johns Hopkins University Press, 1977.

Mayer, Martin, "Uncharted Seas of Reserve Currencies," *Financier: The Journal of Financial Affairs*, February 1977, pp. 15–18.

Petroleum Industry Research Foundation, Inc., *Outlook for World Oil Into the 21st Century*. New York: Electric Power Research Institute, 1978.

Pollock, John C., *The Politics of Crisis Reporting*. New York: Praeger Special Studies, a division of Holt, Rinehart and Winston, 1978.

Rose, Sanford, "The Global Slowdown Won't Last Forever," *Fortune*, August 14, 1978, pp. 92–111.

Solomon, Robert, *The International Monetary System 1945–76*. New York: Harper & Row Publishers, 1976.

Strauss, Simon D., "Why Commodity Cartels Won't Work," *Business Week*, June 30, 1975, pp. 20, 22.

Vogl, Frank, "Illusion of Power, Crisis of Identity, at the International Monetary Fund," *Financier: The Journal of Financial Affairs*, February 1977, pp. 15–18.

Media
Requirements

III

Covering Economics for ... NEWSPAPERS, LARGE AND SMALL

12

WILLIAM E. GILES

T HE PITCHER REARED BACK and zipped a perfect strike to the lonely end on the 20-yard line, who scampered the remaining 80 yards upfield, leaped high in the air, and dunked the ball for the winning two-point touchdown.

What?

Good question. It is sports, and more obviously nonsense than much of the mishmash that has passed for economic and business coverage in many newspapers. Reporting is erratic. Much of the writing is imprecise and too often inaccurate. Articles have been short and meaningless, or long and meaningless.

In the imperfect world of newspapering, these perhaps have not been intolerable offenses. They reflect, in fact, the fuzzy ways and the arcane language of economics. Moreover, economics has possessed little attractiveness for newspapers, which, according to folklore, thrive on sensationalism. Have you ever read a really racy account of a tax bill in Congress, a philandering dollar abroad, or a gallivanting gross national product?

If sensationalism sells newspapers, you might ask, who needs business and economics? The answer would appear to be that millions need business and economic news. Many newspapers are increasing the amount of space devoted to business and economics coverage. Economic news is getting more prominent play on the front pages of newspapers. Reporting staffs of many large daily papers are being upgraded and expanded.

This activity suggests that the low state of economics coverage in newspapers, long tolerated by publishers and editors, is changing. And it is about time. Most newspaper readers, who show uncommon good sense in selecting what they read, historically have skipped business and economic materials, even though it usually has more direct impact on their lives than most other news.

Moreover, newspapers have certain advantages over radio and television, on one hand, and over magazines and other periodicals, on the other. Reporters work under deadlines and their stories must fit into "news holes" that never seem big enough, but far more time and space are available to them than to television and radio news reporters. Still, the newspaper business is exciting because its reports have an immediacy and urgency that are not normally found in a weekly, monthly, or other periodical. These advantages of newspapers are particularly important in reporting economic and business news that is urgent and yet needs comprehension by the reporter and by the readers.

Students who are still in college have asked me, "What can I do to get into business journalism?" They are bright enough to pick up the newspaper and see what is on the front page. They know that the running story is the President's budget or the governor's budget or oil prices or a fight over electric rates—and those are economic and business stories.

In the United States there are some 1,800 daily newspapers with a total circulation of more than 60 million and there are more than 7,500 weeklies with a total circulation of some 38 million.[1] Not all have economic and business news specialists on their reporting staffs, to be sure, but the opportunities for business and economic reporting on large and small newspapers are expanding and will continue to grow.

NEWSPAPERS AND ECONOMIC JOURNALISM

Economic journalism has suffered in general circulation newspapers on several counts. Articles have been difficult to read and writers have made little attempt to make them readable. Many stories have made little sense to readers, and editors have done little to highlight their significance. Economic and business reporting too often has produced stories with inflated verbiage and minimal fact.

It does not have to be that way. A journalist can make stories readable by focusing on people rather than things, by probing for natural, colorful quotes, and by exorcising pretentious, imprecise, and irrelevant wordage. *The Wall Street Journal* perhaps does the best, most consistent work on this kind of article with its page one "leaders." Consider, for example, a piece concerning a company's expenditures of $18 million and two years in the development of a new roll-on antiperspirant. The lead of the story read:

> Most associates credit Derwyn Phillips, the 48-year old president of
> Gillette Co.'s personal-care division, with a sense of humor. But when
> he speaks of the ambition that has been driving him and scores of

Gillette researchers and marketers for the past year or so, his blue eyes harden and his shoulders hunch with intensity.

"We're going to be the dominant marketer in the underarm business," Mr. Phillips asserts. "This company," he says, "knows more about armpits" than any of more than a dozen major competitors in the $11 billion-a-year personal-care-products business.[2]

The arresting quote in the lead promises that the story will be readable and the significance of the story to many readers is implicit in the fact that Americans spend $11 billion annually to buy antiperspirants and other personal care products. High in the article its significance to readers is stated explicitly in a paragraph which says that the story of the development of the new product "tells a lot about how and why such products are conceived, developed, tested and sold in a highly competitive industry."

Obviously, not every business or economic story can, or should, be constructed in this style, even in a newspaper such as *The Wall Street Journal.* On the inside of the *Journal,* writers produce effective news stories with a quite different style, emphasizing short, authoritative, to-the-point leads. For example:

Chrysler Corp. quietly canceled previously announced plans to offer diesel engines in some of its 1979-model pickup trucks and vans.[3]

And another example:

President Carter reversed an earlier stance and decided to raise import duties on industrial fasteners from Japan and other countries.[4]

These, too, are readable in the sense that they get to the heart of the news quickly and smartly. They can be understood on first reading. And, most important, the news in the lead is solidly supported in the body of the story.

The reasons for the generally inferior quality of business and economic reporting in most newspapers stem from the peculiar nature of news, the peculiar nature of economics, and some peculiar notions about the purposes of economic news.

There is, of course, fierce competition each day for news space in most newspapers. "Big" news that is frequently unpredictable and sometimes sensational squeezes less compelling news down or out, and this fact usually works against sustained, systematic coverage. The result is that business and economic news in newspapers usually comes in bits and pieces over days or weeks. Newspaper coverage of business and economics thus suffers from frequently erratic reporting and episodic presentation.

Economic and business news, by its nature, tends to be more complex and unfamiliar than, say, political or sports news. It relies heavily on abstractions, statistics, or ratios and thus is often more difficult to grasp and more difficult to write under pressures of time and news space. While political and sports news is made by politicians and sport figures, reporters often must dig behind the abstractions, statistics, and ratios to find the business people and the arresting quotations that help make economic and business news come alive. Moreover, the journalists who report and edit business and economic news consider themselves, by and large, news generalists rather than economic or business specialists. This is as it should be, insofar as journalists should be good reporters and writers before they are specialists in economics and business or in any other field of coverage. But specialization also demands specialized knowledge, and the absence of such knowledge in traditional newspaper staffing has increased the possibilities of inept and uninteresting handling of economic and business facts.

Business and economic coverage historically has been subject in many newspapers to sensitivities that have little to do with professional judgments of news reporting. Because newspapers are in business, reporters and editors are not immune to pressures applied both internally and externally to shape business and economic news in certain ways. It is not uncommon for business people to object loudly to the printing of "bad" news, even if true, and the upshot is that until recently business coverage on many newspapers has neither attracted nor held the very best journalists.

Because of those and other shortcomings, the traditional business page in the average newspaper often has consisted of little more than stock market tables, puff pieces, mug shots, and the latest crop report from Liechtenstein. The large potential for improvement and for increased reader acceptance is being recognized, however. Business and economic news frequently appears nowadays on page one of many papers. Editors have included more commentary by nonstaff economic specialists. Some have redefined the traditional concepts of "business news" and have put increased emphasis on consumer-oriented coverage of news that is of practical use. Many have carved out space for new facets of economic news and have used more visual materials, such as charts, graphs, tables, and color to illustrate and illuminate articles.

The *Chicago Tribune* began producing a bright new "Midweek Business Report" in the spring of 1978. *The New York Times* started a hefty new "Business Day" section. Other major newspapers, including *The Detroit News, The Washington Post,* and *The Philadelphia Bulletin,* have given business and economics news more space and bigger play.

This new thrust into expanded business and economic coverage by local newspapers reflects a conviction that this field can produce news of genuine interest to people who read general newspapers. The recognition has come primarily because newspapers are aggressively seeking new markets—and rediscovering old ones.

As they look for areas of circulation growth, newspaper publishers and editors are impressed by the spectacular gains registered over the past couple of decades by national publications editorially focused on news of business, industry, trade, and commerce. The prime example, of course, is *The Wall Street Journal*, whose national circulation has scooted from 200,000 or so in the early 1950's to more than 1.8 million in 1979. *Forbes, Business Week, U.S. News & World Report*, and other more specialized business publications have posted similar gains. This kind of growth has suggested there is an appetite for business and economic news which has not been satisfied by local news media.

Obviously, no daily general newspaper could suddenly become a national, specialized *Wall Street Journal*. But just as plainly, *The Wall Street Journal* cannot become a community's daily newspaper serving the varied interests of each community's readers. What is possible and appears likely from current trends is that the more resourceful newspapers, recognizing the growing interest in economic affairs, will be aiming to cover their local economic universe with the talent and fervor normally reserved for sports, crime, and scandal.

As more and more newspapers try to improve their economic coverage, they are wrestling with the need to develop:

1. a concept for covering economic affairs which is logical, workable, and productive;

2. meaningful and fresh techniques of reporting and methods of writing about business and economics;

3. a cadre of knowledgeable reporters, writers, and editors who understand business and economics and possess the journalistic talents to produce readable copy;

4. an editorial conviction that business and economic news is legitimate news of wide interest and must be told straightforwardly and accurately.

A CONCEPT OF ECONOMIC AND BUSINESS NEWS

On many newspapers, reporting on business is one thing; reporting on economic affairs is quite another.

Business is nitty-gritty; the economy is big. Business is local; the economy is national or international. Reporters cover business; journalists cover economics.

Or so it seems from any perusal of a dozen larger, more aggressive dailies. Economic news—inflation, employment, trade, government budgets, the dollar abroad—often gets up-front play. Local business news—which could have far greater impact and interest for the community—usually shows up on the business pages, just ahead of classified advertisements. Business stories generally seem softer, more like features; economic stories reek of authority and importance, but often they are incomprehensible.

The perceived difference in content and play between "economic" and "business" news may have no great significance to casual readers, but it reflects a widespread confusion among newspaper editors about the proper criteria for judging business and economic news on subject matter, on content, and on display. At the least, it suggests that the working concept for handling business and economic news needs refining.

To do this, it is useful to consider both the newspaper and the newspaper audience.

The Nature of News and Newspapers

Because there is in every town and city, in the nation and in the world, more news than can ever be printed daily, some standards for the selection and evaluation of stories are necessary and each newspaper editor has his or her standards. Even a paper as large as *The Detroit News,* with 300 people on its staff, does not have enough reporters to cover everything. While 12 of those staff members normally are involved in covering the business beat in Detroit, there are 41 companies with world headquarters in the Detroit area, plus 569 other companies doing business in the area. There is no way that this group of reporters, relatively large for a metropolitan daily but small relative to the size of their beat, could constantly be on top of everything.

Logic would seem to suggest that local newspapers naturally would stress local economic and business news, just as most emphasize local sports, accidents, and other happenings. But it has not happened. In my random survey of a dozen large dailies, fully two-thirds of the business and economic news that was published originated from distant sources and nonstaff writers.

Much of the published material consists of economic stories from Washington, New York, or abroad. They usually are wire service stories, mostly from Associated Press or United Press International, but sometimes from such specialists as the Dow Jones or Reuters News Services. They usually deal with things—the Consumer Price Index, the dollar, the Federal Reserve Board, inflation, trade, the stock market. They are chock full of statistics and percentages, each tumbling over the other. For the average human being scanning the average daily newspaper, these stories simply cannot be read, let alone understood.

Consider the average reader in Indianapolis, for example, who sees typical dispatches such as these:

Washington—The Commerce Department said inventories rose 0.6 percent in September as businessmen continued a close watch on their stocks in anticipation of an economic downturn next year. . . .

New York—The Federal Reserve Board reported a modest increase in the nation's basic money supply in what analysts see as a hopeful sign that short term interest rates may stabilize.

The nation's chief monetary authority said M-1, which represents money in circulation in checking accounts, rose $1.1 billion to $362.1 billion in the week ended Nov. 8. . . .[5]

Much economic news is made in Washington, of course, and actions taken there on such matters as taxes, interest rates, product safety, tariffs, and the like eventually have an impact on people. But decisions by local employers on such things as prices, payrolls, new plants, and new products have far more immediate impact on a newspaper's community.

The most common reason why local newspapers use more copy generated in Washington and elsewhere is that the wire services deliver it at relatively low cost and it is presumed by copy editors to be important and authoritative. But that is a risky presumption. Moreover, national and international economic stories that tend to substitute for coverage of local business and labor fall far short of the interest and impact of local business and economic material.

There is another and perhaps more fundamental reason why local business and economic coverage in many local newspapers has not been nearly so complete as, say, local sports coverage: The newspaper itself is a business that necessarily relies on the goodwill of its advertisers. Business and economic reporters, therefore, have not always been free and independent of pressures from the business side of newspapers themselves, from the preferences of large advertisers, and from the influence of other community leaders, be they corporate or union executives.

Even some major newspapers with large business news staffs are not immune from what is known in the trade as BOM—a business office must—that frequently is a puff story concerning a major advertiser.

Everybody wants a favorable press, of course, and all kinds of news media are subject to all kinds of pressures, in the form of favors or threats, from politicians and sports figures as well as from business people. At least one press critic has charged that there has existed an "all too pervasive willingness of the press to be had."[6]

Journalists worth their salt are not willingly or knowingly "had." But local newspapers probably are more subject to pressures than large national news organizations, and even papers that are part of such organizations are not immune. For example, after *The New York Times* in early 1976 ran a five-part series on medical incompetence, certain pharmaceutical companies canceled advertising worth $500,000 from *Modern Medicine,* a magazine owned by The New York Times Company.[7]

Business and economic news in local newspapers may be most subject to these pressures simply because such news, if it is covered properly, affects business daily. These pressures, actual and perceived, have been at least partially responsible for the pallid and meaningless nature of much business and economic news, a result that has served neither business, journalism, nor readers.

Some confusion over newspaper coverage of business and economics has resulted because editors have not defined their audiences and thus have not refined the aims of coverage.

The Nature of Newspaper Audiences

There are two major newspaper audiences for business and economic news. The first consists of people who are in business and who want or need to know what is going on in business. The second consists of people who may or may not be engaged in business activity but who are interested in or affected, directly or indirectly, by business and economic activity.

The first group is understood to be knowledgeable about business, but it is distinctly smaller even though it includes interested members, such as advertisers. The second group usually is less informed, although not less intelligent, and it is far larger. A greater effort obviously must be made to attract the attention of the latter group.

The two audiences seem to pose a dilemma. If newspapers aim to serve only the business community, then the presentation of business and economic news often is esoteric, of limited interest, and of more limited impact. If, on the other hand, they aim more independently for a wider audience, they risk offending the business readers either by telling them what they already know or by telling them what they do not need to know in what may be a patronizing style.

While the dilemma may pose some practical problems for newspaper editors and publishers, it is more perceived than real. Business and economic news can be reported and written thoroughly enough and skillfully enough that it interests the casual reader without offending business people. *The Wall Street Journal* almost every day demonstrates on its front page how to do it.

Consider again, for example, the story about the antiperspirant development by a company that "knows more about armpits" than its competitors. The lead of the story certainly was well written to interest the casual reader and, inasmuch as it publicized the company's new product, "Dry Idea," the story presumably did not offend Gillette Co. At the same time, however, the story was no puff piece. In the third paragraph, the story said quite frankly:

The company concedes that "Dry Idea" won't stop perspiration any better than at least five products on the market for some time, but no matter. For Gillette says its product "goes on dry," feels better—and thus leads the user to feel it is more effective.[8]

Business and economic journalism should keep in mind not only that honesty is the best policy but also that there are all kinds of businesses and all kinds of business people. Expertness in preparing and selling pizzas does not automatically qualify the pizza businessman as an expert in steel production, or vice versa. Similarly, a banker, a car dealer, a farmer, a store manager all are in business but cannot be assumed to know or have any pecuniary interest in anyone else's business. It is necessary, therefore, to find common denominators of news interest, whatever the business.

What are common denominators? Success, failure, challenge, conflict, drama, surprise, change, to cite just a few common themes in the world of business and economics. Individuals doing things are unbeatable as subjects of stories whether they are in business, sports, or politics.

Consider just a few samples of business story leads, from *The Detroit News, Chicago Tribune,* and *New York Times* respectively, that grab for universal interest:

The City of Troy has a classic name. It is also the scene of a classic struggle pitting suburban sprawl against establishment of a city center.[9]

What measures 4 by 4 by 5 feet, weighs next to nothing, and is yours for only $10 a month![10]

For a lot of people's money—a great deal of money, in fact—Rodeo Drive is fast becoming the world's most prestigious shopping area.[11]

Editors of business and economic news should assume that readers have little knowledge about the business at hand, a potentially high interest in reading about it, and more than enough intelligence to follow an authoritative lead. Editors also should assume that readers have the common sense to spot a weak, inept effort.

It is hazardous in a general newspaper to pitch stories to specific audiences. The best newspapers provide a wide and varied menu from which readers can pick and choose. But the editorial assumption must be that each item can stand on its own professional merits, whatever the subject matter.

There are, of course, audiences that have a more definable interest in business and economic affairs; they include consumers, stockholders, and wage earners, as well as business people and farmers. But these groups are not sharply defined. A farmer, for instance, is a consumer, a producer, and a laborer who also could be a stockholder. A newspaper reader "belongs" to many groups. A general newspaper therefore must constantly seek to do the most good for the largest number of readers. In business and economics, this boils down to making stories as readable and meaningful as possible to all readers.

A Useful Concept

If newspapers then are to seek and find wider readership, business and economic news cannot continue merely to cater to particular audiences, be they business people, farmers, stockholders, advertisers, or whatever. Business and economic news, like all other news, must be fresh and interesting to a general readership. Wedded to impact, business and economic news thus is freed of its traditional narrowness and parochialism. It means jobs, security, well-being, growth—or the opposite. Thus recast, business and economic news becomes unarguably important and competitive with sports, scandal, and crime for newspaper space.

Space alone obviously is not enough. Business and economic news needs to define its own merits and will do so as it abandons narrowness and parochialism. It will be defined in terms of relevance to the individual, the family, and the community, and not simply in terms of a corporation or the government.

In sum, newspapers that seek wider readership through improvement of business and economic coverage should stress hard news first, especially in local coverage. They must define business and economics broadly as, for example, "the way people make a living and spend their income," must attempt to personalize the news, must write it interestingly, and—above all—must get it right. All that may seem obvious enough, but it has not been so.

REPORTING AND WRITING ECONOMIC AND
BUSINESS NEWS

How shall a logical, workable, and productive concept for reporting business and economic news be applied by newspapers and their reporting staffs?

The first and foremost answer lies in the admonition that the reporter of business and economic affairs cannot set out to boost or knock nor can he or she, through a lack of information or knowledge, be used by others to boost or knock. The job is to get facts and information, make sure they are right, and produce a fair, understandable, and readable report. That advice applies to all journalism, of course, but it applies with particular force to business and economic reporting.

In economics, the facts are not always easy to get or to understand because the beat is loaded with land mines—tricky language, slippery statistics, and unfamiliar concepts. Add to this the problem with some sources—many are too aloof to respond, some are only too eager to propagandize—and it is not surprising that news reporters often are accused of being overly aggressive (arrogant) or unfriendly (properly wary).

Good reporters learn to appreciate both the usefulness and the limitations of helpfulness—from corporations, unions, trade groups, and other sources. A press release understandably reflects the vested interest of the people who put it out. Obviously, that sort of information should never go into a newspaper without independent checking and editing but, sad to say, it sometimes does.

That practice has contributed to unreadable and unread business and economic news. It also has obfuscated the need for authority in business and economic reporting, an area in which authority is especially required simply because business and economic news usually does not explain itself to the reader who is not that interested. The reporter must convey to the reader that he or she knows the subject matter and can write about it with confidence.

Techniques of Reporting

The background knowledge that a reporter needs to cover any story, be it one concerning a national issue such as Social Security or a local matter such as a company's annual profits or a mayor's budget, can be found in all the familiar places—the newspaper's morgue of previous news stories, other articles, documents, and perhaps books. In the substantive chapters of this book, source materials have been suggested for major issues in the news.

In the day-to-day coverage of business and economic news, the ubiquitous press release is not to be overlooked. In large cities and certainly in Washington, even sizable news staffs cannot keep up with everything and always know what is newsworthy in government, companies, or unions. Press releases therefore are useful means of trying to keep abreast of developments and coming events. Some contain news and some contain leads that intentionally or unintentionally will yield news stories.

But the press release should be the beginning, not the end, of a business and economic reporter's work. The information that a reporter learns from a press release, a press conference, or a meeting of say the city council or company stockholders probably will answer who, what, when, and where, but probably will not answer why. Frequently the "why" of a news development is its most pertinent and readable part, but the answer may require digging. Why are a company's profits down? Why are a city's taxes up? Why did the president of a company resign? Why did a union lose a representation election? Why have hospital costs gone up faster than prices generally? Why is Social Security in trouble? Why has inflation persisted?

If an experienced journalist were to offer one most important and obvious piece of advice to young reporters, it would be this: Never hesitate to ask questions, and the higher the authority you question in business, labor, or government the better, but make sure that you have done your homework by getting solid background on the subject before an interview.

When a reporter has questions for a large company, or a union or a government agency or bureau, he or she is apt to be channeled to the public relations office or to an outside public relations firm—to the folks who write the press releases, in other words. This can be good or bad, depending on the caliber of the public relations people and their ability and willingness to talk.

Some public relations men and women can speak with authority; others cannot. If the reporter's questions are not answered satisfactorily at the public relations office, he or she should have no hesitancy to request an interview with an official who does know the answers. Even if the public relations office can answer specific questions, reporters should talk from time to time with top company, union, or government officials to keep abreast of developments and policies that may never be the subject of press releases.

You may not get an interview immediately with the president of a major corporation or the head of a local or federal government agency, but most top officials are willing to talk at some time, especially to reporters who have done their homework.

If you cannot talk with a top official, or even if you can, keep in mind that usually there are at least two sides to a story. Secondary sources are important, for verification or for balance. In business and economic reporting, a company's story might be checked or balanced by a union's views and vice versa. A government agency's story concerning a product's safety or an environmental issue, for instance, might be checked or balanced by the views of the company or community affected by the government regulations. There are many other possible secondary sources in business and economic reporting. Outside lawyers, accountants, bankers, or suppliers, for example, frequently know what is going on inside a company. Business, labor, and consumer interest groups generally know what is going on inside local or federal government bureaus. A company may be a source of information concerning its competitor companies. A government agency probably will know quite a lot about other government agencies.

Reporting techniques are limited only by the motivation and ingenuity of reporters. Devices such as Freedom of Information Acts also can be used in reporting governmental economic affairs. But it must be emphasized that the availability of top news sources also turns on the degree to which reporters themselves are judged to be knowledgeable and informed.

Personalize and Localize the News

Perhaps a few business and economic stories, such as a story in Detroit newspapers of the temporary closing of a local General Motors plant to reduce auto inventories, may explain themselves sufficiently to attract readers. On the other hand, that same story, distributed nationwide by a wire service, offered no explanation of why it was of interest to general newspaper audiences in other cities and its readership undoubtedly reflected little or no interest.[12]

If they are to be read in general circulation newspapers, most business and economic stories must tell why the story has significance or importance to the reader. If the piece has neither, then obviously it should not be published. Many newspapers assume that their readers appreciate the fact that a story, if it is published, must have some inherent value and thus interest. That just is not always so.

The lead of a story should at least suggest its significance to the reader and, if the connection between the story and the reader cannot be made explicit in the lead, then its significance should be explained explicitly high in the story and preferably in the third or fourth paragraph. Unfortunately, that has not been the rule in business and economic reporting. Indeed, the bigger the story, the more likely the reporter's assumption that it needs no explanation. Economic stories that are written in Washington and that run on and on under big headlines in many newspapers typically assume no need of explanation or attraction; consequently, such stories are uninteresting and unreadable.

Consider this not untypical, 43-word lead in a single sentence:

> Washington—The Administration has decided to publish before Election Day a long-delayed study that criticized prices of the aluminum industry, but without the authors' recommendation that the Government consider "possible remedies" which could be implemented if this industry continues to resist competitive behavior.[13]

All the techniques of good writing—an anecdote, a direct quotation, a question, an incongruity, for example—are useful to business and economic reportage in attracting readers by suggesting and explaining the significance of stories to them. In applying those techniques, a basic rule of thumb is this: The more complex the material, the simpler the lead should be.

The rule of thumb has been used repeatedly in *The Wall Street Journal.* The question "When is a potato chip a potato chip?" was the lead of a story about a complicated Food and Drug Administration regulation concerning chips made of dehydrated potatoes.[14] A story about corporations' social responsibilities began with this short question: "What is a corporation's job?"[15] A story about government's difficulties in reducing the inflation rate followed this lead: "Barry Bosworth, the government's chief inflation fighter, may be the most frustrated man in town."[16]

Such leads are attractive not only because they are short, but also because they suggest something that is familiar to and thus interesting to general readers. Everyone is familiar with potato chips, for instance, and almost everyone has some familiarity with frustration. In the story about Barry Bosworth, the reporter attempted to make the significance of the anti-inflation program's frustration more explicit with this sentence in the third paragraph: "The sense of frustration tells the story of what many government and private analysts say is the weakest link in the administration's economic policy: the lack of an effective anti-inflation program."[17]

Localizing and personalizing a story may be difficult in extremely short leads, but there are ways of interesting a reader in a story. Even *The Wall Street Journal* with its national circulation tries frequently to attract readers by localizing and personalizing its stories. An article concerning the paperwork burden imposed on companies by federal, state, and local governments, for instance, carried a small-town dateline and began with this lead:

> Latrobe, Pa.—Ed Nemanic, secretary-treasurer of Vulcan, Inc., is a sweet-tempered, charitable man. He doesn't hate bureaucrats and he doesn't believe politicians are out to destroy the free-enterprise system.
>
> But the government is beginning to try Mr. Nemanic's patience.[18]

The personalized lead has been used by local newspapers too to introduce complex economic stories. One article in a *New York Times* series concerning the financial difficulties of New York's welfare system began with this lead:

> The elderly woman had been sitting in the drab offices in East Harlem while a young man with Project Access, a voluntary agency, made many telephone calls, trying vainly to find someone in the vast bureaucracy of New York City's Human Resources Administration who could handle her problem.
>
> As he began dialing again, she murmured, almost to herself: "I try to see what I can do for my life."[19]

Local stories can be colloquialized and thus personalized. For example, *The Cape Codder,* a twice-weekly paper published in Orleans, Massachusetts, takes local business and economic news seriously, but not too seriously. A lengthy story of local social and economic interest, concerning the cutting of trees on public land by one Charles Weeks, ran under this lead:

> Charles Weeks and his attorney walked into a small, angry nest of residents last Thursday afternoon, when the Harwich Parks and Recreation Commission called a special meeting to talk about Larsen Park and the trees that used to be there.

The sessions began at 3:30 and went on until the cows came home, but nothing was resolved.[20]

There are opportunities for localizing and to a degree personalizing even national economic news that is assumed by Washington reporters to be of significance to newspaper readers simply because it flows from the White House and other lofty places. Many national economic news stories, concerning esoteric matters such as housing construction trends, interest rates, employment patterns, transportation services, and the like, can be used by enterprising reporters to find out what is happening locally in those same areas. Many Washington agencies and bureaus also have regional offices that can be of assistance to local reporters in search of local or regional stories.

The monthly release of the national consumer price index by the Bureau of Labor Statistics in Washington is a continuing national economic story, for instance, although the national statistics may or may not be of local significance or interest. To help local reporters, the bureau has released the national index simultaneously in Washington and in its regional offices in Boston, New York, Philadelphia, Atlanta, Chicago, Dallas, Kansas City, San Francisco, and Los Angeles. Also, recognizing that the national index may not reflect local consumer price movements, the bureau has developed local consumer price indexes for New York, Philadelphia, Detroit, Chicago, and Los Angeles.

The growth of public interest in prices and inflation is reflected in informal tallies, maintained by the Bureau of Labor Statistics, of inquiries received by its regional offices concerning the consumer price index. According to the bureau, the regional offices in 1977 received 308,000 such inquiries, compared with 54,500 inquiries received in 1967. Some inquiries were from the press, but others were from lawyers, accountants, union leaders, and individuals, many of whom have very personal interests in the consumer price index because their wages or pensions are tied to the cost of living.

Explain, Explain, Explain

Business and economic reporting is unlike sports reporting in that sports news ordinarily does not have to be shown to be interesting to the average newspaper reader. On the other hand, the two areas are similar in that sports news often is significant only when placed in context. It is hardly exciting news when the local football team loses another game in a disastrous season. Similarly, a decline in auto sales is less significant when sales have been falling than when they have been rising.

One definition of news is "change," and that applies as much to business and economic news as to all other news. Change relates the present to the past and therefore a business and economic reporter must understand what went before in corporate profits, government taxes, and other matters. Current profit, tax, and other figures are not very meaningful when standing alone; they take their significance from past trends.

Trends that are regarded by news sources as "good" are easily spotted, usually with the help of press releases and press conferences. Higher corporate profits and lower government taxes are obvious examples. Some other trends are simply too large to be ignored. In the early 1970's, for instance, price inflation soared to double-digit levels at the same time unemployment was higher than it had been in 40 years. In many areas of business and economic reporting, however, the news is not so easily placed into the context that reveals its significance. The responsibility then falls to the reporter and his or her knowledge and experience.

Because press releases may give only current statistics, the reporter must dig into documents or interviews to find what went before in company employment, production, wages, and profits, for example. The results of an employee representation election are more meaningful if it is known whether the union previously won or lost an election. When a city council, state legislature, or Congress votes to increase or decrease taxes, the action takes significance largely from the past trend of taxes.

There are many ways in which news can be placed into context and perspective without slant or distortion. For example, there is no way of telling where the writer stood in this interesting lead from *The Chicago Tribune:*

> A new battle in the war between the nation's railroads and truckers will break out next month. The opening shot will come when a Santa Fe piggyback train—laden with lettuce and oranges—pulls out of Los Angeles, bound for Chicago.
>
> On the surface, the event appears unremarkable. But transportation experts say that train, and others like it, could reverse the railroads' decades-old loss of perishable freight traffic to the trucking industry.[21]

In business and economic journalism, more than in other areas of reporting, it is also necessary for the writer to explain the meanings of terms that may be unfamiliar. Perhaps sports writers can assume that their readers know all they need to know. But business and economics reporters can make no such assumption. The reader can hardly be expected to have any interest in what he or she does not understand; many business and economic terms, such as gross national product, balance of trade, earnings per share, cost of living differential, gross income and net income, do not explain themselves. If you have any doubt about readers' understanding, then define and explain.

Even for its relatively sophisticated audience, *The Wall Street Journal* defines terms that many general circulation newspapers might think need no definition. In a *Journal* story about a government official's warning that, if inflation were not curbed then a depression might follow, this explanation was offered:

> Unlike recession, which is defined as two consecutive quarters of declining economic activity, a depression hasn't any generally accepted definition. The council official described it as a "severe and prolonged economic downturn" that results in widespread unemployment.[22]

Reporters obviously must understand terms they are explaining. A glossary of business and economic terms is at the back of this book and additional glossaries can be found in other books and pamphlets. However, reporters also can and should ask business and economic news sources to define the terms they are using.

All of this is not to say that you should tell everything you know, of course. Business and economic stories often tend to be long and unreadable as well as short and meaningless. The trick in this type of reporting, as in all good writing, is to tell the readers all they want and need to know. No less and no more.

BUILDING A NEW CADRE IN JOURNALISM

Not too many years ago any newcomer who arrived in the newsroom with a college degree was regarded with a certain contempt. A cliché of the trade was that a good reporter could cover any kind of news; no special training was needed because good newspapering came with experience, not book knowledge. Much newspaper writing reflected that arrogance.

Even though many reporters with bachelors degrees and some with masters degrees now populate most news staffs, some resentment still lingers about people who come into newsrooms with specialties. They sometimes are looked upon as narrower people than general assignment reporters, as people whose potential is limited by their specialties.

That attitude is changing, as it must. Newspapers have changed as television and radio have become purveyors of the kind of variegated, abbreviated, "spot" news that made the general assignment reporter useful and indeed necessary. So long as newspapers compete head-on with television and radio in stressing the immediacy of news, the general assignment reporter will continue to be useful. However, as newspapers more and more compete for audiences by offering in-depth reporting, investigative reporting, and news interpretation and analysis, newspapers will tend to be staffed more by specialists and less by generalists.

Journalism may never become as specialized as, say, the medical or legal professions or even professional football. But specialization necessarily implies more knowledge and training than were needed in general assignment reporting. Specialization implies authority and it bears repeating that the writer must convey to the reader a knowledge of the subject at hand and an ability to write about it with confidence.

The need for specialization, knowledge, and confidence in business and economic reporting is apparent enough simply from the lack of those qualities in much past business and economic reporting on many general circulation newspapers.

After that is said, however, it must be said again that the first quality an editor normally seeks in *all* aspiring reporters is the ability to write properly and clearly for a widely diversified audience. The ability to do this is most often found in young people with liberal arts background. We need liberally educated young people who can write.

The necessary knowledge of business and economics can be obtained in many ways. Learning can be as simple as reading readily available and free booklets such as "How to Read a Financial Report," published by Merrill Lynch Pierce Fenner & Smith Inc. Or learning can be extensive; journalism majors can and do take courses in economics, business administration, labor relations, accounting, and so forth. Seminars are available to student and working reporters and the cost of attending them frequently is picked up by employers, colleges, or foundations.

However the journalist acquires knowledge of economics and business, he or she will continue to read journals and books in order to broaden his or her horizons and perhaps to discover trends and leads that can be developed into continuing stories. In short, serious business and economic journalists will informally continue their education.

How much knowledge you will want or require will depend on you and your position. On *The Wall Street Journal* and some other large daily papers, beats are specialized and different reporters cover banking, transportation, the stock market, retailing, and so forth. On many smaller newspapers, on the other hand, there is no business beat as such. The reporter who writes business may be called upon to cover politics and other areas as well. This spreads a reporter out but it doesn't diminish the necessity to cover business and economics authoritatively.

To sum up, a new cadre of economic and business journalists will consist of reporters who, first, are able to write and second, have a knowledge of business and economics that enables them to write with authority. They will have liberal arts or journalism degrees simply because they are writing for a general newspaper audience, not for economists or business people or labor leaders. It is for that reason that good reporters rarely hold degrees in economics, business, or labor relations; they maintain an independent perspective of those disciplines and sources.

THE LEGITIMACY OF BUSINESS AND ECONOMIC NEWS

Business and economic news, as we have defined it at considerable length for newspaper purposes, fundamentally is news of how people earn and spend their money and thus how individuals, communities, and the nation strive to improve their economic and social lot. Thus defined, business and economic news is at least as legitimate as many other kinds of news.

Yet, the legitimacy of business and economic news has suffered, partly from perceptions that it is impersonal and complicated but probably more from perceptions unique to the newspaper and business communities themselves. As we have seen, business reporting too often has been viewed as an extension of the newspaper's business and advertising departments. That attitude perpetuates the BOM, it generates various other kinds of puff pieces, and results in the publication of unquestioned and unedited press releases. It gives rise to the attitude that news is "bad" or "good." Given that attitude, any story that is perceived to be even slightly critical of a local company sets off repercussions and the editor, and perhaps reporter, invariably is subjected to flak. The attitude persists in much of the business community that bad news, ignored by a newspaper, somehow will disappear and cause no harm. Good news is supposed to create confidence. Neither, of course, works that way.

That view of business and economic news has been self-defeating within both the newspaper and business communities. Reporters who merely write puff pieces and paste up press releases need no particular knowledge or understanding of business and economics, of course, and the news is self-serving to the business community and meaningless to the general public. It is, in a word, dull. It attracts no worthwhile newspaper audience and thus is of no use to the newspaper or to business.

A newspaper's business is news. Whether the news is "good" or "bad" is a matter of judgment properly left to editorial page writers. Our function is not to make business or labor or any other interest appear good or bad. Our audience is the general readership, and when a newspaper plays to any other interest it diminishes the product and defeats itself.

The caliber of a newspaper can be gauged by the independence of its news staff—by its freedom to pursue legitimate news and get it into the paper. Independence in news reporting and writing ultimately serves the best interests of readers, of business, and of the newspaper itself.

It is neither practical nor necessary that all newspapers be headed by executives from the news side, but superior business and economic news coverage requires independent as well as informed reporting and writing, and these qualities more likely will be found on the news side, rather than the advertising and commercial side, of most newspapers.

If newspaper editors are going to do a respectable job for their readers—and increase the audience, which is their aim—they will have to treat economic reporting and writing with the respect accorded other areas of high reader interest. That is, they will need more newspeople capable of understanding and writing about economic affairs, proper space to display their work, and the competence to let professional work speak for itself.

NOTES—CHAPTER 12

1. In 1976 there were 1,762 daily newspapers published in the United States with a total circulation of 61 million, according to Editor and Publisher, New York. The number of dailies was 1,878 in 1940 and 1,763 in 1960, according to the same source. According to the National Newspaper Association, Washington, D.C., there were about 7,500 weeklies in 1976 and 7,405 in 1975, and their 1976 circulation of 38 million represented an increase of nearly 3 million from 1975.

2. Neil Ulman, "Time, Risk, Ingenuity All Go Into Launching New Personal Product," *Wall Street Journal,* November 17, 1978, pp. 1, 41.

3. *Wall Street Journal,* December 27, 1978, p. 5.

4. *Wall Street Journal,* December 27, 1978, p. 4.

5. The Washington story was distributed by United Press International and the New York story by Associated Press. Both appeared in the *Indianapolis Star* on November 17, 1978.

6. Theodore J. Jacobs, writing in *The New York Times Book Review,* July 30, 1972, p. 17. The comment was made in Mr. Jacobs's review of *The Effete Conspiracy and Other Crimes by the Press* by Ben H .Bagdikian.

7. *New York Times,* February 10, 1976, p. 10.

8. Ulman, "Time, Risk, Ingenuity", pp. 1, 41.

9. *Detroit News,* December 27, 1978, p. 1.

10. *Chicago Tribune,* December 27, 1978, Section 5, p. 1.

11. *New York Times,* December 14, 1978, p. D-1.

12. The story, datelined Detroit, January 29, 1975, was distributed by United Press International.

13. *New York Times,* August 31, 1976, pp. 37, 38, in a story headed "Administration, After Delay, to Publish a Report Criticizing Aluminum Pricing."

14. *Wall Street Journal,* November 25, 1975, p. 4.

15. *Wall Street Journal,* October 26, 1971, p. 1.

16. *Wall Street Journal,* April 11, 1978, p. 1.

17. *Ibid.*

18. *Wall Street Journal,* July 16, 1976, p. 1.

19. *New York Times,* December 8, 1976, p. 1.
20. *Cape Codder,* November 14, 1978, p. 3.
21. *Chicago Tribune,* January 11, 1979, Section 3, p. 1.
22. *Wall Street Journal,* November 16, 1978, p. 6.

SOURCES OF INFORMATION

American Newspaper Publishers Association
The Newspaper Center
Box 17407
Dulles International Airport
Washington, D.C. 20041

American Society of Newspaper Editors
Box 551
1350 Sullivan Trail
Easton, Penn. 18042

Associated Press Managing Editors
50 Rockefeller Plaza
New York, N.Y. 10020

*Editor & Publisher, and Editor & Publisher
Yearbook*
575 Lexington Avenue
New York, N.Y. 10022

National Newspaper Association
1627 K Street, N.W.
Suite 400
Washington, D.C. 20006

National Newspaper Publishers Association
770 National Press Building
Washington, D.C. 20006

New York Financial Writers' Association
Box 4306
New York, N.Y. 10017

*Society of American Business and Economic
Writers*
c/o Robert Corya
Indianapolis News
Indianapolis, Ind. 46206

SUGGESTED READINGS

Banks, Louis, "Memo to the Press: They Hate You Out There," *The Atlantic,* April 1978.

Cooney, John E., "Does Business Want a Sophisticated Press or a Favorable One," *Wall Street Journal,* July 21, 1977, p. 1.

Green, Mark, "How Business Is Misusing the Media," *New York Times,* December 18, 1977.

Hage, George S., Everette E. Dennis, Arnold H. Inmach, and Stephen Hartgen, *New Strategies for Public Affairs Reporting.* Englewood Cliffs, N.J.: Prentice-Hall, 1976, pp. 236–50.

Holland, Robert C. (president of the Committee for Economic Development), "Census-Building, the Press and the Economy," a speech before The Evening News Association, Detroit, October 17, 1977.

Hubbard, J. T. W., "Business News in Post-Watergate Era," *Journalism Quarterly,* Autumn 1976.

Idaszak, Jerome, "The Business News Boom: Today's Money Is on the Money Beat," *Quill,* June 1978.

Jones, William H., and Laird B. Anderson, "The Newspaper Business," *Washington Post,* a 12-part series, in the Business/Financial section, July 24–August 7, 1977.

MacDougall, Curtis D., *Interpretative Reporting.* New York: Macmillan Publishing Co., 1977, chap. 18.

MacNaughton, Donald S., "The Businessman Versus the Journalist," *New York Times,* March 7, 1976, p. F14.

Otwell, Ralph, "Big, Bad Business in the Hands of the Devil Press," *Quill,* April 1977.

Seib, Charles B., "Business and the Media," *Washington Post,* March 26, 1976, p. A27.

Silk, Leonard, *Economics in Plain English.* New York: Simon & Schuster, 1978.

Sulzberger, Arthur Ochs, "Business and the Press," a speech before the Economic Club of Detroit, March 14, 1977.

Udell, Jon G., and contributing authors, *The Economics of the American Newspaper.* New York: Hastings House Publishers, 1976.

Covering Economics for...
MAGAZINES AND PERIODICALS

13

JAMES W. MICHAELS

No AREA IN MODERN JOURNALISM presents a more open-ended opportunity for creativity and personal advancement—for satisfaction and money—than business reporting. The chief business of journalism in times past was not business and economics but government and politics. This has changed. The tremendous success in recent decades of *The Wall Street Journal,* of *Business Week,* of *Forbes* has not been lost on other publishers. Magazines that cater to particularly defined general audiences now weigh in heavily with articles about business and business people. The newsmagazines have devoted more and more space to business and economics. So, of course, have the newspapers.

Do not think of business and economic reporting as a narrow, specialized occupation. Business journalists are covering the biggest continuing story of the day, the year, the decade, and perhaps the remainder of the century. Ask any politician or public opinion poll to identify the most important issues and chances are the answer will be jobs and inflation. That's business and economic journalism!

How do you go about breaking into this profession? My advice is: Aim for the top, but take what you can get. Start wherever you can. Prospective employers want something more than an academic record upon which to judge a person. An editor wants to know whether you are persistent, capable of thinking for yourself, capable of developing as a writer, and good with people.

If *Time* is not interested in you first time around, don't panic. Get something more to put on your resume than just where you went to school. A job, any kind of job, where you have established a track record will help.

Get a job on a newsletter or a trade publication. The job need not even be in journalism; a leading trade publisher has said that he likes to hire young people who have worked a few years in a business and want to switch to journalism. At least two of the current senior editors at *Forbes* started that way.

A job on a newspaper? Okay, but remember that newspaper writing is quite different from magazine writing.

MAGAZINE JOURNALISM IS DIFFERENT

Magazines and other weekly, fortnightly, or monthly periodicals have deadlines, but they are not the daily deadlines of metropolitan newspapers or the still more urgent deadlines of television and radio news. Don't assume from this, however, that magazine writing is a leisurely occupation. If magazine writing normally allows extra time, it also makes additional demands upon the writer. Besides, a deadline is a deadline whether it is two weeks away or 20 minutes away; in either case you are working against time and you never have enough of that. If you are working on a story for *Business Week,* say, and *The Wall Street Journal* gets it first, your story will have lost much of its attractiveness in your editor's view.

Because they have more time, magazine journalists have both the opportunity and obligation to report more broadly and deeply, to write more carefully, and to place issues and events in a more comprehensive context than most newspaper journalists. In sum, magazine writing places a greater value on the journalist's judgment, interpretation, and intuition—on his or her ability and willingness to think a subject through to a conclusion—than most other forms of journalistic endeavor. You must give the reader not only the news but the meaning of the news.

Let us say that, as happened a few years back, American Telephone & Telegraph reports for the first time profits of $1 billion in a single quarter. That milestone was reported widely in the daily press. *Forbes,* coming out a week after the news broke, was able to put the event into better perspective, to point out that the seemingly huge profit represented a modest return on the company's investment; the profit was huge only because the investment required to produce it was so huge. Magazines are more likely than newspapers to supply this kind of perspective. Magazine journalism may not be literature, but it can come close; many authors of books also have written for magazines, certainly including business magazines. The great Lincoln Steffens, for example, covered business and finance early in his career and his understanding of how business and politics interacted helped make him one of the great muckrakers. More recently, in 1951 William H. Whyte, Jr., explored business sociology in a *Fortune* story about management wives, and his later research into the complex interrelationships between corporations and their managements led to his classic book, *The Organization Man*.

This of course is not to say that magazines and newspapers are as different as day and night. In the face of television and radio competition in reporting spot news, many newspapers in recent years have carried much more magazine-type feature material in their business and other sections. Magazines, on the other hand, certainly do not ignore news developments and trends and pegs. Some trade magazines and newsletters supply their specialized audiences with a great deal of specific news that is not available in general circulation publications. Furthermore, many larger newspapers publish their own Sunday magazines, such as *The New York Times Magazine,* which is written in large part by contributors who are not on the newspaper's staff. A good deal of the excellent reporting that goes into *The Wall Street Journal* would be at home in a magazine. More than once we at *Forbes* have dropped a subject because *The Wall Street Journal* got there first and left little of significance unsaid. The line between newspaper and magazine journalism is becoming blurred.

Still, there are fundamental differences between magazine and newspaper journalism that reflect the different functions of the two types of publications. Magazine reporters have more time and frequently more resources than are available to newspaper reporters. At *Forbes* and some other large business magazines, for instance, reporters and editors often have the assistance of staff researchers, statisticians, and junior reporters.

We pride ourselves on brevity at *Forbes,* but magazine articles tend to be longer than most newspaper stories and certainly contain more information than even the longest television documentary (although, of course, the TV documentary may be at times more convincing because of the camera's ability to show rather than merely tell).

But at its best, magazine journalism can do what television cannot do and what newspapers can do only in serial form, thus interrupting the readers' attention span. I am talking about the treatment in depth and in detail of a major subject. An example at *Forbes* was our publication in 1976 of an essay which challenged traditional economic thinking about the causes of inflation. It was titled "Inflation Is Now Too Serious a Matter to Leave to the Economists."[1] The article was six months in preparation and involved a half dozen members of our staff. The persistence of inflation amidst relatively high unemployment confounded traditional economic theory and we were not satisfied with what other people were printing on the subject. During much of 1976, our editors and staff talked about how we should cover inflation and the talk led to a good deal of tension and a bit of shouting.

Our staff writer, David Warsh, then 33 years old, took the sweeping view that, in reporting the inflation story, journalistic skepticism should extend to ideas as well as to events and people, and that ideas should be followed to their source. In other words, don't accept the accepted wisdom. David argued that most contemporary journalists were spending months proving that a president or a businessman was sinning or blundering, but journalists should be willing to tackle the sins and blunders of "the big thinkers as well as the great doers." In his enthusiasm for tackling economists' inflation theories, David insisted: "Only a better theory replaces an existing theory."

David Warsh was a Harvard College graduate, a Vietnam War veteran, and a reporter with a dozen years of experience on publications including *Newsweek* as well as *Forbes*. His collaborator on our staff was Lawrence Minard, 27, who had been reporting for *Forbes* for two years and was a doctoral candidate in economics at the New School for Social Research. They were shouting at me. I took the conventional view: that one investigates events and what important people are saying and doing, and these are the limits of journalism. I argued that David's approach to inflation was not reporting but advocacy. After nearly 30 years in journalism, I thought I knew what journalism was.

I finally surrendered.

Lawrence Minard found a way to change my mind. On the Late Show one night he was watching an old Clark Gable movie which, if you wanted to see it that way, explained economics in terms of the price of beans, Western movie style. I surrendered to the elegant simplicity of the concept. Why shouldn't we get ahead of the thinkers instead of merely reporting on them?

The article was published in November 1976 by Messrs. Warsh and Minard. It was inspired fundamentally by the obvious failure of the economics profession to provide a satisfactory description of the causes of inflation and it rejected both the "too much money chasing too few goods" and the "administered pricing" theories of inflation. Our authors traced rising prices to the increased complexity of society and the ever increasing division of labor within it. They outlined a "complexity" theory, as opposed to the theory that quantity of money is the root cause of inflation, and they drew parallels between contemporary inflation and similar events going back a thousand years in Western history.

Their argument essentially was that new divisions of labor have been created by government welfare programs, by technology, and by the rising aspirations of common man. As the costs of these new programs and new products are diffused among older costs, the prices of goods rise. Thus, inflation of money supply was seen as a consequence, not as a cause, of the growth of social and economic complexity.

The article was almost twice as long as anything that had been published in *Forbes*. Would our readers bother with so long an article on so seemingly arcane a subject as inflation theory? We did not know, but we published it because it had something very important and unique to say.

Our readers most certainly did bother. Never in recent memory had any *Forbes* article drawn such a volume of mail and never had the response been of equally high intellectual caliber. The mail still was coming in six months after publication and we made 20,000 reprints of the article, all of which sold out.

Our business readers by and large were enthusiastic. The majority of economists, not unexpectedly, were hostile. However, one professor of economics who approved wrote: "Your exaltation of Clark Gable as a better economist than Smith, Marx, Keynes, Samuelson and Friedman combined is a stroke of genius and hopefully will so irritate the cognoscenti that they will attempt to flatten you—and thereby risk conversion."

It had not been *Forbes'* purpose to write the ultimate chapter to a thousand years of economic history. As an organ of business and economic journalism, we saw it as our purpose to enlarge and enlighten public debate on a vital issue, and in that we seemed to have succeeded. Anyway, our article won the Gerald Loeb Award in the national magazine field for 1976.

This isn't the kind of project that the typical young business writer will get involved in at first, but it does show the possibilities. They are legion.

THE BROAD HORIZONS OF PERIODICAL JOURNALISM

Business and economic coverage in magazine and other periodicals embraces a large universe of many hundreds of publications.

The largest in circulation are the weekly newsmagazines, *Time, Newsweek,* and *U.S. News & World Report. U.S. News & World Report* has long been oriented toward business and economic coverage, but the others also paid more attention as the interest in business news quickened. A manifestation of interest was a 1971 *Newsweek* cover story about "Corporations Under Fire." The *Newsweek* cover pictured a worried-looking collection of corporate directors seated at a board table on which rested a bomb with a burning fuse.[2] The bomb was plastered with newspaper headlines such as "Students Rap Business," "Nader Attack," and "Consumers Demand Quality." This was not a "news" story but an essay on corporate responsibility, one of the great issues of our time.

At the other extreme from the newsmagazines, in circulation but certainly not in numbers, are newsletters. There may be as many as 5,000 newsletters sold on a subscription basis and many of them deal with some one aspect of business and economics.

Between the extremes of newsmagazines and newsletters are many more publications, large and small. *Business Week, Forbes,* and *Fortune* in the late 1970's each had a circulation in the 600,000 to 800,000 range. Many more magazines and trade journals with more closely defined business and consumer audiences, such as *Broadcasting* and *Editor & Publisher,* had circulations of between 25,000 and 50,000 copies.

Magazines

General interest magazines, along with metropolitan daily newspapers, were injured in the 1960's and early 1970's by competition from television for audiences and advertisers. Some very large magazines, including *Life* and *Look,* folded and were only later revived. Demographic changes also adversely affected some segments of the magazine industry. Declining farm population, for example, seriously hurt farm magazines. In 1950 six leading farm magazines carried 5,568 pages of advertising; in 1969 the number of such magazines was down to three, which carried 1,916 pages of advertising.[3] The surviving farm publications are stronger than ever but the population they serve is no longer big enough to support six. Meanwhile, the farmer has become a businessman and many farmers now read *The Wall Street Journal* and the general business magazines.

The impact of television on the magazine universe, as on the newspaper industry as a whole in the quarter-century from 1950 to 1975, can be overdrawn and misunderstood, however. Magazines and newspapers that catered to clearly defined audiences and interests not served by television's mass audience appeal did not go the way of *Life* or the *New York Herald-Tribune.* A *Forbes* article would turn off most TV watchers, for example. More recently, the ability of magazines to appeal to such specialized audiences has led to a new boom in magazines and particularly in consumer and business magazines. In the consumer field, for example, *Rolling Stone* and *Playboy* are every bit as successful as the old general interest magazines but much more specialized in content and in point of view.

The total number of magazines published in the United States, as counted by the Magazine Publishers Association, did not change greatly in the quarter-century. There were 91 general and farm magazines in 1950, and 102 in 1953. The total dipped to 82 in 1961 and rose to 93 in 1975.[4]

Total magazine circulation and advertising did not decline over the quarter-century. Using the broader measure of circulation based on Audit Bureau of Circulation membership, in 1950 there were 249 magazines or groups with a combined average circulation per issue of 147 million copies in the first six months of that year. The comparable circulation figures were 188 million in 1960, 245 million in 1970, and 249 million in 1975.[5] Magazines killed by television? Far from it.

Magazine circulations increased despite the higher retail cost. For the nation's 50 leading magazines, the average single copy price rose from 39 cents in 1960 to 87 cents in 1975, and the average yearly subscription price increased from $4.58 in 1960 to $10.14 in 1975.[6] The increases have continued. That the public has been willing to pay the higher prices indicates to us in the business that people are willing to dig deep if the material interests them. We are meeting the ultimate test, the test of the marketplace. We are not, like TV, giving our product away to the consumer.

Advertising pages grew along with revenues. The number of advertising pages carried by 91 general and farm magazines in 1950 totaled 73,550 whereas the number of advertising pages in 93 magazines in 1975 came to 79,628. Advertising revenues of the same numbers of magazines totaled $458 million in 1950 and $1.3 billion in 1975.[7] The magazines are not dying. They are changing and booming.

The magazine market grew rapidly after 1975. For example, advertising revenues increased 48 percent from $1.3 billion in 1975 to nearly $2 billion in 1977. As television advertising became more and more expensive, many advertisers took a new look at magazines—and they liked what they saw. The Magazine Publishers Association reported that 67 of the top 100 TV advertisers increased their magazine advertising in the first half of 1978. Amid the boom, *Life* reappeared.

Moreover, the tremendous growth in the numbers of working women may have had a negative effect on the growth of daytime television audiences while increasing the potential audience of magazines.

In spite of the greatly increased subscription and newsstand prices, however, magazines have been hurt by costs, which have risen faster than the inflation rate, particularly in paper, printing, and postage. Therefore, only those magazines that provide a vital advertising audience are thriving. This explains why about half a typical magazine's pages are devoted to advertising; the proportion has not changed greatly since the 1950's.[8] This makes sense: The advertiser pays the larger part of the cost, perhaps two-thirds, and is entitled to get his message across.

In addition to the fact that circulations of magazines with business audiences increased, many newer magazines catering to business and consumer interests, broadly defined, were introduced. Time Inc.'s *Money* is an example of such a hybrid. According to *Folio* magazine, which keeps track of new magazines, 272 new or revived titles were introduced in 1977 and 166 of them were classified as consumer publications. Launching a new magazine or reviving an old one can be a risky proposition and many do not survive, but certainly the number of introductions was one indication of the state of the magazine industry's health.

The trait that linked most of the magazines introduced in the late 1970's was that they catered to closely defined audiences, lifestyles, problems, and issues. New titles catering to business audiences included *Financier* and *World Business Weekly*. The many more catering to consumer interests, closely defined in terms of how specific groups make and spend their money, included *Working Mother, City Woman, All in Style, Crafts, Marathoner,* and *Professional Women*. Other new titles extended the proliferation of magazines that devote themselves to specific cities or regions and for the most part dwell on housing, food, travel, and other matters of local or regional consumer interest. Most of them pay close attention to how people make money and spend money. They have at least a partial business orientation.

Magazines, in sum, have survived the challenge of television and emerged, if anything, stronger and leaner than before, with business magazines emerging as one of the strongest areas. Hence my firm belief that a talented and motivated young person can make his or her mark quickly in business and economic journalism. It is a growing field and there always is more opportunity in a growing field than in a static one.

Trade Press and Newsletters

David Branch, an executive of Fairchild Publications, a leading publisher of trade journals, has referred to trade journalism as "community journalism." He means that, like a local paper, it covers broad subjects in terms of specific interests. He has drawn the analogy of a newspaper in Peoria that might give little or no space to a foreign revolution, unless a local boy or girl, say a Peace Corpsman or a tourist, was killed in the revolt. In that event, the paper probably would put the story on the front page. So with trade journalism: It covers events with particular reference to the interests of its trade community.

To take an imaginary example, suppose you work for a magazine in the mattress trade and a story breaks that the divorce rate is rising. The story would be of no interest, unless it could be shown or suggested that the higher divorce rate would help, or hurt, mattress sales. (It would probably help: new marriage, new bed.)

There are two reasons why journalists generally should not ignore the many magazines that are written for particular trade, business, and professional groups, no matter how parochial they may sound. First, the magazines often are authoritative sources of detailed information about an industry and they can be useful as sources of story ideas and for research and background purposes for general journalism. Second, the trade magazine field offers many job opportunities. It also offers excellent training because trade magazines teach their reporters to be specific and to look for an "angle," and these attitudes are as useful in writing about war or politics as in writing about the garment business.

For example, McGraw Hill, Inc., one of the largest publishers of business, technical, and scientific magazines and of books, publishes more than two dozen magazine titles in addition to *Business Week*. Its magazines include monthlies such as *Architectural Record, Coal Age, Construction Con-*

tracting, Data Communications, and *Modern Plastics* in addition to such week-lies as *Aviation Week and Space Technology, Chemical Week, Electronics,* and *Engineering News Record.*

Many newsletters cater to even more specialized audiences or communities, and they too should not be overlooked as sources of information and of employment. The newsletter field probably is the least familiar to young journalists, but it is the fastest growing field, at least in numbers of publications started in recent years.

Newsletters are published by both large and small news organizations. McGraw-Hill, for example, publishes newsletters in the energy, health, construction, and other areas, in addition to its magazines. According to a McGraw-Hill official, the company's Washington news-gathering operation employed 97 persons in late 1978, compared with about 50 five years earlier, and much of the growth reflected an expansion of McGraw-Hill newsletter publishing.

In a time of soaring publishing costs, newsletters have had the advantage of being relatively inexpensive to produce and yet capable of conveying highly specialized information for which the demand may not be large enough to support a conventional magazine. Since they are less expensive to produce than magazines, newsletters do not require advertising and therefore are much easier and less risky to start than magazines.

Many newsletters are captive publications of business, labor, or other trade associations and organizations and are distributed free to their members and often to the news media. While the quality of such newsletters varies greatly, some can be useful to reporters, as sources and for job opportunities. Remember that you have to start somewhere. One of the brightest young women reporters on *Forbes* came to us from a labor union newsletter. Reporters should be aware that there is an amount of phoniness in some independent newsletters, just as there is an amount of bootlicking of client industries in some trade magazines. The breathless, confidential style of some newsletters can be used to warm over news that has appeared elsewhere. But many and probably most independently published newsletters contain genuinely useful information that is not available elsewhere and is highly useful to business and industry. Indeed, some of the more sophisticated and useful newsletters ask and get $200, $300, and more for a yearly subscription. Since knowledge is money, such specific information and trade-oriented viewpoint can be worth every penny of it to interested parties.

THE PARTICULAR DEMANDS OF PERIODICAL JOURNALISM

The fact that magazines and similar periodicals have the time and other resources necessary to thoughtful and detailed reporting, researching, and writing presents obvious opportunities and satisfactions for journalists.

At the same time it puts certain responsibilities on business and economic reporting generally.

Many years ago a wise old owl of a Boston financier was asked what, in his opinion, we could do to make *Forbes* a better magazine. He did not hesitate in answering. "Give us the bad news about business," he declared. "The stuff people are trying to hide. The good news we already know about." The old man was not suggesting that we should be destructive or negative, but simply that we should view business realistically and not through rose-colored glasses—that we should dig out the facts that our subjects prefer to hide.

That advice should apply to all kinds of news reporting, although, as has been said in other contexts, honest reporting is quite different from hostility. Business people have accused the press of emphasizing bad news and ignoring good news, and their wariness of the press has been returned in reporters' wariness of business people. Both sides have a point.

The way to break down this mutual suspicion is for business people to be open and honest with the press and for the press, on its part, to take seriously its responsibilities to give thoughtful and informed judgments. Doing a "hatchet" job merely for the sake of irritating a news source or amusing the reader is as irresponsible as doing a "puff" job for the sake of pleasing a source or advertiser. Both are wrong. A magazine writer generally has enough time to do more than a surface job and he or she should regard that resource as an obligation as well as a privilege.

Demands of Corporate Reporting

Reporting broadly and deeply about corporate affairs—about the things that people are trying to hide—necessarily involves matters that the subject would rather not see in print. Beyond that, magazine journalism uniquely involves the journalist in matters of judgment that are more in the nature of informed conclusions than personal opinions. This is an important distinction.

Lewis H. Young, editor-in-chief of *Business Week,* made the point in the theoretical setting of a corporate board room after a raucous closed meeting of directors:

> Interviewing a half-dozen directors, a journalist will hear as many meetings described as there are board members, leaving him to wonder if the members had attended the same meeting. Which meeting does the journalist put into print? Using his judgment, experience and intuitive sense of which director was closest to the truth, the journalist synthesizes his best interpretation of what really happened. It may be a unique view of that meeting, putting it into a perspective that nobody who was close to it could see, because the journalist does not have a vested interest in the

outcome. Or it can be dead inaccurate because the journalist was swayed too highly by an articulate director with a sharp axe to grind. The same risks apply to every story. What is important is that a good journalist does more than just record what many people tell him. A tape recorder will do that. He brings insight, interpretation and meaning to every story he reports.[9]

Those qualities can be illustrated in a less dramatic, but real, setting.

Many publications could and did write interesting stories about Levi Strauss & Company, the San Francisco maker of blue jeans. This firm was founded by a penniless Bavarian immigrant who peddled clothing and pots and pans in the mid-nineteenth century, and it rode to glory a century later when blue jeans became the uniform first of the counterculture, later of all youth. Phyllis Berman, a staff writer for *Forbes,* set out in 1978 to determine whether Levi Strauss could continue to keep up with the shifts of fashion, especially when high fashion was moving into jeans. She was not simply describing. She was analyzing. And, yes, predicting.

The resulting article ran under this heading: "With Fashion Coming In, Can Levi Strauss Branch Out?" The subhead read: "Or, put it this way, Can a fifth-generation Berkeley-&-Harvard intellectual continue the success saga started by an immigrant peddler?"[10]

The conclusion that Berman reached was that "Aggressive competition from others had made Levi a follower in the fashion jeans market rather than a leader." Judgment and insight entered into her writing in many other ways too. Consider, for instance, her observations concerning Robert D. Haas, 36, the fifth-generation heir who was trained at the University of California at Berkeley and the Harvard Business School to lead the company—and to meet the challenge it faced in 1978 from fashion jeans. "He seems," Berman said, "superintense and businesslike, perhaps because he is afraid people might think he inherited his present position solely because of his family connection. The same diffidence made him avoid wearing Levi jeans when he was at Berkeley and lived in a virtual sea of jeans."

She concluded with a favorable judgment on young Haas. He was no rich dilettante. She wrote: "It's not only the kid who came up on the wrong side of the tracks who has the drive to make it in business. Sometimes the kid from the *right* side of the tracks can be even hungrier."

Is this reporting? Yes, but it is also judgment-making.

Another rather blunt illustration of judgmental reporting was provided in *Fortune* in 1978 by Peter W. Bernstein, an associate editor. His article about the Great Atlantic & Pacific Tea Company, a giant among supermarket chains, was titled "Jonathan Scott's Surprising Failure at A&P" and it began this way:

> When Jonathan Scott took over as chairman and chief executive of A&P almost four years ago, the company was in desperate straits. It still is. On the record so far, Scott's performance at A&P has been one of the most disappointing management failures of recent years.[11]

There it was. No mistaking the writer's conclusion. No hiding behind "either-or" pseudo-objectivity.

The article may well have been bad news for Jonathan Scott and A&P, but that is immaterial to readers, including A&P stockholders, who have a right to know. The writer functioned as judge as well as reporter.

Publicly held corporations may not want to tell what knowledgeable reporters want to know, but that should not stop the reporter. At *Forbes,* Paul Gibson, an associate editor, did an article about corporate spending on entertainment at sales meetings, conventions, and other business gatherings frequently held at posh resorts in pleasant places such as Hawaii and Bermuda. Corporations were not anxious to talk about them, although the article estimated that such corporate entertainment spending in 1978 hit $1 billion, roughly double the level of five years earlier. The article began:

> It's unusual for an International Business Machines Corp. spokesman to be flustered. But clearly the PR man was embarrassed as he kept insisting that IBM just does not go in for this type of thing. In Detroit a spokeswoman for General Motors was equally touchy. At Ramsey, N.J., a vice president of Okonite, Inc., the smallish wire and cable maker, huffed, "I don't care to discuss this matter with an outsider."
>
> What skeletons in the corporate closet was *Forbes* trying to uncover? Corporate bribery? The purloining of trade secrets? Hanky-panky in the executive suite? Nothing that sinister. We only asked how much money companies are spending nowadays for singers, comedians and other professional entertainers to perform at business functions such as conventions, trade shows and sales meetings.[12]

They did not want to say, but *Forbes* felt its readers ought to know.

Demands of Issue Reporting

Editor-in-Chief Lewis Young of *Business Week* has said:

> Too many reporters and editors hold the naive belief that any information from a government agency is accurate and unbiased. In fact, bureaucrats can be as wrong and as prejudiced as anybody; a bureaucrat often has such vested interests in a program, law or regulation that any views expressed are totally one-sided.[13]

Amen. If business people are often money-hungry, can't bureaucrats and consumer advocates be power-hungry? For example, there are daily occurrences representing a clash between business interests and the wishes of governmental or private environmentalist groups. In the real world, neither side is wholly right in the majority of cases. But some reporters are so biased on one side or the other that they deliver personal opinion rather than informed judgment. This badly serves the reader. The reader should be able to look to the reporter for more than an echoing of propaganda from just one side. Do not take lightly the responsibilities that go with your freedom to interpret the facts.

One may cite in this regard a recent example of terrible issue-reporting in one of our leading newspapers. The article told of a lawsuit launched by a federally funded organization to stop research on labor-saving agricultural machinery. The article told readers that such machinery deprived poor people of jobs. Nowhere did it mention that such machinery also helped bring food to the supermarkets at a cost that is so low relative to our incomes that our overeating has made us a nation of waistline watchers. Nor did it mention that machinery like this has helped lift large parts of the human race from back-stooping drudgery. The writer copped out. In the name of writing "news" he allowed himself to be used as a conduit for propaganda. He failed to examine the motives of the plaintiffs. He failed to bring judgment and perspective into the story.

There comes a time in reporting on issues, however, when even the best reporter, even the most determined editor, realizes that the issue involved is too complex or technical for the staff to handle in the usual way. One way out is through the use of nonstaff experts. *Fortune* in 1978 had Everett Ladd, a professor of political science at the University of Connecticut, explore the apparent inconsistencies in public distrust of big government and public demand for many government services. In an article titled "What the Voters Really Want," Professor Ladd concluded that the voters' wrath did not reflect a truly conservative trend, but what voters really want is not less, but better, government.[14]

Forbes and some other business magazines also use outside columnists on a regular basis to discuss issues and give advice on stock market trends, commodities, and other matters. It also from time to time carries an interview or "conversation" with an expert who has something special to say.

We also have used another technique for discussion of a particularly emotional issue, and in that instance offered no conclusion but left readers to make up their own minds on the basis of personal philosophy and on the relative persuasiveness of the contending factions. In one such article the issue involved a clash between two reasonable but irreconcilable points of view. The issue was the sale by American corporations of goods and services to South Africa, where the minority white government ruled over the majority black population.

At *Forbes's* request, the magazine was given the opportunity to sit in on a meeting where the issue was to be discussed by William C. Norris, chairman of Control Data Corporation, and church groups that owned shares in Control Data and wanted the company to stop doing business in South Africa. The leader of the church representatives was William P. Thompson, then president of the National Council of Churches of Christ in the U.S.A.

We printed excerpts from their discussion under the heading "Revolution, Sayeth the Churchman; One Soul at a Time, Says a Businessman."[15] We offered no conclusion, but merely the observation that in the two-hour discussion "the two sides ended up farther apart than they had started."

Two excerpts summed up their position. Mr. Norris, an electrical engineer by profession and a thoughtful man who did not fall back on the "business is business" argument, said: "We really believe we are a force for good in South Africa. . . . We put in the first black custom computer engineer in South Africa . . . that just hadn't been done." The Reverend Mr. Thompson: "I don't think we're being realistic to talk about computer education of young people who are giving their lives in the interests of freedom."

The point is this: Magazine journalism is flexible. It is not formula-bound as newspapers so often are. At one extreme it can stick very close to the news. At the other extreme it can break new ground and itself *make* news. A classic case was *The New Yorker*'s publication in 1951 of excerpts from Rachel Carson's *The Sea Around Us*. With these articles *The New Yorker* virtually launched the environmentalist movement. We thought that the article on inflation by David Warsh and Lawrence Minard would, somewhat similarly, have a long-range influence on the way people look at economics.

WHAT EDITORS SEEK IN REPORTERS

Because magazine writing differs from newspaper writing, magazine editors and newspaper editors look for different kinds of journalistic talent. At *Forbes,* for example, about half of the younger writers and editors have advanced degrees. A graduate degree is not essential, however. While those who do have graduate degrees tend to have a head start, it should not be forgotten that they have spent several years and a great deal of money getting that head start.

In the long run it is talent and energy and curiosity and breadth of vision that count, not specific training. This can be illustrated by the diversity of backgrounds among people on *Forbes*'s staff. The managing editor began his journalism career as a sportswriter for *Newsweek*. One of the executive editors had a distinguished career on *The Wall Street Journal* before coming to *Forbes;* he is by academic training a lawyer but found that journalism was his true calling. A talented editor began as a researcher at *Glamour* magazine, moved into newsletter writing and reporting and thence to *Forbes*. The Chicago bureau manager went to journalism school, started in trade publishing, and became a foreign correspondent in Vietnam before joining the staff. The associate editor who did the Levi Strauss article studied political science at the University of Michigan and began her working career as clipper of newspapers for *Sports Illustrated*. She started at *Forbes* near the bottom of the editorial ladder as a researcher. Within six years she was an associate editor and in 1978 did more cover stories than any single member of the staff. She was only 33. Another staff member, an economics major from the University of Wisconsin, became an associate editor at 26. As you can see, there is an almost bewildering diversity of backgrounds. What they have in common is talent, a belief in their own powers of judgment, and a fascination with business.

The difference between magazine and newspaper reporting, reflected in the talents editors seek, has been described by Willard C. Rappleye, Jr., editor of *Financier, The Journal of Financial Affairs:*

> Magazine writing differs fundamentally from daily journalism in that judgment and selection of information play a far greater part in magazine writing. Whereas newspaper stories essentially write themselves, in the classic priorities of lead sentence followed in orderly progression by facts in diminishing importance, a magazine article is an expression of choices by the writer, starting with the very selection of the story.
>
> The "why" of most daily newspaper stories is usually self-evident; the "why" of most magazine stories is more often an exercise in individual judgment.
>
> The nature of the magazine of course will determine much of the shape of the story. For a more general circulation publication, there will be greater need to attract the reader's attention and explain what is happening. For an audience more sophisticated in business and economics, the emphasis shifts to greater depth and more arcane information. But always, awareness of the reader's strengths, weaknesses, and needs should inform the writing; and the realization that the business reader is both very busy and very curious creates a nice tension in the writing process and a fine opportunity for forceful writing.[16]

Speaking for Magazine Editors

If you are considering business journalism, be honest with yourself. Not everyone has the personality to be a journalist. You will be dealing with people; they are your sources. Are you good with people? Can you get them to talk with you? Remember that most of the people you interview will not be anxious to tell all you want to know. Do you have the persistence, the curiosity, the self-confidence to keep probing even after you have met with rebuffs? Does the position of observer rather than doer appeal to you? There are many who would rather be in business than write about it. If you are one, you probably will not do well in journalism.

Breaking into the magazine field is not easy for a recent college graduate. The best way to break in at *Forbes* is as a researcher. We generally look for people who have had several years of experience in some field that is important to us, such as business, finance, or newspaper reporting.

A graduate degree is not essential. With regard to formal education in general, an ideal candidate is someone with a major in economics or in business who has taken a good deal of literature and worked on the college newspaper, or an English or history major who has taken a fair amount of economics. The major does not matter as much as the broadness of education.

English and literature are important because business writing requires clarity and must be as free of jargon as you can make it. The ability to write is the ability to make your subjects come alive and to hold your readers' interest. Broaden your vocabulary. Soak yourself in good writing. Courses in composition and short story writing are valuable. You will be surprised at how many top business and economic journalists started not as economics majors but as English or history majors.

An understanding of history is necessary because, to know where we are going, you have to know where we have been. Journalists will put their American history and modern European history to use and should include in their preparation at least a smattering of Asian history. I personally would not want to hire a reporter whose sense of the world starts around 1960.

A few examples tell why. When the environmental movement was at its height, a *Forbes* editor, remembering the moral fervor of the Prohibition experiment, suspected that, just as there was a great backlash against the high moral fervor of the saloon movement, so there would be a similar reaction against the extremes of environmentalism. We predicted, correctly, that this would happen. Again, when the Carter Administration put forth its tax reform proposals in 1977, we recalled the fate of a similar sweeping reform attempt during the administration of President John F. Kennedy. Under President Kennedy, Congress took the tax-cut bait but refused to swallow the reform hook. This sense of history helped us to put the Carter Administration's 1977 tax proposals into perspective.

Anyone who aspires to a career in business and economic journalism today also would do well to learn something about computers and about science. Even some familiarity will help you to understand the changes that sweep through business and the economy. And do not neglect accounting. Double-entry bookkeeping was one of the more ingenious creations of the human mind. Generally accepted accounting principles are the shorthand of business. Unless you understand at least the fundamentals of this shorthand, you will not know what questions to ask businessmen or how to engage in research that goes beyond interviewing.

All of that suggests a fairly ambitious curriculum. It requires a good amount of mind-stretching and may even alarm your faculty adviser, but it is based on experience in hiring, training (and sometimes firing) literally hundreds of young journalists.

If you are serious about a career in business journalism, you will not restrict yourself to formal courses. Outside reading is important too. Expose yourself to *The Wall Street Journal* to see how clarity and sophistication can be achieved even under the pressures of daily reporting. Read the *London Economist* for a slightly different and brightly opinionated perspective on business and economics. Read *Forbes,* because we cover the corporate scene with a unique thoroughness in terms of corporate strategy and personalities. To see how witty yet penetrating financial writing can be, read Alan Abelson in *Barron's.* To see how bright even the trade press can be, get to know *Institutional Investor, Women's Wear Daily,* and *Home Furnishing Daily.*

Do not read these publications just for information. Analyze their techniques. What are the editors trying to do? What devices are they using to achieve their goals? Such publications are among the standard-setters in the profession. You will be competing with and maybe working for them.

Think of business not as an abstraction but as a part of life. Look around you. Some of your best story ideas will come from personal observations. For example, many years ago *Forbes* did the first national magazine article predicting the rise of what became known as consumerism. Where did the idea come from? From our Washington bureau manager who was having trouble getting his car repaired.

Are skirts getting shorter? Are health foods gaining ground? Are fewer young people going to college? Is downhill skiing going downhill and cross-country skiing going uphill? What do these trends tell you about our society? What will they mean to business and the economy? You must bring not only all your formal academic training to bear if you are going to succeed in this competitive profession, but your personal powers of observation as well.

Finally, adopt a skeptical attitude toward what you hear and see. Do not be awed by authority, whether academic authority or the authority of money and success. You will be surprised how often a healthy skepticism is rewarded with a superior story. For example, in 1978 *Forbes* did a highly critical article on a large conglomerate, and the genesis of this article is interesting. A reporter interviewed the company's chief executive, who was glib and convincing, suspiciously so, considering the company's spotty record. His curiosity and natural skepticism aroused, Senior Editor Robert Flaherty began digging and found plenty that was wrong. We printed the story. The company was outraged. This wasn't the story it expected. But it was in our view a truer picture than the one the company had tried to peddle.

Speaking for Newsletter Editors

Editors of newsletters look for much the same abilities and talents as those sought by magazine editors. These include "curiosity, attention to detail, competitiveness and skepticism about both businessmen and bureaucrats," according to David Swit, a former Washington reporter who established a successful small business publishing a half dozen newsletters. Many of the qualities required for newsletters will serve you well in any kind of journalism. Mr. Swit said:

> Being an investigative reporter, in effect, a newsletter writer also must be willing to dig deeply into dull and lengthy documents, for many stories are sparked by written material rather than interviews. However, in addition to this attention to documents, a newsletter writer must have the patience and personality to build rapport with leaders of industry and government, for they have the "inside" information the publication promises its readers. That information usually is shared only after a source has grown to respect the reporter's knowledge and has developed a sense of trust in his or her judgment and reliability in handling confidences.
>
> The actual writing for a newsletter has several distinctive features. Foremost is the need for greater-than-usual precision, because readers often act on the information—and may make a costly business decision if the reporter errs. Another aspect of this need is keeping the confidence of readers who know the field well enough to spot mistakes in fact or judgment.
>
> Also vital is the ability to see and convey the meaning behind official statements or actions. This is what newsletter subscribers primarily buy, for much of the raw information is available with relative ease.
>
> Another essential skill for a newsletter reporter is remembering to look at developments, in effect through the readers' eyes, and to seek what is important to a government agency or the general public. Linked to this is a talent for dealing professionally with news sources who, as often happens, also are subscribers and may feel that they should get special consideration because they have bought a subscription.
>
> While there may not be the glory of writing for a big city daily, the newsletter reporter usually is highly respected in his or her small but cohesive circle. Often, his or her writing has direct influence on policies set by government or industry.
>
> On the practical side, most newsletters are published by small firms, in

which a bright reporter can advance faster than at a publication which has many employees "ahead" of you.[17]

WHAT IS BUSINESS NEWS?

A young journalist, having read this catalogue of personal and educational talents sought by editors of business and economic periodicals, might be discouraged. However, many young journalists with many kinds of talents, and with perseverance, perception, and judgment, have made their marks in the periodical press and gained the satisfactions it offers.

That conclusion could be illustrated in the careers of dozens of reporters and editors at *Forbes* and other publications. Such periodicals are, to be blunt, hungry for talent and energy. A business magazine requires huge amounts of material. You would be surprised at the amount of effort that goes into even a brief article, 1,000 words or so, which may represent as much as two or three weeks' work, involving not only the writer–reporter but researchers, art people, statisticians, and editors as well. This article, which demands no more than a few minutes of the readers' time, may represent thousands of dollars worth of time and effort.

Let's consider one single issue of *Forbes*. The one dated October 30, 1978, contained 27 articles, 15 features, and 10 stories about people that we call "Faces Behind the Figures." Our masthead for that issue listed the names of about 85 staff members who were responsible for the magazine's editorial content, including editors, reporters, researchers, columnists, librarians, and others responsible for art, photocomposition, and production.

On that issue's cover was a drawing of the Statue of Liberty surrounded by a scaffold on which men were cleaning and polishing. The cover line said "Immigration—Why the lady still beckons." The cover story inside explored the great wave of immigrants who were entering the United States legally and illegally and considered what, if anything, should be done about it.[18]

At *Forbes* we rarely start out with the idea that a particular story on a particular subject will be featured on the cover. More often we select a cover subject after looking into a story and judging on the basis of exploratory reporting that it will be of unusual interest to our readers. It quickly became obvious to the editors that immigration was such a story. Items about illegal immigrants appeared in the newspapers almost daily but no one had put the whole subject into perspective. We resolved to do so. Our conclusion: "Maybe with a willingness to mow people down, we could seal the border, but given a humane attitude, we'll have to live with a border that leaks like a sieve."

Is immigration a business subject? You bet your life it is. It touches on many things that have a huge influence on business: the labor force, the composition of the market, and by no means least, on the vitality of the U.S. economy in attracting and providing a livelihood for people from less fortunate areas.

Business and the economy are, in short, concerned with everything that happens in our society. It is a business reporter's job to be aware that culture, style, philosophy, and technology are as important to business, if not more so, than are such purely economic subjects as money supply, interest rates, unemployment figures, and Gross National Product. Business, in short, is as broad as life itself.

Traditionally the press has preferred to cover politics without reference to business and the economy, but we have come to realize that politics is often little more than a pale reflection of the great social and economic realities—business—that underlie it all.

NOTES—CHAPTER 13

1. "Inflation Is Now Too Serious a Matter to Leave to the Economists," *Forbes,* November 15, 1976, pp. 121–41.

2. "The American Corporation Under Fire," *Newsweek,* May 24, 1971, pp. 74–83.

3. Magazine Publishers Association, Inc.

4. *Ibid.*

5. Figures supplied by the Magazine Publishers Association from Audit Bureau of Circulation records.

6. Magazine Publishers Association.

7. *Ibid.*

8. Data from Magazine Publishers Association and Russell Hall Magazine Editorial Reports.

9. Lewis H. Young, in an address delivered at the ITT Key Issue Lecture Series, Columbia, Mo., September 21, 1978.

10. *Forbes,* August 21, 1978, pp. 41–45.

11. *Fortune,* November 6, 1978, pp. 34–44.

12. Paul Gibson, "Two on the Aisle," *Forbes,* October 31, 1978, pp. 86–87.

13. Young, in the ITT Key Issue Lecture Series.

14. Everett Carll Ladd, Jr., "What the Voters Really Want," *Fortune,* December 18, 1978, pp. 40–48.

15. *Forbes,* February 6, 1978, pp. 31–33.

16. Interview with Willard C. Rappleye, Jr., December 1978.

17. Interview with David A. Swit, December 1978.

18. Phyllis Berman, "Does the Melting Pot Still Meld?" *Forbes,* October 30, 1978, pp. 63–67.

SOURCES OF INFORMATION

Forbes
60 Fifth Avenue
New York, N.Y. 10011

New York Financial Writers Association
Box 4306
New York, N.Y. 10017

Magazine Publishers Association, Inc.
575 Lexington Avenue
New York, N.Y. 10022

Newsletter Association of America
900 17th Street, N.W.
Washington, D.C. 20006

McGraw-Hill, Inc.
1221 Avenue of the Americas
New York, N.Y. 10020

Time Inc.
Time & Life Building
Rockefeller Center
New York, N.Y. 10020

SUGGESTED READINGS

Baughman, James P., ed., *The History of American Management*. Englewood Cliffs, N.J.: Prentice-Hall, 1969.

Drucker, Peter F., *The New Society*. New York: Harper & Row, 1950.

Galbraith, John Kenneth, *The Affluent Society*. Boston: Houghton Mifflin Co., 1969.

Mackay, Clarence, *Popular Delusions and the Madness of Crowds*. Wells, Vermont: Fraser Publishing Co., 1932, by arrangement with L. C. Page & Co., Inc.

Macrae, Norman, *America's Third Century*. New York: Harcourt, Brace & Jovanovich, 1976.

Riesman, David, *The Lonely Crowd*. New Haven, Conn.: Yale University Press, 1961.

Schumpeter, J. A., *Capitalism, Socialism and Democracy*. New York: Harper & Brothers, 1942.

Sloan, Alfred, *My Years With General Motors*. Garden City, N.Y.: Doubleday & Co., 1963.

Toffler, Alvin, *Future Shock*. New York: Random House, 1970.

Whyte, William H., Jr., *The Organization Man*. New York: Simon & Schuster, 1956.

Wilson, Sloan, *The Man in the Gray Flannel Suit*. New York: Simon & Schuster, 1955.

Covering Economics for...
TELEVISION
AND RADIO

14

DAN CORDTZ

BROADCAST JOURNALISM AND THE NEED FOR MORE ECONOM-
IC NEWS

THE PARTICULAR DIFFICULTIES OF BROADCAST JOURNALISM
The Nature of Broadcasting's Audiences
A Model for Broadcast Journalism

THE DIFFERENCES BETWEEN RADIO AND TELEVISION
Reporting for Radio
Reporting for Television
The Visual Demands of Television

THE DIFFERENCES BETWEEN NETWORK AND LOCAL COVERAGE
Network Broadcasting
Local Broadcasting

HOW TO OVERCOME THE OBSTACLES
Developing Sources
Developing Story Ideas
Presentation of TV News
Writing Skills, Brevity, and Simplicity
Techniques for Getting and Holding an Audience

A SUMMARY AND CONCLUSION

MOST OF THE CHAPTERS of this book have been devoted to an overview of what constitutes business and economic news, together with substantive information about various aspects of the economy and advice on how to go about covering different kinds of issues. That basic information is applicable to whatever medium you choose.

This chapter will focus on the peculiar demands of business and economic reporting on radio and television. True, the odds are somewhat against your chances of becoming a broadcast/economics specialist. Nevertheless the awareness on the part of the radio-TV audience concerning pocketbook issues is of growing importance. As of this writing, there are only five such specialists on the three commercial networks, and a relative handful on big metropolitan stations around the country.

BROADCAST JOURNALISM AND THE NEED FOR MORE ECONOMIC NEWS

It seems clear that coming events will compel broadcast news directors to pay more attention to business and economic news, and it is reasonable to hope that some of them will appoint specialists to cover the beat.

Certainly the need is clear. According to a survey by Burns Roper, television news is named by 83 percent of the public as its main source of news about business.[1] If that figure is anywhere near accurate, it means that a large proportion of the country is receiving an inadequate and even inaccurate understanding of how the economy works.

One of my colleagues argues that television's treatment of business is the same as its treatment of other news subjects. As an analogy, he points out that we broadcasters report only the occasional school bus accident, not the millions of safe trips. But this analogy is flawed. Our emphasis on school bus accidents does not distort the public's image of reality, because everyone knows from direct, personal experience that almost all school buses arrive safely almost all of the time. So even if the accident stories are overplayed, they do not cause the public to believe that school buses are death traps. But when news of business or labor misbehavior, incompetence, greed, or outright illegality is presented on television, the public's image of reality can be distorted because the average American does not have the background knowledge needed to put the negative stories into proper perspective. People automatically put the bus crash into perspective; they cannot do the same with most business and economic news.

The solution is not, as some business people would prefer, to ignore or downplay the bad news. The solution is to give enough news—good, bad, and neutral—to enable the public to judge all of the news in its overall context. In order to do that, all the news media, and especially radio and television, which have lagged behind the rest, must do a better job of reporting on the economy (which is another word for the competitive market system) and on business (which is the main mechanism by which the economy functions).

THE PARTICULAR DIFFICULTIES OF BROADCAST JOURNALISM

The task of the business and economic reporter in broadcasting is, in many ways, even more difficult than that of the specialist working for general circulation newspapers and magazines.

The Nature of Broadcasting's Audiences

Radio and television have one characteristic that is of overriding importance for a journalist. Their audiences are so large and such a cross section of the public that they include many people with no perceived personal interest in business. That is, most radio listeners and TV viewers are neither investors, managers, nor owners of companies. Their relationship with the business world is overwhelmingly that of employees or customers. Events and trends in business therefore must be presented in a manner that appeals to a general audience.

Moreover, to a much greater degree than readers, the broadcast audience is a distracted audience. The heavy radio listening period is generally during what is called "drive time," the rush-hour traffic period in the morning and evening when millions of automobile drivers are on their way to and from work. Those listeners have their minds on many things—most of all, one would hope, their driving. Few of them are closely attending to every word that comes out of their radio speakers.

The problem of the distracted audience is probably even worse where television is concerned. In the morning hours, TV is frequently treated like radio: people who are shaving, dressing, or eating breakfast merely listen with one ear and occasionally glance at the screen. In the evening the news coincides with the confusion of workers and children arriving home, of dinner being prepared, and of other activities that divert attention from the tube.

But there is another side to that coin. Newspapers and magazines can rarely intrude on the audience's attention. It takes a deliberate act on the part of a reader to absorb the information being offered, and about the only means a publication has of getting the reader to make that decision is a screaming headline or a striking cover picture. In most American homes the television set is on while the news is being broadcast, whether anyone is actively watching or not. And most of the audience has at least one ear and one eye attuned to the set. If people see or hear something that they perceive as important or interesting, their full attention can be captured. That is one important reason why advertisers value television so highly.

Broadcasting has another advantage, and it will probably increase over the years. Most day-to-day human communication is oral, not written. Oral communication is what people are most comfortable with and what, for all too many, is easiest to understand. Hence it has a special effectiveness.

A Model For Broadcast Journalism

In the foreword to the book version of his TV series, "The Ascent of Man," Jacob Bronowski, in explaining why he agreed to use the medium for such an ambitious project, writes of television's strength. "A spoken argument is informal and heuristic," Bronowski explains. "It singles out the heart of the matter and shows in what way it is crucial and new; and it gives the direction and line of the solution so that, simplified as it is, still the logic is right."[2]

A broadcast journalist, and particularly one covering economic and business news, can hardly do better than use that description as a model. Except perhaps for the word "solution," it is a nearly perfect definition of the ideal radio or TV spot story. The most important rule for the economic news broadcaster is to avoid getting bogged down in detail and to stick to "the heart of the matter." It is not necessary to explain everything, so long as "the logic is right."

There are a number of techniques that will help a correspondent achieve this goal, but before getting into them, let's consider first some of the differences between radio and television, at the local and network levels.

THE DIFFERENCES BETWEEN RADIO AND TELEVISION

Many journalists employed by the networks and by local stations work in both the radio and television fields. There certainly are similarities between the two kinds of broadcast media, but aspiring journalists also should recognize the differences.

Reporting for Radio

Reporting on business and the economy on radio is both easier and harder than on television. It is easier for at least three reasons. First, the audiences for individual radio news programs are usually somewhat smaller than those for TV news shows. That means it is not necessary that each story have such a broad general appeal. Indeed, there are many local radio news shows devoted entirely to business and economic news, and this number is growing.

Second, the total amount of time available for news on many radio stations is considerably greater than that devoted to news on all but a handful of TV stations. A few radio stations, of course, air nothing but news and they are naturally the most promising for aspiring journalists. Many other stations carry five minutes or more of news every hour, with longer programs three or four times a day. Almost all of these stations report the closing stock market quotes. Although the stock quotations frequently are "rip and read" summaries taken from press wires, they can provide a framework for other business news.

The third way in which radio reporting on business and economics is easier is that radio has no pictures, so there is no need for a correspondent to strain the imagination in an effort to make a story visual. All that is necessary is to tell the news in a clear, straightforward fashion.

Reporting for radio in some respects is harder than TV reporting. For one thing, the absence of pictures eliminates any visual reinforcement of the message being conveyed in the narrative. Audience research confirms that TV viewers respond more to what they see than to what they hear; they retain and understand it better, too. Even the simple and obvious device of putting numbers on the screen while they are being spoken by the correspondent helps a great deal to impress them on a viewer's consciousness and memory.

Perhaps more important, most radio stories are much shorter than TV spots. The practice varies from station to station and from network to network, but at ABC the outside limit for a radio news spot is 40 seconds.

Even when no numbers are needed, it is often a difficult task to tell a story in half a minute, particularly if the facts are intrinsically hard to grasp and the information is unfamiliar to the listener. It is a mistake to assume that the listener has any background, especially when a technical or specialized term must be used. Such terms have to be defined in every spot and it takes a lot of thought to devise terse, clear definitions that are simple without oversimplifying to the point of purveying misinformation. Yet the challenge of communicating within those tight time limits is one of the fascinations—and professional satisfactions—of radio journalism.

Reporting for Television

Reporting business and economic news on television involves some of the same problems as radio journalism, of course. Time is still at a premium, but TV spots are rarely shorter than a minute and usually they run between a minute and a half and two minutes. Sometimes they can be much longer, particularly in the case of background reports such as those featured on some nightly network news shows.

The most formidable obstacles to getting business and economic news on television are closely linked. The viewing audience is large, it regards the tube as primarily a medium of entertainment, and, it views the news show as an entity. Economic news is sandwiched between the more general items. Except for Public Broadcasting's "Wall Street Week," there have been no regularly scheduled national news shows devoted exclusively to business and economic news.

Audience research strongly suggests that a large share of the viewers, once they have selected a channel, are inclined to stay tuned to that channel unless an item appears on the screen that prompts them to switch. In other words, they do not normally change channels in order to see something, but in order not to see something. That makes television producers extremely fearful of putting on a spot that will offend or bore viewers, because once they switch away they may not be prompted to return to that channel again. In that case, audience ratings would fall for the news show and for all the shows that follow.

The Visual Demands of Television

To overcome these fears, it is essential that stories prepared for television be made broadly appealing—and on TV, that means making them visual. Television's main attraction, its *raison d'être,* is pictures. That is an article of faith with TV news executives and producers. In the view of some television reporters, the emphasis on television as a visual medium before all else is often overdone. But it cannot be denied that pictures are important, and there are no signs whatever that the people in charge are losing their devotion to pictures. So the business and economic correspondent must be prepared to work within those rules.

Lester M. Crystal, president of NBC News, has said, "In TV, if you don't go out and report with a camera, dullness becomes a self-fulfilling prophecy."[3] So the unending challenge to a TV reporter of business and economic news is to figure out how to report a story with a camera. Sometimes this is simply a matter of spending money. Consider, for example, a spot story that was carried on the ABC Evening News about the problems facing the paper industry. The story concerned soaring costs and low profits that were holding back industry expansion and posing the threat of paper shortages and higher prices in the future.

Visual elements were easy to find: trees being felled in the forest, giant machines that swallowed up whole tree trunks and ground them into chips, plants for cooking the chips to make pulp, quarter-mile-long mills that turned the watery pulp into huge rolls of paper, the complex equipment needed to get the pollutants out of the air and water, and finally examples of the incredible array of paper products that the typical viewer uses every day. But to film all that, it was necessary for ABC to send a three-man camera crew, a field producer, and an economics correspondent up to the northeast corner of Maine for three days, and then to process and edit hundreds of feet of film. The final spot was a success, but it cost thousands of dollars to put those two minutes on the air. Even at the network level, news executives do not throw around such sums willingly except for coverage of wars, political campaigns, presidential trips, and natural disasters.

Business stories ordinarily do not lend themselves so readily to visual treatment. Indeed, there are times when there is no way to make an economic story a film spot. If the story is important enough that it must be told anyway, there are frequently things that can be done with graphics. This is still a largely untapped opportunity in TV, which displays none of the imagination of, say *Fortune* magazine when it comes to employing charts, diagrams, and graphs. In the future, as image-creating technology develops, there will be many things television artists can do, even with animation, and undoubtedly graphics will be used more and more if TV increases its economic coverage as it should.

THE DIFFERENCES BETWEEN NETWORK AND LOCAL COVERAGE

So long as the number of commercial broadcast networks remains small and their audiences are huge and amorphous, the networks may not find it advantageous or even possible to specialize to any great extent in business and economic news. The development of business and economic news coverage by the broadcast media might well begin with local stations, which have better defined and less amorphous audiences.

Network Broadcasting

The defining characteristic of network news, of course, is that it must be of national interest or at least have the sort of universal appeal that will make it almost as interesting to a housewife in Seattle as to a bricklayer in Atlanta.

In practice, much network news tends to be news of national economic policy emanating from Washington, or of national unemployment, consumer price, and other statistics. Other obvious network stories are those concerning major industries and their prices, profits, labor disputes, and the like. However, the meaning of national events and trends in the economy can often be most effectively made clear by using individual families, workers, consumers, and companies to illustrate them. In that sense, a local story is made to represent the country as a whole.

The other main characteristic of network broadcasting, and especially of network TV, is that it embodies in an extreme form the problems of large audiences and scarce time that are shared to some degree by all broadcasting. The "CBS Evening News," for example, has been watched five nights a week by some 18 million viewers.[4] The other two commercial TV networks also have audiences that dwarf the readership of almost all publications. Each of the three network evening news programs contains, outside of commercials and introductions, only 22 minutes of news. Written out, that would not begin to fill the front page of a full-sized daily newspaper. In effect, the typical network TV news show is a paper with only a small front page. Consequently, the business and economic news specialist is in a fierce competition for time. Ordinarily, each story on the program must be important enough to make page one. So the correspondent must have the skill to make each story's importance clearly and even dramatically evident.

Local Broadcasting

Local broadcasting is in many ways a more promising field for the development of the business and economic beat. To begin with, local television stations have much more time. Some have begun to carry as many as three hours of news a day, concentrated in the morning, evening, and late at night. The availability of that time is particularly important because the only way to make an impact on viewers and attract their interest is to develop an appetite for business and economic news—and that requires regular, almost daily, exposure. The audience simply cannot absorb more than a few pertinent facts and figures at a time, so it must be fed information in small servings. Ultimately, those morsels will add up to real nourishment.

Moreover, network television tends to use national policy development as the focal point for reporting about the economy, but the economy of the nation is made up of much more than national policy. It is shaped by the aggregate of millions of individual private decisions. Historically, neither Congress nor the President has decided if or when or how much prices or wages will be raised, for instance. Business people and labor leaders have decided those matters.

Because of the competition for time and the need to appeal to a substantial share of an enormous audience, very few stories about individual companies and industries have made the network news programs. But there are many business and economic stories of significant interest to local audiences.

On the other hand, there is an important obstacle to developing business and economic coverage on local television and radio. Very few stations have devoted significant financial or staff resources to news. Most local radio stations have no real news staffs at all. They carry little or no news, and what they carry is simply ripped off the wire-service teletypes and read by professional announcers. Of the remainder, the overwhelming majority are fearfully shorthanded and feel they must concentrate on the staples of local news such as police, politics, and schools. They cannot afford to have a trained specialist who cannot handle general news assignments.

A relative handful of large, profitable stations have news staffs big enough to permit them the luxury of a business specialist. They tend to be in cities where business is clearly important to the local economy; an example is Detroit, where the news of industry is of overriding importance.

The most voracious consumers of business news are the country's more than 100 all-news radio stations.[5] These stations use enormous quantities of material and ought to be the best single market for economic information. They have not filled that role, however. In fact, many of them rely on the substantial quantities of news provided by the networks, the wire services, or the independent syndicators of news shows and commentaries. For the most part, rather than develop local business news, they settle for national news. They also take the traditionally narrow approach to business news instead of seeking out local angles and treating business stories in a way that will make them interesting to a broad audience.

Local television stations normally have larger news staffs, but turning out a TV spot is also much more time-consuming. Typically, every correspondent has to crank out two or more film spots each day. And there are very few stations that can afford, or are willing to pay for, a correspondent doing nothing but business and economic stories. That is why anyone who wants to cover business and economics on television had best be prepared to do other stories as well.

At present—unfortunately—most local television coverage of business, when it has been done at all, has been done by the typical TV general assignment reporter. Many of them are totally lacking in any knowledge of economics, business, and labor. They are largely responsible for the anger directed at television news by business people and labor leaders. If there is any hope of remedying that situation, it lies in the possibility of providing a significant number of television correspondents with the sort of fundamental information contained in this book.

HOW TO OVERCOME THE OBSTACLES

Assuming that you do land a job in which at least part of your responsibility is to cover the business/economics beat, how do you go about it in broadcasting? The first thing that has to be faced is the fact that you will be too busy to cover the beat the way a full-time specialist on a daily newspaper does. You probably will not discover and develop many original stories. You will have to accept the need to rely heavily on other media as your initial sources. In other words, you will have to read your local newspaper and national publications such as *The Wall Street Journal, Business Week,* and *Forbes* carefully to keep abreast of events.

Developing Sources

Obviously, you must cultivate your own sources among local officials, executives, bankers, union leaders, and academics the way any reporter would. You will quickly discover that some of these people—in particular, business people—are extremely wary. For what they regard as very good reasons, they mistrust broadcast reporters. It will take time, patience, and skill to persuade them that you know what you are doing and are not out to get them. And this will be all the harder because your own bosses will be interested mainly in the kinds of stories that businesses frequently would rather not see on the air.

In many ways, your best sources will be the consumers, workers, and other ordinary citizens in your town, for they are also your viewers and listeners. What are they interested in? What are they worried about? What are your own colleagues, friends, family, and neighbors talking about? In the long run, those are the things they want to hear and see on the air. If you and your colleagues are alert and listen consciously for such hints, you will come up with many story ideas and you will also find it easier to locate the real people whose experiences and situations make the stories come alive.

Developing Story Ideas

Potential story ideas are endless. The starting point is the proper definition of economics. "Economics," for present purposes, is anything that has to do with your viewers' work, finances, and standard of living. Louis Rukeyser, who is the host of "Wall Street Week" and was previously network TV's first economic correspondent, puts it this way: "Mention economics and people's eyes glaze over. Mention money and their eyes light up."6 What's more, the networks will never have enough time to cover all the stories, so even if you work for a local station you will have a lot of room to move around in.

For that reason, you can probably do even the sort of explanatory stories about national statistics or trends that are occasionally done on the networks. Certainly you can do "big picture" stories about what is happening to your local economy. Are you gaining jobs? Losing jobs? Are wages and retail sales and savings and consumer debt and delinquencies and bankruptcies rising as much as they are nationally? More? Less? How come?

What about local companies? Are they doing well? Are sales up? Profits up? Enough? Are they expanding, modernizing, turning out new products, breaking new technological ground, trying new approaches to working conditions or employee relations? A large number of companies have introduced programs of remedial economic education for their workers. It may be pure propaganda, but even that is interesting.

The economy of local government is a huge subject that almost never has been done well on the air, and it is going to be a bigger story every year. Is your city making the same mistakes that New York made? How much has the payroll grown? Why? Is the local government trying to boost productivity, trim costs, cut services, contract out more work? How about government employees' wages? How do they compare with private wages? Even if they are low, what has happened to fringe benefits? If your city does not have a hidden pension liability, it is unusual. In many cities, those inadequately funded pension liabilities are going to threaten to bankrupt local and possibly state governments sometime in the future.

What about taxes. Not only are taxes as certain as death, but they probably make most of your audience furious. And unless your city is a rare exception, there is probably a lot to be furious about. Network television has paid a fair amount of attention to federal income taxes, but federal taxes probably annoy people less than local taxes and especially property taxes. The property tax structure across much of the country is inconsistent and inequitable. In many communities, a knowledgeable reporter can find comparable property assessed at different values. You may find certain organizations and companies given special treatment. The comparison of your local tax structure with that of the statistically average American city may also be revealing.

Keep in mind, however, that economic and business stories on radio and television must be related to people. TV viewers are interested in other people almost as much as in themselves, and there is nothing that most people would rather do than peek into the keyhole of other people's houses, especially to find out how they live and earn and spend their money.

You can do stories about rich folks, poor folks, the always-disgruntled middle class, young marrieds, swinging singles, blacks, other ethnics, divorced parents. Many stories can be centered around how these people cope with their economic problems and opportunities.

Stories about how people earn their livings in interesting and different ways are limited only by the reporter's imagination. For instance, what kinds of jobs are working women getting, how are they doing, and what are the problems involved? Why can't teenagers get jobs? Does it really matter to anyone but them? Do retirees moonlight to supplement their Social Security checks? Are they willing to work but unable to find jobs? Families with more than one breadwinner represent a significant phenomenon to which people relate, sympathetically or otherwise.

Presentation of TV News

There are many ways in which economic and business stories can be presented on the air. On TV, most normally will be done as film spots, but there is boundless room for innovation. For example, the veteran TV news executive and producer Fred Friendly believes the most effective way of communicating economic information is through a two-way conversation between an anchorperson and a correspondent who is qualified to answer the questions that naturally occur to someone who does not understand.[7]

An extended interview with an expert can be useful at times, although there is no denying the fact that many experts, and especially economists, do not express themselves well in interviews. Another possibility is an adversary exchange between experts with sharply opposed views, but this also runs the risk of being too arcane for the audience.

As the technology of image-creation improves, it may be possible for a correspondent to do what amounts to an illustrated lecture. The notion will probably horrify most TV executives, but a lecture need not be dull. People pay to go to many of them.

In the setting of the typical local television news show, with its emphasis on making the news as painless and entertaining as possible, a business and economics news correspondent could readily be developed as an on-camera personality. The correspondent could be cast in a variety of roles, ranging at one extreme from the friendly expert patiently explaining matters to, at the other extreme, the viewer's alter ego, mystified by the complexities of the world we live in and seeking out answers to his (and the viewers') questions.

There is no reason why many stories cannot be dealt with in a light, even humorous manner. Not all business and economic developments are heavy, and a catchy phrase or illustration can often make them more understandable and memorable without doing violence to the facts.

Writing Skills, Brevity, and Simplicity

What are the techniques and skills you need in order to do a good job of communicating information about business and economics to listeners and viewers? The first, which frequently does not receive the credit it deserves among print journalists, is a high level of writing skill. This is important in all economic reporting. It is even more essential in broadcasting, because almost all of the audience will lack any specialized information.

Louis Rukeyser has three rules about writing for radio and television:

1. You must write in English, not jargon.

2. Because you must write in English, you must understand very clearly what it is you are trying to say; you cannot just have a general idea.

3. In order to capture and hold the audience, you should do it with a bit of flair. "I have never believed," Mr. Rukeyser has said, "that being on TV gives you a license to bore people."[8]

The first requirement of broadcast writing is brevity—and only careful thought, ruthless self-editing, and practice will achieve it. There are many broadcast journalism textbooks that discuss the general technique of writing for the ear, but there are a few specific rules that apply with special force to business and economic reporting.

For example, in a radio spot and in most television stories as well, you simply cannot tell all you know. In fact, in a 30-second radio spot, you can make only one major point. Even in a minute and a half on TV, more than a couple of points will overwhelm a viewer. And you must avoid like the plague the kind of "on the one hand this and on the other hand that" construction that leaves the audience confused about just what it is you are saying.

Numbers should be used judiciously. Obviously, statistics are sometimes the point of the story, but hold them to a minimum. For example, if unemployment went up half of one percentage point to a rate of 6½ percent, you will probably have to report that. But use approximations that are easy to grasp in place of precise figures that are likely to be forgotten. For example, if the consumer price index for clothing went up 0.7 percent, do not say, "seven tenths of one percent." Say, "almost three fourths of one percent." It is easier to absorb quickly, and it is close enough for any listener's purposes.

In a spot that absolutely must touch on several numbers, such as the components of the consumer price index, it is better to characterize most of them with an adverb: "The price of eggs and milk went up slightly, while flour and baked goods came down a trifle, and poultry and pork dropped sharply." Of course, nobody will agree on precisely what those words mean, but if you used actual numbers almost nobody would remember them. Worse yet, many people would get them entirely wrong.

On television, where it is possible to reinforce the viewer's retention of figures by putting them on the screen, you can get by with employing numbers more freely. But in my judgment, they are now used far too much, and frequently they are not really needed.

In reporting about business and economics, it is often impossible to avoid using technical terms. In that case, they should always be explained, and you should make a great effort to devise an explanation that is simple and clear. It may not satisfy an academic economist, but it must be understandable to the listener. Moreover, once you have come up with a definition that satisfies you, use the same definition every time. Do not alter it for the sake of variety. It will be much more effective if the listener hears it the same way every time, so that if it does not completely register the first time, it will later.

As an illustration, every time I do a spot about the gross national product, I use this definition: "The gross national product is the value of all the goods and services turned out in a year by all of us." Other definitions could be used; indeed, some might be better. But that is mine, and I always use it the same way. Another that I use is this: "Real disposable income is take-home pay adjusted to show how much it will actually buy."

In all good writing for a mass audience, it is obviously better to use straightforward, colloquial language. But it is more important in broadcasting than in print. The reader of a newspaper or magazine can, if need be, reread a sentence or paragraph that is not quite clear or even go back after reading further and finding what seems to be an inconsistency or ambiguity. But the listener or viewer must understand what is being told right away, or not at all.

So the most successful technique is to tell the story as much as possible the way you should relate it to a friend. There is one problem with that: you do not have time for a rambling, redundant tale, as you might have in casual conversation. So you have to balance the two requirements, by tightening up your account but keeping a simple, straightforward construction.

Techniques for Getting and Holding an Audience

Because you must capture the audience's attention quickly, in most cases you should say immediately what the story is about, rather than trying to tease viewers or listeners. Here are three examples of such leads from my ABC scripts:

The general tone of the President's economic message is decidedly upbeat—but the most striking thing about the details is the fact that Mr. Carter has lowered his sights from earlier targets.

The year-long slide in the stock market has been caused by inflation—*and* the suspicion of a lot of people that the government can't do anything about it.

None of the individual parts of Mr. Carter's program—taken by themselves—will have much impact on inflation.

Sometimes not even the central point of a spot can be stated that briefly. It may require several sentences. But the first sentence still must be an arresting statement, and it must flow directly into the rest of the explanation. For example:

The average cost of a day in the hospital is now about $150—not counting tests, medicine, and doctors' bills. Only a little over half of that charge is for direct patient care. The rest is the cumulative cost of dozens of activities—from linen distribution to running the power plant. So the only way to cut hospital costs is by whittling away at every department—and that's exactly what Johns Hopkins Hospital in Baltimore has done.

However, as I argued earlier, the best way to construct a television story is around real people or companies. The focus of the lead then is not on the overall development but on the example. In that case, it is a good idea to follow the practice urged on his correspondents by Av Westin, executive producer of the "ABC Evening News." Mr. Westin suggests that most spots open by focusing on the smallest specific element of the story and then expanding from the particular to the broader, more general point.[9]

To use an obvious example, suppose the consumer price index shoots up in a given month, largely because of higher meat prices. Rather than launching the story with the news of the inflationary acceleration, we open with a shot of a woman at the supermarket meat counter, and the following narration:

Mrs. Hattie Simmons just paid $7.50 for this two-pound steak for her family's dinner. That's a dollar more than she paid for the same amount of beef last month at this time. The same thing is happening across the country, and because steak is the symbol of good living for most Americans, it's driving food budgets through the roof.

Then the story can go on to explain the importance of food prices in the cost of living, what is pushing them up, what the outlook is, and what the political implications of an inflationary speedup may be. But the spot opened with a specific, everyday element to which viewers can relate directly, not an abstraction such as inflation or the cost of living.

When a spot opens on a real person, even an ordinary citizen who is obviously just an example, viewers respond better than to a scene of general action; they will keep watching while you relate a good deal of information, as long as it does not seem irrelevant. That is another good reason to build stories around people.

Economic stories, more than most others, should *explain* events, not simply *relate* them. And since what they are explaining is often difficult for viewers to understand, they must unfold logically and simply. Here is an example that was singled out by *The New York Times* television critic as a "model of clarity."[10] (It may appear to have too many figures, but in this case they were almost unavoidable and they were reinforced by a series of graphics that put the numbers on the screen.)

> The Social Security System is not like a private insurance plan, where people set aside money in individual accounts that later pay their retirement benefits. There's only a remote connection between the amount of money a worker pays in and the Social Security pension he receives.
>
> Social Security is really a huge income transfer system. It transfers income from working-age people to the elderly and from middle-income people to those nearer the bottom.
>
> Each month, a hundred million working Americans and their employers contribute more than $7 *billion,* and that money is then paid out to 33 million retirees.
>
> Relatively more of the money is collected from middle income workers and relatively more is paid out to those who have earned less during their working lives. For example, a person earning the maximum covered income pays in four times as much as a person earning the minimum amount. But when it's time to retire, the person who paid in four times as much gets back only twice as much in benefits.
>
> In spite of that fact, up to now nobody has had any reason to complain—because everybody collects more than he'd get if his contributions had been put into a private pension program.
>
> But that situation may be reversed in the future. Under the new law, in a few years many Americans will be paying $2,000 a year into the fund, and their employers will be matching that. If a person put $4,000 a year into a private program, at current interest rates, over the next forty years he would accumulate almost $840,000—and that would provide him with a lifetime pension of $7,200 a month! Nobody looks for Social Security benefits to go that high—even by the year 2017.
>
> Whatever the benefits are, the tax bite to pay for them will have to go up even faster. That's because the number of retirees collecting pensions will grow a lot faster than the number of workers paying taxes to

finance those pensions. And that means the next couple of generations will really be socked.

That script also demonstrated another suggestion of ABC's Av Westin. He likes all his correspondents, whenever possible, to end their spots by answering the question: "What does this event or trend or development mean?" In many cases, he wants correspondents actually to use the question or its declarative equivalent ("What this means is . . .") in the script. It is a valid, useful device and especially so in spots about business and economics. The main reason people find such news boring is that they seldom see its significance or a direct connection with their own lives.

For example, in a story that said President Carter's 1978 economic message to Congress lowered its inflation and unemployment goals, the closing paragraph was:

> So what the message means is this: President Carter now recognizes that our economic problems are tougher than he thought, and that progress toward solving them will be slower than he hoped.

In another example, a story that said steelmakers are reluctant to expand capacity because of low profits, the closing paragraph was:

> But unless a lot of them start to invest more, they may bring on exactly the kind of economic slowdown they're afraid of. And a slowdown would mean fewer jobs, lower incomes, and the kind of recession spiral we learned about a couple of years ago.

It is not always easy to perceive precisely what a news development means to the typical viewer or listener. But if the correspondent cannot puzzle that out and make the meaning crystal clear, why should the audience pay such a story any attention? Obviously, most items will not be matters of life or death, but unless they have some real significance to an important segment of the audience, they should not be put on the air. It is the journalist's job to uncover that meaning and point it out.

A SUMMARY AND CONCLUSION

Remember that a majority of the broadcast audience consists of people who are not actively interested in business and economic news; who have little or no background knowledge of the subject matter; and who are likely to be giving the news only part of their attention. If you are to have any hope of reaching them, and informing them, you must:

1. Tell them in an arresting way exactly what the spot is about.
2. Explain the event you are reporting, rather than merely describing it.
3. Avoid technical terms whenever possible; otherwise, define them simply.
4. Write everything in unembellished colloquial English without jargon.
5. Err on the side of oversimplification, and on the side of leaving out figures and details.
6. Point out in an explicit way how the development you are reporting will or may affect the viewer/listener.

That adds up to a difficult assignment, but nobody said broadcasting business and economic news is easy. It is not. When it is done well, though, it is important and the rewards are great.

NOTES—CHAPTER 14

1. August 1976 survey, Roper Organization Inc., New York, New York.
2. Jacob Bronowski, *The Ascent of Man* (Boston: Little, Brown and Co., 1973).
3. Interview with Lester M. Crystal, June 1976.
4. The average evening audience of the "CBS Evening News" for the season running from September 1977 to April 1978 was 18,510,000, according to CBS Inc. Public Information Office, New York.
5. There were approximately 110 all-news radio stations throughout the country in 1978, according to the National Association of Broadcasters, Public Relations Office, Washington, D.C.
6. Interview with Louis Rukeyser, June 1976.
7. Interview with Fred Friendly, October 1976.
8. Interview, October 1976.
9. Avram Westin, memo to ABC news staff, September 13, 1977.
10. John J. O'Connor, *New York Times*, January 1, 1978, p. E-14.

SOURCES OF INFORMATION

Action for Children's Television
46 Austin Street
Newtonville, Mass. 01260

American Broadcasting Company
1330 Avenue of the Americas
New York, N.Y. 10022

National Broadcasting Company
30 Rockefeller Plaza
New York, N.Y. 10022

National Cable Television Association
918 Sixteenth Street, N.W.
Washington, D.C. 20006

CBS Inc.
51 West 52nd Street
New York, N.Y. 10022

Maximum Service Telecasters Inc.
1735 DeSales Street, N.W.
Washington, D.C. 20036

National Association of Broadcasters
1771 N Street, N.W.
Washington, D.C. 20036

*Radio and Television News Directors
   Association*
1735 DeSales Street, N.W.
Washington, D.C. 20006

Television Information Office
National Association of Broadcasters
745 Fifth Avenue
New York, N.Y. 10022

SUGGESTED READINGS

Bliss, Edward, Jr., and John M. Patterson, *Writing News for Broadcast.* New York: Columbia University Press, 1971.

Brown, Lester L., *Television: The Business Behind the Box.* New York: Harcourt Brace Jovanovich, 1971.

Cole, Barry, and Mal Oettinger, *Reluctant Regulators: The FCC and the Broadcast Audience.* Reading, Mass.: Addison-Wesley Publishing Co., 1978.

Epstein, Edward J., *News from Nowhere.* New York: Random House, 1973.

Hage, George S., Everette E. Dennis, Arnold H. Ismach, and Stephen Hartgen, *New Strategies for Public Affairs Reporting.* Englewood Cliffs, N.J.: Prentice-Hall, 1976.

Harrington, Stephanie, "What's All This on TV?" *New York Times Magazine,* May 27, 1975, pp. 41–91.

Head, Sydney W., *Broadcasting in America: A Survey of Television and Radio.* Boston: Houghton Mifflin Co., 1976.

Johnson, Nicholas, *Test Pattern for Living.* New York: Bantam Books, 1972.

MacDougall, Curtis D., *Interpretative Reporting.* New York: Macmillan Publishing Company, 1977.

Noll, Roger G., Merton J. Peck, and John J. McGowan, *Economic Aspects of Television Regulation.* Washington, D.C.: The Brookings Institution, 1973.

Stevens, John D., and William E. Porter, *The Rest of the Elephant: Perspectives on the Mass Media.* Englewood Cliffs, N.J.: Prentice-Hall, 1973.

Whiteside, Thomas, "Annals of Television: Shaking the Tree," *New Yorker,* March 17, 1975, pp. 41–91.

GLOSSARY

A

accounts payable: the amounts owed by a company to its suppliers of goods and services. The accounts normally are called "open accounts" and are payable in 30, 60, or 90 days.

accounts receivable: the amounts owing from customers to whom goods were shipped in the regular course of business. Customers are usually given 30, 60, or 90 days in which to pay.

administered price: a price set under conditions of imperfect competition in which an individual company or small group of firms has considerable degree of control over market prices.

aggregate demand: the total quantity of all goods and services purchased in an entire economy, expressed in terms of the dollars expended.

antitrust: being against monopolistic agreements to control prices or markets. Government antitrust policy, which originated when certain business trusts attempted to monopolize markets, is designed to curb numerous monopolistic and anticompetitive practices.

antitrust laws: legislation principally designed to protect competition by outlawing numerous monopolistic and anticompetitive practices. In the United States the major federal antitrust law is the Sherman Act of 1890 and amendments thereto.

B

balance of payments: a record of all the international economic transactions of a nation and its people; included are exports, imports, government transactions such as foreign aid and expenditures abroad, international investments, and monetary transfers.

balance of trade: the dollar value of the difference between the goods and services exported and imported by a country during a given period of time. If exports are less than imports, a trade deficit results; if more, a trade surplus.

balance sheet: an itemized financial statement showing assets, liabilities, and net worth of any economic unit on a given date.

bid and asked: a stock market term often referred to as a quotation or quote. The bid is the highest price anyone is willing to pay for a security at a given time; the asked is the lowest price anyone will take at that time.

blue sky laws: a popular name for state laws (as opposed to federal securities laws) enacted to protect the public against security frauds. The term reportedly originated when a judge ruled that a particular stock had about the same value as a patch of blue sky.

bond: a written certificate of indebtedness obligating the issuer to pay interest coupons at regular intervals and to repay the principal on a specified date. Bonds are usually issued to provide financing for a fixed asset.

business cycle: a recurring pattern of expansion and contraction in the level of business activity. The phases of the typical business cycle include recovery, prosperity, decline, recession, and then recovery again as the economy moves into another cycle.

C

capital: financial assets, land, facilities, and equipment used in the production of goods and services. Capital is also defined as the amount invested in an enterprise.

capital expenditures: money spent for property or other fixed assets, including land, buildings, machinery, and other equipment, used in the production of goods and services.

capitalism: an economic system that relies heavily on previous accumulations of wealth (capital) to produce the nation's standard of living. The term "capitalism" is often used in reference to an economy in which the means of production are owned and controlled primarily by private individuals or groups of individuals (see **free enterprise**); however, *state capitalism* also exists, such as communism.

capitalization: total amount of the various securities issued by a corporation, including bonds, debentures, preferred and common stock, plus retained earnings.

collective bargaining: a method of reaching a labor agreement in which representatives of the employees and the employer negotiate proposed changes in the terms of a labor contract.

commodities: goods such as wheat, corn, copper, and hides that are used in trade or industry and can be transported; however, the term is also used to refer to all economic goods.

common stock: securities representing an ownership interest in a corporation, generally entitling the owner to vote for directors and on certain policy matters and to receive any dividends declared. Common stockholders have the last claim on the earnings and assets of a corporation, after all creditors and preferred stockholders.

communism: a political and economic system in which a nation's productive resources and property are owned collectively and in which major economic decisions are made by central authority. The term, as used to describe the economy of the Soviet Union and of certain other nations, usually refers to a form of socialism that comes about through military or revolutionary means rather than through ballot procedures.

conglomerate: a corporation that has grown by purchasing and merging with other corporations in diverse rather than related lines of business.

consumer price index: a measurement at the retail level of the cost of living, prepared by the U.S. Bureau of Labor Statistics.

corporation: a legal entity or organization that is granted authority by a state government to engage in business or some other activity. A business corporation is entitled to issue stocks and bonds and theoretically exists in perpetuity. The liability of its owners is limited to their investment.

cost of sales: the total cost of goods sold during an accounting period. In retailing, the cost is based upon the prices paid for the items sold; in manufacturing, it is based upon production costs including materials, labor, and energy.

cumulative preferred: a preferred stock protected by a proviso that, if one or more dividends are omitted, the omitted dividends must be paid before dividends may be paid to the company's common stockholders.

cumulative voting: a method of voting for corporate directors by which the shareholder may multiply the number of his or her shares by the number of directors being elected and cast the total for one or more directors.

currency devaluation: action by a government or by market forces that reduces the value of a nation's currency in relation to the currencies of other nations.

current assets: unrestricted cash and other assets which, in the normal course of business, may be turned into cash in the reasonably near future, usually within a year.

current liabilities: a company's debts and other obligations that fall due within the coming year and are to be paid out of current assets.

D

debenture (bond): a security ranking ahead of preferred stock, backed by the general credit of a company but not secured by a mortgage or lien on any specific property.

deficit: in the case of government it is the amount of money that the governmental unit pays out in excess of the amount received in a given period of time. In the case of a company it is a net operating loss due to the fact that expenses exceeded income during an accounting period.

deficit financing: borrowing to cover a deficit.

deflation: a protracted decline in the general level of prices; the opposite of inflation.

demand deposit: a deposit in a financial institution which may be withdrawn at any time without notice, usually by the writing of a check. Demand deposits make up the largest part of U.S. money supply.

depreciation: the reduction in the value of a fixed asset such as machinery and other capital goods that occurs over time because of aging, wear and tear, and technological obsolescence.

depression: a protracted period of greatly reduced economic activity characterized by widespread unemployment and a reduced level of production and income; a very severe recession.

director: a person elected by shareholders to represent their interests in the management of an enterprise. The directors appoint the president, vice-presidents, and other chief operating officers and act on major policies and decisions of the enterprise.

discount rate: the interest that Federal Reserve banks charge on funds borrowed by commercial banks that are members of the Federal Reserve System.

dividend: a payment to shareholders for their investment in corporate stock. Dividends normally are paid in cash from the retained earnings of the corporation; however, there are also *stock dividends* (see definition) and *liquidating dividends* upon the dissolution of a corporation.

dumping: selling goods, usually in international trade, below market prices while maintaining higher prices in major market areas such as the domestic market. The practice is usually used to dispose of surplus inventories or to beat foreign competitors.

E

emerging nation: a country that is only beginning to develop its economic potential. Also called less developed countries, or LDC's, these nations frequently are poor and have only recently been given their political and economic independence.

F

fascism: a political and economic system which may permit private ownership of property but has highly centralized economic and political decision making by an authoritarian government which places the state above the individual.

fiscal policy: a planned course of action by government in which expenditures, taxes, and debt management are used to influence economic activity.

fixed assets: the tangible assets of a business not intended for sale which are used to produce goods and services or otherwise operate the business.

fixed costs: costs that do not vary with the volume of output, such as unavoidable overhead expenses, property taxes, interest costs, and depreciation charges.

free enterprise (system): a political and economic system which emphasizes private initiative, freedom of choice, and the competitive forces of a free market in the creation and distribution of goods, services, and wealth. Also called a "free market" and, inappropriately, a "capitalistic" economy.

fringe benefits: items such as vacations, pension, and insurance benefits that are not deducted from an employee's pay but are paid for by the employer for the benefit of the employee. It is not unusual for fringe benefits to exceed 25 percent of an employee's pay.

full employment: a condition of the economy in which there is sufficient aggregate demand to employ almost all those who wish to work and are qualified for jobs. In the United States full employment usually is said to exist when the unemployment rate is less than 4 percent.

G

gross national product: the total market value of all final goods and services produced in a nation during a given period, usually a year.

H

horizontal combination: a merger of two or more companies that produce like goods or services. Some refer to a horizontal combination as the merger of competitors.

I

import quota: a limit on the quantity of a product that may be imported into a country during a specified period of time.

inflation: a protracted rise in the price of most goods and services. Inflation over a significant period of time usually is associated with an increase in the money supply.

interlocking directorates: a situation in which members of the board of directors of one company are also members of the board of directors of other companies. It is generally illegal to have interlocking directorates among competing companies.

inventories: raw materials and supplies, goods in process, and finished goods that a business has on hand, usually to meet production and customer needs as they arise.

investment banker: an organization that buys entire new issues of stock and bond securities and distributes them to security dealers (brokers) for resale or to investors. Investment bankers are also called "security underwriters."

investment company: an organization that uses its capital to invest in other companies. Often such companies or trusts bring together the savings of individuals for investment.

L

labor force: includes those over 14 years of age who are working, are looking for work, or are absent from work for unavoidable reasons such as labor disputes, illness, or vacation.

labor union: an organization of employees which acts in their behalf in negotiating with management concerning wages and other matters.

liabilities: the amount owed to others by a business, government, or individual.

liquid assets: cash and other assets that easily can be converted into cash, such as government treasury notes and other easily marketable securities.

M

macro-economics: refers to the economy as a whole rather than individual economic units.

management: the board of directors and officers of an organization; those in whom executive authority and responsibility are vested.

mercantilism: an economic system, popular in Europe in the sixteenth, seventeenth, and eighteenth centuries, which was characterized by a highly controlled economy with numerous government regulations designed to increase the flow of precious metals into the treasury of the mother country.

merger: the combination of two or more formerly independent business units into one organization with a common ownership.

micro-economics: refers to the economic behavior of individual units in the economy, such as business firms and households.

monetary policy: the policies of government and/or banking authorities concerning the supply of money and credit and interest rates, usually to influence the level of economic activity and prices.

monopolistic competition: a market situation in which there is rivalry among competing sellers but one or more sellers has a definite degree of control over its prices because of customer preference for its products and services.

monopoly: the domination of a specific market by one seller who has no competitors.

municipal bond: a bond issued by a state or a political subdivision, such as county, city, town, or village. In general, interest paid on municipal bonds is exempt from federal income taxes and, frequently, state and local income taxes within the state of issue.

N

net income or **net profit:** the revenues of an enterprise less all associated costs during a given period of time. It is the balance remaining for the owners of the enterprise, i.e., the compensation of equity capital.

net sales: the total sales of a company in a given period less allowances for returned or damaged goods and discounts provided to purchasers.

nonprice competition: competitive tactics of rival sellers other than price adjustments, such as improved quality, advertising and promotions, extended warranties, and other services offered to buyers.

O

oligopoly: a market in which there are so few sellers that each must consider the potential reactions of others when making price or level-of-output decisions.

over-the-counter market: the market for securities sold by brokers outside organized stock exchanges. All securities not listed on an organized exchange are sold over the counter.

P

preferred stock: a class of stock that has prior claim over common stock to the earnings of a corporation and, usually, a prior claim upon assets in the event of liquidation. The dividend on preferred stock is usually at a rate prescribed at the time of issuance.

price discrimination: the charging of different prices to various buyers even though the conditions of sale are similar. If the effect of price discrimination is to lessen competition or foster monopoly, antitrust laws may have been violated.

price-earnings ratio: the current market price of a share of common stock divided by earnings per share for the previous year. A stock selling at $20 and earning $2 per share has a price-earnings ratio of 10.

prime rate: the interest rate that commercial banks charge to their preferred customers, usually large customers having a low degree of credit risk.

productivity: the relationship between a nation's output (the quantity of goods and services produced) and input (the amount of labor, material, and capital expended to produce those goods and services). The productivity of labor is usually measured in terms of output per man-hour.

profit: in general terminology profit is the excess of revenue or selling price over all the costs involved. In economics, profit is the reward to an entrepreneur or group of business owners for undertaking the risks of engaging in a business enterprise.

prospectus: a written offer to sell securities. The Securities and Exchange Commission and state blue-sky laws require that a prospectus disclose to potential investors essential facts pertinent to the security.

protectionists: those who favor high tariffs and other restrictions on imports so that domestic goods will not have to compete with foreign goods.

proxy: written authorization given by a shareholder to someone else to represent him and vote his shares at a corporate shareholders' meeting. Proxy statement disclosures are regulated by the Securities and Exchange Commission.

public utility: a business that provides essential public services and tends to be a natural monopoly. Such utilities operate under a franchise from government and are regulated by a commission or other body representing the public.

R

recession: a period of declining economic activity, typically defined as two or more calendar quarters of reduced real gross national product. That is, after adjusting for price changes, the final consumption of all goods and services is decreased from the preceding quarter. A severe and prolonged recession is usually called a *depression*.

restraint of trade: any business action or conduct that interferes with the free functioning of a competitive market or that tends to reduce competition.

S

single proprietorship: the oldest and most common type of business ownership, one in which the business is owned by an individual.

socialism: a political and economic system in which much or most of the means of production is owned and controlled collectively, usually by government, and in which central planning is substituted for the marketplace in the allocation of resources.

specialist: on a stock or commodity exchange, a specialist is one who specializes in a given stock or commodity, executing brokers' orders and attempting to maintain an orderly market for the transactions involved.

stock: the ownership or equity capital of a corporation, divided into shares and represented by certificates.

stock dividend: a dividend paid in securities rather than cash. The dividend may be additional shares of the issuing company, or in shares of a subsidiary company held by the company.

stock split: the division of the outstanding shares of a corporation into a larger number of shares. For example, if a stock splits three for one, each shareholder receives two additional shares for each share held. While not increasing the value of stockholders' equity, there *may* be price appreciation due to the increased marketability of the securities.

T

tariff: a tax levied on goods imported or exported. In the United States, tariffs may apply only to imported goods; a tax on exports is prohibited by the Constitution.

U

union shop: a business in which the employer may hire only those workers who are or will become a union member after a specified period of time. In other words, the employee must join a specific union to maintain his or her employment.

V

variable costs: costs that vary directly with the level of output, such as materials and direct factory labor.

W

working capital: assets, generally cash, available to pay current operating expenses and obligations such as wages and salaries, materials, and energy bills.

INDEX